GATHERING A HERITAGE

Ukrainian, Slavonic, and Ethnic Canada and the USA

Since the 1970s and 1980s, the study of immigration and ethnicity has grown to become an essential aspect of North American history. In *Gathering a Heritage*, Thomas M. Prymak uses the essays and articles he has written over the past thirty years as a historian of Ukrainian and Ukrainian Canadian history to reflect on the evolution of ethnic studies in Canada and the United States.

The essays included in this book explore the history of Ukrainian and Slavonic immigration to North America and the literature through which these communities and their historians have sought to recapture their past. Each previously published essay is revised and expanded and several more appear here for the first time – including the fascinating story of French Canadian writer Gabrielle Roy's connections with Ukrainian Canadians and her tumultuous affair with a Ukrainian Canadian nationalist in pre-war London.

THOMAS M. PRYMAK is a research associate of the Chair of Ukrainian Studies at the University of Toronto.

Cover illustrations: (front) A Quadriga, or Chariot of the Gods, pulled by four horses carrying Winged Victory. It is taken from the cover of *Ukraina* magazine (Winnipeg, January, 1918), the month that the Ukrainian People's Republic declared its state independence. *Ukraina* was edited by a former student of Mykhailo Hrushevsky, Oleksander Sushko. There are numerous Quadrigae gracing the capital cities of modern Europe, the most famous being that on top of the Brandenburg Gate in Berlin, but only one has survived from classical antiquity. It consists of the four horses atop the Church of San Marco in Venice, stolen from Constantinople by the Crusaders in 1204; (back) Author photo by Cyrus Vladimir Prymak.

ІСТОРІЯ
УКРАЇНИ

КИЇВ–ЛЬВІВ–ВІДЕНЬ,

в другому році відбудування Української
держави.

Т-ВО „ВЕРНИГОРА"

Title page of Ivan Krypiakevych's short *History of Ukraine,* published in Saskatoon, Saskatchewan, 1920. The page shows Ukrainian national symbols accepted by most Ukrainian Canadians of that time. On the upper left, the Archangel Michael, Patron Saint of Kiev; on the upper right, the Lion of the City of Lviv and western Ukraine; and, below, the Trident of Saint Volodymyr, adopted by most Ukrainian governments in 1918 and after. Above the symbols, the title reads simply "History of Ukraine." Below the symbols read the ostensible places of publication: "Kyiv–Lviv–Vienna." Below that, the year of publication: "In the Second Year of the Reconstruction of the Ukrainian State." Below that, the publisher: "'Vernyhora' Society." Krypiakevych's short history was reprinted in Canada many times and was used as a textbook in Ukrainian Saturday Schools in both Canada and the United States right through to the 1970s.

THOMAS M. PRYMAK

Gathering a Heritage

Ukrainian, Slavonic,
and Ethnic Canada and the USA

UNIVERSITY OF TORONTO PRESS
Toronto Buffalo London

ISBN 978-1-4426-4635-3 (cloth)
ISBN 978-1-4426-1438-3 (paper)

Library and Archives Canada Cataloguing in Publication

Prymak, Thomas, M., 1948–, author
  Gathering a heritage: Ukrainian, Slavonic, and ethnic Canada and the USA / Thomas M.
Prymak.

  Includes bibliographical references and index.
  ISBN 978-1-4426-4635-3 (bound)   ISBN 978-1-4426-1438-3 (pbk.)

  1. Ukrainians – Canada – Historiography. 2. Ukrainians – United States – Historiography.
  1. Title.

FC106.U5P79 2015   971.004'91791   C2014-905554-4

This book has been generously supported by the publications program
of the Shevchenko Society Scientific Society of Canada.

Канадська
фундація
українських
студій

Canadian Foundation
for Ukrainian Studies
Fondation canadienne
des études ukrainiennes

This book has been generously supported by the Canadian Foundation for Ukrainian
Studies.

This book has been generously supported by the Ukrainian Studies Fund.

University of Toronto Press acknowledges the financial assistance to its publishing program of the Canada Council for the Arts and the Ontario Arts Council, an agency of the
government of Ontario.

Canada Council   Conseil des Arts
for the Arts   du Canada

ONTARIO ARTS COUNCIL
CONSEIL DES ARTS DE L'ONTARIO
an Ontario government agency
un organisme du gouvernement de l'Ontario

University of Toronto Press acknowledges the financial support of the Government of
Canada through the Canada Book Fund for its publishing activities.

For Cyrus, Shari, and Yassy

Contents

Library Studies and Reference Works

Concluding Thoughts

Preface

In recent years, monumental changes have been occurring in the ethnic composition and immigration history of most of the industrially developed countries of the world, including both Canada and the United States. In particular, the beginnings of a new mass migration of people from various countries to Canada and its southern neighbour can be traced back to changes in the immigration laws in both countries enacted in the 1960s. These changes eliminated certain restrictions placed on immigration from Third World countries, and, by the late 1970s, a massive new immigration from them was fully underway. The movement gathered strength steadily over the course of the next few decades and began to level off only during the economic downturn that began in 2008. It was soon realized that this new immigration from countries that had previously supplied very few immigrants to Canada and its neighbour – that is, countries in Asia and elsewhere in the Third World – signalled a change in the ethnic makeup of the receiving countries, the like of which had not occurred since the Great Economic Migration from eastern and southern Europe to the Americas that had taken place from the 1880s to 1914. The earlier immigration had expanded the sources of the Canadian and American populations southward and especially eastward across all Europe; this later immigration is presently expanding them southward and eastward across the whole world.

There is, however, one constant: from very modest beginnings in the 1930s, through the expansion in the educational systems of the 1950s and the "roots" phenomenon of the 1960s, through the multicultural movement of the 1970s, the 1980s, and beyond, to the exciting new developments of the early twenty-first century, interest in "ethnic studies" and immigration history has been steadily growing among both the general population and scholars. The present book seeks to address this interest with regard to one of the most prominent groups constituting the earlier Great Migration to Canada, and, in places, makes some modest comparisons with later developments.

The book contains a collection of my essays dealing with Ukrainian Canadian subjects and related themes, Slavonic and ethnic, written over the course of the last twenty-five years. (Certain parallel or divergent American developments are also considered in various places.) During this period, my interests expanded considerably from Ukrainian Canadian history with an emphasis on the pioneer immigration to the Canadian prairies at the end of the nineteenth and the beginning of the twentieth centuries, through the experiences of the children of this pioneer immigration, the generation of the 1940s, which lived through the Great Depression and the Second World War, to Ukrainian Canadian and Ukrainian American cultural history of later times, with an emphasis on scholarship and higher education, especially history writing and the lives and careers of various historians. Thus, the pre-1914 pioneer immigration, the children of the pioneers, the interwar immigration, their children, and, later on, the post-1945 immigration, the highly political so-called Displaced Persons immigration, which the earlier immigrants, mostly economic in nature, welcomed to Canada and the United States, are the major subjects of the present book.

The oldest contribution to the present collection is the essay on the distinguished Ukrainian writer Ivan Franko and the emigration question in old Austrian Galicia (Franko's homeland, a region inhabited by many Ukrainians), which was written in 1983, prior to the defence of my PhD thesis in Ukrainian history at the University of Toronto. I wrote this Franko essay on the basis of some revealing new documents that I had come across by chance in the course of researching my dissertation on Franko's friend and close collaborator, the historian Mykhailo Hrushevsky. It was published in a rather severely abridged form under the title "Ivan Franko and Mass Ukrainian Emigration to Canada" in the journal *Canadian Slavonic Papers* at the end of 1984 when I was Visiting Professor of Ukrainian History at the University of Saskatchewan. A much fuller and completely updated version of this essay appears here for the first time. One of the very last essays to be written and placed in this collection is the paper on the influential French Canadian writer Gabrielle Roy and her connections with the Ukrainian Canadians, especially the mysterious "Stephen" with whom she fell thoroughly in love and to whom she devoted two full chapters in her autobiography. This autobiography is now generally considered to be a classic in the genre in Canadian literature.

Much of the material in *Gathering a Heritage: Ukrainian, Slavonic, and Ethnic Canada and the USA* has already been published, at least in part, in various journals, some of them highly specialized and rather obscure to the general Canadian or American reader. Indeed, two of the articles were even published in far-off Kazan, the capital city of Tatarstan in the Russian Federation! Consequently, with a view to making these essays more available to Western readers, I have taken this opportunity to gather, revise, and update much of this scattered material, especially the older material dealing with various immigration questions, and, thus, these materials have become somewhat "new." Similarly, other materials, which, like the Franko essay mentioned above, were published only in a shorter form, appear for the first time in full here. Also, the essay on library studies titled "Scholarship on Mykhailo Hrushevsky during the Early 1980s: Ukrainian Books and Libraries in Canada and the United States," the substantial essay on reference materials, "Ukrainian Canada in the Encyclopedias, 1897–2010: An Historical Overview," and the above-mentioned essay titled "In the Shadow of a Political Assassination: Gabrielle Roy's 'Stephen' and the Ukrainian Canadians" make their first printed appearance in this volume.

The heritage gathered here is, of course, primarily Ukrainian Canadian, and all the essays included reflect this fact. But, as indicated in the title, related themes, Slavonic and ethnic, are treated as well. Thus, while there is a geographical focal point for the work – western Canada and the prairie provinces – the material radiates outward to include all of Canada and, indeed, even all of North America and the New World. The essays on Ukrainian émigré scholarship, for example, take in the entire Western world, as, indeed, do some of the essays on the early waves of emigration from Europe to the Americas. With regard to questions of migration to the New World, social and political factors influencing emigration from eastern Europe come to the fore, as also do immigration policies and conditions in North America. Moreover, in places, international relations and European power politics impinge directly on the very Canadian issues and events discussed here. Perhaps the best example of this sort of thing in this volume is the essay on Gabrielle Roy and her connections with the Ukrainian Canadians. In this particular essay, the rise of Hitler, the spread of Stalinism, and the European political crises of 1938–9, which led to the Second World War, are of central importance to Roy's personal life of the time and her decision to become a writer. Although Roy first gained fame as a Quebec writer, it should be emphasized that she always remained a French Canadian writer from the ethnically diverse province of Manitoba of the 1930s. This fact affected her political opinions in later life and gave her a certain cosmopolitan streak, which included an interest in the Ukrainian Canadians. Thus, there is both a local core and a universal framework to the present book.

On a slightly different level, I should point out that all the essays contained in this book were written by a scholar trained in historical method and usually working in the field of European history; in particular, the history of "Russia and Eastern Europe," as the discipline was once geopolitically defined. Thus, the linguistic skills and historical consciousness of the author vary somewhat from that of the typical Canadian or American historian whose linguistic skills are generally restricted to English and French and whose emphasis is most definitely on this continent. This different approach to the sources comes out quite clearly, I think, in the essays in this volume on the writer Ivan Franko, the historian Dmytro Doroshenko, and, perhaps most of all, the political leader/historian Mykhailo Hrushevsky. All three men were giants in their fields and very important to their nation but are little known to most North American historians and to the North American public at large. It is my hope that the European training and interests displayed here bring a refreshingly new perspective to the history of an important Canadian/American ethnic group and also make a contribution to European history in its connection with this continent.

Finally, I think it would not be untoward to mention that the reprinted part of the articles and essays collected here, although generally updated and expanded, are still witnesses to their own times. They document some of the interests and conditions that prevailed during the last years of the Cold War, the Soviet reform period of perestroika and glasnost, and the first years of Ukrainian independence. Thus, as witnesses of those times, they are not entirely without interest in and of themselves. Of course, though the essays in this book are arranged chronologically with the historical materials first and more general materials later, it is not necessary for them to be read in this order. The general reader may choose what interests him most (biography, library studies, or whatever) and read it first and turn to the older materials only later, if they catch his interest. With all these considerations in mind, I entrust this volume to the hands of the reader and hope that he (or she) may enjoy going through it as much as I have enjoyed putting it together. *Lege filiciter!*

Acknowledgments

I should first like to thank the various publishing houses and their editors and manuscript reviewers, often anonymous, who, earlier on, helped me to see some of these essays into print in their original editions. The possibilities they first offered me to share my ideas with others were a great encouragement to the writing and eventual revising, expanding, and updating of these pieces. I should also like to thank the editors and publishers of the various journals in which they first appeared for permission to reprint them here. It was the distinguished historian of eastern Europe, the late Professor Peter Brock of the University of Toronto, concerned that for too long I had limited my writing to articles and reviews, who pushed me into publishing still another book. With fond memories, I acknowledge him here. I would also like to thank the eminent sociologist Professor Wsevolod Isajiw (University of Toronto Emeritus) for his helpful comments on the manuscript, the respected folklorist Dr Robert Bohdan Klymasz of Winnipeg (formerly of the Canadian Museum of Civilization in Ottawa) for encouraging me to write on certain little-known but important Ukrainian Canadian topics, and my colleagues at the Canadian Institute of Ukrainian Studies, Toronto Office, Roman Senkus and Andrij Makuch, for their encouragement and many a useful bibliographical lead. I also thank Professor Frank Sysyn of the Peter Jacyk Centre for Ukrainian Historical Research at the University of Alberta for certain services rendered that helped to see this book into print. My editor pro tem at the University of Toronto Press Len Husband, my copy editor Pat Sanders, and my associate managing editor Frances Mundy expertly guided it forward to press. Some important funding for the book came from the Shevchenko Scientific Society, Toronto Branch, the Canadian Foundation for Ukrainian Studies, also in

Toronto, and the Ukrainian Studies Fund in Cambridge, Massachusetts. I thank all three of these institutions for their generous support.

But, most of all, I should like to thank my wife Yassy and my children Shahram and Cyrus, who were witnesses to the joys and travails of a (then relatively) young academic setting out to explore his ethnic roots in western Canada. The journey has been a long one, and one that has not yet ended, but it is one in which each of you has intimately participated, through numerous conversations about ethnicity and heritage, through homework assignments that you chose to do on Ukrainian or Ukrainian Canadian themes, or through simple attendance at Josef Cardinal Slipyj Ukrainian Catholic School in West Toronto. I especially thank my beautiful Iranian wife Yassy (or Yassaman, as formal Persian would have it) for the respect she has always shown for her husband's somewhat exotic (to her) Ukrainian Canadian heritage, which even included going to Kyiv and Soviet Ukraine to study Ukrainian in the bad old days when the KGB was constantly breathing down our necks but when Solidarity was already raising its banners in Poland and John Paul II had already blown the trumpet that would knock down the walls of Jericho and set such a large part of our world free. I also especially thank Shahram and Cyrus for bearing with their parents each time we met an interesting foreigner, or Canadian with a "foreign" accent in Toronto and elsewhere, and inquired about his or her background to the dismay of our somewhat more reserved children. It has been all part of the same cosmopolitan cultural quest, for true respect for, and knowledge of, one's own heritage, with all its manifold and diverse sources, I have learned, often leads to respect for, and knowledge of, that of others. And so, with love and fond memories, I dedicate this book to all three of you.

[1] **hĕ'rĭtage**, n. What is or may be inherited;
(fig.) portion allotted to any one.
Concise Oxford Dictionary of Current English (1951)

The principal office of history I take to be this:
to prevent virtuous actions from being forgotten,
and that evil words and deeds
should fear the judgment of posterity.
Tacitus, *Annales*

To history has been assigned the office of judging the past,
of instructing the present for the benefit of future ages.
To such high offices this work does not aspire:
It wants only to show what actually happened (*wie es eigentlich gewesen*).
Leopold von Ranke

Obviously, the cooling of raw emotion and substitution of tepid intellectual
discourse for the language of attack and defense tends to immerse any historical subject in ambivalent complexities. The most vital history is likely to be written during the period when emotion remains strong enough to be recollected
in tranquility (Wordsworth's definition of the well-spring of true poetry) and
before anger or love have been completely obscured by intellectual constructs.
William H. McNeill

Introduction

Bernard of Chartres used to say that we are like dwarfs standing on the shoulders of giants so that we can see more and farther than they....

John of Salisbury, twelfth century

Before presenting the varied essays contained in this book, I think it appropriate to say a few words about the title and some of the concepts used throughout the volume. First, the title: *Gathering a Heritage* is a familiar concept to most national historians of eastern and central Europe, but is less well known to mainstream Canadian and American historians and to Canadians and Americans in general, or, at least, less well known to such people in the way that I have used it here. For some time now, eastern European historians who write the histories of their respective countries, many of them missing from the political map of Europe before 1918, have divided into several stages the history of the national movements in their parts of the world; most of these movements were eventually successful to some extent, and the result was national independence and the final appearance of these countries on maps. Thus interpreted, the stages of these national movements were, first, "heritage gathering" by a relatively small elite of intellectuals of various sorts, then mass mobilization in various cultural and social organizations, and then political action sometimes resulting in military conflict and "wars of liberation."[1]

The first great wave of Ukrainian or "Ruthenian" (as it was called at the time) immigration to Canada and the United States (which originated for the most part in the Habsburg Monarchy) occurred before 1914 and, to a certain degree, falls in-between the first and the second of these three stages; at least, for most of these immigrants, if not for the elite in their European homeland. In other words, "heritage gathering" and mass cultural organization were especially important for this initial wave of Ruthenian/Ukrainian immigrants to Canada and the United States. (The building of churches and the formation of religious communities are cases in point, as were the establishment of *prosvita* or popular "enlightenment" societies striving to promote literacy in the native language and education in a national spirit.) Political involvement and the national movement existed both on the right and on the left of the political spectrum, but in Canada, at least, they were still in an embryo form to some degree. Indeed, the very name "Ukrainian," with all its promising (or disconcerting, as the case may be) political and national implications, did not become predominant in Canada until the 1920s, and, more universally, in the 1930s, some twenty-five or thirty years after the immigration had begun. It was only then that this new name almost completely replaced older terms such as "Ruthenian" (applied previously to the new settlers by themselves) and "Galician" (applied previously to the settlers by many of their new Anglo Canadian neighbours). Indeed, as late as 1937, the *Encyclopedia of Canada* contained the article "Ukrainians" (which acknowledged that by that time they constituted the fourth-largest ethnic group in the Dominion after the British groups, the French, and the Germans), but also the somewhat scurrilous article "Galician Immigration," which made no reference to the "Ukrainian nationality" of most of these "newcomers" to the Prairies, while, among the Ukrainians themselves, the largest religious institution of the Ukrainian Canadians, the Ruthenian Greek Catholic Church of Canada, retained its old name on the statute books until 1951.[2]

At this point, it is necessary to get personal. Three of my four grandparents belonged to this first pre-1914 "pioneer" wave, and I identify with it quite closely. When I was a boy in the western Canadian city of Winnipeg in the 1950s, I learned that I was of Ukrainian background, but knew nothing of the highly politicized Ukrainian "nationalist" movement that came to dominate Ukrainian political life in the western parts of that country between the wars and afterwards. Thus, the third, more political, stage outlined above was somewhat alien to me. In fact, aside from a few folk customs observed by my family, I knew very little of Ukrainian culture and even language. Consequently, many years later, when I became interested in this background of things Ukrainian, I had to start almost from scratch. In fact, I consciously began to "gather a heritage," about which I learned more and more over the course of the following years. Most of my scholarly career and the present book are just an extension of that long-lasting and serious but also very enjoyable enterprise. An unintended by-product is that this enterprise has also turned me somewhat more political and aware of "nationalist" versus "Communist" influences on, and conflicts concerning, my ethnic heritage.

From a different viewpoint, of course, some Canadian and American observers might see this as an exemplary manifestation of the principle conventionally called "Hansen's Law" once formulated by the American historian of immigration Marcus Lee Hansen (1892–1938), who famously wrote that "what the son wishes to forget, the grandson wishes to remember." Hansen is now often interpreted to have meant a return not exactly to ethnicity but rather to a recollection of it. Moreover, more recent observers have pointed out that this recollection or "rediscovery" of things past by the third generation is highly selective in nature, some things being deliberately forgotten while other things, especially those of a positive symbolic nature, purposefully cultivated. The elements cultivated greatly vary from folk dancing and various kinds of music to genealogy and history. In my particular case, study of the immigrant experience of my grandparents never quite squelched the feeling that I was "other" and "ethnic" but not "immigrant." Indeed, I was aware at all times that Canadian history as I had been taught it – Mackenzie down the Mackenzie River, Fraser down the Fraser, representative government followed by responsible government in the two Canadas, and a Great War from 1914 to 1918 in which neither of my grandfathers, though resident in this country, in any way participated, or, presumably, were in support of – was a history that was at some distance from my family's experience. In fact, I always considered the Great War to have been a futile and indescribably wasteful enterprise, its contribution to Canadian "nation building" inadvertent and not all positive. And, when I did consider pre-twentieth-century Canadian history, I usually identified with the conquered Catholic French and not the conquering Protestant English or Scots; thus, I found Champlain and Montcalm to be congenial figures and preferred Louis Riel, the controversial Métis leader and founder of Manitoba, to John A. Macdonald, the foremost father of the Canadian Confederation and first prime minister of Canada. (My regional background and early education in a Manitoba Catholic school with its particular ethnic mix, which included both French and assimilated French Métis, were probably partly responsible for this orientation. Moreover, it was this particular background that most certainly led to my early university studies in medieval history and the history of the Crusades, an international phenomenon in which the country that we today call "France" played an especially significant role.) In general, however, my distance from what can be called the "triumphalism" of English Canadian history was probably due most of all to the fact that before the 1970s, "ethnic" history in the sense of the histories of the non-French and the non-British – that is, my history in particular – was not a part of the Canadian history curriculum and virtually no "ethnic" topics or even surnames appeared in the history textbooks. Moreover, though today, "ethnic studies" are very much a flourishing branch of Canadian sociology, the political and cultural historians still lag very far behind the social scientists and no proper ethnohistory of this country as yet exists, though partial immigration histories in English, and preparatory studies of various other sorts, including collections of source materials, have been done in several languages, of which Ukrainian, Polish, and German, not to speak of French, are very important for the prairie region. Indeed, Canadian ethnic history is still too often lumped together indiscriminately with immigration history and no significant distinction is made between the two. This is an obfuscation, gleefully promoted by certain unsympathetic establishment and assimilationist historians, which completely ignores the evolution of Canadian ethnicity through the generations and is in desperate need of correction. My personal journey from textbook Canadian history through European, medieval, and world history, to immigration history, and finally to Canadian ethnic history lies at the base of the present book and forms the essence of this heritage-gathering project at its core.[3]

Of course, heritage gathering of the type in which I have long been engaged has certain implications for Canadian history as a whole. Writing before 1939, the famous English Canadian humorist Stephen Leacock, who was not known to have much sympathy for "continental" immigrants to this country, could already foresee such a development and seems to have objected to it. "Leave them alone," he declared, "and pretty soon the Ukrainians will think that they won the battle of Trafalgar." In fact, as indicated above, I make no claims about the Battle of Trafalgar, but I do think the history of my own family and that of my ethnic confreres, as well as of many of those in parallel groups sometimes considered "others," forms a good part of Canadian history, and an understanding of the historical myths that formed these particular ethnicities is necessary to develop a more balanced understanding of Canadian society as a whole. As the Austrian Canadian historian Franz Szabo boldly put it: Cossacks as well as *coureurs-de-bois*![4]

As to Canadian history and the heirs of the Cossacks, one might add that the link between the two recurrently bubbles to the surface at certain crucial times. For example, not only were the Ukrainians important in the settling of the Prairies, but it was they who were among the first to raise the ire of Anglo Canadian "nativists" (to use the polite term) at the beginning of the twentieth century; it was they and their fellow "ethnics" (usually called "foreigners" at the time) who complicated the Manitoba school question; it was they who formed the bulk of the unjustly interned "enemy aliens" during the Great War; they, among others, who were the butt of the rightist reaction during and after the Winnipeg General Strike of 1919; they who provided much of the rank and file of the Communist Party of Canada during the Great Depression and who volunteered in numbers to join the international brigades fighting the royalists/nationalists during the Spanish Civil War; they who were blamed for much of the "no" vote on the Prairies after the acrimonious Conscription Plebiscite of 1942 that split the country down the middle; they who inspired John Diefenbaker's fiery September 1960 United Nations speech condemning the evils of Communism and calling for the freedom of the "captive nations," and Ukraine in particular; they who formed one of the most prominent parts of the ethnic alliance that brought Ed Schreyer's NDP to power in Manitoba in 1969 and rejoiced when, several years later, he was appointed the first non-British, non-French, that is, "ethnic," Governor General of Canada (Schreyer was actually of Galician German ancestry; his wife was of Bukovinian German ancestry); it was they who led the boisterous protests that shook Toronto and embarrassed Prime Minister Trudeau during the state visit of Soviet Premier Alexei Kosygin in the early 1970s; it was they who led the fight for a multicultural Canada at the time of the Royal Commission on Bilingualism and Biculturalism, a fight that they legally won with the federal government's proclamation of official multiculturalism in 1971, and that they symbolically won with Schreyer's appointment to Ottawa, reiterated a decade later with Ray Hnatyshyn's appointment as the second Governor General of "ethnic" origin and the first of Ukrainian ancestry; and finally, in a partial reversal of their predominantly leftish tendencies before 1939, it was they, or at least some of their most active political leaders, who most openly bucked the Jewish and left-wing lobbies and insisted on a wider historical perspective, due process, and a fair hearing for those Canadian citizens accused of being involved in Nazi war crimes, generally one of the worst libels that any innocent individual or ostensibly implicated community could endure during the last decades of the

twentieth century and the first decade of the twenty-first. Their political
spectrum was always exceedingly broad, their politics always exciting;
their social life was always lively, and their religious life tumultuous as
much as tranquil. During most of their time in this country, they formed
a seriously divided but very vigorous Canadian community with politically opposed but perennially recurring traditions; and, throughout the
twentieth century, this community and these traditions repeatedly provided some very colourful chinks, red and white, blue and yellow, in the
ever-changing kaleidoscope that is Canadian society. They are a Canadian
ethnic group, an "ethnicity," if you will, with a story to tell, and those establishment historians, either political elitists on the "right" such as Jack
Granatstein or social homogenizers on the "left" such as Gerald Friesen,
who would cross them out of Canadian history for the sake of a more
narrow national narrative, do a serious disservice to their country.[5]

Of course, the history of Canada itself in relative terms is not all that
long and, though the Ukrainian Canadians have been a part of it throughout most of its time as a self-governing dominion within the British
Empire, and all of its time as an independent country, the freshness of
their experience and a certain pioneering mentality permeate their culture, which is almost stereotypically designated as "ethnic." Witness the
fiery Ukrainian dancers who, over many decades, almost always performed for Queen Elizabeth II on her state visits to western Canada and
the girls with their embroidered Ukrainian costumes with ribbons flow-
ing who ceremoniously offered her bread and salt. Though only dating
back to the royal visit of 1939, which was aimed to bolster Canadian support for the coming war in Europe, such traditions are fairly old in relative terms; that is, both the custom of offering bread and salt and the
monarchy and civic tradition that they honour are centuries old. It is the
coming together of the two that remains fresh and striking and particularly Canadian.

On a different level, it has to be admitted that, in a certain sense, the
general concept of "ethnicity" and, indeed, the very word itself, is also
new. It does not appear, for example, in Walter Skeat's famous *Concise
Etymological Dictionary of the English Language*, which was first published at
the turn of the nineteenth century (the time when a particularly famous
Canadian postage stamp bore the proud motto: "We hold a vaster empire than has been!"). This dictionary, however, does list the word "ethnic" and tells us that it is derived through the Latin *ethnicus* from the
Greek *ethnikos*, meaning "national." The Greek noun *ethnos*, from which
the adjective derives, at one time had the double connotation of "nation"

and "foreign people," as is revealed in the Greek version of the Bible, where it is used to translate the Hebrew term *goy*, meaning a non-Israelite or "gentile" nation. For about three centuries, in the English language, the "foreign" or more strikingly "heathen" meaning of the word seemed to predominate, but by the middle of the nineteenth century, the simpler meaning of "a people" began to hold sway. The term "ethnicity" itself seems to have been first applied to so-called "immigrant groups" and their descendants in 1941 by the American anthropologist W. Lloyd Warner, who may have felt something of the original double meaning of the root word.

Traditionally, the term "ethnicity" has some relation to the concept of "race," but is also somewhat distinct from it, since, in commonsensical terms, a person can at times cultivate or discard his or her ethnic background, but cannot do quite the same for race. Of course, as the sociologists assure us, "race," too, is largely a social convention or construct, since, for example, a person of a certain racial type in the United States may find himself placed in a different racial category in Brazil or some other country. Moreover, both "ethnicity" and "race" are concepts that were constantly changing throughout the twentieth century and the former ever more frequently replaced the latter since its misuse by the Nazis in the middle of that century. For example, the Canadian census once counted people of various "racial origins" but now discusses only "ethnic groups" and "visible minorities."

There are, at present, generally two different uses of the term "ethnic" in North American scholarship. One restricts usage to persons of non-English background (or, in Canada, to persons of a "non-charter group" – that is, non-English and non-French background), while the other acknowledges that all people have some kind of ethnic background or other, and this includes elite White Anglo Saxon Protestant Sons (WASPS) as well. In the title of the present work, the word "ethnic" appears and is used in the narrower sense, which excludes the English and also, to some degree, the other British groups. I do this consciously, not because I wish to deprive English Canadians of their heritage (it is well stated in most mainstream Canadian history books), but rather to emphasize what these books have generally ignored or belittled: the history of us "others."[6]

It must be acknowledged, however, that ethnicity is a variable thing, culturally learned as much as genetically inherited, and can be put on or taken off at various times. It is created over time, and sometimes, as the asssimilationists constantly remind us, it passes away. In North America, many immigrant groups typically at first often had only local, regional, or religious identities, which were later wielded into national or broader "ethnic" identities by the social pressures of North America and the influence of events occurring on the international stage. For example, as mentioned above, the Ukrainian Canadian identity and even the "Ukrainian" name itself developed out of earlier regional and religious identities, and, on the Prairies, firmly congealed only in the 1920s. Other groups such as the Polish and the Italians also went through this process of transformation from local to national identities, though for the most part without the striking change of name that was characteristic of the Ukrainians. Some groups never did completely congeal, as, for example, "German" Canadians and Mennonites, who to this day remain seriously divided along religious lines that impede the emergence of a single ethnic identity.

Boundaries are also important. In other words, how do ethnic groups define themselves and mark themselves off from their neighbours? Leaving this question unanswered sometimes leads to puzzling problems. For example, through most of the twentieth century, the Canadian censuses showed there were significantly more Ukrainian speakers in the country than there were Ukrainians. This would be unremarkable for a prominent group with an internationally recognized language like the Germans or even the Russians. But for a little-known group, which throughout most of the century did not even possess its own state, like the Ukrainians, it was indeed remarkable. Ukrainian Canadian historians typically explained it by saying that for a long time, citizens of Ukrainian background were still often incorrectly registered as Austrians, Russians, or even Poles.[7] But it also could be that the Ukrainians, being by far the largest Slavonic group in the country and comprising the third-largest group on the Prairies after the British groups and the Germans, exercised an assimilative effect on their Slavic neighbours, especially those Roman Catholics from Galicia, and their children, who, in Europe, the United States, or even in eastern Canada, would be usually counted as "Poles." Thus, throughout twentieth-century Canada, the ethnic markers were in this particular case not always clear.

In addition to this, it should be noted that, in western Canada at least, when newspapers, politics, and political pamphleteering are put aside, on the personal level this Ukrainian–Polish relationship was usually positive. Intermarriage was always quite common and the large numbers of Canadian Roman Catholics who today adhere to Ukrainian ethnicity are, at least in part, evidence of it. Once again, this throws light on the element of choice in the acquisition of ethnicity. Children of mixed parentage can usually openly choose which ethnicity to adopt. In my own family, which is the typically mixed Ukrainian and Polish, I always felt myself Ukrainian, though I was aware that one of my grandfathers was Polish and subscribed to the famous Winnipeg Polish weekly *Czas* (Time). Indeed, even he hailed from pre-1914 eastern Galicia, southern Podillia, to be exact, a predominantly Ukrainian region that was incorporated into the Ukrainian SSR in 1944 as part of the Ternopil region. By contrast, one of my sisters, who visited Poland during a very formative part of her life, identifies more closely with a Polish identity, and I had a close uncle (my mother's brother Edward Miedzybrocki) who attended a Ukrainian church, spoke a bit of Ukrainian, knew practically no Polish at all, and still considered himself to be Polish and not Ukrainian. For a time, he was, in fact, president of the Canadian Polish Professional and Businessmen's Association in Manitoba.

This mixing is, as I have said, a typically western Canadian phenomenon, but such situations are not unique to Canada. They also occurred in late nineteenth- and early twentieth-century eastern Europe. Thus, the foremost spokesman for integral Ukrainian nationalism, Dmytro Dontsov, an extremist if there ever was one, who actually immigrated to Canada after 1945, ironically had a brother who declared himself "Russian," while in western Ukraine under Poland from 1919 to 1939, the leader of the Ukrainian Greek Catholic Church, Metropolitan Andrei Sheptytsky, who was a national hero of no little import, came from a prominent Polish family with quite distant "Ruthenian" roots. His brother became a Polish general. All this would seem to push the explanation for ethnicity into the "chosen" or "invented" rather than the "inherited" or "primordial" camp, and, among social scientists today, supporters of the "invented" concept seem to hold the upper hand.[8] Certainly, in the writing of the articles in this book, I have sometimes felt myself constrained to bypass the vagaries of real life and, to no little degree, accept the given boundaries of a well-defined ethnic group. Nevertheless, I remain a Ukrainian Canadian with a significant and valued Polish heritage, and it occasionally shows in this volume dedicated to heritage gathering.

Of course, heritage gathering never ends and, with the passage of time, new material sometimes comes to the fore. This is particularly true in times of great political and social change, and there is no doubt that East European, Ukrainian, and Ukrainian Canadian studies in the 1980s and 1990s were deeply affected by such changes. For example, the first draft of the essay on Ivan Franko in this volume was written when the Cold War was still underway and Soviet materials were still very heavily censored. Since that time, Franko's literary, scholarly, and journalistic corpus has been much more fully published and new nuances added to his biography. In fact, for readers in Ukraine itself, this biography has been completely reinterpreted. With regard to Franko and Canada, suffice it to say that we now know for certain that the great writer himself once considered emigrating to this country. Thus, on 18 May 1895, Franko wrote to his political mentor Mykhailo Drahomanov that things were going badly for him in Galicia and that he was ready to emigrate to some other country. He continued: "At this time, we are talking a lot about Canada here with Dr Oleskiv. In the middle of July, he is going there to seek a place for Ruthenian colonists, and if an appropriate place can be located and the possibility of founding a nice colony demonstrated, I will be the first who is ready to go across the ocean."[9] This letter was unknown to me in 1983 when I wrote my first essay on Franko and Canada. It has been integrated into the updated and much expanded essay appearing here.

On a somewhat different level, I think it necessary to consider some terms that occur repeatedly in this book and may need some explanation for readers unfamiliar with the subjects considered here. The first two are the terms "Slavonic" and "Slavic." These two terms are used interchangeably in the present work to refer to the largest ethnolinguistic group of peoples in eastern Europe and their descendants in North America. Many writers approaching Canadian and American ethnic history use the term "Slavic" and avoid the term "Slavonic." This is probably because, among academics on this continent, "Slavic Studies" are now an established discipline and the term "Slavonic" is generally restricted to the medieval world where the liturgical language of the early South Slavs is referred to as "Old Church Slavonic," and its derivatives in the eastern Slavic world are referred to as forms or "redactions" of "Church Slavonic." By contrast, in Britain, the parallel discipline is referred to as "Slavonic Studies" and the relevant modern languages and modern peoples of eastern Europe are often referred to as the "Slavonic languages" and the "Slavonic peoples." My choice to mix the two terms is a conscious one, not only because the potential readership of this book extends past Canada and the United States to Britain and beyond, but also because I feel that the term "Slavonic" somewhat restores a bit of the medieval *gravitas* that emigration to the New World cut off for so many poor immigrants of earlier times. Indeed, the children and grandchildren of these early immigrants were often so very alienated from their ancient European roots that one prominent Polish American historian, John J.

Bukowczyk, even titled his master work on this subject as *And My Children Did Not Know Me: A History of the Polish Americans.*[10] My use here of the term "Slavonic" is a road sign indicating the direction in which the descendants of older immigrants may go to find and recover some little-known but very profound parts of their ancestral heritage. Furthermore, as is well known to philologists and medieval historians, the apparently unrelated words "Slavic" and "slave-like" are, in fact, etymologically related (both are derived from the medieval Latin word *sclavus*, meaning first "Slav" and then later "slave"), and the use in this book of the (for some North Americans) literary and archaic-sounding term "Slavonic" is an attempt to put somewhat more distance between the two and restore a certain pristine dignity to the root of this word, which, in its origins, was almost certainly positive.[11]

The second term or phrase that may be unfamiliar to some readers is what I, inspired by several American and Canadian writers on the subject, call "the Great Migration," or "the Great Economic Immigration," or variants of these forms. As is repeatedly explained in the essays that follow, this term refers on one level to the great eastern and southern European immigration to the Americas that occurred between the 1880s and the outbreak of the Great War in 1914. American historians often call it the "New Immigration," which contrasts, in their view, with the preceding "Old Immigration," which was predominantly from the British Isles and northwestern Europe. (This was a period of enormous change in the ethnohistory of North America and caused a certain amount of panic in some quarters.)[12] In my view, however, and not in my view alone, this language of "old" and "new" is now somewhat obsolete. This is because, after a long period in the first half of the twentieth century of relatively limited immigration to the United States from Europe (less limited in Canada), and a short period of resettlement of refugees at the end of the Second World War, in the 1970s, a still newer mass immigration from the Third World, particularly Asia, began. As did the Great Economic Immigration from 1880 to 1914, this new immigration, largely of people who joined the so-called visible minorities in North America, greatly changed the ethnic and cultural makeup of Canada and the United States. Thus, it, too, can be referred to as a "New Immigration," though, for many groups such as the Chinese and certain others, it had precedents in earlier times.

With regard to specifically Prairie Canadian history, and the history of the Ukrainian Canadians, the pioneer or Great Economic Immigration is a very apt designation, for it was in numerical terms by far the greatest immigration of eastern Europeans in general, and Ukrainians in particular, to this region, and it distinguishes very clearly between this immigration and the much smaller interwar immigration (still largely economic), and the smaller still, politically motivated, refugee immigration post-1945, which is usually referred to as the Displaced Persons (DP) immigration. The more recent post-Soviet immigration to Canada has also been relatively small in numerical terms, though, to some extent, it is undoubtedly important in rejuvenating certain institutions of the organized Ukrainian community in the country. (It provides Ukrainian-fluent staff for certain museums, libraries, and academic institutions founded by earlier waves of Ukrainian Canadians whose children and grandchildren are now mostly assimilated and English speaking, though many undoubtedly retain a clear memory of their "ethnic" origins and identify in some ways with things Ukrainian.) These four "waves" of Ukrainian immigration to Canada, as it were, form the paradigm around which Ukrainian Canadian history is usually organized, and the pioneer or Great Economic Immigration was the first and by far the largest of these waves.

Finally, this terminology again varies with geographical emphasis. When the "push" factors in Europe are paramount, the term used for the pre-1914 period is the "Great Economic Emigration," since the stress is on leaving; when the "pull" factors in North America are more important, the term becomes the "Great Economic Immigration," since the stress is on arriving. This distinction between emigration and immigration is often glossed over by historians dealing in an unequal way with either Europe or the Americas who usually reveal either a Euro-centric or American-centred view. In this way, for example, some historians often write of political "émigrés" while others write about economic "immigrants."

This question of émigrés versus immigrants is manifested in various forms in different ethnic communities. Among the Ukrainian Canadians, for example, the distinction between the first two waves of economic immigrants and the third or DP wave was often remarked on in earlier times by participants in these waves and was later noted by historians. In western Canada in the 1970s, I myself noticed the appearance of young "nationalist" missionaries from the East, children of the DP immigration, who had come to western Canada with the noblest of intentions to spread the national gospel among the largely assimilated grandchildren of the older economic immigration. This elitist tenor of a good part of the DP immigration, throughout the second half of the twentieth century, was particularly strong in Toronto, the metropolitan centre of the DP immigration, and produced a certain amount of friction with its somewhat less political confreres. Moreover, western Canadian regionalism and resentment of Toronto's cultural pretensions and important role in Canadian society may have deepened this divide. Certainly, Torontonian civic pride and sometimes dismissive, sometimes good-natured, joking about provincial and frosty "Winterpeg," which was, to the 1970s, the metropolitan centre of the older economic immigration, did not help.

But the division was not limited to Canada's Ukrainians or even to Canada, riven as it is with various regional tensions. More generally, among some eastern European communities in the United States, where regionalism among these groups is much less pronounced, this friction still reached remarkable proportions. For example, in the 1980s, a sharp exchange occurred on the pages of the *New York Times Book Review* between the Nobel Prize-winning Polish poet Czesław Miłosz (a newer, post-1945 political émigré who had lived for a while under the Communist dictatorship) and Stanislaus Blejwas (an historian of the older, economic Polish immigration). Miłosz bemoaned what he called "the incredible cultural crudeness of Polish-Americans" and Blejwas replied to the poet by noting "that intolerant prejudice unique to intellectuals, namely, the contemptuous condemnation of the masses who do not read or understand him." The Polish American historian James S. Pula concluded that this peculiar debate reflected the old divide between the nobles or *szlachta* and the peasants who lived under them in pre-Communist Polish society in eastern Europe. Among the Ukrainian Canadians, the friction between the older immigrants and the DPs, to my knowledge, never reached the same intensity or, at least, literary levels as among Polish Americans, but the difference in ambience was, for several decades at least, very real. The use in this book of the term "Great Economic Immigration" attempts to remove from the picture all condescension of the Miłosz type and its concomitant frictions.[13]

The third term or phrase that may require some explanation is what I call the "Long Cold War." By this term I mean the long-standing conflict between the Soviet Union and the West that occurred between the defeat of Nazi Germany in 1945 and the final collapse of the Soviet Union in 1991. Certain historians who advocate the concept of a shorter Cold War date the beginning of this conflict somewhat later – for example, with the Communist coup in Czechoslovakia in 1948 – and end it somewhat earlier – for example, with the fall of the Berlin Wall and the liberation of "eastern Europe" in 1989. But for the Ukrainian Canadians, as one of the anonymous readers of this manuscript pointed out to me, the Cold War was already in full swing by the 1920s and 1930s, and, after a brief period of suppression from 1941 to 1945 (the period of the "Grand Alliance" between the Western democracies and the USSR), certainly took on a new vigor after 1945; and, for Ukrainians in Europe, it was 1991 and the declaration of national independence from the USSR that was the great turning point and not the 1989 fall of the Berlin Wall. The year 1991 actually meant that "eastern Europe" now extended some 800 kilometres further east to the new border between independent European Ukraine and a somewhat different "Eurasian" Russia. Most importantly, the term "Long Cold War" also puts to rest the illusion that the Sino–Soviet conflict and other events of the 1960s and 1970s somehow diluted or ended certain aspects of this conflict, especially the ideological aspects, that directly concerned the population of Ukraine and were of great import to almost all of the organized Ukrainian community in Canada and the United States. This view was widespread among Western historians of international relations right until 1991, but it was never shared by most Ukrainian scholars working in the West who were always well aware that political repression in Ukraine and the censorship of political materials and of scholarship of all kinds continued right through to the Gorbachev Reforms of the late 1980s.[14]

In this way, the term "Long Cold War," like other terms frequently used in this book, such as "ethnic," "ethnicity," "ethnic history," "Slavonic," "Slavic," "emigration," "immigration," the "Great Economic Migration," and "heritage gathering," takes on a special meaning. It is to be hoped that this meaning adds something to the understanding of the reader to whom these concepts may be less well defined and to whom the debates surrounding them may be somewhat new.

Finally, it is necessary to say a few words about the organization of the book. It is divided into four separate sections, each reflecting a certain connection between Europe and the Americas and using the concepts described above. In the first section, "Emigration Studies," the materials are set in chronological order and pass from the general to the particular. Thus, the first essay on the Great Migration in the literatures of the Slavs treats the oldest emigration from eastern Europe to the Americas before 1914, the so-called pioneer era, and takes in all of both regions; the second essay concentrates more specifically on the Russian Empire and North America; and the third zeros in on the old Austrian Crown Land of Galicia, the Ukrainian emigration from this land to western Canada, and the role of the writer Ivan Franko in helping to prompt this emigration. The fourth essay in this section takes the story out of the pioneer era and treats the interwar emigration from the Republic of

Poland to Canada. But, in many ways, this later interwar emigration was merely an extension of the earlier pioneer emigration. The new immigrants to Canada had largely the same social profile as the earlier ones did and they mostly came from exactly the same part of Europe: old Austrian Galicia, which was annexed to the Republic of Poland in 1918–19 and offically renamed Eastern Little Poland by the new Polish government and its agencies. With regard to my particular heritage, I should point out that although three of my grandparents came to Canada before 1914 with Austrian passports from old Galicia, the fourth, my maternal grandmother, although an ethnic Ukrainian, came from this same region in 1925 with a new Polish passport.

On a different level, post-1945, this same region underwent further political change and was annexed to the Ukrainian SSR; by then, its emigrants to Canada were fleeing the advance of the Red Army westward and were, therefore, quite political, which was very different from most of their predecessors, who were, by and large, purely economic immigrants. This comes out in the present book in the essays dealing with anti-Communist Ukrainian émigré scholars, many of whom, such as the philologist J. B. Rudnyckyj or the historian Lubomyr Wynar, hailed from this same area, though, as the recent and exhaustive study of Wynar's Ukrainian Historical Association by Alla Atamanenko has shown, Wynar himself tried very hard to have all of modern Ukraine represented on the pages of the association's journal, *Ukrainskyi istoryk* (The Ukrainian historian).[15] Thus, the spectacular and repeated border changes in twentieth-century eastern Europe played a role in forming the character of Ukrainian and eastern European immigration to North America, but did not change it completely.

The second section in the book, "History, Historians, and Others," also has an emphasis on pre-1945 developments, but goes on to deal with some of the contributions of post-1945 immigrants. It starts with a consideration of the career of the historian Dmytro Doroshenko, who visited Canada twice in the 1930s and finally immigrated to this country in the late 1940s. It continues with treatments of the Canadian historian George W. Simpson and his relations with the Ukrainian Canadians; it then turns to an examination of how the subject of Ukrainian history was treated in the 1930s, then during the war of 1939 to 1945, and then again during the Cold War period. The general theme here is one of slow but steady growth and constantly increasing professionalism, the shift from the spread of literacy and popular education (as, for example, in the *prosvita* or "enlightenment" societies) to scholarship and higher forms of learning (as, for example, in various post-1945 émigré academic institutions). The emphasis on the origins of Ukrainian Canadian scholarship in the pioneer, interwar, and Second World War eras reflects my own family background, while the treatments of the DP emigration post-1945 and its contribution to historical and other scholarship reflects my professional training under the influence of some of these DP scholars. The final essay in this section, that on Gabrielle Roy, ties in to interwar developments and reflects the yearning for higher education among the earlier immigrants as well as the striking political developments of the 1930s and the personal life of the principal protagonists, Gabrielle Roy and Stephen Davidovich, the latter of whom ended as a professor of public administration at York University in Toronto.

The third group of essays, "Library Studies and Reference Works," continues some of the themes raised in the second section. The career of the distinguished Winnipeg philologist J. B. Rudnyckyj is examined with regard to his contributions to "Library Science," as the field was called at the time, and reflects the state of Ukrainian émigré scholarship during the Cold War era, especially the central years of this long period. The second essay in this section (on Mykhailo Hrushevsky) is my own personal assessment of what I discovered about Ukrainian history and Ukrainian émigré scholarship towards the end of this Long Cold War and continues the "books and libraries" theme. The third essay in this section on the Ukrainian Canadians in the encyclopedias sums up the general history of this group and says a lot about how its members were viewed throughout the various periods of Canadian history from the 1890s to the present. The evolution described here in certain ways parallels points made in the earlier essays and puts them within a more general context.

These three essays are followed by a final section consisting of a single essay with some concluding ruminations comparing the Ukrainian experience in Canada with that in the United States. This piece makes some general remarks on the idea of multiculturalism as it has developed in Canada over the last few decades and how this has diverged from ethnic experiences in the great American Republic to Canada's south, where the idea of the melting pot has always been very prominent, though not necessarily all-encompassing.

In sum, all the essays included in this volume reflect the heritage I have been collecting over the course of the last few decades. They move from basic questions of emigration and immigration, to the first fragile fruits of education in the New World, and then to the fuller development of Ukrainian scholarship on this continent. This process began with popular education and the national movement as expressed by "popular enlighteners" such as the writer Ivan Franko and other Slavic figures, continued through further enlighteners such as Mykhailo Hrushevsky and Dmytro Doroshenko, was transferred to Canada and given a special Canadian spirit by men such as George W. Simpson, was observed and commented on by no less a writer than Gabrielle Roy, and reached a certain maturity in the work of émigrés such as the Ukrainian American Lubomyr Wynar and the Ukrainian Canadian J. B. Rudnyckyj. Of course, Ukrainian culture on this continent has progressed considerably since the end of the Long Cold War, and, it must be said, the heyday of Ukrainian émigré scholarship is now long gone. Nevertheless, I am, in part, most definitely a product of certain of these developments and, like Bernard of Chartres so many years ago, I acknowledge that the heritage I have gathered here clearly reflects that state.

Emigration Studies

1 The Great Migration: East-Central Europe to the Americas in the Literatures of the Slavs, Some Examples

Iterum. Ubi bene, ibi patria.
(Again. Where it's good, that's where the homeland lies.)

With apologies to
Emily Greene Balch

The century that preceded the First World War saw one of the greatest voluntary movements of population in world history. Quite literally, millions of European citizens, some city people, but mostly townsfolk and villagers, deserted their homelands and boarded trains and then ocean-going ships for the New World. They headed for both North America and South America. The movement began in western and northern Europe, but, by the 1850s, had encompassed Germany and central Europe, and, by the end of the century, engulfed southern and eastern Europe. During the first years of the twentieth century, Italy, the lands of the Habsburg Monarchy, and the western borderlands of the Russian Empire became the principal focal points of the emigration movement.[1]

By the middle of the nineteenth century, this mass movement of ordinary people, labourers from the towns and agriculturalists from the villages, had already touched certain territories inhabited by the Slavonic peoples of Europe. The westernmost of the ethnographically Slavic territories were, of course, the first to be affected. Thus, the first mass migration of Slavonic peoples to the Americas emanated primarily from Polish-speaking lands such as Pomerania, the Poznan region, and Prussia in imperial Germany, and from Czech-speaking Bohemia and the Croat lands in the Habsburg Monarchy. Afterwards, this so-called emigration fever caught Slovakia and Trans-Carpathian Ukraine (or "Upper

Hungary," as these territories were called at the time), "Austrian Galicia" (which was inhabited for the most part by Poles in the west and by Ukrainians or "Ruthenians," as they were then usually called, in the east), and also the land known as the Congress Kingdom of Poland within the Russian empire. Finally, the movement spread to the western borderlands of Russia itself and encompassed the territory inhabited by Belarusans, Ukrainians, and, to a lesser degree, by Russians.[2]

In a pattern that was common throughout most of these lands, isolated individuals, political émigrés, and colourful adventurers of various sorts preceded the mass migration of country folk. Among the Slavs, the Poles are definitely the best example, with political émigrés and military men such as Tadeusz Kościuszko and Kazimierz Pułaski playing significant roles in American revolutionary history and Sir Cazimir Gzowski playing a prominent role in nineteenth-century Canadian public life. Polish political émigrés were also early arrivals in Latin America, and, for example, the Brazilian emperor Pedro I, while visiting Paris, even shouted out *"Vive la Pologne"* when he found himself at the theatre, by chance, at a play put on for Polish émigrés from the November Insurrection. The audience reciprocated with a shout of *"Vive l'Empereur du Brézil'."*[3] Other examples of early Slavic political refugees and assorted adventurers include the Czechs Augustine Herman (c. 1605–1696) and Frederick Philipse (1616–1701), who emigrated to colonial America, the Slovak inventor Jozef Murgas (1864–1929), who emigrated to the United States in the late nineteenth century, the Slovene Roman Catholic missionary Frederick Baraga (1797–1868), and Ferdinand Konščak (1703–1759), the Croat Jesuit explorer who helped demonstrate that Baja California was a peninsula and not an island. Finally, there was Ahapii Honcharenko (Agapius Goncharenko) (1832–1916), who came to America from the Kiev region of the Russian Empire, founded the *Alaska Herald*, the first Russian-language newspaper in the United States, and tried to establish a Ukrainian socialist colony in California during the early years of the twentieth century. Both Russian and Ukrainian historians include Honcharenko in the history of their respective communities in America, though undoubtedly he was a nationally conscious Ukrainian.[4]

When, in the 1870s, emigration from the Slavonic countries in Europe began to take on a new, more plebian, and much more massive character, there were, once again, a few exceptional personalities. These included a small number of intellectuals and writers who witnessed this mass exodus of eastern European country folk, in some cases even visiting or planning to visit the New World themselves, and sat down to describe what they believed to be this unique migration in travellers' tales, memoirs, fictional accounts, and poetic works of various sorts.

By far the most famous name among these literary observers is that of Henryk Sienkiewicz (1846–1916), who attracted world attention by his historical novels of seventeenth-century Poland and of Christian heroism in ancient Rome. His grand trilogy of historical novels on the fall of the old Polish Lithuanian Commonwealth, which were published between 1883 and 1888, are tales replete with love and war, and made him the most popular Polish writer of his time. In 1905, his *Quo Vadis*, a tale about the persecution of Christians in ancient Rome, won the Nobel Prize for literature. Sienkiewicz, who was of lesser gentry origin, had begun his career as a journalist for the Warsaw newspaper *Gazeta Polska* (Polish gazette) where, under the pseudonym "Litwos," he published a series of "letters" or feuilletons in which he described the petty episodes of ordinary life and paid some attention to what nineteenth-century observers euphemistically called "the Social Question." In these early writings, one can find a "realistic" and very touching picture of the hard life of the Slavic country folk.[5]

It was on a romantic whim, it seems, that Sienkiewicz and a group of his Polish intellectual friends, including the famous Polish actress Helena Modrzejewska (who came to be known in the English-speaking world as Helen Modjeska), decided to leave Warsaw to live a freer, ostensibly more "natural" life on a frontier commune in far-off California. Sienkiewicz's experience with this ill-fated socialistic experiment, his descriptions of American life in the 1870s, and his observations of the beginning of organized Polish life in America and the initial phase of the mass migration of the Polish peasantry were published immediately in the form of a series of "Letters" to the readers of the *Gazeta Polska*. In turn, this Warsaw paper paid for the cost of the expedition.[6]

Sienkiewicz and his friends knew that other European intellectuals had preceded them in the voyage to the New World. In his *Listy z podróży do Ameryki* (Letters from my travels in America, published in English as *Portrait of America: Letters of Henry Sienkiewicz*), the Polish novelist mentioned both the *American Notes* of Charles Dickens and *Democracy in America* by Alexis de Tocqueville. The former had been translated into Polish in 1844; the latter was widely read throughout Europe in the nineteenth century. Certain Polish writers, too, had dealt with American themes: Julian Horain dispatched enthusiastic reports from California; Christine Narbutt published the account "In America," and Roger Lubieński, Sygurd Wiśniowski, and Kalikst Wolski all printed several articles on the subject.[7] But it is in Sienkiewicz that can be found the best-known descriptions of the initial stages of mass Polish economic migration, and it was Sienkiewicz who produced the first important work of fiction in Polish dealing with this migration.

Most of Sienkiewicz's *Listy z podróży do Ameryki* dealt with the author's impressions of the New World and of American life and character. Only one letter (number thirteen) directly treats the mass migration of the Polish peasantry and the new Polish communities in America. But even in this brief letter, Sienkiewicz makes several observations that become major themes in his fictional tale about the Great Economic Migration. Sienkiewicz deals first with the difficulties of the ocean crossing and the motivations of the peasant travellers: "In search of bread and freedom which we did not have back home," they tell him. Then came the delight followed by the shock of landing in bustling New York and the sudden realization that "there would be no one with whom they could speak in the Catholic language." Sienkiewicz does not minimize the horrendous physical and psychological difficulties the new immigrants had to face, and concluded that "their lot is a severe and terrifying one and whoever would depict it accurately would create an epic of human misery."[8] This is exactly what Sienkiewicz was to do in his intensely moving short story "Za chlebem" (For bread).

"Za chlebem" was written after Sienkiewicz had returned to Poland from his travels in America. It was first read publicly in 1880 at a gathering in the Warsaw City Hall held for the financial benefit of poor country folk who had gotten in trouble with the law. Afterwards, it was printed in the *Gazeta Polska* and the *Dziennik Poznański* (The Poznan daily), two of the leading Polish newspapers. The press notices stressed the emotional power and cruel reality of Sienkiewicz's tale. It was obvious that he had written this piece as a warning to all who would venture from hearth and home in search of fortune in unknown lands far away.[9]

In this particular case, the story did not attribute emigration to political conditions, but, rather, Sienkiewicz's protagonists, old Vavron Toporek and his beautiful daughter Marysia, went to America as a result of a curious combination of local crop failures, a frustrating legal dispute with a neighbour, and the none-too-fortuitous arrival of a cunning German emigration agent. After a difficult ocean crossing marked by overcrowding and fear of death by storm, Vavron and young Marysia arrive in New York City, where ignorance of the language, lack of money, and the generally terrible living conditions throw Vavron into such a fit of despair that he almost kills his daughter. However, a chance meeting with an established Polish gentleman leads to their resettlement in a Polish colony on the Arkansas frontier. Such an opportunity to plough the virgin soil of the West was the dream of almost all Slavic immigrants of rural background, and Sienkiewicz allows the colony to flourish. For a brief time, Vavron's and Marysia's health and hopes are restored. But, once again, a string of disasters, ending in a flood in which Vavron perishes, puts an end to all hope, and Marysia eventually returns to New York, where, unable to return home or to find work, she reverts to penury and dies.

The cunning emigration agent, terrible ocean crossing, language difficulties, and horrible living conditions in New York were all themes that first appeared in Sienkiewicz's *Letters* and correspond to his impressions of the lives of the poor Slavic immigrants. However, the disasters on the frontier do not; for, in his *Letters,* Sienkiewicz makes it clear that if a Polish farmer can find the money to get to the far West, he will eventually do well. The Polish writer's portraits of the existing Polish communities of Chicago, Detroit, and Milwaukee, again, are anything but depressing. Thus, it is clear that the didactic purpose behind "Za chlebem" was to discourage the Polish country folk from venturing on the great journey to the New World. Sienkiewicz produced other works based on his experiences in America: *Przez stepy* (Across the plains, 1878) dealt with the love between a sweet American girl and the Polish captain of an immigrant party, and *Latarnik* (The lighthouse keeper of Aspinwall) is the tragic story of a Polish political refugee who is unable to find peace in the New World – but none of them had as their central theme the Great Migration of the eastern European peasantry. This theme did clearly emerge, however, in the works of other Slavonic writers.

One of the most important of these writers was the Slovak novelist Martin Kukučin (1860–1928). Born Matej Bencur to parents who were small farmers of the Lutheran faith and of petty gentry origin, Kukučin grew to become one of the best and most cosmopolitan Slovak writers of the turn of the century. At first, he wrote short stories that dealt realistically and sympathetically with Slovak village life. But he later composed a number of novels that stand among the greatest monuments of modern Slovak literature. One of these, *Dom v stráni* (The house on the hillside), was set in Dalmatia and dealt with the social gulf and conflicting responsibilities of the large landowner and the impoverished peasant farmer; another, the five-volume *Mat' volá* (The motherland is calling), was destined to become one of the most important works of Slavonic literature dealing with the emigration theme. Like Sienkiewicz, Kukučin also wrote a travelogue detailing his experiences in South America. But this three-volume *Prechádzka po Patagonii* (Travel sketches of a trip through Patagonia) was published in full only after his death in 1928 and never became well known outside the world of Slovak literature.[10]

The emigration theme appears quite early in Kukučin's work, for migration was an important aspect of life among the Slovak villagers of the High Carpathians. Indeed, at the turn of the century, Slovaks had the highest per capita emigration rate among all groups from the Habsburg Monarchy. In 1899, they represented 25 per cent of all immigrants to the United States from the monarchy and 45 per cent of those from Hungary. One in every four people among the almost two million members of this group had already been to America before World War I.[11] Thus, Kukučin's short story "Z teplého hniezda" (From a warm nest) (1885), which was his first attempt to deal with the emigration theme, hit on an important aspect of life in the Slovak village. This autobiographical tale dealt with the departure from the Slovakian mountains of a young son, Matej, for work, not in America but in a far-enough-away Hungarian city. Emigration themes, personal separation, broken family life, and the economic stagnation of the village all appear in this story. Its main theme, however, is the attractive ceremonialism of the villagers in their ritual of saying goodbye to Matej, and, in this way, Kukučin emphasizes the wholeness of the community and its public morality. The tale is widely regarded as one of the best early stories of Slovak village life. A second early Kukučin story, "Dies irae" (The day of wrath), deals with the social power of money and plainly anticipates his long masterpiece on the emigration theme, *Mat' volá*.[12]

Kukučin's five-volume *Mat' volá* is a novel about the life of Croatian immigrants in South America and details aspects of a Slavonic immigrant group that Kukučin, who served for many years as a medical doctor both in Dalmatia and then in Punta Arenas, Chile, knew very well.[13] Although Kukučin was able to describe precisely the daily life and economic struggles of these southern Slavic migrants, with their attendant desire to return to their native "motherland," he also wove into his story a great moral lesson about the use of money. Kukučin evaluated each of his characters according to their use of money. The shopkeeper Simon Katovič, a man who considers that his shop belongs not to the person whose name appears on the sign but, rather, to all the customers trading in the shop, became the central figure of the novel. Two characters especially exemplify the search for happiness in the New World: the demoralized Andrija, whom greed makes a usurer and who is, in the end, rejected by the entire community; and Kreśimír, who, on the contrary, succeeds in retaining his integrity and returns ultimately to his native land, which he was never able to forget. What is especially remarkable about Kukučin is not his innovative realism but, rather, his ability to tackle difficult class, economic, social, and psychological questions without either diminishing their intensity or reducing them to the mechanical formula of class struggle. Even when describing the most extreme conditions of immigrant life, Kukučin never lost his humane and gentle touch.[14]

The Slovak Martin Kukučin, who had spent many years in Latin America, produced the most important novel on the emigration theme in the Slavonic literatures, but it was the Polish writer Maria Konopnicka (1842–1910), who had never once visited the New World or even sailed on an ocean-going ship, who penned the greatest contribution in the poetic field. Konopnicka is well known in contemporary Poland as a poet, a writer of short stories and children's tales, and as a political and social activist who made many contributions to the women's movement. She was born into an intelligentsia family, educated at a Catholic school for girls in Warsaw, married, had six children, divorced, and was compelled to make her living by writing. For a time, she edited a Polish women's magazine, *Świt* (The dawn), but her radical program soon alienated many – both potential contributors and others – and difficulties with the censor compelled her to resign. She spent a great deal of time travelling in western Europe and, in 1891, during a visit to Zurich, met by chance a group of ragged Polish peasants who were making their way home across Europe. They were emigrants who had been enticed to Brazil but had been completely disillusioned by their stay in the New World. The wanderings of these disoriented Polish country folk, who travelled from Brazil to Marseilles, then to Geneva, Zurich, and eventually Cracow, inspired Konopnicka to write an epic work on the emigration theme. Her long poem *Pan Balcer w Brazylii* (Mr Balcer in Brazil) was the result.[15]

It was Konopnicka's long-standing dream to write an epic poem dealing with the life and fortune of the Polish peasantry. Polish literature already possessed an epic poem focused on the lives of the gentry (Adam Mickiewicz's *Pan Tadeusz*), and Konopnicka wished to complete the national literature and to make it truly national ("*prawdziwie narodową*") by writing an epic on the peasantry. The sudden mass migration of the Polish peasantry to Brazil at the turn of the century, the "Brazilian fever," as it was called at the time, provided her with the unifying theme she needed. Immediately after her encounter with the Polish peasants in Zurich, she began gathering material for *Pan Balcer w Brazylii.* The first part of the poem, "On the Sea," was published in the spring of 1892. Other parts appeared during the following years, and the entire epic was completed and published by 1909. Thus, it took her all of seventeen years to complete her great project.[16]

It was not scarcity of material that delayed the completion of *Pan Balcer w Brazylii.* The Brazilian fever was an important phenomenon of the day, and the Polish intelligentsia, both in Galicia and in the Congress Kingdom, which, by the turn of the century, were the major focal points of the emigration movement, avidly discussed the matter in books, pamphlets, and the daily press. Factors such as rural overpopulation, parcelization of the land, unscrupulous emigration agents, and advertising by labour-hungry Brazilian state governments who had just experienced the abolition of slavery were all openly broached. The mass migration of perhaps some 275,000 people to Brazil was often seen to be a popular – that is, democratic – phenomenon that widened the perspective of the villagers, but, at the same time, it was also acknowledged that the emigrants endured unspeakable sufferings and that the mass migration, in the short term at least, caused economic as well as demographic losses to the homeland. The conservative gentry usually opposed emigration because it increased the price of labour, while the radical intelligentsia generally criticized it because seemingly it dulled the edge of the class struggle. Konopnicka, like Sienkiewicz before her, was in accord with this negative majority view.[17]

Pan Balcer w Brazylii is the story of a group of Polish peasants who set off for Brazil at the height of the Brazilian fever. They are immediately beset by difficulties: the terrible ocean voyage in the tight, prison-like quarters of a ship that was not meant to carry people and the filth and oppressive heat that cause the first deaths. In Brazil, they are not given the land they were promised but, rather, are immediately divided into groups, some to work on a coffee plantation, others to work in the depths of the jungle. Amidst the steaming heat of the tropics, Pan Balcer, who is an artisan, not an ordinary peasant, arises as a leader and advises the suffering country folk to return home. Balcer leads them through jungles and over mountains, where many succumb to heat and thirst, but they eventually make it to the port. The dock workers, however, are on strike, and Balcer again is the first of the country folk to join the strikers. Eventually, the suffering peasants succeed in sailing for their native land. The final part of the poem is a hymn of praise to Mother Poland.[18]

Like her Slovak contemporary Martin Kukučin, Maria Konopnicka is a master of description, and her depiction of the various peasant types is detailed and accurate. Her use of Pan Balcer as a narrator provides an opportunity to describe nature and the villagers with the simplicity and authenticity of folk language. Her major theme is a patriotic one, steeped in the religious language of the devout country folk. The difficulties of the journey and the return home transform the protagonists from peasants (sing.: *chłop*) to the people (collective: *lud*) and from people into a real part of the nation (*naród*), and, in so doing, complete the social profile of the Polish nation of which only the gentry had hitherto been depicted on such a scale.[19]

The appearance of *Pan Balcer w Brazylii* was greeted enthusiastically by Konopnicka's early critics. Sienkiewicz immediately saw the vividness and accuracy of Konopnicka's descriptions of the ocean voyage and the New World, while Aleksander Brückner and Wilhelm Feldman both conceded that "Konopnicka has enriched the national Pantheon with the people."[20] More recent observers are far more severe, with the slow pace, lengthy descriptions, and dated material (emigration to Brazil ceased to be a current event after the Russian revolution of 1905) becoming critical themes. "The ideology of Pan Balcer," wrote Julian Krzyżanowski in 1979, "is the mechanical clustering of various uncoordinated parts and has little to do with the epic parts of the poem which are its [true] value."[21] However, as a testament to the emigration fever that struck the Slavonic lands at the turn of the twentieth century, Konopnicka's work remains unsurpassed. *Pan Balcer w Brazylii* has been translated into both Russian and Ukrainian, and, because of her treatments of patriotism, class consciousness, and alliance between peasant and worker, Soviet critics, in particular, to the demise of the USSR, continued to rate her work highly.[22]

Even during her lifetime, Maria Konopnicka's work was not unknown among the eastern Slavs. She was particularly familiar to the Ukrainians with whom the Poles shared the Austrian province of Galicia, and she attracted the special attention of the western Ukrainian writer Ivan Franko (1856–1916), who reckoned her "among the most talented women not only in Polish but also in all the Slavonic literatures." Franko liked Konopnicka's dedication to the peasantry, her lyrical talents, and her lack of national exclusiveness – what were probably ethnically Ukrainian Eastern Rite Catholics ("Uniates," as they were then called) play an important role in *Pan Balcer* – but at the same time, like so many later critics, he thought that *Pan Balcer w Brazylii* fell far short of an epic poem on the level of *Pan Tadeusz*.[23] Franko's opinion was of considerable significance because the Ukrainian peasantry of eastern Galicia was also very severely struck by the Brazilian fever, and, like Konopnicka, Franko himself composed a memorable poem on this theme.

Franko was certainly the man to do this job. Not only was he the most outstanding literary talent among the Galician Ukrainian intelligentsia of the turn of the century – shortly before his death in 1916, he was nominated for the Nobel Prize in literature – but he was also a gifted journalist and social critic who had written frequently on the emigration theme and had even been personally involved in the effort of some members of the Galician Ukrainian intelligentsia to redirect the emigration movement from Brazil to North America, most especially to western Canada. Like Sienkiewicz before him, Franko was a severe critic, though not an absolute opponent of mass economic migration. He seemed to believe that the emigration to the New World could be beneficial to both the emigrants and to the nation as a whole so long as it was well organized and wisely carried out.[24]

By the end of the nineteenth century, however, the mass migration of Galician Ukrainian country folk had reached truly astounding proportions. Overpopulation, famine, and educational, national, and other legal disabilities caused thousands to sell whatever they had and leave. According to Soviet reckoning, 212,000 Ukrainians deserted Galicia between 1890 and 1910. In the first decade of the twentieth century, another 35,000 left the neighbouring province of Bukovina, while emigration from Trans-Carpathia was correspondingly large.[25] Among the very poorest, fantastic rumours sprang up; for example, in 1891, quasi-messianic hopes were aroused by the mysterious death of the emperor's son, Crown Prince Rudolph, at Meyerling. In 1895, the emigration agent Gargoletti took advantage of this credulity. Disguising himself as a peasant-farmer, he pretended to be the beloved Archduke Rudolph and bought up the villagers' land in exchange for promises of cheap passage to places such as Brazil. A sudden and irresistible surge in emigration of poor folk was the result.[26]

The vain hopes and tragic situation caused by the unscrupulous Gargoletti was the spark that fired Franko's imagination. In the following couple of years, he composed a cycle of poetry on the Brazilian theme and published it in his own periodical and in the prestigious Galician Ukrainian journal *Literaturno-naukovyi vistnyk* (Literary-scientific herald).[27]

Franko's cycle *Do Brazilii* (To Brazil) may be divided into three parts. The first part takes the form of a letter from a group of Galician Ukrainian villagers to the Archduchess Stephanie, the wife of the late Crown Prince, in which they assure her that Rudolph was not dead but alive, was sending her greetings, and wished the country folk to follow him to Brazil. This faraway land, they informed the archduchess, was truly a peasant paradise without landlords or money lenders, a land where the faithful Ukrainian villager (*virnyi Rusyn*) simply captured a few monkeys to do whatever work had to be done. The second part of the cycle tells of the hardships of departure, the struggle across the Austrian Empire to a port city – Fiume, Genoa, or Hamburg – and across the high seas to the famous Brazilian state of Parana. The third part of the cycle again takes the form of a letter, this time from one of the emigrants who has succeeded in making it to the New World. This letter again tells us of the perils of travel and of the many who had died on the way. It ends with equally bad news about life in Brazil, where tropical weather, poisonous snakes, and other difficulties had taken their toll. The poor Ukrainian emigrants were even forbidden to use their own language; Brazil, they were now told, was a "Polish" country.[28]

Other Galician Ukrainian writers also devoted a great deal of attention to emigration motifs. In 1899, Vasyl Stefanyk published a collection of stories on the departure theme entitled *Kaminnyi Khrest* (The stone cross); in 1896, Andrei Chaikovsky printed one with the ironic title *Braziliiskyi harazd* (Brazilian prosperity); in 1901, Osyp Makovei wrote *Tuha* (Grief) and, in 1903, *Hist z Kanady* (The guest from Canada); and Tymofii Borduliak contributed three more titles to the genre. But, with the possible exception of Stefanyk's tales, none of these works ever enjoyed the prestige and popularity of Franko's *Do Brazilii*. Under the Soviets, where the cult of the "revolutionary democrat" Ivan Franko was very well developed and the social utility of literature was considered to be its most valuable quality, the renowned Ukrainian writer's criticism of the Brazilian fever was taken to highlight his intense social consciousness and his loyalty to the underprivileged masses of the Ukrainian villagers.[29] The simple humanity of his tale is its lasting quality.

Ivan Franko spoke for the impoverished villagers of western Ukraine under the Habsburg Monarchy, but, farther east, in the Ukrainian lands under the Romanovs, other authors took up the cause of the simple Ukrainian country folk and directed attention towards the Great Migration to the New World. Of these, by far the most important was the famous Russian writer, journalist, memoirist, and radical populist Vladimir Korolenko (1853–1921). Although he was of mixed Ukrainian–Polish ancestry and always retained a special interest in his native land, Korolenko was brought up in an atmosphere that caused him to choose Russian literature as his calling and, like many writers of Ukrainian background, he made an important contribution to Russian culture. Korolenko was educated in Saint Petersburg, joined the "movement to the people" in the 1870s, was exiled to eastern Siberia in the 1880s, edited the widely circulated populist journal *Russkoe bogatstvo* (Russian wealth) after his return, and eventually settled in the town of Poltava in eastern Ukraine, where he spent the remainder of his days. He was especially well known for his "progressive" and humane approach to social questions and was a defender of disadvantaged minority groups such as the Votiaks, Jews, and Eastern Rite Catholics (Uniates). He opposed the death penalty, both under the tsars and under the Bolsheviks, and, during the last years of his life, addressed a series of letters to A. V. Lunacharsky, the Bolshevik commissar of education, condemning the Bolsheviks as enemies of civilization. Korolenko also wrote a novelette entitled *Bez iazyka* (Without the language) on the question of peasant emigration to the United States.[30]

The idea of writing a piece on the subject of the Great Migration originated in Korolenko's own experiences in the United States during his visit to the Chicago World's Fair in 1893. He had long been interested in seeing America, a land of both economic progress and civil liberties, and, in places like London and New York, he knew that he could find exiled Russian revolutionaries who would be of interest to him. Travelling as a correspondent of the newspaper *Russkie vedomosti* (Russian news), Korolenko and a friend sailed to Scandinavia and to England, and then on to America. The whole journey took three and a half months and, during this time, the Russian writer managed to visit London, New York, Buffalo, Niagara Falls, and Chicago. While in London and New York, Korolenko did, in fact, meet some Russian exiles, and his steps were closely followed by the Russian secret police. In New York, moreover, the press sensationalized the arrival of this "victim of the Tsar" and expounded on his desire to take asylum in the United States. Shaken by this news and frightened by the possible reaction of the Russian authorities, Korolenko, who knew no English and who had no intention of remaining in America, hurried on to Chicago. Once again, minorities such as the African Americans and the native Indians aroused his special sympathies. On his return home, he learned of the death of his young daughter, and guilt over his absence during this critical time forever darkened his memories of the voyage to the New World.[31]

During his visit to America, Korolenko could not help but notice the large numbers of Slavic and eastern European immigrants who were beginning to fill the cities of New England and the Midwest. Indeed, by the end of the 1800s, the emigration fever had definitely touched the western borderlands of the Russian Empire and, between 1899 and 1916, some 2,651,000 Russian citizens, primarily Poles and Jews, but an ever-increasing number of Belarusans, Ukrainians, and Russians as well, were to arrive in the United States as immigrants.[32] Thus, Korolenko was able to gather a great deal of material for literary work. Some of this he used in his short story "Fabrika smerti" (Factory of death), which mirrored what he saw in a giant Chicago meat-packing plant; other materials he worked into travel notes, and still others entered into his principal creation on the emigration theme, *Bez iazyka.*

The main character in *Bez iazyka* is Matvei Lozinsky, a strong but gentle young farmer from Volhynia in Ukraine. Volhynia was then one of the most westerly provinces of the Russian Empire. Matvei, with his sister and his friend Dyma, sets out to go to America, to Minnesota, where, they are told, empty agricultural land, cows that give much milk, and some strange thing called "liberty" await them. Separated from his sister in Hamburg, during the ocean crossing, Matvei meets and befriends Anna, a young girl also from his country. In New York, Matvei, Anna, and Dyma go through all sorts of adventures and Matvei is again separated from his friends. He stumbles into a meeting in Central Park where the famous labour leader Sam Gompers is speaking, and, inspired by the emotional power of the orator, rushes forward to thank him. A New York policeman stands in the way, however, and Matvei, unable to speak the language, according to the custom of his own country, bows low to kiss his hand. Misunderstanding the gesture, the officer, who thought he was about to be bitten, strikes the simple Volhynian villager with his club, and a commotion ensues. But, with the help of some Italian working-men, gentle Matvei escapes to the American West, unaware that the sensationalist papers have branded him "the wild man of New York." Matvei is eventually saved by the mysterious Russian émigré Nilov, who speaks English and is able to explain the misunderstanding to the proper authorities. In the end, Matvei is reunited with Anna and settles down to a new life in America.[33]

Korolenko's story, despite its exposition of the harshness of the immigrants' initial experiences in the New World, is basically optimistic. Of all the major literary works dealing with the great migration, only those of Korolenko and Kukučin end on a happy note. Much in Korolenko's story is taken from real life. For example, Matvei's difficulties with English and consequent misunderstandings with the press mirror the unfortunate experience of Korolenko himself. Korolenko, in fact, took much of his basic material from the experience of a certain Latvian immigrant from the Russian Empire whose language problems in America had caused him to be taken for a madman. At first, Korolenko thought to tell the story of this Latvian immigrant. Later, he played with the idea of changing his protagonist to an American Pole, then to an Eastern Rite Catholic (Uniate) Belarusan gentleman. In the end, he settled on a man whom he knew the best, his countryman Matvei Lozinsky, who was an Eastern Rite Catholic Volhynian villager; that is, what today we would call an ethnic "Ukrainian." Once again, the choice of Matvei is characteristic, for the Ukrainian and Belarusan Catholics were a persecuted minority in the Russian Empire and their emigration to the New World, as in the case in *Pan Balcer w Brazylii*, reflects a vague but very real desire for personal and religious liberty. (The majority of Volhynian and other Eastern Rite Catholics in the Russian Empire had been converted to Orthodoxy only on government order after the failure of the Polish insurrection of 1830–1.) The fact that Korolenko chose one of the few Volhynians to remain true to Catholicism in the face of such government pressure underlines his sympathy for such persecuted minorities; thus, he seems to have retained his humanitarian ideals to the end.[34]

Korolenko and his contemporaries Sienkiewicz, Kukučin, Konopnicka, and Franko all had a number of characteristics in common. All were important writers within their own cultural sphere; all held certain humanitarian values in common; and all had a sympathetic interest in the Slavonic country folk of eastern Europe. Thus, it is no surprise that, at one time or another, all of them turned to the emigration theme and related their impressions and opinions of the Great Migration that was then sweeping across the Slavic lands.

Most of these writers were very critical of the emigration movement and expressed this criticism in the woeful tales they told of the voyage to the New World. Konopnicka and Sienkiewicz are probably clearest in their condemnation of peasant emigration. Konopnicka's *Pan Balcer w Brazilii* certainly was a literary reflection of the fact that about one-third of the emigrants eventually forsook the promises of the New World and returned to their native land. On the other hand, while Sienkiewicz was obviously depicting peasant emigration in its worst possible light in "Za chlebem," in his *Letters*, he had a few good things to say about the new Polish communities in the United States. Franko, too, in his poetry, painted a bleak picture of the fate of the emigrants, but, in his public life, tried to divert the direction of the emigration from Brazil to Canada rather than trying to stop it altogether. Longing for the European homeland and the difficulties of migration play major roles in the works of both Korolenko and Kukučin, although it is they who hold out the most hope for prospective emigrants. *Bez iazyka* does not overlook the civil virtues of democratic America, while *Mat' Volá* is more a tale about morality than a polemic against the New World. Both of them end on a happy note. Taken as a whole, therefore, it might be concluded that the writings of these major literary figures paint a varied picture of the trials and tribulations, the hopes and the dreams, the disappointments and the discoveries of the emigration side of the Great Migration of the eastern European peasantry to the New World. For the immigration side – that is, the life of these same villagers in the Americas – one must look to the literatures of the Slavs produced in the New World itself. But that is another story.

2 A Little-Known Book from the Late Soviet Period on the Economic Emigration from Imperial Russia to Western Europe and North America, 1880–1914

Emigrare ex loco in locum.

The nineteenth and early twentieth centuries saw one of the greatest voluntary movements of population in world history. This movement began modestly with the migration of labour from village to city and from certain countries in Europe to certain others, but, with time, it took on greater proportions with many millions of Europeans, some city people, but mostly country folk and villagers, leaving their homelands and boarding trains (which were a relatively new phenomenon) and then ocean-going ships (ever bigger and faster) for the New World. The movement began early in the nineteenth century in western and northern Europe but, by the 1850s, had encompassed Germany and then, later, central and eastern Europe.

By the 1880s, there was already significant "mass" internal "trans-European" migration; that is, movement from Italy, certain provinces of the Habsburg Monarchy, and the western borderlands of the Russian Empire to the newly created and economically dynamic German Empire. By the first years of the twentieth century, the western borderlands of the Russian Empire were not only providing seasonal workers and farm labour for imperial Germany, but were also exporting large numbers of people to the Americas.[1]

With regard to the eastern European part of this Great Migration, considerable scholarship has been done on certain nationalities and ethno-cultural groups and very little has been done on others. A significant body of scholarship, much of it in the English language, has been produced on emigrants from imperial Russia, the Jews, Poles, and Finns. In general, scholarly writing on the emigration of members of these groups has tended to take an "ethnic" or "national" approach, with the bulk of the scholarship being produced in the central and eastern European successor states of the old Habsburg and Romanov empires, or by the descendant members of these nationalities who had earlier emigrated to North America.[2] By contrast, scholarship taking a supra-ethnic "regional" or "geopolitical" approach has been less abundant, with studies of emigration from the Habsburg Empire predominating.[3]

Those eastern European nationalities, which, to the time of the collapse of the USSR, were not successful in establishing successor states to the Habsburg and Romanov empires, for a long time were less prolific on the question of emigration, but, during Soviet times, even they produced a certain amount of respectable scholarship. Most of this work, however, was written either in the languages of the eastern European nationalities themselves, or was written in Russian, which was the lingua franca and the primary language of science in the Soviet Union. Thus, within the USSR, studies appeared on both Baltic and eastern Slavic – that is, Belarusan, Russian, and Ukrainian – emigration to the New World. Some of this scholarship took the form of chapters or sections within larger histories of the various "union" republics such as the Lithuanian and the Ukrainian Soviet Socialist Republics,[4] while some of it took the form of specialist studies of various aspects of the emigration movement. A great deal of this work seems to have been done in the Ukrainian republic, with A. N. Shlepakov producing a title on pre-1914 Ukrainian economic emigration to Canada and the USA, and A. A. Strelko producing one on the Slavic populations of the various countries of Latin America.[5] A number of articles also appeared on the emigration movement as reflected in Ukrainian literature, most especially on the works of the Galician Ukrainian writer Ivan Franko.[6] Studies by Shlepakov, Sh. A. Bogina, and others dealt with general immigration themes in American history, though Bogina's study strangely ignored the Slavic and eastern European contribution to this history.[7] On a different level of discourse, however, general, synthetic treatments of emigration to the Americas from imperial Russia were long lacking. Thus, the appearance of such a book was a real event in Soviet scholarship.

The book in question, N. L. Tudorianu's *Outline [History] of the Russian Toiling Emigration of the Period of Imperialism (to Germany, the Scandinavian Countries and the USA)*, appeared, characteristically, not in Moscow or Leningrad but, rather, was published in Moldavia (today Moldova) by the Kishinev State Pedagogical Institute.[8] The Moldavian Republic, a largely ethnic "Moldavian" or Romanian area, which was known as "Bessarabia" in the nineteenth century, witnessed a massive emigration to the New World of its very large Jewish population during the last years before the First World War, and so, like the Baltic, Polish, Belarusan, and Ukrainian lands, formed a part of those western borderlands from which the majority of Russian subjects emigrated.

Tudorianu's book is based on a wide variety of sources. Not only did he make use of previous Soviet scholarship and the few scholarly studies of the emigration movement produced during the late imperial and early Soviet era, but he also made extensive use of unpublished imperial Russian sources preserved in various Soviet archives. Thus, his notes sparkle with references to the numerous "fonds" or collections of the imperial Russian foreign ministry, preserved in what was then called the Central State Historical Archive of the USSR, and also sources from the Central State Archive of the October Revolution, and the Central State Historical Archives of the Lithuanian, Latvian, Moldavian, and Ukrainian republics. These major archives contain the reports and personal observations of Russian diplomats in western Europe, the United States, and Canada; Russian governors in the various provinces of the empire; and police officials both at home and abroad. They also contain documents of other ministries and departments interested in the emigration question, including the Ministry of Trade and Commerce and the tsar's Holy Synod, which supervised religion and the affairs of the Russian Orthodox Church. Some of these Russian officials were assigned to gather German and American statistics on the migration question, and Tudorianu makes good use of German port and naval statistics and American immigration statistics. The latter, he points out, had long registered country (i.e., sovereign state) of origin, but had begun to register the ethnic composition of the immigrants only in 1898, and did not record return migration until 1908. It is these last years before the war, however, that saw the peak of emigration from the Russian Empire, and American statistics are, therefore, of considerable use.

Tudorianu begins with a discussion of the socio-economic situation of European Russia during the second half of the nineteenth century, during the era that followed the great reforms of Tsar Alexander II. The most important of these was the emancipation of the serfs, which increased the personal liberty and horizontal mobility of the general peasant population. This was especially true in the western borderlands of the empire, where there was no repartitional peasant commune to hold the villagers to the land. These territories, of course, and not the central Russian provinces, formed the focal point of the emigration movement.

Tudorianu argues that landlessness and "the proletarianization of the peasantry" were the primary causes of peasant migration. He maintains that this problem was more severe in the Baltic and Polish provinces than in central Russia, and that while the Belarusans and Ukrainians were somewhat better off in this regard than the Balts and Poles, they, too, suffered from land hunger. Other "push" factors in these regions included poverty caused by inefficient agricultural techniques; persecution of Jews, Eastern Rite Catholics, and others by the Russian Orthodox state; compulsory military service; and the lack of industrial growth in the western borderlands. In the Polish lands, only certain areas (e.g., the Warsaw region) were sufficiently developed to absorb their excess agricultural population.

"Pull" factors were also important. Tudorianu points out that wages for agricultural workers in Germany exceeded wages paid in the Russian Empire's northwestern region (Belarus') and the southwest region (Ukraine) by about a time and a half. American wages exceeded wages in these areas by three and four times. Improved postal and rail systems, successful returning emigrants, letters from relatives abroad, remittance payments to families left at home, and the systematic spread of word of the New World by professional emigration agents in the employ of major shipping companies all fostered a growing interest in life in the United States, Canada, and western Europe.[9]

Emigration to Germany began in the 1880s. It started in the most westerly provinces of the empire, where the peasant population was purely Polish in composition, and it moved eastward, eventually reaching territories where the rural population was predominantly Belarusan or Ukrainian. During this period, a number of German-speaking colonists living in the Lower Volga and Ukrainian steppe region also migrated west (38–9). In general, among the Slavs, this was a seasonal migration concerned with agricultural work in Prussia and other parts of the new German Empire. Each year, several hundred thousand people were involved, and soon the scope of the migration was widened to include Denmark, where there was also a growing demand for agricultural labour. The dynamics of the migration are given in table 2.1 (64).

The small minority that did not return to Russia did not possess German citizenship and did not stay in Germany. It seems that most of them heard of opportunities elsewhere and eventually made their way to the great German port cities of Bremen and Hamburg, and from there travelled to the USA, Canada, Argentina, Brazil, and other countries (65). The national composition of this seasonal emigration from the Russian Empire is difficult to determine with any precision. However, Russian

Table 2.1 Dynamics of migration.

YEAR	LEAVING RUSSIA	RETURNING TO RUSSIA
1902–6	348,205	336,926
1909	513,184	499,193
1912	797,716	766,505

statistics provide information on the region of origin of emigrants from the empire and, from these, the national composition may be inferred. Again, the pattern is from Polish west to Baltic, Belarusan, and Ukrainian east. Tudorianu breaks down the percentages of the emigration of so-called Russian (*Rossiiskie*) workers to Germany in table 2.2 (68).

Emigration to the New World was a much more complex phenomenon. First, it entailed a voyage across the ocean, which required considerable investment. Because of the time and money required, it could not be a seasonal migration. None of the emigrants could return to Russia yearly and a great number never bothered to return at all. Second, ocean travel meant the involvement of the large naval companies, and the politics of marine competition and of the recruitment of emigrants. In general, the American and Russian merchant marines were unable to compete with the great German and English steamship lines, and most of the emigration from central and eastern Europe was directed through the great German, Belgian, and English ports at Bremen, Hamburg, Antwerp, and Liverpool. Competition between the British and the Germans was especially fierce, with fare wars occasionally breaking out. Thus, in October 1904, the Russian embassy in Berlin reported to the Ministry of Foreign Affairs in Saint Petersburg that "during the present year, when the mutual competition of English and German steamship companies has caused a significant reduction in ship fares and led to huge losses to both parties, the activities of German emigration agents on the Russian borders has taken on an especially sharp character" (121). These agents were especially active along the borders between Russia and the Habsburg Empire, and, of course, it was this same general area that saw the most intensive movement abroad.

With the exception of the Congress Kingdom of Poland, however, mass emigration from European Russia did not begin among the Slavic country folk, but, rather, among the non-Slavic elements. According to Tudorianu (124), the first to leave for America were the Mennonites from the provinces of Saratov and Simbirsk. These German-speaking

Table 2.2 Origin of "Russian" workers in Germany, %.

Territory	1890	1900	1910	1911	1913
Kingdom of Poland	92	85	64	48	45
Baltic Lands	7	12	15	17	20
Northwest Region (Belarus')	1	3	12	20	20
Little Russia (Central Ukraine)	–	–	6	10	9
New Russia (Southern Ukraine)	–	–	3	5	6

Protestant colonists were pacifists who objected to the compulsory military service that was being imposed on them after the reforms of Alexander II. The Jews were next to leave. They, too, suffered under restrictive legislation directed specifically against their group. Then, Belarusan and Ukrainian peasants began to leave, and, finally, peasants from the other parts of European Russia. Emigration of national and religious minorities and of country folk from the western regions of the empire continued to increase steadily until the outbreak of the First World War.

From the American perspective, this general trend from western and northern Europe to southern and eastern Europe was often referred to by the terms "old" immigration and "new" immigration. In 1870, at the beginning of this gradual shift, immigrants from Italy, the Habsburg Monarchy, and Russia made up only 1 per cent of all newcomers to the United States. In 1880, they comprised 19 per cent, but, by 1905, had climbed to 75 per cent (167). At the turn of the century, the Russian Empire trailed both the Habsburg Monarchy and Italy in providing immigrants to the United States, but, by the last years before the outbreak of war, had climbed to first place. Table 2.3 is based on American statistics and illustrates the phenomenal growth of immigration to America from the Russian Empire (171–2).

When the intervening years are added on to the figures given in the table, it can be established that, between 1820 and 1913, about 3.2 million people immigrated from the Russian Empire to the United States, with the great majority of these arriving around the turn of the century. Furthermore, according to a March 1917 report prepared by the Russian embassy in Washington, some 2,877,746 Russian-born immigrants were then living in the USA (172, 301). Thus, by the first years of the twentieth century, mass migration from the Russian Empire to the American Republic was a fact of life recognized by the governments of both countries.

Table 2.3 Immigration to America, 1820–1913.

Year	Total Immigration	From "Russia"
1820	8,385	14
1830	23,322	3
1840	84,066	1
1850	369,986	31
1860	150,237	156
1870	387,203	1,130
1880	457,257	7,191
1890	455,302	35,698
1900	448,572	90,787
1905	1,026,499	184,897
1907	1,285,349	258,943
1913	1,197,892	291,040

In 1899, American officials began to keep records about the national composition of immigrants and, although these records were far from perfect, they give a certain idea of the general trend. Table 2.4 shows the national composition of immigrants from the Russian Empire from 1899 to 1913. Numbers of immigrants are given in thousands and in the percentage of the immigration from "Russia" as a whole. The "others" in this table refer to Armenians, Romanians, and other smaller nationalities from the Russian Empire. Latvians were counted as Lithuanians, Estonians as Finns, and Belarusans and Ukrainians as Russians. In general, it will be observed that Jews led fairly consistently, making up about 40 per cent of the immigration; Poles followed, making up about a third; with eastern Slavs, who were, of course, counted as Russians, trailing far behind.[10]

At the time these statistics were collected, in Russian bureaucratic circles, it was generally thought that the emigration had a definite non-Russian (*inorodcheskii*) character and that eastern Slavs played an insignificant role. But Tudorianu believes that this was not the full story and quotes A. I. Shcherbatsky, an official at the Russian embassy in Washington, to the following effect: "Considered separately, the emigration movement of Russian people is growing quickly, more quickly than the general movement out of the empire, and one can assume that if our economic situation and that in the United States does not change, this

Table 2.4 Immigration to America from the Russian Empire, 1899–1913, in thousands (%).

Nationality	1899–1903	1904–1908	1909–1913	Total
Jews	185 (38)	482 (50)	297 (32)	964 (41)
Poles	133 (28)	237 (25)	305 (33)	675 (29)
Lithuanians and Latvians	50 (10)	82 (8)	90 (10)	222 (9)
Finns and Estonians	61 (13)	61 (6)	52 (6)	174 (7)
Germans	35 (7)	48 (5)	55 (6)	138 (6)
Russians	9 (2)	45 (5)	111 (12)	167 (7)
Others	8 (2)	6 (1)	9 (1)	23 (2)
Total, Russian Empire	481 (100)	961 (100)	919 (100)	2,361 (100)

growth will continue" (p. 173). He further quotes a 1914 report of the Russian consul at Seattle on the nature of this east Slavic immigration. "Not less than 80% of the Russians in America," states the Russian consul, "are people who have come here to earn a living and they suffer more than others in the conditions of the [economic] crisis. They are almost exclusively peasants, agricultural workers. During my five months here, I have seen people from most of the provinces of European and Asiatic Russia. Recently, there have been a great many Belarusans and Little Russians, and of the Great Russians there have been natives of Kursk, Riazan, Nizhegorod, Viatsk, Saratov, and especially Simbirsk provinces" (177). Tudorianu adds that while the Jews and the Germans had come to stay, the Belarusans, Ukrainians, Russians, Poles, Balts, Finns, and others looked on emigration as a temporary matter and one day hoped to return to their European homeland.

There were exceptions, of course; for example, from 1900 to 1905, some 10,000 country folk from Kiev Province (Kyiv Province in modern Ukrainian orthography) migrated to North Dakota with no intention of ever returning to the empire (179). But this group, which settled into ranching in the western parts of the state, belonged to the Protestant "Stundist" sect and so fit into the category of a religious minority.

According to Tudorianu, different nationalities settled in different parts of the United States. He states that while Jews settled in the large cities of the East and the Midwest, where they founded numerous successful Jewish institutions, the Slavs tended to settle in the great industrial centres and mining towns, where they worked as urban labourers. The Germans, however, who had arrived somewhat earlier, seemed to prefer the plains states where they could still find empty land and engage in farming or ranching.

From the Russian imperial point of view, the emigration was not wholly undesirable. Not only did the movement somewhat relieve rural over-population and the land hunger of the peasantry, but remittance payments to family left back home aided in the reduction of the imperial balance-of-payments deficit. Although exact figures on the amount of money sent back to Russia cannot be found, the Russian Ministry of Trade and Commerce reckoned that it amounted to about 100 million rubles a year, and it seems certain that American immigrants sent more money back to Russia than did seasonal workers in Germany.

Tudorianu's final chapters deal with the lives and organizations of the various emigrants from Russia in the United States. He discusses the efforts of the Russian Orthodox Mission, which was financed by the tsar's Holy Synod, to bring the immigrants, including ethnic Ukrainian and Belarusan Eastern Rite Catholics, into the fold of the Russian Orthodox Church. (Russian officials saw this as one aspect of the general Slavophile movement, which was aimed at reducing the power of the Catholic Habsburg Monarchy and increasing the power of the Orthodox tsar.) He also describes the role of the various "fraternal" organizations in protecting industrial workers from financial uncertainties, mentions the role of the Greek Catholic clergy in the formation of such bodies, and dwells on the effort of secular-minded members to free themselves of both church politics and clerical control. Finally, Tudorianu discusses the role of various groups from "Russia" in the American socialist movement – in particular, the language federations of the American Socialist Party – and stresses the strength of Social Democratic leanings among the Jews, Latvians, Finns, and Russians. Though Tudorianu's account of eastern European immigrant life in America provides little new information for the Western reader, his general imperial Russian perspective and supra-ethnic "geopolitical" approach is unfamiliar and seems to shed new light on the subject.

There are, of course, some very real problems with Tudorianu's study. Since it was published in 1986, on the eve of the implementation of Mikhail Gorbachev's new policy of glasnost, or "openness" in public and intellectual life, Tudorianu's book suffers from the tight prescriptions and ideological baggage that were characteristic of Soviet scholarship during the Brezhnev years. Thus, his introductory chapter begins with the traditional quotations from Marx and Lenin on subjects concerning which there is already general agreement, and the citations of authorities from the turn of the century are wholly unnecessary. It is interesting, however, to know that Lenin was intrigued by the subject of the economic emigration to the New World and actually asked his comrades to gather materials about it for him and, in the end, did produce a minor article on this subject.[11]

Other problems linked to the Soviet censors of his time seem to have caused Tudorianu more severe problems. Since emigration from the homeland was generally seen by Soviet authorities in a very negative light, a kind of betrayal of the land of one's birth, Tudorianu was compelled to emphasize the negative factors of the old regime that caused people to emigrate. He was also compelled to stress what he considered to be the specious or misleading nature of the "pull" factors that drew the emigrants to the New World. Such an emphasis, which reflects the quality of "Soviet patriotism" at the time that Tudorianu was writing, was not entirely new, for even the eastern European intelligentsia of the so-called period of Imperialism, at the turn of the last century, was already aware of the dangers to the nation posed by uncontrolled emigration of the peasant masses and often drew a negative picture of the movement in various analytical and fictional works dealing with the theme.[12] It is worthy of note that these sentiments were codified and institutionalized in the rules of censorship that still prevailed during the early Gorbachev years. Similarly, Tudorianu was unable to use or cite the extensive scholarship produced in the West or even in other Soviet Bloc countries over the period that he researched his book. Works of synthesis published at that time in the United States and Canada make it clear that even then, the contributions of Western scholars of immigration and ethnic history were extensive.[13] Nevertheless, the contribution of Tudorianu to the development of the migration history of eastern Europe was generally sound. He tackled a subject on which Soviet scholarship had hitherto produced no synthesis and used sources and archives that had long gone unused. The result was the opening of a new area of research to Soviet and subsequent scholarship, and the necessity for Western scholars to take note of it.

3 Ivan Franko and Large-Scale Ukrainian Economic Emigration to Canada before 1914

Sapientia in exitu canitur.
(Rozum khvaliat pid kinets spravy.)
(They praise wisdom when it's all over.)

Iu. V. Tsymbaliuk, *Latynski pryslivia i prykazky*

After the poet Taras Shevchenko, Ivan Franko (1856–1916) is perhaps the best-known Ukrainian literary figure of modern times. During his lifetime, he was a widely acclaimed poet, writer, and scholar, and a political and social activist of considerable importance. By the time of his death, he was already a national hero and was especially beloved in western Ukraine, or "Eastern Galicia," as the major Ukrainian region of the Austrian Empire was then called. Both in Soviet Ukraine and among Ukrainians living abroad, his cult long remained undiminished and, during the Cold War, his works were often reprinted by the Communist state and its émigré opponents alike.[1]

Franko took an interest in most of the major cultural and social questions of his time, but his greatest responsibility, as he often said, was service on behalf of the impoverished and oppressed "Ruthenian" or Ukrainian country folk of Austrian Galicia. "As the son of a villager, brought up on rough peasant bread," he confessed to the western Ukrainian intelligentsia who had gathered to honour the twenty-fifth year of his literary activity, "I have felt it my duty to devote my life's work to this simple people."[2] Franko carried out his pledge on at least two different levels: cultural work, both literary and scholarly; and organizational work, both social and political. It was first in his capacity as a social and political mentor of his people that he became interested in the question of mass emigration from overcrowded Galicia.

Emigration from Galicia was not new. In the days of the Polish Lithuanian Commonwealth, Galician peasants had often fled eastward to escape oppressive taxation and cruel landlords. The partitions of the old Polish Lithuanian Commonwealth among Prussia, Austria, and Russia had only temporarily halted the exodus; in 1848, the abolition by the Habsburgs of the residues of serfdom was a step towards opening the gates anew. Twenty years later, the land laws were amended to allow unrestricted division of land among one's heirs. Thereafter, constant subdivision of the limited land produced a spectacular growth in the number of small holdings, and these became so small that they could barely support the population. Many small landholders were being forced to sell out to the owners of large estates, and these had a tendency to diminish in number but grow even larger. In addition, modern industrial development was practically non-existent, so there were no new cities to which the excess population might migrate.[3] The result was emigration abroad; at first, to the factories and coal mines of Germany or the American Midwest; later, to the southern provinces of Brazil and the beckoning prairies of western Canada. There was also considerable migration within the Austrian Empire itself.[4]

Franko was no more immune to the call of distant lands than were his land-hungry Galician compatriots. In 1888, he was without a steady income and disappointed by the failure of his short-lived journal *Postup* (Progress). Moreover, he had been working together with Polish socialists and writing in Polish for many years, but longed to put his talents at the service of his own people. He was also curious about the ways of democracy in the New World. Thus, when a friend, Volodymyr Simynovych (1859–1932), invited him to come to the United States to edit the Ukrainian language newspaper *Ameryka*, Franko informed his political mentor, the émigré from Russian Ukraine Mykhailo Drahomanov (1841–1895), that he was "preparing to go to America, to Shenandoah where I am asked to take over as editor of *Ameryka*."[5] Franko knew that by running a Ukrainian newspaper in the United States, he would not have much more financial security than by continuing his work at the Polish daily *Kurier Lwowski*. "But all the same," he told Drahomanov, "I would not be working for foreigners but for my own people, and I would be breathing free air. Moreover, I think that the American school would be an important and valuable thing for me and to go through a five-year course there would do me a lot of good."[6]

Drahomanov had mixed feelings about losing his most talented protégé to the New World. He thought that Franko's projected journey might bring some benefits, but he also feared the conservative influence of the Greek Catholic Church, which provided intellectual leadership to the new Ukrainian communities in America. "Your journey to America is of great interest to me," he replied to Franko, "and I expect a lot of good to come of it, both for yourself and for the cause; but I fear that from the very first moments you will run into difficulties with the priests. It is enough that you are going, to have them crying out against you as some kind of 'red' and the thing will go right up to the metropolitan. But all the same go. Just watch out for the wolf, and do not go into the woods."[7]

Drahomanov's advice was not without effect. Franko's wife was sick and this, combined with disquieting news about *Ameryka*'s financial state and, more ostensibly, bad news about the character of Ivan Voliansky (1857–1926), the Greek Catholic priest who was making arrangements for the paper, caused Franko to delay his departure. "In any case," he assured Drahomanov, "I still have to think the whole thing over very thoroughly."[8] In the end, Franko never did go to the United States of America.

But others did. At first, it was a trickle, but the trickle turned into a stream and then a torrent. Overpopulation, famine, and educational, national, and other legal disabilities (restrictions on peasants) caused thousands to sell whatever they had and leave. According to Soviet reckoning, between 1890 and 1910, 212,000 Ukrainians deserted Galicia. In the first decade of the twentieth century, another 35,000 left the neighbouring province of Bukovina; emigration from mountainous Transcarpathia, which was the smallest and poorest Ukrainian region in the Habsburg Monarchy, was correspondingly large.[9]

The prospective emigrants did not have an easy time of it. Lacking the overseas colonies possessed by other European states, the Austrian government in Vienna did nothing to encourage the emigration or help the emigrants. Moreover, the provincial bureaucracy, which had been controlled by the Polish gentry since the 1860s, was generally hostile. Polish landowners were especially critical of peasants leaving for the empty steppe lands said to be awaiting them in the Russian Empire. In the conservative press, the movement was usually referred to as a "plague," a "disease," or by some other such term of opprobrium. As late as the first years of the twentieth century, the influential Galician Polish lawyer Leopold Caro was still seriously arguing that illiteracy, gullibility, and drunkenness "not only among the peasants in Eastern Galicia and Bukovina, but also among the [Polish] Mazurians" were the real causes of mass emigration. As a result, local authorities would often deny the villagers passports, and police and lower-level administrators would hinder them at every step. On a higher level, too, the authorities feared that agents of various shipping companies, out to make a quick profit, could easily mislead the country folk. Thus, in January 1892, when Ivan Pylypiw, the very first Ukrainian peasant to settle in Canada, returned home with stories about free land across the ocean, he was promptly led off to jail at bayonet point.[10]

The phenomenon did not go unnoticed by the Ukrainian intelligentsia. On 21 October 1892, in the same year that Ivan Pylypiw was arrested, Franko penned a spirited defence of the peasant's right to emigrate, and he published it in the Viennese social democratic *Arbeiter Zeitung*. Franko argued that necessity was driving the population abroad and that the Polish newspaper stories about foreign agents, especially "Muscovite agents," provoking peasant migration to Russia and elsewhere were pure nonsense. Franko thought the causes of the emigration were clear enough: parcelization of the land and the absence of industrial growth. These factors had led to extreme poverty, overpopulation, and even famine. Major famines had occurred in 1847, 1849, 1855, 1865, 1876, and 1889. Thus, Franko remonstrated, "it is no secret that Galicia is overpopulated." And what was the meaning of overpopulation? Franko explained:

It really means that the population living on the land in Galicia, with its given state of culture and present division of the means of production, cannot maintain the necessary level of subsistence. For anyone to whom these elementary facts are not a secret, this peasant emigration from Galicia, which has been swiftly increasing recently, can come as no surprise. On the contrary, such a person must consider emigration to be an entirely natural, necessary, and irreversible process.[11]

In Franko's eyes, administrative harassment of the departing villagers was caused by the Polish gentry, who wished to keep wages down through a captive labour supply. The gentry, he wrote, "has seen, and will only see harm in the emigration of the country folk. For when the peasants flee, the submissive labourer and the household servant are no longer cheap."[12]

Franko painted a very sorrowful picture of peasant attempts at emigration. Conditions were so bad that the country folk not only willingly migrated to Hungary, Germany, and North America, but also latched onto the slimmest of hopes and left for the forests of Brazil and the empty steppe lands of Russia-in-Asia. Among the very poorest, fantastic rumours sprang up, giving rise to intense emotions of various sorts. Sometimes, eschatological expectations emerged. For example, quasi-messianic hopes were aroused by the mysterious death of the emperor's son, Crown Prince Rudolph, at Meyerling. Franko writes:

> And so, last year, that is, in 1891, the population [of those poorest areas] was seized by a veritable emigration fever. For weeks on end the peasants crowded around the offices of His Majesty's local officials, demanding passports to Brazil. News of unnatural events circulated. It was said that Archduke Rudolph had not died, but was alive in Brazil where he was founding a new state that he wanted to populate with Ukrainian peasants. The pleading and persuasion of the authorities and the clergy did not help. It took many weeks of penal confinement to dampen the fiery ardor and love for the late archduke, and all the same, it did not work ...

The next year, the rumours concerned the Russian tsar. It was said that the tsar was expelling all the Germans and Jews from his country and had promised every Ukrainian peasant ten morgs of good land. (A morg was a little less than an English acre.) The Russian border patrols, concludes Franko, were kept very busy trying to turn back the tide.[13]

The situation became critical after 1893, when a depression began to close down factories in the American Midwest. Many immigrant workers were even compelled to return home. Under such conditions, the Galician peasantry did, indeed, become prey for unscrupulous agents offering cheap passage to places like Brazil. The most famous incident occurred in 1895, when the emigration agent Gargoletti crossed practically all of eastern Galicia. He was on foot and disguised as a peasant-farmer pretending to be the beloved Archduke Rudolph. Gargoletti was assisted in his plan by the village innkeepers who bought land from the duped villagers and then shared the ill-gotten gains with him. "The proof of the great confidence that this swindler could arouse," writes a student of the case, "are the numerous letters written to the Archduchess Stephanie by the villagers from many parts of Galicia. In these letters they assured her that the Archduke, her husband, was not dead but alive, and was sending her greetings, and wished them to follow him to Brazil."[14] When horror stories about exploitation by coffee plantation owners, about Indian massacres and the unhealthy Brazilian climate, began to reach Galicia, the Ukrainian intelligentsia became truly alarmed.

The desperate dilemma of the peasantry, who were caught between messianic dreams and bitter realities, captured the imagination of Franko. Being at the height of his literary powers, he did not restrict himself to journalism, but, like the influential Polish poetess Maria Konopnicka, whom he greatly admired, also devoted a cycle of poetry to it.[15]

The poem *Do Brazilii* (To Brazil) tells the story of the promised kingdom set aside for the Ukrainian villagers; it describes the hardships of the journey and the disappointments of arrival. Perhaps one of the most touching parts of the cycle is the first section of the poem, which consists of Franko's paraphrase of the numerous enthusiastic letters received by the Archduchess Stephanie from her loyal Ukrainian country folk. Rudolph was alive and the villagers could not keep such important news for themselves. In the end, after much debate, they felt it necessary to address the archduchess and ...

Pro n'oho zvistku podaty,
Shchob z namy i ty vtishala sia, iak maty.

Tell the happy news about him so that you too
Can rejoice with us, like a mother ...[16]

During 1895, Franko even began to write a play in three acts on this same Brazilian theme. For some reason, he never completed the project and only a brief introductory note has been preserved. It was titled "This Is Happening in Our Time."[17]

Franko's celebrated poem and projected play did not grow out of a void, and neither did they embellish the fundamental emotions at work beneath the phenomenon of sudden and massive emigration; they only paralleled the rough songs of the country folk who gathered in the marketplaces. One of the most popular songs of the time, which reflected these very same feelings, summed up the role of the archduke, of the commercial world represented by the Jewish tavern-keeper, and of the villagers themselves. It achieved this in only a few short lines:

Nash tsar Rudolf narod do Brazylii vzyvaie,
Ale Izraylia tsilkom ne puskaie ...
Pokydaimo toi krai prokliatyi,
Ydem do Brayzlii – budem panuvaty!

Our Tsar Rudolph calls us now to Brazil,
But he does not call out to Israel . . .
Leave this place so cursed and damned,
We go to Brazil, to rule over the land![18]

With the depression in the United States and political obstacles to emigration eastward, for a few years, Brazil seemed to be the only alternative for the land-hungry Galician peasantry. But the dangers were so great that many figures among the Ukrainian intelligentsia felt they could not encourage such adventures. The best-known opponent of Brazilian schemes was Professor Osyp Oleskiv (1860–1903), a friend of Franko's and an agricultural expert with a deep concern for the fate of the departing villagers.[19] Oleskiv had happened upon some literature about Canada and began to investigate the possibilities of diverting the emigration in this direction. He made some preliminary inquiries, and, in July 1895, his booklet *Pro vilni zemli* (About free lands) was published by the Prosvita Educational Society.

In this booklet, Oleskiv urged the villagers to give up the idea of Brazil and consider going to Canada, where the immigrant farmer regularly received 113 morgs of land and, in Oleskiv's own words, where he can get "the patent of ownership after three years, provided he can prove that he has been residing on the land at least six months each year, that he has built a house, and that he has brought under cultivation a certain amount of land."[20] As for Franko himself, on 18 May 1895, he wrote to Drahomanov that things were going badly for him in Galicia and that he himself was ready to emigrate to some other country. He continued: "At this time, we are talking a lot about Canada here with Dr Oleskiv. In the middle of July, he is going there to seek a place for Ukrainian colonists, and if an appropriate place can be located and the possibility of founding a nice colony demonstrated, I will be the first who is ready to go across the ocean."[21] We do not know the reason, but Franko never did go to Canada; Oleskiv, however, did. After an interview with the Galician governor Count Kazimierz Badeni, who was highly esteemed by Emperor Franz Joseph and who was soon to become Austrian prime minister, and after establishing contact with Canadian government officials, Oleskiv and a peasant representative set out to discover in person the possibilities of the new land.[22]

While Oleskiv was thus negotiating with Canadian officialdom, braving the North Atlantic, and exploring Manitoba and the Northwest, Franko and others among the Ukrainian intelligentsia did not stand idly by. Franko, in particular, wrote a number of articles about the various dangers of emigration.[23] After Oleskiv had returned to Galicia on 14 November 1895, a conference was held on the subject of emigration, and the radical politician Viacheslav Budzhinovsky, Franko's old acquaintance, the schoolteacher Cyril (Kyrylo) Genyk, Franko himself, and many others attended.[24] Oleskiv gave a very favourable report of the prospects for mass emigration to Canada and set out his plan for changing the

direction of emigration from Brazil to the Canadian Prairies. Oleskiv wanted to see the emigration better organized. He wanted the emigrants to be
adequately provisioned when they left, to travel in groups, and to have
proper guides and translators, or, at least, experienced leaders. As a result
of these proposals, a permanent Emigrant Aid Committee was formed.[25]

This same day, the first in a series of Franko's articles on emigration
appeared in *Kurier Lwowski*.[26] Throughout November and December
1895, the writer became directly involved in the plan for transferring the
direction of emigration to the Canadian Northwest. He wrote frequently
on the subject, attended conferences, and spoke at mass meetings of as-
sembled peasantry. It was at one such conference that the young and as-
piring literary critic Mykhailo Mochulsky (1875–1940) first saw Franko,
who was then at the height of his powers. The appearance of the famous
writer left an indelible impression on Mochulsky and, many years later,
he described it thus:

> Perhaps the first time that I saw Franko was during the winter of 1896. It was
> at the "Academic Society" where some student was delivering a speech
> about the emigration of our villagers overseas. At that time I did not listen
> very closely to the content of the speeches, but was more occupied with the
> person of Franko. He left the room where the lecture had been read in the
> company of Professor Oleskiv. His appearance so affected me that I remem-
> ber it as if it were today: he was of medium height with a handsome high
> forehead and slightly curly, rust-colored hair. He had a small rust-colored
> moustache and grey steel-like eyes. Understanding and energy were written
> across his face. His eyes and mouth showed enthusiasm and conviction. He
> wore an embroidered shirt. His clothes were unpretentious, even poor. His
> manner was modest; I would even say a little shy. Franko and Oleskiv sat
> together with a group of students. When the lecture had ended, there was
> a discussion. Some students were against emigration, considering it to be a
> loss of the best national forces; others were for emigration, giving as a rea-
> son that in emigration people acquire a broader point of view and usually
> return from emigration better off financially and arrange their affairs bet-
> ter in the homeland. Franko, so far as I remember, was not against emigra-
> tion, but insisted that it be well organized and wisely carried out. He spoke
> quietly and when he touched upon the order of things in Galicia, he did so
> with irony....[27]

Mochulsky's memory did not fail him. Franko did indeed defend the
Galician peasantry in its attempts to emigrate abroad and criticized the

Galician administration for its attempts to limit it. Throughout the winter of 1895–6, Franko continued to write and speak on the subject.[28] In fact, at this point, Franko and the Radical Party that he led were intensely involved in the organization of the countryside. The 1890s were a period when, all over eastern Europe, political parties were being formed and political life was beginning to touch the peasantry. It was the goal of Franko and his colleagues to turn the "Ruthenian" country folk (to use the terminology of the day), who were still very much an amorphous peasant mass, into an organized political force of nationally conscious Ukrainians. The Radical Party was the instrument they used and, three times (in 1895, 1897, and 1898), Franko himself was to run for public office under its banner.[29]

In general elections to the Galician provincial assembly held in September 1895, Badeni's administration used unusually vigorous strong-arm tactics (beatings, mass arrests, stuffing of ballot boxes) to ensure the defeat of the two Ukrainian opposition parties, the peasant-based Radicals and the intelligentsia-based Populists or *narodovtsi*. By a policy of "self-reliance" – that is, mass meetings and mass organization of the villagers – the Radicals still managed to get two members elected. However, when Franko ran in a by-election to the central Austrian Parliament, or *Reichsrat*, shortly afterward, the same government tactics, including the arrest of Franko himself, foiled the poet's candidacy. The stormy elections of 1895 were the first of the so-called bloody elections for which Galicia became known throughout the Austrian Empire. They were the immediate background to the emperor's appointment of Badeni to the post of Austrian prime minister, and they immediately preceded the series of mass meetings that occurred in the countryside during November and December of 1895.[30]

The phenomenon of mass public assemblies (*vichovyi rukh*) was quickly becoming an important factor in the politicization, and even the social life, of the villagers. At these meetings, several thousand villagers would gather to hear speeches on both practical concerns of immediate interest to them and the general questions of political life. During the winter of 1895–96, a major political topic was the recent "bloody election," and a major practical concern was mass emigration to Brazil and to Canada.[31]

Franko was a frequent speaker at these mass meetings. In particular, he spoke several times during the winter of 1895–96, and more than once he discussed the question of emigration to Canada. On 3 December, at a place called Velyki Mosty, for about two hours, Franko spoke to the massed peasantry on the subject of emigration to Brazil and Canada. On

26 December, at a similar meeting at Zbarazh, he spoke on the same subject. On 8 January, he addressed crowds at Peremyshl on the necessity for universal, direct, and secret balloting and the abolition of electoral curia, and, on 15 February at Drohobych, he discussed other topics of interest to the peasantry.[32]

At the meeting at Velyki Mosty, Franko compared the relative merits of emigration to Canada and to Brazil. His peasant audience heard him discuss the civil order in each country and conclude that people live much better in Canada. In Brazil, Franko said, immigrants receive 40 morgs of forest, while, in Canada, they receive 100 morgs of good wheat-growing land. Moreover, in Canada, a man's property and life were safe; in Brazil, they were not. The main problem with Canada, the writer informed his audience, was that it cost 120 Austrian guilders to get there, while passage to Brazil was free. Franko advised those who could afford it to go to Canada. But he cautioned them that they should wait until spring because there would be no work in Canada in the winter and one should have enough money of one's own to live through this cold season. "Those people who do not have the money to go to Canada," he concluded, "must also wait at home for a while. At this very moment in Lviv they are trying to arrange for free tickets. Then all those who are set on emigrating must turn to Canada because it is a thousand times better there than it is in Brazil."[33]

The efforts of Franko, Oleskiv, and the others involved in redirecting the emigration to Canada were not in vain. In the following months, several well-organized groups of villagers left Galicia to settle in Manitoba and the Northwest. In the fall of 1896, a Canadian official reported to the Commissioner of Dominion Lands in Winnipeg that there had been a large increase in the number of new "Ruthenian" settlers from Austrian Galicia. The official ascribed the increase to the efforts of Oleskiv, who was now well known to the Canadian government, and he stated that already "upward of one hundred families, in all 630 persons, have settled, principally in Manitoba and Alberta...."[34] It was an auspicious beginning.

But, like many new ventures, the emigration movement to Canada was not without problems. The political ones came first. In 1895, a group of conservative Polish members in the Austrian *Reichsrat* proposed a ban on all activities that would promote emigration.[35]

This idea threatened to interfere with the work of Oleskiv and his committee, and Franko decided to speak out against it. In a major article published in the Viennese weekly *Die Zeit* (no. 115, 12 December 1896), the writer again attacked the government for ignoring social and economic factors and blaming the movement abroad on emigration agents. At one time, said Franko, Badeni had blamed the Ukrainian clergy; at another, Badeni and his friends accused the Radical Party of stirring up dissatisfaction and setting the villagers in motion. Standing by the position that he had first taken in 1892, Franko repeated that economic need was the basic factor in the mass migration of the Galician peasantry. He then accused the local administration of being the real culprits. "Is it not characteristic," the writer asked sternly, "that the first news about Ukrainian peasant emigration to North America, which reached the newspapers in 1884, concerned the money that had been sent home from America but which the postal officials in the Galician Post Office had kept for themselves?" The situation had changed little since, but, all the same, administrative barriers could not quench the thirst for free lands abroad.[36]

On 21 January 1897, the emperor, in accord with the views of Badeni and the conservatives, signed a law restricting the promotion of emigration. However, in the case of the Canadian emigration, this legislation does not seem to have been strictly enforced, and, over the next few years, Oleskiv and his committee continued their work and even increased its intensity.[37] Organized groups of peasant farmers, clad in rough sheepskins and with a few agricultural implements and a modest capital of perhaps a few dollars stuffed into their pockets, left for Canada every year and were soon supplemented by emigrants attracted by letters from friends or relatives. Franko's old school companion and political sympathizer Cyril Genyk led Oleskiv's second organized group of settlers, which arrived in Winnipeg on 25 July 1896.[38] At Oleskiv's suggestion, the Interior Ministry of the Canadian government hired Genyk as an interpreter, and in this capacity the new Canadian civil servant greatly helped the immigrants; in the early years, Genyk met virtually all new arrivals and, as a result, he eventually became a nearly legendary figure among the Ukrainian settlers of western Canada.[39] By 1902, according to an official report drafted by Genyk, some 38,435 Galicians, the vast majority of them ethnic Ukrainians, were settled in Manitoba and the Northwest.[40] Indeed, between 1898 and 1909, Galicians grew to make up 73.19 per cent of all immigrants from the Habsburg Monarchy to Canada.[41] With the help of Genyk, Franko, and other Radical Party activists, Oleskiv's project was beginning to bear fruit.

Once settled in the new country, the Galician immigrants, in spite of the remoteness of their location across the Canadian prairies, did not immediately break all ties with their former homeland. Genyk, in particular, tried to keep in touch with Franko and the Old Country Radicals.

The new government interpreter, whose Winnipeg home soon became a meeting place for the immigrant cultural elite, was one of the founders of the first Ukrainian newspaper in Canada, *Kanadiiskyi farmer* (The Canadian farmer) (1903). He wrote to the Radical leaders, Franko and Pavlyk, asking for their assistance. "Perhaps you have heard from Pavlyk," Genyk wrote to Franko, "that we are publishing a newspaper in Winnipeg under the name *Kanadiiskyi farmer*. We are in a very poor state for publishing a newspaper and thus I would ask you to write something for us. I think that we can pay you for each of your contributions. You would be able to write about the most touchy subjects without any fear of the censor."[42]

It is quite probable that Franko replied to Genyk's letter, but until Genyk's personal archive is discovered, the nature of Franko's reply will remain unclear. It is known, however, that *Kanadiiskyi farmer* reprinted many of Franko's works, and this might have been done with his permission. Moreover, in spite of the fact that *Kanadiiskyi farmer* was financed by the Liberal Party of Canada, Genyk and many other contributors continued to carry on the Radical Party traditions they had brought with them from Austrian Galicia. In particular, Genyk, like Franko to an extent, was an anti-cleric of sorts and an opponent of the conservative Greek Catholic clergy. Thus, it is not surprising that he kept Franko informed of the first efforts to found an independent Eastern Rite Church organized along Protestant lines.[43] Genyk also wrote to Franko concerning an idea for a fraternal agricultural society he hoped to establish. Genyk meant this *Zemelne Volne Bratstvo* (Free agricultural society) to be a cooperative undertaking, independent of the churches, and based on the pooled capital of several farmers. Franko thought Genyk's letter worthy of publication and expressed sympathy with the humanitarian ideals that it contained, but he had grave doubts as to whether conditions in North America were conducive to such an enterprise.[44]

Genyk's correspondence with Franko is an early example of the famous writer's considerable prestige in the fledgling Galician colonies in North America. Other examples abound. In Scranton, Pennsylvania, Franko was chosen as patron of a secular and nationally oriented mutual-benefit society, the Ukrainian Workingmen's Association; in Winnipeg, Manitoba, various works of his were reprinted. For example, the immigrant intellectual Oleksander Sushko reprinted Franko's popular-style synopsis of scientific opinion on biblical legends about the creation of the world. In 1913, on the fortieth anniversary of Franko's literary activity, greetings flowed back to the Old Country from organizations of various sorts located in all parts of Canada where Ukrainian immigrants lived. Commemorative concerts were held in Winnipeg, Vancouver, Montreal, and elsewhere, and the proceeds were sent back to Lviv. Thus, even before his death in 1916, Franko had already become a cult figure among the Ukrainian Canadians. With the revolution of 1917 and the rise and fall of independent Ukrainian governments in Kyiv and Lviv, the cult was strengthened, so that, for many years, in Canada as well as elsewhere, both Moscow-line Communists and convinced nationalists venerated the figure of the eminent Galician writer. This cult is but little diminished today.[45]

It was natural that Franko should so quickly become a cult figure among the Ukrainian Canadians, who, by the eve of the First World War, numbered well over 150,000 people. The late nineteenth-century mass immigration from Galicia to the Canadian prairies was no accident. The necessity for emigration was established beforehand, the destination investigated, and the prospective immigrants properly informed and organized. Franko, Oleskiv, and their colleagues played an active role in the entire process. Franko, in particular, was well aware of the momentous social and demographic forces at work in the Galician countryside. He knew that in the absence of industrialization, large-scale emigration was the only alternative to overcrowding and famine. He was deeply moved by the quasi-messianic dreams of the impoverished villagers, but cautioned them against dangerous voyages to inhospitable places like Brazil and Russia-in-Asia. When Oleskiv returned from Canada, Franko, who earlier had himself considered visiting North America, and perhaps even emigrating to Canada, joined him in redirecting the course of an exodus that was now believed to be nearly unstoppable. The concerted effort of these social activists coincided with a general drive to organize the Galician peasantry into a coherent political force. The phenomenon of mass public assemblies of the country folk helped to hasten the rise of modern political parties in Galicia, but it also helped to produce a large-scale and orderly immigration to Canada. The Galician settlers did not quickly forget their Old World benefactors. This is certainly one of the reasons why the portrait of the western Ukrainian writer Ivan Franko today hangs in so very many community halls scattered across the length and breadth of the Canadian prairies, and, indeed, all of Canada.

4 A Polish Scholar on Polyethnic Emigration from the Republic of Poland to Canada between the Wars

In varietate concordia.

(Motto of the European Union)

The general outlines of the great eastern European migration to the Americas, which began in the 1880s and grew in intensity until the outbreak of the First World War, have long been known. During this period, literally millions of central and eastern European country folk left their villages and boarded trains for the bustling port cities on the western coasts of the European continent. From Hamburg, Bremen, Antwerp, and Liverpool, they crossed the ocean on one of the large German or English steamships that plied the Atlantic and took them to the various ports of North and South America. Thereafter, they travelled by rail to the Canadian prairies, they dispersed to the industrial states of New England or the American Midwest, or, in South America, made their way from Rio de Janeiro and Buenos Aires to agricultural settlements in Argentina or the fertile and temperate southern provinces of Brazil.[1]

In 1914, the outbreak of the Great War brought this unprecedented emigration to an abrupt end. During the 1920s, the movement was partially renewed, but severe quotas on the entry of eastern Europeans enacted in 1921 and 1924 in the United States, and stringent entrance requirements, which, in 1919, designated eastern Europeans as "non-preferred" people in Canada, restricted the flow of migrants to a trickle. In the mid-1920s, however, economic conditions improved. Canadian immigration policies changed and soon the numbers of people emigrating from eastern Europe began to increase. The movement remained strong until the world economic downturn of the 1930s. The newly created Republic of Poland, which arose out of the ashes of the Romanov, Habsburg, and Hohenzollern empires, and the young Dominion of Canada, which was still completing the settlement of its western prairie region, played a large part in this general process.

Writers and scholars both in Canada and in the Polish Republic began to pay attention to this extraordinary movement of people while the phenomenon was still underway. On the receiving end, the changing ethnic mix was most visible on the Canadian prairies, which, even in the 1920s, still were not completely settled. Thus, it is not surprising that the socially concerned Prairie schoolteacher Robert England devoted some serious attention to the subject, while the Protestant social worker Charles H. Young penned an important sociological study of the largest eastern European immigrant group, the Prairie Ukrainians.[2] In a similar way, a "literature of emigration" began to appear in the languages of eastern Europe, and this literature described the qualities, prospects, and problems of Canada and the New World. In Poland, the most detailed treatments of Canada were written by consular officials posted to Canada; in particular, Józef Okołowicz, who was the first Polish diplomatic official assigned to Canada, and Roman Mazurkiewicz, who was for a time vice-consul of Poland in Montreal. Both these men, but Mazurkiewicz in particular, held positive beliefs about the New World and supported the idea of Polish emigration to Canada.[3]

During the period following the Second World War, scholarship about Canadians who trace their origins to eastern Europe began to develop more thoroughly, and, of course, almost all this literature in some way dealt with the realities of the immigration experience. Of the major ethnic groups of the interwar Polish Republic, the Poles were the subject of a pioneering work by Victor Turek and the Ukrainians were first examined by Paul Yuzyk and Vladimir Kaye.[4] Thereafter, numerous other works appeared and, by the 1980s, major synthetic histories came out that rested on the studies carried out during the 1960s and 1970s by scholars of Polish and Ukrainian background. For the Poles, the study by Henry Radecki and Benedykt Heydenkorn, which had a strong sociological slant, was most notable, and, for the Ukrainians, the collection of essays edited by Manoly Lupul held a somewhat parallel place.[5] Specialist studies also appeared on Polish Canadian diplomatic relations, on immigrant workers before the Depression, and on the difficulties of Jewish immigration to Canada during the late 1930s and 1940s.[6] On still another level, for the sake of Polish readers, a Polish Canadian scholar summarized Canadian immigration policies during the pre- and interwar periods in a serial publication of the Catholic University of Lublin.[7] Thus, it comes as no surprise that a first major study of polyethnic emigration to Canada from the interwar Polish Republic was also sponsored in Poland by a group of similarly interested scholars, this time in Cracow by the Polish Academy of Sciences, Institute for the Study of Poles Abroad.

The work in question is Anna Reczyńska's *Emigration from Poland to Canada during the Interwar Period*, which focuses on the migration question itself rather than on the history of the immigrant communities in the new country.[8] Reczyńska's study is derived from a wide variety of sources. Statistical materials, upon which a good part of the book is based, were gleaned from both Canadian and Polish publications and archives. Important Canadian sources include the annual reports of the Department of Immigration and Colonization (1918 to 1935) and the Department of Mines and Natural Resources (1937 to 1940) as well as the Canada Year Books (1920 to 1940). Canadian census statistics were also used, as were various statistical annuals published by the government of the Polish Republic from 1920 through to 1938. Reczyńska also examined important Polish archival collections including the records of the foreign and internal ministries, the Polish Association for the Care of Relatives Abroad, the World Union of Poles Abroad, and some of the records of the Polish consulates established in Canada – especially the consulate general in Montreal and the consulate in Winnipeg – which, being accredited to a British Empire dominion, were formally under the administrative jurisdiction of the Polish embassy in London. Canadian archival collections used include the Public Archives of Canada in Ottawa, and the Multicultural History Society of Ontario and the Canadian Polish Research Institute, the latter two of which are located in Toronto.

The interwar Republic of Poland, known in Polish historiography as the Second Republic, was very much a multinational state. The collapse of the German Empire (1918), a successful war against the Western Ukrainian People's Republic (1918–19), and a compromise peace with Soviet Russia (1921) left large Ukrainian, Belarusan, German, and Jewish minorities within the new Polish state. About one-third of the country's population was now made up of national minorities. Most significantly, the former Austrian Crown Land of Galicia, which had seen very intensive emigration to Canada during the period from 1896 to 1914, was now completely absorbed into the Polish Republic, largely against the wishes of the Ukrainian population, which formed an absolute majority in the eastern half of this ethnically mixed territory. This factor was of great importance because, during the interwar period, this same area continued to provide a substantial proportion of emigrants to Canada and remained the area of most intense out-migration to Canada until the renewed outbreak of war in 1939. Ethnic Ukrainians, therefore, play an important role in Anna Reczyńska's story.

This story begins with some general observations about the character and extent of emigration from the Second Republic. First, the emigration movement was very extensive, a continuation of the Great Economic Migration, which had reached its climax in the years before the First World War. Between the wars, it involved well over a million people, of whom the majority were seasonal migrants who left for work in western Europe. France was the target country of most of the workers, although, after 1926, Germany also occupied an important position. In the first years after the war, the United States held a prominent place as a destination for trans-Atlantic emigrants, but severe quotas against migrants from Poland enacted in 1921 and 1924 severely reduced traffic to the USA. This left Canada and Latin America, specifically Argentina and Brazil, as major targets. Due to the vagaries of Brazilian immigration policies during this period, most of the emigration was directed towards Canada and Argentina. During the entire period from 1919 to 1939, over 140,000 people holding Polish passports emigrated to Canada; by 1928, over 40 per cent of all the trans-Atlantic "Polish" emigration was directed to the North American Dominion. National minorities, including Jews, played a large part in this movement, but the Ukrainians played a clearly dominant role (7–8). Because only Argentina and Canada still had quantities of empty land to offer to prospective immigrants, in general, they remained the principal target countries during the interwar period. Also, it seems that while Polish industrial workers, artisans, and Jews tended to go to Argentina, Polish country folk and Ukrainians tended to head for Canada (8). By the beginning of the twenties, writes Reczyńska, the Polish vice-consul in Montreal suggested there were about 400,000 people in Canada who traced their origins to the territory of the interwar Polish republic. Of these, there were about 100,000 Poles and 300,000 Ukrainians.[9]

The erection of the new Polish Republic also had an effect on the character of the interwar emigration. No longer could German emigration agents who worked for the great German shipping companies freely roam the Galician, Volhynian, and Mazurian countryside and more or less openly spread propaganda and recruit unsuspecting peasants for the difficult journey to the New World. Emigration procedures were now formalized under the control of the Polish state, and the entire process was now overseen by Polish officials both in Canada and in the European homeland. The steady spread of the Polish system of public education meant there were fewer cases of illiteracy among emigrants, and, together with new literacy regulations enacted in Canada, ensured that the old English Canadian stereotype of the illiterate "Galicians," the men in sheepskin coats, began to pass away (11).[10]

The reasons for emigrating from the "Old Country" (and this was the term used by most of the immigrants themselves) remained more or less the same as for the pre-war period: overpopulation in the countryside and parcelization of the land into ever-smaller plots. During the interwar period, Poland had one of the highest birthrates in all of Europe and the population increased by over seven million people, from 27.2 million to 34.8 million. Meanwhile, Polish industrial production grew very slowly, not surpassing its pre-war level until 1938. Thus, there were no cities to which the surplus agricultural population could migrate (18–19).

In spite of these pressures, it was not the most severely impoverished, or the destitute, who formed the majority of the emigrants. Studies of individual villages by Polish social historians (such as Franciszek Bujak and others), as well as the testimony of the migrants themselves, make it clear that this search for a new life was a matter of social improvement ("for a better life") and not of necessity. It is clear that the cost of rail and ocean travel eliminated the poorest, while, in the case of Canada, it was necessary to possess a modest sum on arrival in order to pass the immigration requirements. (It was assumed that a certain amount of money was necessary for the purchase of land.) This financial factor, speculates Reczyńska (23), is the probable reason for the difference in character between the "proletarian" emigration to Argentina and the "agrarian" emigration to Canada.[11]

Other factors were also important in drawing people specifically to Canada. First, the existence of a large migration to Canada during the period from 1895 to 1914 acted as an example for the next generation. Many villagers in eastern Galicia and elsewhere had relatives or neighbours in the new country, and news gleaned from letters home, remittance payments to family, and return visits by former emigrants tended to spread information about opportunities in Canada. Second, in books, pamphlets for emigrants, and newspaper articles, Canada was described in positive terms, so much so, in fact, that the word "Canada" in Polish came to be a synonym for well-being, abundance, and wealth (25). Third, the earlier wave of emigrants had established institutions that were particularly attractive to the various minority nationalities inhabiting the

Polish state: Ukrainians in Canada possessed their own ecclesiastical and, in part, educational systems, and they founded a variety of social and political institutions that operated more freely in the new country than in the old; the German churches in Canada worked with the big railroad companies to attract and even help finance German settlers from Poland; and the Jews, even at this early date, had a small parliamentary lobby that tried to ease the entry of individual and, in some cases, entire groups of, Polish Jews (31). Finally, some emigrants, especially among the Jews, were attracted to Canada as a stepping stone to the United States, which, of course, was also seen as a land of plenty.

Polish statistics clearly show the importance of Canada as a destination for emigrants during the interwar period. The general trend is from a period of no emigration to Canada during the first years of the new republic to a modest emigration of a few thousand per year during the early twenties, to a climax of about 20,000 per year during the late twenties. The numbers decline once again during the post-1930 Depression years. During the peak years, Canada was the destination of just under 15 per cent of all "Polish" emigrants and 40 per cent of all trans-Atlantic "Polish" emigrants (9). Reczyńska's figures are shown in table 4.1(9).

Statistics are also available on the locality from which the emigrants came. In general, the areas of most intense emigration lay in the southeastern quarter of the interwar republic. The Province (*województwo*) of Tarnopol (Ternopil in Ukrainian), which was carved out of old Austrian Galicia, was the focal point and was the only province from which over 25,000 people emigrated to Canada. (During the period before 1914, this was also the area of most intense out-migration to Canada.)[12] Lwów (Lviv in Ukrainian) Province, which had also been a part of Austrian Galicia, came second with over 20,000 emigrants; then came Volhynia, which had been a part of the Russian partition, with over 10,000 emigrants. These were followed by the provinces of Stanisławów, Polesia, Lublin, Kielce, and Cracow, each of which contributed about 5,000 people. Northern Poland and western Poland did not see statistically significant migration to Canada (59).

Most of these emigrants declared their destination to be western Canada; in particular, the prairie provinces of Manitoba and Alberta. However, the Canadian census of 1941 clearly revealed that a good part of the new arrivals either did not settle in the Prairie West, or lived there only for a certain period, afterwards moving east to the industrial cities of southern Ontario or to mining towns located in the northern Ontario bush country (63–4). This information tends to support the conclusions

Table 4.1 Emigration from Poland.

Year	Total Emigration	Trans-Atlantic Emigration	To Canada
1918	4,629	4,629	–
1920	88,303	74,121	4,306
1922	70,089	38,716	3,717
1924	74,539	22,511	2,271
1925	81,218	38,449	4,268
1926	167,509	49,893	15,810
1927	147,614	58,187	22,031
1928	186,360	64,581	27,036
1929	243,442	65,310	21,703
1930	218,387	46,534	16,940
1931	76,005	11,770	1,326
1932	21,439	9,667	1,118

of those Canadian social historians who point out that numerous immigrants who came to Canada in search of inexpensive land or a homestead actually found themselves part of an ethnically diverse Canadian proletariat.[13] On another level – that of gender – statistics compiled by the Canadian Department of Immigration and Colonization reveal that men in their twenties tended to predominate during the late 1920s, while women in their thirties tended to be more numerous in the 1930s. The late 1920s, it will be remembered, were years of economic prosperity and high immigration, while the 1930s were years of depression and low immigration.

Throughout this period, Polish officials collected a considerable amount of information about the religious affiliation of emigrants to Canada. Since most Roman Catholics considered themselves to be Poles, most Greek or Eastern Rite Catholics considered themselves to be Ukrainians, most Protestants considered themselves to be Germans, and most Greek Orthodox considered themselves to be Ukrainian, or, in some cases, Belarusan, these figures also tell us something about the ethnic composition of the emigration. In general, for the period from 1926 to 1938, which included the years of most intense emigration, Roman Catholics numbered 39,953 emigrants, making up 34.5 per cent of the total; Greek Catholics numbered 41,113 people, making up another 35.5 per cent of the total; and the remainder was divided among Jews (16,169 or 14 per cent), Orthodox (10,703 or 9.2 per cent), and Protestants (6,266 or 5.4 per cent). The numbers of Roman and Greek Catholics tended to be large in the 1920s but declined to a few hundred per year in the 1930s. The numbers of Orthodox, Protestants, and Jews also declined during the 1930s, but, in percentage terms, the numbers of Jews rose spectacularly and, in 1934 and 1935, they formed the single largest group (1,052 people) emigrating from the Polish Republic to Canada (71–2). This seems to indicate that the unofficial Canadian immigration restrictions on Jews were not impregnable and that Jewish lobbyists in Canada enjoyed at least some success at getting some individuals into the country.

Religious confession, however, is not always a sure indicant of national affiliation. Certainly, many Greek Catholics, Orthodox, and Jews who considered themselves to be Poles in the Old Country would not identify with the Polish community in Canada. The case of the Belarusans is particularly difficult, for, throughout the interwar period, their national consciousness remained quite low and the name "Belarusan" does not appear in many religious, linguistic, and ethnic origin statistics. However, many people did come to Canada from the Belarusan regions of interwar Poland and they do have to be taken into account in any reckoning of the national breakdown of the immigrant population. When religious, linguistic, and geographical factors are all taken into account, Reczyńska concludes that the national structure of the Polish immigration to Canada from 1918 to 1939 was made up as shown in table 4.2 (81).

From these figures, it is clear that the national minorities of the Second Republic were vastly overrepresented among the emigrants, while the Poles, who made up about 66 to 68 per cent of the citizenry, contributed less than a third of the emigrants. The case of the Ukrainians was most striking, for they are estimated to have made up only from 13.9 to 16.2 per cent of the population, while they made up over 40 per cent of the immigration to Canada. Similarly, Belarusan emigrants exceeded their proportion of the population by a factor of two, and Germans exceeded their proportion by a factor of three. Canadian immigration policy, speculates Reczyńska (82), which favoured agriculturalists, was probably at work in attracting the large numbers of Ukrainian and Belarusan country folk, while the existence of a large, established Ukrainian community in Canada may also have been a factor. "The tradition of Ukrainian emigration to Canada," she concludes (82), "as well as the fact that the Ukrainians met the requirements set up for immigrants to this country, meant that Canada was the main goal of Ukrainian emigration from Poland between the wars."

Table 4.2 National structure of Polish immigration to Canada

Ukrainians	40.4%	59,500
Poles	29.4%	43,300
Jews	14%	20,600
Germans	7.8%	11,400
Belarusans	7.4%	10,900
Others	1%	1,500

It is important to add, however, that Canada was the exception in Polish emigration history during this period. In general, Jews, not Ukrainians, were the most active participants in the emigration movement in proportion to their part of the population, while Ukrainians and Belarusans were the most reluctant to leave (82). Similarly, Ukrainians were more likely to return to the Polish Republic than were Germans or Jews. Although the percentage of people leaving Canada to return to the Old Country was relatively small when compared to re-emigration for the Polish emigration as a whole, Ukrainians from Canada did continue to return to "Poland" right into the 1930s (94).

All these factors operated within the general context of Polish emigration policy, which changed slightly with the passage of time. During the period before 1914, before the establishment of the Polish state, many public figures opposed the emigration movement, believing that the population and economic loss was harmful to the Polish national cause and that the emigrants endured considerable physical hardship. The large Polish emigration to Brazil was widely discussed. During the pre-1914 years, Józef Okołowicz, later Polish consul general in Montreal, spoke out against emigration; J. Siemiradzki criticized the Ukrainian professor Józef Olesków (Osyp Oleskiv in Ukrainian) for dispersing what he considered to be the "Polish" emigration by initiating a "syphoning off" of Ukrainian emigrants from Brazil to the Canadian prairies; and Leopold Caro postulated that seasonal migration was better than permanent emigration, that continental was better than trans-oceanic, and that colonies were better than the simple export of labour abroad (98–100).[14] These negative attitudes towards the emigration movement also appeared in works of literature composed in Polish and the other Slavic languages.

They did not, however, carry the day. Before 1914, certain publicists such as the populist writer Jan Stapiński spoke positively about the benefits of peasant emigration to Canada, while other writers were aware that their ideas merely reflected the existence of a mass phenomenon but did not greatly influence its course. With the erection of the new Polish state, however, public opinion turned decisively in favour of the movement. It was recognized that the movement of people would increase traffic at the new Polish ports on the Baltic Sea, that remittance payments to family in Poland would help with the balance-of-payment problem, and, of course, the problems of hunger and rural overpopulation would be somewhat reduced. The Polish Ministry of Labour and Social Welfare favoured emigration because it tended to reduce internal tensions in the country; and the Ministry of Foreign Affairs liked it because it was hoped that the flow of Poles abroad would help extend Polish influence in far-off lands (103). Most Polish political parties took an interest in the emigrants and wished to see the Polish government set up agencies to look after them (105). By 1925, Michał Straszewski, the Polish consul in Montreal, was reporting to the embassy in London on the excellence of Canada as a target for future emigration (107).

Care of the emigrants in Canada was a specific concern of the Polish diplomatic corps in the Dominion. The Consulate General, which had been set up in 1919 under the supervision of Józef Okołowicz, who continued to write and publish on immigration questions, was supplemented in 1920 by a second consulate in Winnipeg, which was to specialize in the care of Polish immigrants. Later, agencies were also established in Regina and Vancouver, and Polish diplomatic intervention with the Department of Immigration and Colonization, especially in cases of discrimination against the "non-preferred" Poles, became frequent (123). The Polish consulates in Canada also made an attempt to control the return of immigrants to the homeland. In the early twenties, there were cases where they refused to issue passports for Ukrainians in Canada who wished to return to Europe, while, in other cases, they directed Poles in France, Belgium, and even Cuba to come to Canada (125).

On another level, the consulates sometimes interfered in the internal life of the Polish community in Canada: in 1931, for example, they helped to establish the pro-Piłsudski – that is, pro-government – Federation of Polish Societies in Canada (*Zjednoczenie zrzeszen Polskich w Kanadzie*) and, shortly afterwards, briefly subsidized the Winnipeg newspaper *Czas* (Time), which had recently been taken over by pro-government Poles but earlier had been very critical of the national minorities policy of the regime of Marshal Piłsudski (125).[15] Moreover, it is almost certain that the Polish consulate kept a close watch on the Polish- and Ukrainian-language federations of the Communist Party of Canada, since these were especially vocal in their criticism of the Polish government, and the Ukrainian leftists, in particular, were so numerous that they formed one of the main bastions of organizational and financial support for Canadian Communism.

The unsettled national question in Poland did, in fact, influence the emigration policies of the Polish government. Though, at first, certain government officials believed that Polish peasants from the centre of the country should be encouraged to settle in the ethnically mixed eastern borderlands of the republic – in particular, in eastern Galicia and Volhynia – and help to "Polonize" these regions, and others argued that favouring Ukrainian emigration might economically harm the overpopulated Polish centre, such negative views did not prevail. Rather, Polish officials quickly reached the conclusion that the emigration of national minorities might, in fact, get rid of certain "undesirable elements" and help strengthen the Polish character of the state. In the eyes of the Polish consul general in Montreal, Józef Okołowicz, the Ukrainians, in particular, were such an undesirable element. Therefore, as early as 1922, Okołowicz informed his ministry that what he called the entirely "natural" wave of Ukrainian migration to Canada should be used by the Polish government to reduce the Ukrainian presence in eastern Galicia, or, as it was now officially called, "Eastern Little Poland." He continued (129):

> Such an action cannot be viewed as a desire to expel the Ruthenians from their ancient lands through deportation abroad, as, for example, to penal servitude in "San Domingo." To the contrary, I am under the impression that such an agitation would even gain the moral and factual support of those Ukrainian circles which are unfavorable to us [and] ... who wish to implement their program for the creation of a "New Ukraine" in Canada. . . . This country is known in every hamlet in eastern Galicia as a synonym for self-sufficiency, freedom, and happiness.

Other consular officials, local authorities in Poland, and Polish specialists writing on the national question agreed with Okołowicz and suggested that the Polish government should actively encourage Ukrainian emigration to Canada, as one report frankly put it, "in order to strengthen Polish control [*Polski stan posiadania*] in eastern Galicia" (132).

The results of all these suggestions are not entirely clear. It seems that while the Polish central government did not interfere or try to limit Ukrainian emigration to Canada, neither did it actively encourage it. Thus, when, in 1924, the Greek Catholic bishop in Canada, Nikita Budka, and the Saint Rafael Immigrant Aid Society in Winnipeg initiated a project for the emigration of some 10,000 Ukrainian agricultural workers from Poland and managed to get some cooperation from the Canadian Pacific Railway, the plan still went unrealized, largely through the indifference of the Polish authorities (130–1). These same authorities were more willing to take action in the later twenties, and, at one point, the Ukrainian case was even studied as an example for the possible emigration of Jews and Germans from Poland; many Jews, in particular, did go to Canada, but, in general, Polish governmental encouragement was not the principal motivating factor behind this movement. Canadian immigration policies seem to have been much more important.

This also seems to have been the case with regard to specifically Polish ethnic emigration to Canada. Nevertheless, many new emigration schemes of various sorts did arise with the establishment of the Second Republic. Since Poland was a principal successor state to the old German Empire, some Poles argued that she had a claim to a portion of the former German imperial colonies; others argued that plans for joint settlement could be worked out with one of the smaller colonial powers such as Portugal, and the idea of a Polish colony in French Africa, perhaps Madagascar, was raised. However, most hopes were placed in a Polish colony in Latin America, and some settlements were actually founded in Brazil and in Peru (137–8). Thus, the idea of establishing vigorous and durable Polish settlements in western Canada was not entirely unique.

Polish government interest in Canada grew through the 1920s as the numbers of Ukrainians and Poles coming to Canada steadily increased. In 1926, Roman Kutyłowski, the deputy director of the Emigration Administration of the Polish State Emigration Council, delivered a report that favoured the idea of expanded Polish settlement in western Canada. He suggested increasing the activity of the Winnipeg consulate, state subsidies for emigrants, and experimental colonies in northern Saskatchewan. Kutyłowski wanted to settle the Poles in large groups separate from the Ukrainians, whom he saw as posing an assimilationist danger to the Polish settlers. In fact, Polish emigration officials generally wished to see group settlements that could preserve a Polish identity and, aware of probable Canadian resistance to such plans, even thought to set up a front organization in Canada that would be able to implement them with a certain amount of discretion. When it was realized that this would entail considerable risk and expense, it was decided to simply expand the activities of the Winnipeg consulate and to encourage Polish Roman Catholic priests to move to Canada. (It was expected that they would act as magnets for scattered Polish settlers.) But even this had to be done with considerable tact, it was observed, since Anglo Canadian Protestants, who were viewed as being suspicious of Catholics, might arouse the country to a negative reaction (143–5).

In 1929, the Polish government's Colonization Society sent a three-man commission under Count Aleksander de Lago to thoroughly investigate the possibilities of large-scale Polish settlement in western Canada. The commission negotiated with the railways and the institutions responsible for the settlement of the prairie provinces. The Prince Albert area in Saskatchewan and the Athabaska area in Alberta were chosen as potentially favourable sites, but Canadian disinterest and the onset of the Great Depression ensured that nothing came of the venture (145–56). It was obvious that Canadian immigration policy was the determining factor in the growth of the emigration movement during the 1920s.

The "non-preferred" status of Canadian immigrants from central and eastern Europe, in fact, was largely suspended during the second half of the 1920s. By 1925, the "open-door" lobby of transportation and resource-based industries succeeded in convincing the Dominion government to enter into an arrangement with the Canadian Pacific Railway and the newly formed Canadian National Railway, which allowed these companies a free hand in the distribution of central and eastern European agricultural immigrants. In many cases, potential immigrants in Poland were initially approached by representatives of the railway companies, generally steamship agents who were paid five dollars for each bona fide agriculturalist. The Polish, Ukrainian, and other prospective immigrants then travelled to the major ports at Danzig (Gdańsk) and elsewhere, where they were screened by railway officials and checked by Canadian immigration officials. Then, they sailed to Canada on Canadian or, in many cases, Polish vessels, and made their way to employment in western Canada or the mining country. Between 1925 and 1930, when the railway agreement was cancelled under the pressure of changed economic circumstances in Canada, some 185,000 central European immigrants entered Canada, many of them coming from the Polish Republic.[16] Polish attempts during the 1930s to route the declining numbers of travellers onto the Polish-owned Gdynia-America Line failed and, for five years, caused tensions in the diplomatic relations between the Second Republic, on the one hand, and Canada and Great Britain, on the other. This dispute probably reinforced the general trend towards low migration levels. Resolution of the dispute in Canada's favour saw a slight increase in Polish emigration to Canada on the eve of the war but the numbers of immigrants involved never approached the volume that entered Canada under the terms of the Railway Agreement of 1925 to 1930 (160–84).

Regardless of the policies of the Canadian government or the Polish government, after the onset of the Great Depression, many Ukrainians, seemingly the largest emigrating group interested in Canada in interwar Poland, appeared to have felt that it was the powers that be – that is, Polish officialdom – that were not allowing them to emigrate to the North American Dominion. Thus, in the winter of 1938–9, a parody of a popular Ukrainian Christmas carol that touched on the emigration theme was published in the humorous Ukrainian weekly *Komar* (The mosquito). The punch lines went:

Bo khlopska nevista vse nese do mista,
Kurku, maslo, syr i iaitsia velmozhnym do tista.
...
Nema na to rady, ne prosy poshchady.
Ne puskaiut' vorizhenky u svit do Kanady.

For the peasant woman is carrying everything to town:
Chicken, butter, cheese and eggs for cake for the rich.
...
You cannot help it, do not even ask for mercy:
Our enemies are not letting us go into the wide world, to Canada.[17]

Thus, the evidence of folklore supports the statistical and bureaucratic evidence compiled by Anna Reczyńska that Canada occupied a prominent place in the hopes and dreams of prospective emigrants in interwar Poland even after the onset of the Depression and the ending of the Railway Agreement of 1925 to 1930.

In general, emigration to Canada from the interwar Polish Republic, as reflected in the work of Anna Reczyńska, reveals a number of characteristics. First, this was a polyethnic migration in which the participation of national minorities from the Second Republic was vastly disproportionate to their respective parts of the composition of the Polish state. Second, during the interwar period, Canada was a principal target country for Polish emigration in general. Third, despite the evidence of certain pieces of folklore, the Polish government in no way hindered the emigration of its citizens to Canada and many government officials considered ways of further encouraging the movement; such considerations were given to both the national minorities, especially the Ukrainians, who were often considered unfriendly to the new Polish state, and to ethnic Poles. Fourth, Canadian government policy was a major causal factor behind the migration, which reached its peak during the railway agreement.

These general points made so clearly by Anna Reczyńska do not exhaust the theme of polyethnic emigration from the Second Republic to Canada. The question of ethnic relations in Poland between the wars is largely ignored in Reczyńska's story, but the national tensions of these years are well known and form an important part of the background to the emigration of the national minorities. Ethnic relations in Canada between groups emanating from Poland are similarly ignored in Reczyńska's study, though it is well known that, for example, Polish Ukrainian relations in Canada during the period from 1918 to 1939 were very good on the personal level (as reflected in communal cooperation, the number of intermarriages, etc.) but often tense in the political arena (as reflected in polemics appearing in the press and in various pamphlets, etc.). In this way, in the 1990s, a few years after the publication of Reczyńska's book, the Polish historian of emigration Edward Kołodziej generalized that interwar Polish Ukrainian relations in Canada "were generally correct, even friendly," and that the most tense years were those between 1918 and 1919 (the time of the Polish Ukrainian war over Galicia) and 1930 (the year of the Polish government's so-called Pacification of this same area, then tendentiously called "Eastern Little Poland" by Polish officialdom). Thus, while Polish diplomats in Canada might have thought that Canada was a good target for the export of its Ukrainian minority, they also kept a close eye on developments in the Ukrainian Canadian community and intervened with the Canadian Department of External Affairs when they thought it politically expedient.[18] Nevertheless, Anna Reczyńska's study was an important contribution to the literature on Canadian immigration when it first appeared and today still remains an important starting point for anyone interested in polyethnic immigration to Canada from eastern Europe during the first half of the twentieth century.

History, Historians, and Others

5 Dmytro Doroshenko and Canada

Vita brevis, ars longa.
Life is short, art is long, but history is longest,
for it is art added to scholarship.

George Macaulay Trevelyan, *Clio: A Muse*

Dmytro Ivanovych Doroshenko (1882–1951) was undoubtedly the most important and most prolific Ukrainian émigré historian of the twentieth century. Writing in the 1920s, 1930s, and the 1940s, at a time when the term "Ukraine" was still relatively new to the Western public and when historical scholarship was very much censored and restricted in the USSR, he popularized the very idea that Ukraine had an identity and independent history of its own. He also espoused a conservative but nonetheless progressive philosophy in which a central theme was care for the well-being and enlightenment of the simple Ukrainian country folk. This he did, in his characteristically quiet and gentlemanly manner, in works popular and scholarly, published in many different languages and in several different Western countries. One of these countries was Canada, with which he had a close and long-lasting relationship.[1]

During the interwar period, Canada was home to a very large Ukrainian community, settled principally in the Prairie West, which had its origins in the Great Economic Immigration from eastern Europe to the Americas in the years before the First World War. This community, which had been fairly well organized before the war with a variety of political, social, economic, and ecclesiastical institutions, was replenished by renewed immigration during the 1920s. However, these first "waves" of immigration, of "Ruthenians," as they were then usually called, were made up largely of poorly educated country folk, impoverished villagers from the Austrian provinces of Galicia and Bukovina (before 1914), and from newly independent Poland, which had annexed the Ukrainian parts of Galicia in 1918. Only a very slight sprinkling of village priests and Old Country intelligentsia accompanied the villagers to the new country, and acquaintance with the higher levels of education and sophisticated scholarship of the kind produced by Doroshenko was still in its initial stages.[2]

By the early 1920s, however, a definite beginning had been made. In fact, as early as 1916, a major Ukrainian student residence and cultural centre, the Petro Mohyla Institute, had been founded in Saskatoon, where it was located close to the University of Saskatchewan campus. The institute immediately became a focus of controversy when the Greek Catholic bishop of Canada tried to exercise control over it. This incident provided the spark that ignited a popular revolt against the Greek Catholic Church. The institute eventually became a major institutional support for the newly founded and vociferously anti-Catholic Ukrainian Greek Orthodox Church of Canada, which claimed the loyalty of some of the most nationally conscious of the new Ukrainian Canadian intelligentsia. Another strong institutional support for the Orthodox movement was the Winnipeg newspaper *Ukrainskyi holos* (Ukrainian voice), edited by the fiery journalist Myroslav Stechishin (1883–1947). *Ukrainskyi holos* generally took a populist or slightly left-of-centre position in Ukrainian politics and supported the Ukrainian "republican" movement led by the pro-Western social democrat Symon Petliura, who was resident in Paris during the early 1920s. By contrast, Doroshenko was a supporter of the conservative movement in Ukrainian politics led by the former Hetman General Pavlo Skoropadsky, who had briefly ruled in revolutionary-era Ukraine as a German-supported monarch. In the period following the revolution, Doroshenko's close friend Viacheslav Lypynsky, who was resident in Vienna between the wars, became the premier ideologist of this conservative Hetmanite or monarchist movement. It is unknown how it happened, but, in 1924, *Ukrainskyi holos*, in spite of its ideological support of Petliura (who, in late 1918, had actually helped to overthrow the Hetman and re-establish the revolutionary republic), published a series of articles by Doroshenko discussing Lypynsky's conservative political philosophy. This material appeared not under Doroshenko's real name but, rather, under the pseudonym M. Zabarevsky.[3] Perhaps the *Ukrainskyi holos* circle showed some tolerance of Doroshenko's conservatism because he was not a Catholic but an Orthodox Christian from eastern Ukraine. Certainly, this circle eventually came to appreciate the historian's attractive style of writing in which he expressed important ideas simply and clearly so that they were easily understood by a wide range of different readers, even those without a higher education. Doroshenko was, in fact, a brilliant popularizer of both Ukrainian historical ideas and Lypynsky's political philosophy.

Some light is thrown on the matter of Doroshenko's contributions to *Ukrainskyi holos* by his correspondence with Myroslav's brother Julian Stechishin (1895–1971). Julian was a central figure in the Mohyla Institute in Saskatoon and, together with his brother Myroslav in Winnipeg, was then elaborating a political philosophy that was intended to be an underpinning for the new Orthodox movement on the Prairies. In 1925, Julian sent Doroshenko, who was then resident in Prague where he was a professor of history at the émigré Ukrainian Free University (*Ukrainskyi vilnyi universytet u Prazi*), an honorarium of twenty-five dollars for his previous contribution to *Ukrainskyi holos* and inquired about further materials. Stechishin particularly wanted to know about the degree of popular support for the Hetmanite movement, both among émigrés in western Europe and in Ukraine itself. Doroshenko responded to this request, but the historian was doubtful whether *Ukrainskyi holos* could publish this material. He referred to the strong "republican" position of *Ukrainskyi holos* and noted that the paper had just recently published some very severe attacks on the Hetmanite movement. In any case, the historian advised Stechishin that the material, if published, should be printed unsigned or under a pseudonym, since he was at that time being vigorously attacked by certain political rivals in Prague and accused of being disloyal to the liberal democratic Czech government, which financed the Ukrainian Free University and protected him. None of this further material ever appeared in *Ukrainskyi holos* and, in 1926, correspondence between the two men temporarily ceased.[4]

For the next few years, contact between Doroshenko and the Ukrainian Canadians seems to have been slight. A brief excerpt from one of Doroshenko's booklets and a reprint of his memoirs about the revolution appeared in another Winnipeg newspaper, *Kanadiiskyi farmer* (The Canadian farmer), but that was about it.[5] More immediate contact was resumed, however, when another Orthodox activist left for Europe in 1932 to undertake Ukrainian studies at the Ukrainian Free University in Prague. Petro I. Lazarowich (1900–1983) had studied education at the University of Saskatchewan and then law at Alberta College in Edmonton before leaving for Europe, and he was already deeply involved in

Ukrainian affairs in western Canada before leaving for the Ukrainian Free University. By this time, Doroshenko was a senior professor teaching history at this institution and it was here that Lazarowich met him.[6]

After his return from Europe, Lazarowich established a law practice in Edmonton, but remained deeply involved in Ukrainian affairs, especially educational matters. He was a leading figure in the Ukrainian Self-Reliance League of Canada (USRL) (*Soiuz Ukraintsiv Samostiinykiv Kanady*), a populist and liberal-oriented lay brotherhood closely affiliated with the Ukrainian Greek Orthodox Church of Canada. This was the quasi-political organization that, during the 1930s, had emerged as a result of the ideological work of Julian Stechishin, his brother Myroslav, and other Orthodox activists; it remained supportive of the Ukrainian "republican" movement in Europe led by Symon Petliura, who had been assassinated in Paris in 1926 and, in consequence, became a widely acknowledged national hero.[7]

In addition to Lazarowich, several leading members of the USRL were devoted to spreading higher education and Ukrainian national consciousness (which went together, in their view of things) among the Ukrainian immigrant population of western Canada. During the 1930s, this group arranged to bring a number of prominent scholars from Europe to deliver public lectures in several different Canadian cities in which there were substantial Ukrainian communities. In 1936, at the suggestion of Lazarowich, the USRL considered inviting Doroshenko to come to Canada on such a tour. Certain USRL members were hesitant about inviting Doroshenko, who continued to be an ideological supporter of Petliura's rival, Skoropadsky (who was resident in Berlin between the wars), but, assured of Doroshenko's abilities and "objectivity" by another Prague professor, the sociologist Olgerd Bochkovsky, who had preceded Doroshenko on a similar tour to Canada in 1936, and undoubtedly with the full support of the Stechishin brothers, the Petro Mohyla Institute in Saskatoon, together with its companion cultural institutions, the Hrushevsky Institute in Edmonton and the USRL, proffered the invitation.[8]

Doroshenko received the invitation in December 1936 in Warsaw, where he had recently moved to accept a position as professor of church history in the Department of Orthodox Theology in the university there; he agreed to come to Canada on condition that the tour be strictly academic and entirely non-political. This presented no problems for the USRL and the arrangements were finalized.[9]

Thus, in July and August of 1937, Doroshenko visited Canada to make his tour. He had a very busy schedule, which began at a conference of

USRL activists in Saskatoon, where he gave the keynote address and aroused the meeting to "lengthy applause." Thereafter, he was supposed to give a sixty-hour course in Ukrainian history at the Mohyla Institute in Saskatoon, but, because of the catastrophic drought that was then hitting Saskatchewan, it was moved to the Hrushevsky Institute in Edmonton. This course was designed primarily for high school teachers. Lazarowich introduced the scholar to the Edmonton public at Doroshenko's inaugural lecture, which was on Mykhailo Hrushevsky as an historian. Seventy-four students, including teachers, university students, businessmen, and even some ordinary workers, enrolled in this course, which had to be transferred to a larger lecture hall at Alberta College to accommodate the unexpectedly large enrolment. After the conclusion of the course, Doroshenko delivered lectures in Saskatoon, Vegreville, Mundare, Regina, Winnipeg, Fort William, Toronto, Montreal, and several smaller towns scattered across the Prairies, where the bulk of the Ukrainian Canadians lived. He also delivered a series of lectures about "famous Ukrainian women" to the Ukrainian Women's Association in Edmonton. In Edmonton, he stayed with a local Ukrainian women's activist, Doris Yanda, and her lawyer husband Dmytro (1892–1969), with whom he later corresponded.

All these lectures were a great success. In the larger cities, some 400 to 500 people, predominantly professional people but also businessmen and workers, would come to hear the famous historian speak; in the smaller towns, the audiences, of course, were somewhat smaller, with farmers, their wives, and sometimes even grandmothers with young grandchildren attending. Doroshenko managed to attract listeners from a wide spectrum of political views and to speak diplomatically and graciously so that he offended no particular viewpoints, neither democratic left nor conservative right, which were every bit as polarized within the Ukrainian ethnic community as within Depression-era Canadian society at large. The Ukrainian Canadian press, including certain rivals of *Ukrainskyi holos*, greeted the professor's presence very positively and this was duly noted by the Winnipeg paper after the scholar's departure.[10] The Ukrainian Canadians generally seem to have been very pleased with Doroshenko's visit. In fact, he was received so warmly that he was invited to repeat the tour in the summer of 1938.[11]

Doroshenko was deeply moved by the warmth and great success of his first Canadian tour. On 24 November 1937, he wrote to Doris Yanda from his home on Narbutt Street in Warsaw that he had been profoundly affected by his "pleasant and unforgettable impressions of Canada." He continued:

Those several weeks which I spent in Canada, especially the time that I spent in Edmonton, belong to the most beautiful days that I have lived through during the whole period of my emigration. My spirit was revived, as if I became many years younger. I began to look more optimistically on our future, and you and your husband contributed to this to a great extent. I am grateful for all this to the depths of my heart....[12]

One month later, Doroshenko informed Yanda that he had delivered a lecture about Canada at the Ukrainian Scientific Institute in Warsaw (*Ukrainskyi naukovyi instytut u Varshavi*) and that over 100 people attended.[13]

Shortly before this, the leading Galician Ukrainian newspaper *Dilo* (Action) published a detailed interview with Doroshenko about his Canadian tour. In this interview, the historian explained the positive re-action of the Ukrainian Canadians to his presence. He stated that, in addition to his course, he had spoken forty-eight times in various places across the country and that both the Ukrainian- and the English-language press had covered the events fully. He then stated plainly:

The goal of my public lectures was to show Canadian Ukrainians that they are a part of a great people with an exceptional historical past and tradition. I tried to raise our Canadian brothers up in their own eyes and also in the eyes of the local English and French population, which has more or less ceased to regard the Ukrainians as a peasant people without its own territory and treats them as the equal of other cultured citizens.

Doroshenko then turned to the subject of the Ukrainian Canadians them-selves and made some positive observations. "Ukrainians in Canada," he said, "are standing on their own feet and whatever they have achieved, they have achieved exclusively through their own hard work. 'Canadian Ukraine' gives us full rights to believe in the creative genius of the Ukrainian people." Doroshenko also was reported to have stated that the Ukrainian Canadians "without exception" retained a deep sentiment for the Old Country, desired an independent Ukrainian state, and were ready to help it morally and materially, "although," he added, "one should not understand this to include help of a military character."[14] The final caution in this statement probably was included to reassure the Polish government, which was then engaged in a fierce struggle against the militant actions of the underground Organization of Ukrainian Nationalists (OUN), which was rumoured to receive funding from its supporting organizations in Canada and the United States. In Canada, the principal organization supporting the OUN was the rightist Ukrainian National Federation (*Ukrainske natsionalne ob'iednannia*), or UNF, which was a fierce rival of the USRL.

In a private letter to the daughter of a close friend, written at this time, Doroshenko somewhat more candidly discussed the situation of the Ukrainians in Canada and Canadian race relations in general. After remarking on his very busy schedule during this tour and the enormous size of the country (it took him four and a half days to get from Quebec City to Edmonton by express train), the historian observed that the train ride was still very pleasant and that "the railway cars are wonderful, artificially cooled, and comfortable." He added: "There are no classes there, and everyone travels in the same way. Only at night, if one wishes, one can get a place in a sleeping car where one is looked after by the Blacks, and it must be said, they serve one wonderfully and look after the passengers like nursemaids after children." He continued:

> In general, in Canada work is divided among the various races: the Blacks serve on the trains and as shoeblacks on the streets; the Chinese serve as laundry workers, the Japanese as porters at the railway stations and they sell vegetables; other functions are carried out by the representatives of various White nations. Only the native Redskin Indians do not work, because they are not suitable for any kind of work; the state has granted them enormous reserves of forests and lakes where they hunt and fish and receive 'support' from the state somewhat like that received by the Ukrainian émigrés in the Czech land, and they go to the train stations where they stare at the passengers from across the ocean, and the passengers look at them.

Doroshenko was similarly candid in his observations about the Ukrainians in particular:

> Canada is an agricultural country and is quiet. It has eleven million people including four million French, six million English (together with the Irish), a half million Ukrainians, and also Czechs, Poles, Jews, Germans, and whatever other people you can think of. Winnipeg has 150,000 inhabitants and 40,000 Ukrainians. You hear the Ukrainian language everywhere and you see Ukrainian signs. I lived in Edmonton for a month and did not have dealings with a single English person: a Ukrainian dentist fixed my teeth, a Ukrainian tailor sewed my clothes, a Ukrainian shoemaker mended my shoes, and I ate at a Ukrainian restaurant, lived with a Ukrainian doctor,

and bought razors for shaving, newspapers, and such at a Ukrainian 'bazaar.' I purchased drugs at a Ukrainian pharmacy. I only sent my bed-sheets to the Chinese laundry and shined my shoes with a Black. In this way, I did not get any practice at all speaking English.... The Ukrainians in Canada strongly hold to their nationality, but the younger generation is already slowly being anglicized. I saw how my audience, male and female students, and school teachers, spoke English among themselves. Indeed, it is difficult to resist such a strong culture as the English.[15]

Such were Doroshenko's uncensored observations of ethnic and race relations in 1937 Canada.

In 1938, Doroshenko returned to Canada for his second tour. At the beginning of this second tour, he gave a five-week course to Ukrainian Canadians in Edmonton on the history of Ukrainian literature. (This time, his inaugural lecture was on the early nineteenth-century Ukrainian poet Ivan Kotliarevsky, and, according to *Ukrainskyi holos*, his course contained "over sixty students.") He then spoke in Montreal, Ottawa, Saskatoon, and Winnipeg. Several speeches were devoted to the promotion of the émigré Museum of the Liberation Struggle of Ukraine in Prague (*Muzei vyzvolnoi borotby Ukrainy u Prazi*), and a collection was made to raise money for it. Doroshenko's presence was widely discussed in the press and he also spoke on Canadian radio programs.[16] The historian lectured as an independent scholar, and the Ukrainian Canadian monarchist party, the United Hetman Organization (UHO), conservative supporters of Hetman Skoropadsky led by Wolodymyr (William) Bossy (1899–1979) and Michael Hetman (1893–1981), did not seem to have any special control over, or contact with, him. Many years later, Olha Woycenko, who was closely associated with *Ukrainskyi holos*, recalled that Doroshenko "was our house guest both in 1937 and 1938."

My husband [Petro Woycenko (1882–1956)], the editor Myroslav Stechishen, the lawyer J. W. Arsenych, and perhaps others often had lunch together at a restaurant nearby the offices of [The] U[krainian] V[oice]. A loyal hetman man and a businessman, A. Malofij, often picked him [that is, Doroshenko] up in his car and drove him home for dinner. But this man was not an extremist; he was a real gentleman and highly respected in the community. He got along with all factions. I don't think Doroshenko was in touch with Bossy or Hetman, at least I never heard. I must mention that members of all factions attended Doroshenko's lectures. This was as it was in Edmonton, Saskatoon, Winnipeg, and Toronto. Doroshenko was very tactful and was aware of the various factions in Canada so he chose to lecture as a high cali-bre scholar should without offending anyone.[17]

During these Canadian tours, Doroshenko also made contact with some English Canadian scholars. The most important of these was George Simpson (1893–1969), a professor of history at the University of Saskatchewan. Simpson's interest in Ukrainian affairs had been sparked by the presence at the university of several students of Ukrainian back-ground who were sincerely devoted to the Ukrainian cause and whom he later described as "nationalistic." As well, by the 1930s, the Petro Mohyla Institute was a thriving institution, and there and elsewhere on the Prairies, interest in establishing Ukrainian studies courses at the univer-sity was growing. Both Julian Stechishin, who was practising law by this time, and the schoolteacher Ivan Danylchuk (1900–1942), two impor-tant figures at the Mohyla Institute, were in close touch with Simpson and it was he who suggested that English-language textbooks were im-perative if such courses were to be launched. Lazarowich, who had be-come dominion president of the USRL in July 1936, concurred, and, during the convention in July 1937 in Saskatoon at which Doroshenko had given his very well-received address, a resolution was passed, delegat-ing the USRL executive to arrange to have such textbooks published in Ukrainian history and language. Thus, it seems, it was natural that a trans-lation of Doroshenko's recently published, master synthesis of Ukrainian history, his two-volume *Narys istorii Ukrainy* (Survey of Ukrainian history), should be proposed. In fact, by the end of 1939, in just two short years, this book had been expanded by the addition of several new chapters by Doroshenko, put into English by the European-based librarian and jour-nalist Hanna Chikalenko-Keller, edited with an introduction and update by Simpson, and published in 686 pages by the Hrushevsky Institute in Edmonton under the title *A History of the Ukraine.* This was the first gen-eral history of Ukraine to be published in the English language.[18]

Doroshenko had been invited to come to Canada for a third tour in 1939, but the approach of the Second World War, which broke out in September, cut off direct contact between the historian and the Canadians. All the same, his name was far from forgotten on the North American continent. His history sold well and, to meet the demand, had to be reprinted in 1940; Vladimir Kaye-Kisylewskyj (1896–1976), the di-rector of the Ukrainian Information Bureau in London, who had mi-grated to western Canada before moving to England and who for a time was a student of R. W. Seton-Watson at London's School of Slavonic

Studies, investigated putting out another "mass-circulation" edition through Everyman's Library in England, but, under war conditions, nothing came of the idea. As it was, however, the Canadian edition of the book was very well received by young Ukrainians in Canada and the United States who were hungry for basic materials about their eastern European heritage, and it was favourably, though not widely, reviewed both in Canada and the United States.[19]

Meanwhile, on the other side of the Atlantic and within Nazi-occupied Europe, Doroshenko did not forget his Canadian compatriots. During the war, he published two significant articles in German on the Ukrainians in Canada. The first of these, published in a German journal specializing in the study of the Eastern Christian churches, was devoted to the history of the Ukrainian Orthodox Church in Canada, the United States, and Brazil.[20] In this article, Doroshenko stressed the popular and national character of the Ukrainian Orthodox movement in the Americas, but also pointed out its weaknesses, primarily the questionable canonical status of the current bishop, Ioan Teodorovych, whose jurisdiction spread across both Canada and the United States, and a preponderance of lay control, which led to some parishes' breaking away from the central administration and forming schismatic-style independent churches. In Canada, this administration was the so-called Winnipeg "Consistory" under the Rev Semen Sawchuk (1895–1983), which had a great deal of local autonomy because Teodorovych was normally resident in Philadelphia in the United States.

The second article was devoted entirely to the Ukrainian Canadians and deserves more detailed analysis. In this article, which Doroshenko published in a well-known German ethnographical journal, our émigré historian gives a brief social history of the Ukrainian Canadians.[21] He starts by describing the difficult economic situation in eastern Galicia before 1914. This situation, he believed, caused the mass emigration of Ukrainians to Canada. A basic reason for this, he wrote, was the inadequate redistribution of land following the abolition of full serfdom in Galicia in 1848. Thus, even after the emancipation, the country folk continued to be oppressed by the local Polish landowning nobility. Doroshenko stressed the enormous difficulties the first settlers had to overcome: lack of education and inadequate knowledge of English, settlement on marginal land far from major centres of commerce, the necessity for clearing the land of bush, and many other difficulties. On the other hand, Doroshenko continued, each settler was given a "quarter section" (sixty-five hectares) of free homestead land and, through hard work, could quickly establish a thriving farm. Doroshenko noted that the prairie provinces of Manitoba, Saskatchewan, and Alberta had originally attracted most of the emigration, but also noted that ethnic dispersion was already occurring and that many Ukrainian farmers and workers had moved to the cities. He pointed out that the city of Winnipeg, in particular, was already the major urban centre for the country's Ukrainians and that, so he claimed, about 40,000 of his compatriots resided there. The eastern cities of Montreal and Toronto followed with about 12,000 each, and then came Edmonton to the west with 8,000.

As in the private letter he wrote shortly after his first trip to Canada, so, too, in this published article, Doroshenko estimated the total number of Ukrainians in Canada in 1939 to be about half a million (*rund eine halbe Million*), though he noted that official Canadian census figures put it somewhat lower, closer to 300,000. Doroshenko believed that the official figure underestimated the true number of Ukrainians because ostensibly it still counted many "Ruthenians," "Russians," and "Austrians" of Ukrainian origin in separate categories and not as Ukrainians. Thus, with the 1937 yearbook of the newspaper *Ukrainskyi holos* (92), which was a major source for him, the historian concluded that the Ukrainians presently formed the fourth-largest ethnic group in Canada, outnumbered only by the "English," the French, and the Germans.[22] Doroshenko next noted that most of these Ukrainians traced their origin to Galicia, with smaller numbers coming from Bukovina, and only a light sprinkling from Carpatho-Ukraine and Dnieper Ukraine. Many of these Galician settlements, however, bore "national" rather than local Galician names. Thus, there were settlements named after national heroes such as Mazepa, Shevchenko, and Petliura. The Ukrainians, he believed, could establish such nationally named colonies because they tended to congregate in large "block settlements" scattered across the Prairies.

Doroshenko then turned to the cultural and political history of the Ukrainian Canadians. He began by stating that their cultural development was somewhat less advanced than that of their compatriots in the United States. As an example, he gave the fact that the first Ukrainian newspaper in the United States, *Ameryka* (America), had appeared as early as 1886, while the first Ukrainian paper in Canada, *Kanadiiskyi farmer* (The Canadian farmer), had appeared only in 1903. He explained this difference as due to the fact that, for a long time, the Ukrainian Canadians possessed no educated elite, which, he believed, was somewhat in contrast to the situation in the United States.[23]

According to Doroshenko, the absence of an educated and secularized elite meant that the first settlers in Canada organized much of their cultural life in traditional religious forms and put a great deal of energy into the formation of religious congregations and the building of churches. He observed that the first settlers, who were mostly of Greek Catholic origin from Galicia, came without priests to serve them and were the object of the attention of Roman Catholic and Protestant missionaries, but, with the 1910 visit of the Lviv metropolitan Count Andrei Sheptytsky (1865–1944), church affairs were put in order and a Greek Catholic bishop, Nikita Budka, eventually was named.

However, there remained considerable dissatisfaction with Rome, which continued to forbid the marriage of Ukrainian priests in the New World. As well, Latinization of the Ukrainian Byzantine rite had already progressed rather far, and the Greek Catholic bishop Nikita Budka was less than tactful in allowing and, perhaps, even promoting such Latinization. Religious tensions and national feelings became mixed and were aggravated by events in eastern Europe. The revolution of 1917 in Russia and Russian Ukraine and the eventual establishment of national governments both in Kyiv and Lviv ignited the tinderbox, and a new Ukrainian national church was born, first in Ukraine, then afterwards in Canada. Doroshenko explained it thus:

> The World War and the establishment of a Ukrainian national state in Kyiv in 1917–18 caused fundamental changes in the ecclesiastical and general folk life of Canada's Ukrainians. When the news about the establishment of an independent Ukraine and the autocephalous Ukrainian Orthodox Church founded in it came to Canada, there awakened in wide circles of the Ukrainian emigration a spontaneous movement with the slogans: "Away from Rome! Unity with the Ukrainian national church in the Ukrainian State!" The latent dissatisfaction with Rome and its ecclesiastical policy, which took no account of the national aspirations of the Ukrainians, now burst forth. Added to this, the point was made that Orthodoxy was the national church which nine-tenths of all Ukrainians confessed.[24]

The result was the foundation, at a conference in Saskatoon in 1918, of what Doroshenko called a new "Eastern Orthodox Ukrainian Church in Canada." Our émigré historian then gave a brief description of this church, once again mentioning its canonical and administrative problems, and the renewed threat to it posed by a post-war resurgent and now more nationally oriented Greek Catholic Church. He then considered Ukrainian secular organizations in Canada. These organizations he listed as follows: the USRL, which, he stated, had some thirty branches scattered across the country and supported the Orthodox Church; the

Ukrainian National Federation (UNF), which had forty branches and was, in his view, primarily an anti-Polish organization; the United Hetman Organization (UHO), which supported Skoropadsky and also, so he claimed, numbered forty branches; and, finally, the Ukrainian Labour Farmer Temple Association (ULFTA), which had a spectacular 100 branches, was pro-Communist, and which, Doroshenko claimed, was financially supported by the Soviet Union. All these organizations had their own women's auxiliaries, youth wings, and press organs.[25]

Doroshenko concluded his survey with a brief account of Ukrainian participation in Canadian political life. He mentioned that the first Ukrainian had been elected to a provincial legislature in 1913 and to the federal parliament in 1926, and that many elected municipal posts were presently being filled by Ukrainians. However, he noted, the younger generation was already strongly assimilated into English Canadian society (*verenglischt wird*), although much was being done by the more nationally conscious Ukrainians to delay this process. The efforts of the latter took the form of the distribution of Ukrainian books, newspapers, and magazines, bringing Ukrainian writers and scholars over from Europe, and moves to establish Ukrainian "chairs" (*Lehrstühle*) or professorships at the universities in Saskatoon, Edmonton, and Winnipeg. The Orthodox and Greek Catholic churches were also important. Doroshenko concluded, however, by cautioning that the entire long-term situation of the Ukrainians in Canada was dependent on what he called "a favourable resolution" of the Ukrainian question in Europe.

However, in the eyes of most Ukrainian Canadians, the outcome of the Second World War did not bring a "favourable resolution" to this Ukrainian question in Europe. The westward march of the Red Army and the Soviet annexation of western Ukraine, formerly under the Poles, Romanians, and Czechs, caused a mass flight of the Galician Ukrainian intelligentsia and the Prague émigrés to western Europe, where they were joined by many refugees from Dnieper Ukraine and elsewhere. Doroshenko himself, who had moved back to Prague during the war, now abandoned his library and archives, complete with their valuable unpublished manuscripts and correspondence, in the Czech capital, and he fled to western Germany, which was occupied by the Western allies. Terror before the Soviet advance was everywhere evident. As early as the summer of 1945, at a time when communications between North America and Europe were still difficult, George Simpson received a note from the historian, who was stranded in Augsburg and wished to move, as he put it, "further west, even across the ocean." Doroshenko asked

Simpson to communicate with Petro Woycenko in Winnipeg and Petro Lazarowich in Edmonton, which Simpson seems to have immediately done. Word of Doroshenko's distress spread quickly among his friends in Canada and J. W. Arsenych, his colleague J. R. Solomon, and others soon got involved. "If the Russians lay their hands on Professor Doroshenko," wrote Lazarowich in a letter of 4 July 1945 to Arsenych, "we will never see him alive again." Simpson, Lazarowich, and, in particular, the Winnipeg lawyer J. R. Solomon immediately made representations to the Minister of Mines and Natural Resources J. A. Glen, who seems to have been in charge of immigration matters at that time, but the Ottawa bureaucracy would not budge. Glen replied to Simpson and the others that there were as yet no Canadian immigration facilities in continental Europe, that it was "impossible to obtain westbound transatlantic passenger accommodation," and, at any rate, Doroshenko was not admissible to Canada under the then-existing regulations.[26]

The general situation of Doroshenko and other Ukrainian refugees in western Europe at that time was, in fact, desperate. Under the Yalta agreement concluded in early 1945 between the Western allies and the USSR, all refugees were to be returned to their homelands at the conclusion of hostilities. There were over two million Ukrainian refugees (the so-called Displaced Persons or DPs) in western Europe at war's end and many of them had no desire to return to a homeland now under Soviet rule. Soviet "repatriation" teams, which included members of the dreaded Soviet political police, were allowed into the western zones of occupation, and British and American soldiers often cooperated with them in the forcible return of the refugees. Doroshenko himself, of course, was in great danger and, as his former student, the historian Borys Krupnytsky, later recalled, had to live for a while "incognito or under a pseudonym." But, it appears, with the help of certain Ukrainian Canadian servicemen in the Canadian armed forces in occupied Germany, he managed to escape the Soviets.[27] It was probably through these same servicemen that Doroshenko eventually got in touch with the church administrator, the Rev Semen Sawchuk of Saint Andrew's College, an Orthodox institution in Winnipeg, which, of course, at that time was the main centre of Ukrainian cultural and political life in Canada. Sawchuk, who, for a brief period, was a chaplin with the Canadian forces stationed in England, sent the historian an invitation to come to Canada and teach at Saint Andrew's but for some time the visa and other problems continued. By 1947, however, communications and Canadian immigration policy had changed such that he was successful in obtaining a Canadian visa.[28]

At this time, the idea of moving to North America was in the course of becoming a reality for many of the Ukrainian DPs stranded in western Europe. From 1945 to 1947, the scholars among these refugees had already been establishing émigré scholarly institutions in the DP camps in Germany, and the question now arose of transferring some of these institutions, together with their personnel, to North America. Doroshenko, who had been elected the first president of one of the foremost of these institutions, the Ukrainian Free Academy of Sciences (*Ukrainska vilna akademiia nauk,* or UVAN), seems to have had these considerations in mind when on 8 August 1947 he wrote to his colleague, the historian Oleksander Ohloblyn:

> I am very sad to leave my countrymen with whom I have lived for more than two years in Bavaria, sharing grief, poverty, and all kinds of emotions and fears. But I take comfort in the thought that I go not only for my own advantage and to work in more formal conditions, but also for the sake of paving the way for the transfer of our scholars and to lay the foundations of a Ukrainian scholarly centre in the States or in Canada.[29]

Several weeks later, Doroshenko went to Paris, where he stayed for two months before boarding a ship for Canada.

On 28 November 1947, at the start of a very cold prairie winter, Doroshenko and his wife Nataliia arrived at the Canadian Pacific Railway station in Winnipeg, Manitoba. They were met by a small delegation of prominent Ukrainian Canadians, including Olha Woycenko, with whom Doroshenko had stayed on his two previous trips to Winnipeg. Woycenko, who had been greatly impressed by the gentlemanly historian during his previous visits, was now shocked at the appearance of the Doroshenkos. "It was a pathetic sight," she later wrote. "They looked tired and aged. They had only one suitcase and a few small bundles, the only possessions after the ravishes of war and years of exile."[30]

Nevertheless, Doroshenko immediately took up his position at Saint Andrew's College and, by 12 December, for the modest salary of $135.00 a month, was teaching the subjects in which he specialized. (His inaugural lecture was on ecclesiastical history as a part of universal history.) Indeed, his teaching load seems to have been quite full. He taught church history within the college's Department of Theology and the history of Ukraine and the history of Ukrainian literature within the Department of the Humanities.[31] Moreover, in spite of the loss of his library and archives during the war, he also once again took up his research and writing. This activity was carried out along five directions. First, he updated his previous synthetic work on Ukrainian history by writing new chapters for Ivan Krypiakevych and Mykola Holubets's *Velyka istoriia Ukrainy* (Great history of Ukraine); these chapters described the Soviet regime of the 1920s and the 1930s, interwar western Ukraine under the Poles, the fate of the Ukrainian lands during the war, and, at its end, what he called the "Great Pan-Ukrainian Emigration" (*Velyka vse-ukrainska emigratsiia*) of the intelligentsia and many others westward. This work was published in large format and very attractive binding in Winnipeg by the Galician Ukrainian refugee Ivan Tyktor (1896–1982), who had headed a large and very successful Lviv publishing house between the wars and now was continuing his profession in the New World by reprinting some of his more important pre-war volumes, including this *Velyka istoriia Ukrainy*.[32]

Second, Doroshenko continued his research on the Ukrainian community in Canada. He did this systematically, beginning with a major bibliography on the Ukrainian Canadians, which he undertook with the help of the young Manitoba scholar Paul Yuzyk.[33] He also edited a large volume of materials on the Ukrainian Canadians for the Ukrainian National Home, an important Winnipeg Ukrainian institution with a very large library and cultural program. In this book, Doroshenko and his Canadian colleagues stressed Ukrainian Canadian connections with, and loyalty to, the Crown. Thus, there is a detailed discussion of Governor General Lord Tweedsmuir's 1936 speech to the Ukrainian Canadians in which he stated that by being good Ukrainians they would also be good Canadians, and there is also a very detailed description of the warm reception the Ukrainian Canadians gave the king and queen during the royal tour of 1939.[34] Third, at the suggestion of Olha Woycenko and in spite of some misgivings about the loss of his archives and records, Doroshenko wrote a new volume of memoirs dealing with his cultural and political activities before the revolution. In these memoirs, which are a real gem in the history of Ukrainian memoir literature, he described the vicissitudes and major figures of the Ukrainian national movement before 1914. Doroshenko knew most these figures quite well and was balanced and moderate in his judgments of them, even those with whom he later firmly disagreed. Time and distance probably played some role in the writing of this particular book.[35]

Fourth, seemingly in tandem with his teaching duties at Saint Andrew's College, he wrote on general church history, and his two short volumes on this subject were eventually published in Winnipeg. The first of these dealt with early church history and the second specifically with

Ukrainian church history.[36] Fifth, he spent the fall and winter of 1949–50, and the following spring as well, writing a popular history of Ukrainian literature, probably for the use of the students of Saint Andrew's. This book was completed and the manuscript submitted to the Rev Sawchuk by Doroshenko's wife Nataliia, but, for some reason, was never published.[37]

Word about Doroshenko's emigration to Canada and this country's welcome reception of Ukrainian refugees spread quickly throughout the Ukrainian emigration in Europe. For example, in 1948, the famous Ukrainian poet and literary critic Ievhen Malaniuk (1887–1968) asked the young scholar Bohdan Budurowycz, who was then in Germany but was about to depart for Canada, to get in touch with Doroshenko there and ask him if he could help him to emigrate to Canada. In the winter of 1948–49, Budurowycz was already in Dauphin, Manitoba, and immediately wrote to Doroshenko in Winnipeg about Malaniuk. Doroshenko promptly replied, but related that unfortunately he was in no position to help Malaniuk. Budurowycz passed the letter on to the poet.[38]

But others did manage to come to Canada. Two particularly important figures were the literary historian Leonid Biletsky (1882–1955), a colleague of Doroshenko's from Kyiv and Prague, and the philologist Jaroslav Rudnyckyj (1910–1997), who was from Galicia but had spent some time in Prague during the war. Both arrived in Canada in January 1949 and immediately began organizing a Canadian branch of the Ukrainian Free Academy of Sciences, the émigré institution founded in Augsburg, Germany, in 1945. Doroshenko, of course, had been the founding president of this organization before leaving Europe, and now, greatly impressed by young Rudnyckyj's energy and enthusiasm, became active in the establishment of the Canadian branch. (Biletsky succeeded Doroshenko as president in 1951, and Rudnyckyj succeeded Biletsky a few years after that.) Woycenko writes that "the three scholars used to meet quite often at Doroshenko's small apartment. The one year and a half that this trio worked together, they accomplished quite a bit."[39] In fact, by the 1950s, UVAN in Canada became a major centre of Ukrainian émigré scholarship, publishing a large number of serials and several weighty tomes of materials in Ukrainian and Slavic studies.[40] The concurrent establishment of a new Department of Slavic Studies at the University of Manitoba headed by Rudnyckyj offered further hope that Winnipeg would be a congenial place for Doroshenko to continue his academic and other work.

It was not to be. Doroshenko, already worn out by the ravages of war and exile and frequent changes of residence, found no peace in

Winnipeg. The day-to-day materialism of certain of the older economic immigrants to Canada and the harsh prairie climate began to take their toll. His previous idealism about, and enthusiasm for, Ukrainian Canadian society now began to disappear. On 1 October 1949, he replied to an inquiry from his colleague Ohloblyn, who was still in Europe, that life in Winnipeg was difficult because of the harsh winter and the constant colds and illnesses that went with it. Moreover, life in Winnipeg was, in his exact words, like "life on a completely different planet.... Your letter returned me to a world of interests that does not exist here in Canada, because cultural life (in our understanding of the word) does not exist here. Materialism rules all."[41]

Doroshenko's depressed psychological state was caused in large part by unexpected developments at Saint Andrew's College. This institution was facing financial problems and, in the spring of 1949, the dean of the college, Professor Martynovsky, informed the historian that from then on he would be paid only for the months actually spent lecturing; that is, from September to April. The rest of the year, he would be left without an income. "To say the least," writes Woycenko, "this was a shock to the Professor as he had no other revenue and no other reserves. At that time he was sixty-seven years of age [and] had a wife to support as well as himself. This upset him to the point that it had a bearing on his health."[42] Over the course of 1949, it became clear that he would not be invited to return to work at Saint Andrew's. At the same time, a throat malady he had recently developed worsened, he began to lose his voice, and he fell into ever-deeper bouts of depression. For some time, he absolutely refused to believe that the Rev Sawchuk and the administration of Saint Andrew's could leave him in such a precarious predicament and, forgetting himself completely, he paced about his tiny apartment, exclaiming: "How could they do this to me? I am not a criminal. They themselves invited me here. I have worked fifty years for Ukraine. Why didn't they tell me about this beforehand?"[43]

Doroshenko's personal relations with Sawchuk also seem to have had a certain bearing on his employment situation and his financial distress. It was rumoured within Orthodox circles in Winnipeg that Sawchuk held a grudge against Doroshenko because of the latter's friendship with another new arrival in the city, Ivan Ohienko (1882–1972), a distinguished churchman and scholar in his own right and a friend of Doroshenko's from pre-revolutionary and revolutionary Ukraine as well as from interwar Poland, but a man with whom Sawchuk was in bitter conflict over local church politics. It is evident that Sawchuk's attitude towards Doroshenko was anything but sympathetic or supportive, and this is clearly reflected in the memoirs of Doroshenko's wife Nataliia.[44] Certainly, Doroshenko's situation was difficult.

It was not, however, impossible. This same year, a UVAN committee was formed to celebrate the fiftieth anniversary of the professor's scholarly and public career and to help him out financially. The committee was headed by Biletsky; Rudnyckyj was one of the vice-chairmen and Woycenko was treasurer. Sawchuk, however, after unsuccessfully trying to co-opt the activities of the committee into Saint Andrew's College, where a small gathering in honour of Doroshenko was held, in the words of Woycenko, "boycotted" the affair.[45] Nevertheless, the committee's activities were a great success. On 13 November 1949, a large banquet was held in honour of Doroshenko, a booklet published describing his scholarly and public career, and over $2,500, a very large sum in those days, raised to support him.[46]

However, Doroshenko's health problems continued. "The stay in Canada was fatal for him," a relative later wrote. "He lived in very difficult material circumstances and did not survive the climate. Already very sick, he yearned [*zabazhav*] to return to Europe: although not to his homeland, but all the same, closer to it."[47] In 1950, after two unsuccessful throat operations, the disappointed and ailing historian shocked most of the DP emigration, of which almost all were in the process of moving west to the Americas, by returning to Europe, where the threat of a new war between the Soviet Union and the West was already looming. He did so by way of the United States, where he stopped in Detroit supposedly to deliver an address to a gathering commemorating the seventeenth-century Cossack Hetman Bohdan Khmelnytsky and to consult a physician concerning his throat ailment; thereafter, he travelled first to France, where he stayed in Paris for a while, and then to Germany.

Meanwhile in Winnipeg, word had gotten out about Doroshenko's difficult situation at Saint Andrew's. The rumours now spread well beyond the Orthodox community, and articles on the subject began to appear in the press. Edmonton's Catholic *Ukrainski visti* (The Ukrainian news) and the rightist UNF's *Novyi shliakh* (The new pathway), both long-standing rivals of *Ukrainskyi holos* and the Orthodox USRL, alluded to the subject in various articles. The UNF organ asked ironically: "Is it not because of that warm atmosphere [*toi pryiemnoi atmosfery*] in our Orthodox centre in Winnipeg that, all the same, the seventy-one year old Professor Doroshenko decided to leave his post as professor at Saint Andrew's and return in his old age (and at this time!), to Europe?!" Stung by what it considered to be a general aspersion on the Orthodox, *Ukrainskyi holos*, in an unsigned article, struck back, saying that whatever the political situation among the Orthodox, Doroshenko had always kept his distance from church politics and had returned to what it called "sunny Europe" for health reasons alone. The paper maintained that through private sources it had recently learned that, in fact, the professor was already beginning to recover.[48]

Unfortunately, these private sources turned out to be mistaken. Although Doroshenko rested and recovered slightly during the return ocean voyage over the Atlantic, his condition did not improve in France and deteriorated even further in Germany. He died in Munich on 19 March 1951, and his loss was sorely felt by Ukrainians scattered throughout Canada and the Western world.[49]

Doroshenko's contacts with Canada and the Ukrainian Canadians were remembered long after his demise. These had taken many forms. First, through his courses at Alberta College and his lecture tours in the 1930s, Doroshenko had participated in the general movement espoused by some leading members of the USRL to raise the educational level, the self-confidence, and the national consciousness of the Ukrainian immigrant community in Canada. His audience was mainly from the second generation of Ukrainian Canadians who, like his admiring younger lady friends, Doris Yanda in Edmonton and Olha Woycenko in Winnipeg, had been born in Canada. Long deprived of intellectual leadership, this generation was deeply inspired by the gracious scholar from central Europe who had taken the time and effort to visit this far-off Ukrainian colony and inform it about the cultural achievements of the Ukrainian political emigration in central Europe. Doroshenko's brilliance as a popularizer of these achievements fit in perfectly with the USRL's plans for popular enlightenment, and these tours were an unmitigated success.

Second, during the war years, Doroshenko informed the scholarly public in Nazi-occupied Europe of the existence and progress of the Ukrainian community in Canada. His remarks on the history of this community were well informed, clearly expressed, and not uncritical. Third, after the war, he contributed to the foundation of higher education and scholarship about Ukraine at Saint Andrew's College and in the new post-war scholarly institutions established by the so-called DP immigration; in particular, the Winnipeg UVAN. In spite of the impediments of his age and hard experiences, Doroshenko remained significantly productive during this last phase of his scholarly career, and books and articles in a number of different genres continued to roll from his pen right through to his final departure from Winnipeg.

In turn, Doroshenko received much from the Ukrainian Canadians. First, of course, during his early tours of Canada, they provided him with an eager audience, which was well able to appreciate his fluid style and his "popularizing" approach to scholarship and lecturing. They re-established, as it were, his contact with the common people, the *narod* from which he had been long divorced during his years in central Euro-pean exile; the warm reception accorded him lifted his spirits, strength-ened his resolve, and gave him a very idealistic picture of Canada. At this time, the Ukrainian Canadians also provided him with financial support to take back with him to Ukrainian émigré institutions in central Europe, especially Prague. Second, shortly before and during the war, the Ukrai-nian Canadians provided him with the financial and technical support necessary for the publication and distribution in the English language of his most widely read book, his masterly *History of the Ukraine*. This book had a powerful effect on public opinion in the North American Dominion and made his name well known in academic circles well beyond the prai-rie provinces of Canada where it was printed. (The lawyer J. R. Solomon, at a farewell meeting shortly before Doroshenko's final departure from Winnipeg, even declared that it was only after the appearance of this English-language *History of the Ukraine* that the English-speaking world ceased to call his people "Ruthenians.")[50]

Third, in the post-war years, the Ukrainian Canadians came to his res-cue in wartorn Germany and made possible the transference of the UVAN to Canada, where, for a brief time, the tired scholar was still able to thrive. The severe blows of exile, war, and emigration, followed by the difficulties of émigré life in a far-off land with an extreme climate and unending factional disputes, eventually wore him out and, during this final period, Doroshenko's idealism about Canada completely disap-peared. But, for many years, his collaboration with the New World was beneficial to both his hosts and himself. In spite of the brevity of his visits and final emigration from North America, the soft-spoken gentleman, ever reluctant to enter into personal or political confrontations with his contemporaries, gave much to Ukrainian Canada. His legacy will not be soon forgotten.

6 General Histories of Ukraine Published in English during the Second World War: Canada, the United States, and Britain

If history repeats itself, and the unexpected always happens, how incapable must Man be of learning from experience.

George Bernard Shaw

History repeats itself. Historians repeat each other.

Philip Guedala

The establishment of Communist dictatorships on the territory of the old Russian Empire after 1917, and throughout eastern Europe after 1944–5, impelled a significant number of scholars into exile in the West. In western Europe and North America, these scholars, and their colleagues who were natives of the Western democracies, began to produce scholarly books on the history, literature, and politics of eastern Europe. Although this process had begun in earnest in central and western Europe in the 1920s and the 1930s, it reached its apogee in North America during the last years of the Cold War, when the institutional arrangements of the relatively new discipline of Slavic Studies were already clearly established and the power and prestige of the Soviet Union and its clients were still considerable. Ukrainian historians were a part of this general process, and the development of Ukrainian historiography in the West, especially English-language historiography, followed the pattern of Slavic and East European studies in general.

The war of 1939 to 1945 was a turning point in this process. Before 1939, the focal point of Russian and Ukrainian émigré scholarship was still in central and western Europe, especially Prague, Warsaw, Berlin, Paris, and London. In North America, there were still very few professional scholars of Russian history and even fewer Ukrainian scholars. However, during the war, a number of general histories of Ukraine appeared in English that made a significant impact on the Western scholarly world. In spite of wartime restrictions, they were reviewed in some of the most prestigious historical journals, were widely read, and continued to be read well into the Cold War that engulfed the world after 1945. Revised or reprinted during the 1960s, 1970s, and 1980s, they were used by students in university-level history courses and cited in more general histories. Their practical use diminished only somewhat when, at the end of the 1980s and the 1990s, new synthetic histories of Ukraine were published that gave more up-to-date and different views. It is these general histories of Ukraine published during the Second World War, but widely disseminated during the Cold War, that form the subject of the present chapter.[1]

Prior to 1939, knowledge of Ukrainian history in the West was virtually non-existent. There did exist some general references in survey histories of Russia and Poland, but these tended to reflect the russophile or polonophile views of their various authors and did not treat Ukrainian history as an independent subject of inquiry.[2] There also existed a substantial body of polemical literature regarding the contemporary Ukrainian question; some of this literature was sympathetic to a Ukrainian viewpoint but, in general, it made only fleeting references to Ukrainian history.[3]

The prominence of the Ukrainian question during the international crises of the late 1930s awakened a new popular interest in Ukrainian history. On the one hand, a number of writers set to work composing popular surveys of Ukrainian history for the general public; on the other hand, a small group of more professional scholars began work on more scholarly treatments of the subject. Almost all these histories were published within a short time of each other during the first years of the Second World War.

Three separate volumes belong to our first general category: popular history. The most traditional treatment of the subject was a small volume bearing the revealing title *The Ukraine: A Russian Land* by Pierre Bregy and Prince Serge Obolensky. The latter co-author, Obolensky, was a moderate liberal and francophile aristocrat, and his book had first appeared in French a few years before. This work was a learned discursive study, reflective rather than scholarly, which exhibited no sympathy for the Ukrainian national idea. Obolensky stressed what he believed to be the geographical unity of all the "Russian lands" and viewed Ukraine as nothing more than a particular region of Russia. For this émigré prince,

Ukrainians were merely a regional variety of Russians, Ukrainian literature did not go beyond the bounds of peasant literature, and the Ukrainian people did not exist as a separate nation. Obolensky acknowledged
the decentralizing tendencies of the Ukrainian national movement of
the nineteenth century but stressed their "federalist" rather than nationalist character. He was, moreover, strongly critical of what he believed to
be twentieth-century German influences on Ukrainian nationalism.
However, he did acknowledge that what he called the "rich and numerous" Ukrainian communities in Canada and the United States were
strong supporters of national independence. Being a popular history
and rather political tract, Obolensky's book was not widely reviewed in
the scholarly journals.[4]

The second popularization to appear at the start of the war reflected a
clearly Soviet viewpoint. This was *Ukraine and Its People: The Essential
Background of One of Europe's Vital Problems* by a little-known writer named
Hugh P. Vowles, an English engineer who had lived and worked in Soviet
Ukraine under Stalin. Unlike Obolensky, Vowles accepted the existence of the modern Ukrainian nationality and stressed the oppression
of the Ukrainian people throughout the ages. He went on to praise the
Bolshevik revolution and Stalin's collectivization program, but, of course,
was very critical of Polish rule in western Ukraine (he called Piłsudski "a
fanatical nationalist") and claimed that Hitler intended to make use of
Ukrainian "separatist" movements in favour of a great Ukraine for the
sake of his own territorial ambitions. Vowles also mentioned the importance of the Ukrainians in the United States where, he stated, they were
one million strong, and in Canada, where they ostensibly formed the
third-largest nationality after the English and the French. Like Obolensky's
book, Vowles's, too, was largely ignored by the scholarly journals.[5]

A third popularization of Ukrainian history was written during this
period, and this was the only one to reflect a Ukrainian national view.
Charles Milnes Gaskell's "A Submerged Nation: The Ukrainian Case"
was authored by a liberal democratic Englishman who, during the 1930s,
visited the various parts of partitioned Ukraine and dedicated his book
"to the memory of Professor Michael Hrushevsky." Unlike Obolensky,
who completely denied the existence of the Ukrainian nation, or Vowles,
who admitted its existence but was unwilling to contemplate its independence from the USSR, Gaskell was sympathetic to Ukrainian national
aspirations. He stated at the outset that he believed the Ukrainians to be
a distinct nation and the Ukrainian language to be an independent
tongue and no mere dialect of Russian. Like his model, Hrushevsky, he

traced Ukrainian history back to ancient times and discussed the glories of Kyivan Rus', the devastations of the Mongol invasions, the transference of the "leadership of the Ukraine" to Volhynia and Galicia, the subsequent troubles of Polish rule, and the military activities of Bohdan Khmelnytsky, who founded "the Cossack state" but was forced by circumstances to submit to the Muscovite tsar. He then went on to describe the unsuccessful attempt of Ivan Mazepa to free Ukraine from Muscovite rule. But Gaskell's real interest was in recent Ukrainian history and he devoted his most detailed chapters to the rise of the modern Ukrainian national movement, the revolution of 1917 to 1920, in which he openly sympathized with the moderately socialist but liberal democratic Central Rada led by Hrushevsky, and was very critical of the German-supported reaction and Soviet republic that followed. Gaskell analyzed Stalin's collectivization program and did not fail to mention that "millions of innocent Ukrainians" perished in a great famine caused by the forced requisitioning of cereals carried out by the Communist dictatorship. Gaskell also gave plenty of space to developments in western Ukraine under the Poles, Czechs, and Romanians. He was very critical of Polish and Romanian rule over their Ukrainian territories; less so of Czech rule. He admitted that the Germans were interested in making use of Ukrainian nationalism for their own ends but did not think that the two were inevitable partners. In general, Gaskell clearly distinguished between what he believed to be an Asiatic-oriented Russia from a European-oriented Ukraine. The publication of "A Submerged Nation: The Ukrainian Case" would have had a definite effect on public opinion in the English-speaking world in 1939–40 had it been published at that time, but, unfortunately, technical and then political difficulties prevented this from happening. Gaskell, who held some official positions during the war, was killed in an air crash on his way home from the Yalta conference and the work was preserved only in typescript.[6]

The various histories of Ukraine by Obolensky, Vowles, and Gaskell, in spite of their different interpretations, had certain characteristics in common: they were all authored by amateur historians, not specialists; they were all popularizations, not scholarly works; and they all gave special attention to recent history and current political events – that is, they all addressed the contemporary "Ukrainian question" from an historical point of view. But none of them could speak with great authority and scholarly nuance to the most fundamental questions of Ukrainian history. For such a treatment, it was necessary to turn to the supposedly more scholarly histories. Three of these appeared during the first years of the war.

Let us once again take the most traditional first. This was undoubtedly W. E. D. Allen's *The Ukraine: A History* published by the Cambridge University Press.[7] Allen was a private scholar of Anglo Irish background who could read Russian and had earlier authored a general history of the Georgian people; he also had a certain interest in the history of the Ottoman Empire. In his preface, Allen acknowledged the aid of "three or four scholars, Russian and Ukrainian [who] have collaborated in the preparation of the material ... [and] wish to remain anonymous ..."[8]

Like Obolensky before him, whom he approvingly cited on one or two occasions, Allen basically accepted the traditional Russian viewpoint on all the main questions of Ukrainian history, both medieval and modern. In fact, in spite of its formal title in which the name "Ukraine" appears, his book was not so much a history of Ukraine as it was a geopolitical history of eastern Europe with a focus on what he called the "south Russian" steppe. Allen saw a geographic unity to the European part of the Eurasian plain, which he believed to be bound together by great rivers, and, for him, Ukraine was simply "South Russia." However, he did give a general outline of Ukrainian history from Kyivan Rus', the Russo-Lithuanian state, Cossack times, and the Ukrainian lands within the Russian Empire to the modern era. His emphasis was not on current politics but, rather, on the sixteenth and seventeenth centuries, and he discussed several traditionally important historiographical questions, such as the meaning of the Treaty of Pereiaslav, which began the process of the absorption of Ukraine into the Muscovite state. At the end of each major section of his book, Allen appended extensive bibliographical notes that contained citations of numerous specialist works and he sometimes gave critical assessments of them. He even had an excursus or two on the use of folksongs as historical sources and compared the nineteenth-century Ukrainian *kobzars* or minstrels to Gaelic Irish balladeers of the same period. Far more detailed and ostensibly more critical than the popular works discussed above, Allen's book was meant to appeal to a more scholarly readership.

Given its expositions of the recurrently tangled web of eastern European geopolitics, with frequent digressions on Ottoman and Caucasian affairs as well as on more exclusively Polish or Russian history, and its citations from the works of major non-Slavic historians such as von Hammer and Iorga, Allen's book must have made interesting reading for anyone unacquainted with the internal history of eastern Europe, especially Ukraine. He threatened no one accustomed to traditional conservative Russian or Polish views with any novel ideas about new nationalities in eastern Europe and their historical claims. As well, Allen's book fit well into the conservative traditions of western European history with their emphasis on political history and the diplomatic relations between states. But, to anyone familiar with the more complex questions of Ukrainian history and the divergent interpretations of them, Allen's bias was also perfectly clear.

In historiographical questions, W. E. D. Allen was a russophile pure and simple. For him, Kyivan Rus' was the first "Russian" state and its inhabitants the first "Russian" people. So, too, the Lithuanian state was largely a "Russian" polity; Ukraine's inhabitants of Khmelnytsky's time, too, were "Russian," as, indeed, even were most of the inhabitants of pre-war Austrian Galicia. This refusal to distinguish between "Russia" and "Rus'," or, later on, between "Russia" and "Ruthenia," is one of the most striking characteristics of Allen's book. Of course, it militated against any recognition whatsoever that Ukraine had any independent history of its own.

Equally disturbing to the modern student of Ukrainian history are Allen's ethnic prejudices and his interpretations of various events. Perhaps his references to "the dark minded millions" who lived between the Urals and the Vistula and to an "addiction to extremes" and "obsession with the ideal" as "a fatality of the Slav character" (82) were typical of their time and place, but they cannot be read today without a certain degree of embarrassment. His characterization of the whole of Ukrainian Cossackdom as "savage" and uncivilized is similarly oversimplified. Moreover, on all counts, Allen takes the Russian side in various historiographical disputes between modern Russian and Ukrainian historians. Thus, Kyivan Rus' was completely depopulated at the end of the Mongol invasions and Ukrainian historians are mistaken to stress the continuity between this polity and Lithuanian and Cossack Ukraine; neither the wars of Bohdan Khmelnytsky nor the agreements between the Hetman and Muscovy created or acknowledged the existence of a Cossack state; Mazepa was a selfish adventurer, not a Ukrainian patriot; local conditions, not Catherine II or the imperial Russian government, were primarily behind the reintroduction of serfdom into eighteenth-century Ukraine (219); Shevchenko did not create or even strive to create "a special Ukrainian language in opposition to Russian"; rather, Russian readers could easily understand "the Little Russian dialect" (241), and it was Professor Hrushevsky who created the Ukrainian literary language out of "the peasant dialect of Galicia" (252). Moreover, as the revolutionary Ukrainian politician Volodymyr Vynnychenko admitted, Hrushevsky's governing assembly, the Central Rada, had no popular support, while Skoropadsky was a puppet of the Germans and Petliura a puppet of the Poles. Petliura's followers were, of course, the worst pogromists of 1919 (309), and the whole Ukrainian national movement between the wars was tinged by its association with Germany.

As to Soviet Ukraine, Allen believed that the entire ukrainianization program of the 1920s was somewhat artificial and, in the famine of 1933, as he put it, perhaps "about ten per cent of the population of southeastern Russia died of hunger" (329–30). To the history of the Ukrainians in interwar Poland, Czechoslovakia, and Romania, Allen gives practically no attention. Moreover, nowhere does Allen quote or paraphrase Hrushevsky, and his notes are heavily tipped towards the works of various Russian authors such as Miakotin and Nolde rather than to Ukrainian historians, many of whose works seem to be listed only in a pro forma manner. Add to this the chaos in the transliteration of Ukrainian and Polish names, which are usually given only in their Russian forms, numerous factual slips, and obfuscations, and we have before us a very problematic book.

Although the many factual slips and transliteration problems escaped the notice of most Western readers, Allen did not completely avoid criticism. For example, B. H. Sumner, a British historian of Russia with some similar interests to Allen's, gave his book a somewhat mixed reception in the *English Historical Review*.[9] On the one hand, Sumner acknowledged that the book had an unfinished quality about it, as if its numerous notes and sources were somewhat "undigested." He wrote: "The impression is given that, despite the wealth of bibliographical references, the author himself is not fully at home with the first hand sources for any particular portion of Ukrainian history and a much fuller discussion of these would have been welcome" (267). Sumner also criticized what he believed to be Allen's insufficient treatment of Ukrainian religious and cultural history of the sixteenth and seventeenth centuries and his lack of interest in institutional history. He also noted that Allen ignored the history of eastern or Sloboda Ukraine.

On the other hand, Sumner was an historian of Russia, not Ukraine, shared most of Allen's russo-centric opinions, and did not think him unsympathetic to the Ukrainians. For example, Sumner approved of Allen's tracing the origins of "Ukraine" only as far back as the seventeenth century, and of his portrayal of the weakness of the modern Ukrainian national movement, especially during the revolution. He also mentioned that he believed Allen to be right when he held that, in the

1930s, the peasants opposed collectivization on other than "national" grounds. On a somewhat different level, Sumner praised Allen's juxtaposition of Turkish, eastern European, and western European history, his attention to detail, and even his use of folksongs as sources. Most telling of all, however, this British historian of Russia quoted Allen to the effect that "the destiny of all the peoples of the USSR 'must be a Russian destiny in the sense that the fluvial network of the Great Eurasian Plain is one geographical and economic whole out of which it is impracticable and would be unreal to attempt to carve out independent national units'" (387). Sumner made no criticism of Allen's marginalization of western Ukraine under the Poles, Czechs, and Romanians.

Sumner's carefully balanced but generally sympathetic review of Allen was only partially countered by a much more critical assessment that appeared in the *American Historical Review*. In this review, Harold R. Weinstein openly accused Allen of bias and stated that his anti-Ukrainian feelings led him to ridicule the whole Ukrainian national movement and underestimate its importance. But Weinstein, who seemed to sympathize with Stalin's USSR, restricted his specific criticisms to Allen's unfavourable treatment of the Soviet Union and the collectivization campaign; he even accused Allen of being too sympathetic to Petliura, who had militarily opposed the Soviets. (Petliura had also been the target of Jewish attacks and had been assassinated by a Jew who was alleged by many Ukrainians to have been a Soviet agent.) Weinstein concluded pointedly that Allen's "ukrainophobia is outweighed by his anti-Soviet feelings."[10]

Allen's book was an important attempt at a scholarly history of Ukraine in English, but it was not the only one. Shortly after Allen's book was published, Mykhailo Hrushevsky's *A History of Ukraine* appeared, edited by O. J. Frederiksen of Miami University in Ohio, a state with a substantial Ukrainian immigrant population.[11] Frederiksen's book was a translation of Hrushevsky's popular-style *Iliustrovana istoriia Ukrainy z dodatkom novoho periodu istorii Ukrainy za roky vid 1914 do 1919* (Illustrated history of Ukraine with an addendum on the new period of the history of Ukraine from 1914 to 1919), which had been published in the early 1920s in Winnipeg, Manitoba, by the pioneer generation of Ukrainian settlers from Austrian Galicia.[12] The English translation was sponsored by the Ukrainian National Association (*Ukrainskyi narodnyi soiuz*) in New Jersey, and the translators were Wasyl Halich, who, during the 1930s, had authored a respectable history of Ukrainians in the United States, Omelian Revyuk, who edited *Svoboda* (Liberty), the most widely circulated non-Communist Ukrainian newspaper in the United States, and Stephen

Shumeyko, who edited the English-language *Ukrainian Weekly*, a supplement to *Svoboda*, and who edited the penultimate draft before it went to the general editor, O. J. Frederiksen. The latter appended a chapter of his own on developments after 1919. Unaware of his connections with Allen, the team then approached George Vernadsky of Yale, who was the son of Vladimir Vernadsky, the first president of the Ukrainian Academy of Sciences in Kyiv; they asked him to write a preface. Vernadsky did this and he then submitted the whole work to Yale University Press for publication. Meanwhile, word of the project got out and Communist front groups in the United States began attacking Hrushevsky's reputation, slandering him as a pro-Nazi anti-Semite. Vernadsky had to assure the press that Hrushevsky had been a reputable scholar and could not be accused of ethnic prejudice.[13] Vernadsky's preface was dated 12 March 1941, and the book was published before the year was out.[14]

This edition of Hrushevsky's *History of Ukraine* – Hrushevsky-Frederiksen, as we shall call it – differed in certain important respects from the Ukrainian original. First, the original had been a truly illustrated history containing dozens of well-selected illustrations, pictures, engravings, drawings, photographs, and maps, all of which were authentically Ukrainian, and all of which were contemporary or near contemporary to the eras discussed; that is, they were in themselves antique artifacts of a sort. These were scattered throughout the book to reinforce various points made in the text. By contrast, Hrushevsky-Frederiksen was a simple survey history without illustrations. True, the editors added a few antique maps prominently displaying the name "Ukraine" in its historical context, but the documentation and general feel for an illustrated history were lost. Second, the translation was not exact. In fact, it was at places so loose as to be considered a paraphrase, and a somewhat poor one at that, rather than a translation. Third, Hrushevsky's original general sections (there were seven of them), which divided his tale into various eras, were missing, and chapter headings invented by the translators were added. Fourth, the translators added expressions and terms that were missing from Hrushevsky's original. Some of these even intruded into the new chapter titles. Thus, for example, in their discussion of Kyivan Rus', they added a chapter title "The Kingdom of Kiev," which was missing from the original, and which Hrushevsky might not have approved. Fifth, of course, Frederiksen added a final chapter updating the history to 1940 and appended a detailed bibliography of historical works in various European languages (with Slavic titles printed in both the original

Cyrillic and English translation) and of recent political literature on Ukraine in English. The general result was that Hrushevsky-Frederiksen varied greatly from the original, both in appearance and in content. In its content, it was considerably less scholarly, though in form, at first glance, it appeared to be more scholarly.

In its general approach, however, Hrushevsky-Frederiksen did no violence to the master's basic ideas, only strengthening and clarifying their national tendencies for the sake of an English-speaking public. Continuity from ancient times to the present was its keynote. It began with the archaeology of the ancient "Ukrainian" steppe and, from Scythians and Greeks, proceeded to what the translators called "the first Ukrainians"; that is, a Slavonic tribe called the Antes. From there, Hrushevsky-Frederiksen proceeded to the "founding of Kiev" (local elements rather than foreign "Varangian" or Viking ones were stressed); then came the "Kingdom of Kiev" and its decline, the Tatar invasions, and the subsequent rise of Galicia and Volhynia. Thereafter occurred the Lithuanian ascendancy, which Hrushevsky basically saw as benign, and the Polish ascendancy, which Hrushevsky painted in darker colours. Then came the rise of the "Kozaks" (the traditional English spelling was "Cossacks") and "national revival in the steppes." This revival took the form of a struggle over the question of church union; Hrushevsky-Frederiksen was loyal to the original in its identification of Ukrainian nationality during this period with Orthodox resistance to the union and the polemics on both sides that grew out of this dispute. The culmination of this struggle came with Bohdan Khmelnytsky's war against the Poles and his reluctant and regretted turn to Moscow; Mazepa is portrayed in a balanced manner both as a patriot who wished to unite and free his country from foreign rule and as a self-interested autonomist. After the defeat of Mazepa came the decline of the "Kozak" host and the last rebellions. However, the nineteenth century brought a "national renaissance"; the national idea brought the beginnings of enlightened democracy. Kotliarevsky, Shevchenko, and the Cyril-Methodian brotherhood initiated a national movement that was characterized by education and progress and that eventually led to national independence in 1918. Frederiksen then added an account of the independence struggle of 1919 to 1921, Soviet rule, the ukrainianization program of the 1920s, and the purges and "great famine" of 1932–3, costing, as he wrote, "the lives of several million men, women, and children." Just as, in earlier chapters, Hrushevsky had devoted considerable attention to the Ukrainians under the Poles and Austrians, so, too,

Frederiksen did not ignore the Ukrainians under post-war Poland, Czechoslovakia, and Romania. The book ends with the 1940 annexation of northern Bukovina and parts of Bessarabia to the Ukrainian SSR.

Like Allen, Hrushevsky-Frederiksen elicits a mixed response among modern readers. On the one hand, Hrushevsky was obviously a very learned scholar who wrote with great authority on his subject. Most striking is his refusal to engage in wide-ranging generalizations. Hrushevsky was a "positivist" in method who stuck closely to the facts and was reluctant to go beyond them to support more general theories. In fact, so striking is this trait of Hrushevsky's that, other than a general commitment to the idea of a national Ukraine, the antecedents of which stretched back into deep antiquity, it is difficult to determine his personal political beliefs from the text. This is generally seen as positive by the community of professional historians, many of whom even today in this "postmodern" era sincerely accept the ideal of scholarly "objectivity." On the other hand, this strict adherence to unembellished fact means that Hrushevsky's style is not conducive to the writing of popular history. It is, quite simply put, a difficult book to read. Moreover, this problem is compounded by the roughness of the translation, which, in spite of its looseness, is inferior.

Other problems also arise for the English-speaking reader. Perhaps the most troubling is Hrushevsky-Frederiksen's tracing of Ukrainian history back to ancient times and calling the Antes "the first Ukrainians." Although there might be some genetic or linguistic link between the ancient Antes and the modern Ukrainians, and the heritage of the Antes, like that of Kyivan Rus', probably belongs more to the modern Ukrainians than to any other modern people, the use of the name "Ukraine" in this ancient context is anachronistic and therefore problematic for many Western readers. (In the minds of some non-Ukrainian scholars, it is the equivalent, I would guess, of speaking of "England" under the Romans, or Roman "France.") The fact that the translators strengthened the use of this anachronism, of course, escapes the notice of most readers.

Other innovations introduced by the translators included the use in personal names of modern Ukrainian rather than more traditional or Russian orthography (thus, Volodimir instead of Vladimir), dropping the definite article "the" before the name "Ukraine" (in English, the definite article is widely used before the names of regions such as "the Pampas" or "the Kuban," but very seldom used for independent countries), and the neologism "Kozak" instead of the traditional "Cossack" (apparently – and here I am guessing – in an attempt to distinguish between Ukrainian "Kozaks" and Russian "Cossacks"). On the other hand, the translators kept to the conventional English forms for major geographical names such as Kiev (not Kyiv) and the Dnieper River (not the Dnipro River).

In general, Hrushevsky-Frederiksen gives a very mixed impression. On the one hand, it purports to be the work of a great scholar and has some of the trappings of a scholarly work. On the other hand, it surprises and sometimes irritates the modern reader with its difficult style, its neologisms, and other untoward innovations. In short, it gives neither Ukraine nor Hrushevsky their due.

Thankfully, a third general history of Ukraine appeared during the war, which offered an alternative to both Allen and Hrushevsky-Frederiksen. This was Dmytro Doroshenko's *History of the Ukraine*, edited for the English-speaking world by George W. Simpson of the University of Saskatchewan in western Canada. (Western Canada, even more than Ohio, was a centre of Ukrainian immigrant settlement.) This book, which we shall refer to as Doroshenko-Simpson, was sponsored by the Ukrainian Self-Reliance League (*Soiuz Ukraintsiv Samostiinykiv*), a Ukrainian Orthodox Brotherhood very active in Canada's western provinces, and was translated into English by Hanna Chikalenko-Keller (1884–1964), a Ukrainian journalist, translator, and librarian at the University of Tubingen.[15] Doroshenko himself was a prominent Ukrainian historian and professor at Charles University and the Ukrainian Free University in Prague, and, after 1936, at the University of Warsaw. He had been active in Ukrainian politics during the revolution and participated in the conservative regime of Hetman Pavlo Skoropadsky, which had overthrown Hrushevsky's Central Rada. In scholarship, he represented a conservative "statist" approach to Ukrainian history.[16]

Unlike Hrushevsky-Frederiksen, Doroshenko-Simpson did not claim to be an exact translation of Doroshenko's original Ukrainian-language *Narys istorii Ukrainy* (Survey of Ukrainian history), which had appeared in Warsaw in 1932–4; rather, it was an abridged version with the very full bibliographies and extensive historiographical sections omitted entirely. Nonetheless, it was a substantial book and the first of the general histories considered here to be published. The translation itself was fairly fluid, the job of the translator being made much easier by Doroshenko's beautiful prose, which combined fluidity with simplicity. Doroshenko himself added two new chapters on the First World War, the revolution, and events up to the early 1930s, while Simpson added a series of maps illustrating the geography of various historical eras, and he penned a lucid general introduction explaining the logic of the concept of Ukrainian history and giving an account of the origin of the name "Ukraine."[17] Simpson also added a brief appendix on the recent momentous events in European politics in which the Ukrainian question played an important role.

In its general approach, Doroshenko-Simpson resembled Hrushevsky-Frederiksen but with certain important differences. For example, like Hrushevsky-Frederiksen, Doroshenko-Simpson traced Ukrainian history back to ancient times and began with a discussion of Ukrainian archaeology, the Scythians, and the Greek colonies on the north shore of the Black Sea. It then considered the "origin of the Ukrainian state," the Varangian or Viking contribution to this state, which the author felt was considerable, and its Christianization and fate under the Mongols. Doroshenko-Simpson stressed the difference between the total subjection of Muscovy to Tatar rule versus what it believed to be the merely partial subjection of Galicia; it took the Ukrainian side on the question of the supposed depopulation of Ukraine following the Tatar invasion and stressed the peaceful accession of the Ukrainian lands to Lithuania. Doroshenko-Simpson, like Hrushevsky-Frederiksen, then treated in detail the question of the church union and the rise of the Cossacks that culminated in the revolt of Bohdan Khmelnytsky. This great Hetman is treated in a very sympathetic manner and his dealings with Muscovy are characterized as merely an "alliance" (a rather loose translation of the Ukrainian word *soiuz* of the original, which can also mean "union"); Hetman Petro Doroshenko's efforts to reunite Ukraine after the Treaty of Andrusovo are stressed and Mazepa is portrayed sympathetically as a Ukrainian patriot. The abolition of Ukrainian autonomy is a tragedy, and the rise of modern Ukrainian nationalism, as in Hrushevsky-Frederiksen, is associated with education and progress. During the revolution, the rise of the Central Rada was followed by a "Russian–Ukrainian war," and, of course, the "Ukrainian Hetman state of 1918" is sympathetically described. But so, too, are the activities of the "republican" Symon Petliura. By contrast, the Soviet regime is given very scant attention. The national achievements of the 1920s are barely mentioned, as, indeed, is the fact that "the Soviet authorities allowed millions of the population to perish from terrible hunger in 1932" (648). Doroshenko-Simpson, in fact, gives somewhat more space to the Ukrainians in interwar Poland than it does to Soviet Ukraine. The Ukrainians in Czechoslovakia and Romania are also mentioned.

To the modern student of Ukrainian history, Doroshenko-Simpson makes a somewhat better impression than does Hrushevsky-Frederiksen.

It reads much more smoothly and contains fewer unexpected innovations. The transition from traditional Slavonic or Russian orthography to modern Ukrainian is somewhat eased in the former by the use of alternate forms in brackets; thus "Vladimir (Volodimir)" and so on, and the "Cossacks" are simply Cossacks and not "Kozaks." Nevertheless, like Hrushevsky-Frediksen, Doroshenko-Simpson omits the use of the article "the" before the name "Ukraine" in the text (if not in the book title), uses the name "Ukraine" in its discussions of ancient times, and obviously sees this country as more than a mere region and claims for it the heritage of Kyivan Rus'.

On a somewhat different level, the reluctance to generalize that is so evident in Hrushevsky-Frediksen also appears to some degree in Doroshenko-Simpson. There are occasional lapses, as, for example, in its discussion of Russian national character, which is supposed to have a "well developed instinct for state building" (67), something that was supposedly not so clear in the Ukrainians; but, in general, Doroshenko, like Hrushevsky before him, is very guarded in the expression of his political beliefs and he obviously values the ideal of scholarly objectivity.

Since Doroshenko-Simpson, Hrushevsky-Frediksen, and Allen all appeared within a relatively short time of each other, there was a certain amount of overlap in the scholarly reviews, which made some comparisons between them and, on occasion, reviewed them together. Perhaps the most balanced and one of the better-informed reviews was that written for the Chicago-based *Journal of Modern History* by Alfred A. Skerpan, an historian of Russia.[18]

Skerpan reviewed both Allen and Hrushevsky-Frediksen but, apparently, was unaware of the publication of Doroshenko-Simpson or, perhaps, it was unavailable to him, since he makes no mention of it. He began by welcoming the publication of both Hrushevsky-Frediksen and Allen, but stated that "neither can be considered fully objective or adequate." He criticized the former for what he believed to be its anachronistic use of the term "Ukraine" prior to the seventeenth century, and for claiming Kievan Rus' primarily for Ukraine, when, he believed, it belonged to "all eastern Slavs"; he also accused Hrushevsky of being a typical nineteenth-century romantic, and claimed that his final chapter was merely a "heated and frequently inaccurate commentary on events of World War I." In general, Skerpan accused Hrushevsky-Frediksen of reflecting an unobjective, nationalist viewpoint.

By contrast, Skerpan recommended Allen as an "antidote to the sometimes egregious nationalism of the translation" and claimed Allen had

made "a strong effort toward objectivity." Nevertheless, Skerpan continued, the result was an overemphasis on "Russian" interpretations of events
and the book was marred by numerous "glaring" errors. Allen over-
looked the independence of the earlier phases of Ukrainian history, vital
developments in church history and law, and the role of the influential
church brotherhoods, which played such an important role in the
struggle over the union. Skerpan concluded that Allen depended on
conventional English-language accounts of eastern Europe such as the
Cambridge histories, the *Encyclopaedia Britannica*, and the older English
outlines of Russian and Polish history. The implication was that neither
Hrushevsky-Frederiksen nor Allen should be read in isolation.

Other reviews of our three scholarly histories were less balanced.
John Shelton Curtiss, an American historian of Russia, wrote in the
American Historical Review that Hrushevsky-Frederiksen had "an anti-
Russian separatist character," used the name "Ukraine" anachronistically, unjustly claimed the civilization of Kyivan Rus' for Ukraine, was
less convincing than his opponent Kliuchevsky on the Norman question, took the side of the Cossack leaders rather than the Ukrainian
peasants in Cossack times, and silently passed over events such as the
Polish uprising of 1863, the economic results of the emancipation of
1861, the radicalism of the 1880s, and the rapid industrialization of the
country after 1890. Curtiss concluded that Frederiksen's update was the
least impressive part of the book.[19]

Perhaps the most unbalanced review, however, came from the pen of
Michael T. Florinsky, a Russian American historian who was the son of
Timofei D. Florinsky (1854–1919), one of the most outspoken opponents of the Ukrainian national movement in pre-revolutionary Ukraine.
Writing in the very first issue of the *Russian Review*,[20] the younger Florinsky
praised what he called Allen's "truly remarkable erudition" and "thorough knowledge of the literature" and agreed with almost all his interpretations, especially his opinion on the recent origin of the Ukrainian
nationality, its supposedly superficial and academic character, and its alleged association with Austria and Germany. Both Hrushevsky and
Doroshenko are dismissed by Florinsky as "a special plea" exercised by
"extreme Ukrainian nationalists."

The supposedly comparative reviews by Florinsky and Curtiss were both
strongly inclined towards a pro-Russian position. But at least one comparative review took the opposite track. George W. Simpson, Doroshenko's
Canadian editor, penned a review for the Colorado-based *Journal of Central
European Affairs*, which not only evaluated Hrushevsky-Frederiksen, but

also looked at three popular-style books on Ukraine that gave interpretations strongly critical of Ukrainian nationalism. These were the popular
histories by Bregy and Obolensky and by Vowles, discussed above, and a
third book titled *Republic for a Day*, on the Carpatho-Ukrainian crisis of
1938–39, by the British journalist Michael Winch.[21] Simpson was positive
in his assessment of Hrushevsky-Frederiksen, praising Vernadsky's preface on Hrushevsky and calling the book "a mine of information," but he
admitted that "the digging is not at all times easy." He thought Hrushevsky-
Frederiksen especially valuable for the modern period and the account
of the Ukrainian national movement. By contrast, Simpson was sparing,
factual, and somewhat skeptical in his comments on Bregy and Obolensky,
while he was downright negative on Vowles, stating that much of the
book "can hardly be called history." As to the journalist Winch, Simpson
thought him entirely biased and handicapped by his ignorance of the
Slavic languages and his dependence on a Polish translator, who, of
course, would not have been sympathetic to Ukrainian concerns.

Scholarly evaluations of Simpson's own work were less frequent than
evaluations of Hrushevsky-Frederiksen or, indeed, Allen. The most positive scholarly review – in fact, the only significant one I have been able to
find in the academic publications – was authored for the newly launched
Journal of Central European Affairs by Stuart R. Tompkins, a Canadian-born
historian of Russia working at the University of Oklahoma.[22] Tompkins,
who seems to have been familiar with Ukrainian immigrants because of
some time spent working at the Department of Education in the province of Alberta in western Canada, thought Doroshenko-Simpson had
achieved what he called "an almost super-human task" in reducing to
manageable proportions the variegated histories of the different parts of
Ukraine, and he characterized Doroshenko as a member of Hrushevsky's
school. Tompkins's only criticism was that Doroshenko-Simpson was
weak on the economic history of eastern Ukraine, which, however, was of
special import because of the current war in eastern Europe.

The reviews by Tompkins and Simpson were, of course, the exceptions.
In general, the question of Ukrainian nationality and its historical claims
was greeted with a certain amount of skepticism by Western scholars.
Several of the reviewers alluded to the problem of the origins of the
Ukrainian people, which stretched into deep antiquity, according to
Hrushevsky-Frederiksen and Doroshenko-Simpson, but was of more recent, indeed, even modern, origin, according to more mainline russo-
centric Western authors. Much of the problem seems to have revolved
around the use of the name "Ukraine" itself, as was alluded to in

Simpson's introduction to Doroshenko. Both Hrushevsky-Frederiksen and Doroshenko-Simpson used it without further question for even the earliest periods. This, it may be assumed, reflected their commitment to the idea of the ethnolinguistic continuity of the Ukrainian people throughout the ages and the claim to the heritage of Kievan Rus' by the modern Ukrainian people. By contrast, W. E. D. Allen used the conventional term "Russia" just as extensively when referring specifically to "Ukraine," and he used it for all periods of Ukrainian history. This, it seems, reflected the low esteem in which Allen held the Ukrainian national idea.

But the problem is more complex than this. It involves, in fact, two different but closely related problems of translation. First, there is the problem of how to translate the Slavic noun *Rus'* (which is more commonly used by Slavic historians for the older periods of eastern European history, especially for the period of what Ukrainian scholars and some others working in English call "Kievan Rus'" or, occasionally, "Kyivan Rus'"), and there is the problem of how to translate the Slavic noun *Rossiia* (which Ukrainian scholars working in English translate as "Russia" and restrict to Muscovy and the imperial era that followed). In the 1930s and 1940s, Frederiksen and Simpson were fighting an uphill battle against a scholarly public that rode roughshod over these distinctions and labelled almost everything "Russia."

The second translation problem concerned the very common Ukrainian and Russian adjectives *Rus'kyi* and *Russkii*, which, when referring to the modern *Ukrainian* people and their *ancestors*, had no agreed-upon solution in the 1940s, as, indeed, they have no agreed-upon solution today. In the 1930s and 1940s, Allen used "Russian" and Hrushevsky-Frederiksen and Doroshenko-Simpson used "Ukrainian." More recent Ukrainian historians working in the West have used the adjectives "Ruthenian," "Rus'ian," and, of course, "Ukrainian" to distinguish Ukrainian history from Russian.[23] The most recent author of an English-language general history of Ukraine suggests solving this problem by using the word "Rus" as both a noun ("the country of Rus") and an adjective ("the Rus people"), thus, on the one hand, making a clear distinction between "Rus'" and "Russia," and, on the other hand, at least partially avoiding both the anachronistic use of the term "Ukrainian" and the misleading use of the word "Russian."[24] But no completely satisfactory solution exists. The choice of the English-speaking writer, translator, or editor invariably reflects his or her views as to the independence or lack of independence of the general course of Ukrainian history. This was strikingly clear in the 1930s and 1940s.

One further point must be made about the reviews. This concerns the distinction between Hrushevsky-Frederiksen and Doroshenko-Simpson and the historical schools they represent. None of the reviewers cited in this paper was able to make this distinction and one of them (Curtiss) somewhat misrepresented Hrushevsky-Frederiksen's position. The fact of the matter is that Hrushevsky represented the populist (*narodnyk*) school of Ukrainian historiography, which was somewhat radical, emphasized the role of the common people in Ukrainian history, and tended to view their leaders as opportunists who were not consistently interested in the national cause. By contrast, Doroshenko-Simpson represented the conservative "statist" (*derzhavnyk*) school of Ukrainian historiography, which stressed the positive achievements of the educated political elite and viewed the masses in a more negative light; for, according to the statists, the masses were at times a drag on the national movement and the struggle for an independent or, at least, autonomous Ukrainian state. The failure of the reviewers to see this distinction between the two schools can be explained only by the fact that both Hrushevsky and Doroshenko were very reluctant to make any wide-ranging generalizations in their histories and stuck closely to the facts. Their ideological assumptions could, thus, be seen only by scholars who were already acquainted with at least the broad outlines of Ukrainian historiography and its debates, and, in the early 1940s, it seems, none of the reviewers concerned was so equipped. Moreover, the position of Hrushevsky changed somewhat over the many years of his long career and the *Iliustrovana istoriia Ukrainy* is not the best example of his populist ideology. In the West, the ideological distinction between Hrushevsky-Frederiksen and Doroshenko-Simpson seems to have been first clearly articulated by O. J. Frederiksen himself, who, in a pioneering *Handbook of Slavic Studies*, edited by the émigré Russian historian Leonid Strakhovsky, also had something interesting to say about his rival, W. E. D. Allen.[25]

We may conclude by restating that the international political crises of the late 1930s led to the publication during the war of several important books in English about Ukrainian history. These books may be divided by genre into popular histories and scholarly works. In both the popular realm and the scholarly realm, several different views were represented. These included conservative Russian, Soviet Russian, and two different Ukrainian national viewpoints. With regard to the popular-style history of Ukraine authored by Gaskell, we admit that this volume was only written and not published. But, by the same token, it should be noted that a book similar to Gaskell's was, in fact, published later in the war. This was W. H. Chamberlin's *The Ukraine: A Submerged Nation*, which was fullest on the Soviet period and gave an eyewitness account of the Great Famine of 1932–3. Chamberlin concluded his book with some idealistic specula- tions about the USSR's eventually transforming itself into a democratic federation of free peoples.[26] Moreover, even the official Soviet view of Ukrainian history changed somewhat during the war with serious con- cessions made towards Ukrainian national sentiment, and this was noted not only by Ukrainian immigrants in the West, both nationalist and Communist, but also by so august a publication as the *American Historical Review*.[27] The final result of this flurry of research, translation, and publi- cation was that far into the Cold War era, which began in 1945 and lasted into the 1980s, Ukrainian historiography in the English language, at least with regard to general histories, continued to be dominated by books published during the Second World War.

7 George W. Simpson, the Ukrainian Canadians, and the "Prehistory" of Slavic Studies in Canada

History is philosophy
teaching by example.

Dionysius of Halicarnasus
Fl. 30 BC

George W. Simpson (1893–1969) was born and raised in Chatsworth and Owen Sound, Ontario, but is best known as a distinguished Prairie Canadian, a long-time chairman of the Department of History at the University of Saskatchewan (1940 to 1957), and first provincial archivist of the Province of Saskatchewan. He was also a pioneer in the field of Slavic Studies and was a charter member of the Canadian Association of Slavists, which was formed shortly after the end of the Second World War.[1]

By the final years of the earlier conflict of 1914 to 1918, Simpson was already living in Saskatoon and, in 1919, received an arts degree from the University of Saskatchewan. The following year, he earned a Master of Arts degree in history from the University of Toronto and, from 1922, began teaching in the Department of History on the Saskatoon campus.[2] It was not long before his occupation as a university teacher brought the young scholar into contact with the many students of Slavic background who were just then beginning to make their appearance at various Prairie universities.

The early immigration records did not use the term "Ukrainian." Instead, the pioneers from the regions of eastern Galicia and Bukovina in the Austrian Empire were generally known in Canada as "Galicians" from the place of origin of the majority, or as "Ruthenians" from their traditional nomenclature in Austria. But, with the collapse of the Romanov and Habsburg empires and the temporary but precedent-setting establishment of national governments in Kyiv and in eastern Galicia, national consciousness and the Ukrainian name rapidly spread throughout the former Galician colonies of North America. By the 1920s, the new Communist left, which glorified the progress of the Ukrainian Soviet Socialist Republic, the populist centre, which stood for progress and enlightenment in the national spirit and an independent Ukraine, and the conservative right, which also supported the struggle for an independent Ukraine, all accepted the idea of the Ukrainian national identity, which they propagated among the former eastern European villagers.[3]

George Simpson may have come into contact with Prairie Ukrainians as early as the closing years of the Great War when he was doing his undergraduate work in history at the University of Saskatchewan. But it was the sudden appearance of modern nationalism among the Ukrainians that first attracted his attention to them. "As a member of the department of history," he wrote many years later, "I became interested about 1924 in the rise of Ukrainian nationalism as part of my modern history studies. This interest was quickened by the presence of Canadian Ukrainian students at the University who were strongly nationalistic in outlook."[4] By 1930, the number of these students was enough to form a club, the Alpha Omega Society, with which Simpson established close and continued contact. About this same time, he learned to read, and considerably more haltingly, to speak, the Ukrainian language.[5]

Simpson's contact with prominent Ukrainians expanded very quickly. In the early 1920s, he got to know the Saskatoon lawyer Julian Stechishin who, for many years, served as rector of the Mohyla Institute, a Ukrainian Orthodox student residence and cultural centre located near the University of Saskatchewan. Stechishin had extensive contacts with the Ukrainian intelligentsia in the Old Country and eventually became an historian in his own right.[6] By 1928, Simpson was in correspondence with Vladimir Kysilewskyj, an early organizer of the conservative Sich organization and the editor of Edmonton's Catholic *Zakhidni visti* (The western news). Kysilewskyj had a growing interest in introducing the study of eastern Europe into western Canadian universities and, in preparation for such a task, in the early 1930s, went to England to study under the famous British Slavist R. W. Seton-Watson at London's School of Slavonic and East European Studies. Simultaneously, however, he established a non-party Ukrainian Information Bureau in London, which was financed by the Ukrainian American millionaire Jacob Makohin (1880–1956). Simpson and Kysilewskyj had many interests in common and when, shortly afterwards, Simpson went to London, he visited Kysilewskyj and queried him on the School of Slavonic and East European Studies. "He impressed me by his knowledge of Slavonic problems," Kysilewskyj wrote many years later. "He also told me of the plans to introduce the teaching of Slavonic languages at the University of Saskatchewan ..."[7]

The Ukrainians of western Canada had long been interested in seeing their language and culture studied in Canadian institutions of higher education. As early as January 1914, Nykyta Budka, the Greek Catholic bishop of Canada, had noted the desirability of "a permanent Lecturer on Ruthenian history, literature and art" to be appointed to one of western Canada's universities. Two years later, a contagion of wartime jingoism closed down the bilingual school system that had existed in Manitoba and in a less formal way in Saskatchewan and Alberta, but in Manitoba, J. W. Arsenych and a delegation urging retention of the bilingual school system took the idea of a university-level chair of Ukrainian studies to the Manitoba legislature.[8] As late as the 1920s, the Anglican bishop of Saskatchewan G. E. Lloyd was still crying out against "a mongrel Canada" and advocating "British blood," "British language," and British supremacy.[9] But Lloyd's program for a purely British Canada was immediately challenged both in the federal parliament by Michael Luchkovich, the MP for Vegreville, and in the press by Watson Kirkconnell, the young linguist who was about to begin the task of translating the "New Canadian" literature into English.[10] The atmosphere for humanistic studies and cultural tolerance was slowly improving. Thus, by 1931, the Winnipeg Prosvita Reading Society, at the initiative of Andrii Hospodyn, was able to again raise the question of a Ukrainian-language department at the University of Manitoba, and, by 1935, Simpson was successful in introducing an elementary course on the history of the Slavic peoples at the University of Saskatchewan. "This was," as the historian later wrote, "the first such course given in any university in Canada."[11]

In the summer of 1937, Simpson again went to Europe, where he visited several Ukrainian academic centres including the Ukrainian Research Institute in Berlin. While visiting the institute in Berlin, Simpson even met Hetman Pavlo Skoropadsky, who had briefly ruled as monarch of a German-occupied Ukraine during the war of 1914 to 1918 and who continued to maintain his claim to rule in any future independent Ukraine.[12] By 1938, Simpson was busy editing *A History of the Ukraine* by one of Skoropadsky's most distinguished supporters, the historian Dmytro Doroshenko, who had retired from politics during the 1920s. In Saskatoon, Simpson was also in close touch with the Edmonton lawyer

Peter Lazarowich, who initiated visits to Canada by Doroshenko in the summers of 1937 and 1938. Lazarowich, Julian Stechishin, and other central figures in the populist and Canadian-oriented Ukrainian Self-Reliance League of Canada (USRL) had elaborated a plan for the translation into English of grammars, dictionaries, and history textbooks for possible use in future courses of Ukrainian language, culture, and history to be taught in Canadian universities. While Stechishin began work on the first English-language textbook of Ukrainian grammar, it was Simpson who stressed that English-language books were a necessity and it was Simpson who initiated the translation of Doroshenko's *History*.[13]

By 1938, international events had put the Ukrainian question on the front pages of newspapers throughout the Western world. Hitler was demanding revisions of international boundaries in eastern Europe and was making use of dissatisfied minorities to achieve his ends. As a result of the Munich Pact of 30 September 1938, Hitler forced Czechoslovakia to accept agreements reached by him in consultation with the leaders of Great Britain, France, and Italy; these agreements resulted in the annexation of the German-populated Sudetenland to the Third Reich and the granting of autonomy to Slovakia and ethnically Ukrainian Subcarpathian Rus'. In the latter province, a Ukrainian government under the leadership of Auhustyn (Augustine) Voloshyn came to power. Non-Communist Ukrainians in Canada reacted enthusiastically as the new autonomous state was seen as the "Piedmont" for the creation of a much larger Ukrainian national state in eastern Europe. On the other hand, among the general public, Ukrainian nationalists in Europe had already acquired a reputation as extremists who were not above the use of terrorist tactics, and Ukrainian Canadian support for an autonomous Carpatho-Ukraine dependent on German favour tended to reinforce the notion once spread by Russian monarchists that the whole Ukrainian question was simply a matter of "German intrigues."[14]

At the height of this speculation about Carpatho-Ukraine, George Simpson decided to speak out on the question of Ukrainian nationalism. He had already been getting inquiries from interested parties such as the education specialist Robert England, who was the author of *The Central European Immigrant in Canada*.[15] Thus, in January 1939, he gave a talk over CBC Radio and defended the Ukrainian nationalists as being no more authoritarian or violent than were their hostile neighbours. Simpson thought that the Ukrainian "national liberation movement" in Europe then moved in harmony with German expansionist aims, but that this was only a coincidence and nothing more. He compared underground nationalist Ukraine's relationship with Nazi Germany to the old alliance between revolutionary America and absolutist France. Just as America would have gotten its independence anyway and eventually have turned against absolutist France, with which it differed in principle, so, too, would Ukraine gain its independence and throw off German influence at the earliest opportunity.[16]

Both moderates and more extreme nationalists among Ukrainian Canadians reacted favourably to Simpson's speech. He received a large number of thank-you letters, both from moderates like the USRL activist Peter Lazarowich and from rightists like the Ukrainian National Federation (UNF) leader Wladimir Kossar.[17] (The UNF members seemed to admire the dynamism and anti-Communism of the central European dictatorships but voiced no objections to liberal democracy in Canada.) The Saskatoon-based UNF organ *Novyi shliakh* (The new pathway) commented approvingly: "With these words, the honorable professor rebutted those opponents of the Ukrainian cause who try to turn Ukrainian nationalism and the whole Ukrainian problem into a 'German intrigue.'"[18]

Insofar as Ukrainians in Canada were concerned, at least, the break between Germany and the Ukrainian national movement came far sooner than even Simpson had expected. In March 1939, German armies marched unopposed into Prague while their Hungarian allies took over parts of Slovakia and all of Carpatho-Ukraine. The latter put up a brief but futile resistance. On 16 March 1938, Lazarowich, who had earlier spent some time studying in Prague, wrote to Simpson from his law office in Edmonton:

> We are all amazed at the rapidity, directness and brazenness of Hitler's destruction of Czechoslovakia. You will understand that naturally we are all more concerned about Carpatho-Ukraine than any other part but of course we realize that the other events are of far greater significance to Europe as a whole than the disappearance of this midget state. The most incomprehensible thing to me is the Czechs, whom I have had the opportunity to study at close range and who, I believe, are a chivalrous and courageous people; [they] have been crushed without even a show of resistance ... It appears now that the little Carpatho-Ukraine is the only portion of the former Republic which had the courage to resist the invader to any extent at all against obvious and overwhelming odds. In my opinion, Roumania will be next to crumble under the heel of Hitler.[19]

These international events had a direct bearing on the efforts of Simpson, Edmonton-based Lazarowich, and others to introduce some kind of Slavic Studies program into the regular Canadian university curriculum. Simpson had suggested that a Ukrainian or Slavic history course be introduced at the University of Alberta; Vladimir Kysilewskyj was finished his studies in London and was ready to teach it; but, when Lazarowich approached the administration, he got nowhere. "The prospect of inaugurating a course in Ukrainian history in the summer session of the University of Albert next year," Lazarowich informed Simpson in his 16 March letter, "has now entirely disappeared."

> Yesterday I was called by The President of University who, in the presence of the Dean of Arts and the Director of the Summer School, informed me that for several reasons the idea must be entirely dropped … From the trend of remarks, it appeared to me that the fundamental reason is … political. I think the University is very timid about starting something which smacks of what might be termed nationalism because the President at one stage pointed out to me that the Ukrainians are not united in Canada, that they do not speak with one voice and that it would be extremely difficult to get someone who would bring to the subject complete objectivity.

Lazarowich concluded with even more bad news:

> Although they assured me that Dr. Kysilewsky, as the proposed instructor, received the highest recommendations from the Slavonic School in London, yet there was the additional information that he was engaged in political propaganda of a certain type and, of course, they could not have him. I am sorry that the University cannot see the necessity of including a course in Ukrainian history or the history of the Slavonic peoples in view of the increasing importance of this part of the world at the present time.[20]

The expansion of university-level Slavic Studies on the Canadian prairies would have to wait.

Meanwhile, Europe lumbered steadily towards war. Eastern Europe continued to make headlines, moreover, and Simpson found an eager audience for a further series of radio broadcasts on the Ukrainian question. In the wake of the Hungarian annexation of Carpatho-Ukraine, he argued in favour of autonomy for that province. He clearly distinguished between what he called the "rampant and vicious" nationalism of Germany and Italy and the nationalism that, as he put it, "represents a stage in the growth to maturity of groups of people, especially those who have long suffered suppression and domination." Then, in the wake of British and French guarantees of Poland's borders, Simpson argued that the Western democracies, and Canada, too, should take an interest in the welfare of the large Ukrainian minority in Poland.[21]

There was no time to test Simpson's proposals in real life. Hitler's abandonment of the Carpatho-Ukrainian "Piedmont" turned out to be only the first step in his rapprochement with Stalin, who greatly feared the disruptive potential of Ukrainian nationalism. In August, a non-aggression pact was signed; by the end of September, Poland had been partitioned between Germany and the Soviet Union, and Britain and France were at war with Hitler.

The occupation of eastern Poland by the Soviet Union was especially troubling to non-Communist Ukrainians in the West. A few of the moderate Ukrainian leaders had, like the Polish government, fled to Romania; there were others in Lithuania and Hungary. In London, Kysilewskyj was trying to arrange for relief for these refugees, while in Canada, Simpson, who, by this time, seems to have acquired an international reputation among Ukrainians, received appeals from Madame Ida de Bachynska of the Ukrainian Red Cross in Switzerland. Simpson advised Bachynska that he was sympathetic to the cause of saving the refugees but that he was in accord with the Ukrainian leaders in Canada who were already active and were working closely with, as he put it, "our own Canadian Red Cross organization."[22] About this same time, the English-language edition of Doroshenko's *History of the Ukraine* edited by Simpson was completely sold out and Kysilewskyj, at the suggestion of Lazarowich, was trying to negotiate an inexpensive London edition in the style of Everyman's Library.[23]

In 1940, the fall of France, Holland, Belgium, Denmark, and Norway created a new crisis atmosphere in Canada. The North American Dominion was now Britain's senior ally and every effort was to be made to rally the population behind the cause. Native Canadian fascist leaders such as Adrien Arcand were locked up, the Communist Party of Canada and affiliated organizations such as the Ukrainian Labour Farmer Temple Association (ULFTA) were banned, and new pressure was put on the feuding non-Communist Ukrainian organizations. George Simpson, who was trusted by both of the two big non-Communist Ukrainian organizations – the populist USRL and the rightist UNF – together with Kysilewskyj, who came from England, and the British emissary Tracy Philipps, played a central role in reconciling the two factions so that a new Ukrainian Canadian Committee (UCC), which united all the major non-Communist organizations, was formed.[24] Government officials were pleased with the merger and James Gardiner, minister of agriculture and, from 1940 to 1941, minister of national war services, wrote to Simpson congratulating him on uniting the Ukrainian population behind the war effort and encouraging him to continue his interest in Ukrainian affairs.[25]

During the war, Simpson's interest in Ukrainian affairs operated on at least two levels. On the one hand, he continued to cooperate with Ukrainian cultural activists in the preparation of English-language books about the Ukrainian question. Ideas were put forth for books on the future of the national state in Europe, the roots of Ukrainian nationalism, and the nature of the Ukrainian emigration to Canada and other countries, and also for a book of maps about the Ukrainian lands. Only the last project worked out and Simpson's modest *Ukraine: A Series of Maps* appeared in 1941.[26] On the other hand, Simpson continued his efforts at promoting the Canadian war effort among Ukrainians. For example, when the influential Ukrainian Greek Catholic bishop Ivan Buchko visited the United States from Europe and South America and suggested that Britain and Germany make peace, but also that Britain did not really care to see the establishment of a strong, democratic Russia or an independent Ukraine, Simpson wrote to the bishop and asked him to give further consideration to international developments from the British point of view. This view, he claimed, supported the principles of national freedom and could, at any time, make an independent Ukraine a matter of active policy.[27] Similarly, Simpson wrote to the volatile but charismatic UNF leader Wasyl Swystun about the necessity for skilful and statesmanlike leadership. This leadership, Simpson wrote, "will undoubtedly affect the future of Canada and it may in a crisis, have a far-reaching effect on the situation in Europe."[28]

Simpson's record in reconciling the two non-Communist Ukrainian organizations, his other activities in the organized Ukrainian community, and his low-key approach to Canadian political life brought him to the attention of the federal Department of National War Services. This department was just then undertaking the task of further organizing Canadians of non-English or non-French background behind the war effort. In October 1941, T. C. Davis, a judge temporarily seconded to the department and holding the position of associate deputy minister, asked Simpson to come to Ottawa and participate in its work. At the end of October, Simpson became senior advisor to the director of public information, and, not long afterwards, a voluntary Committee on Cooperation in Canadian Citizenship was formed. Tracy Philipps and Vladimir Kysilewskyj were brought in to serve under Simpson. Kysilewskyj was to handle relations with the ethnic press and Tracy Philipps remained a so-called European advisor.[29]

In the following months, Simpson's Committee on Cooperation in Canadian Citizenship took action of several sorts. Materials were supplied to the ethnic press, links were established with the Canadian Red Cross and with various friendship councils and unity councils, an attempt was made to encourage the Poles to follow the Ukrainian example in forming a common committee to aid in the war effort, newspaper stories on members of various ethnic groups who had enlisted or performed an outstanding service were circulated, efforts were made to fight discrimination by Anglo-Saxon employers, and a project was elaborated for the translation into English of the classic literatures of the various European-origin peoples of Canada.[30] As well, in cooperation with the National Film Board, motion pictures were circulated about the various Canadian ethnic groups.[31]

The strenuous work in Ottawa, plus a regimen that required constant travel between Ottawa and far-off Saskatoon, had an adverse effect on Simpson's health. By July 1942, he was so sick that his doctor advised him against further travel. Simpson, therefore, retired from active direction of the committee and returned to his position as professor of history at the University of Saskatchewan. He remained formal chairman of the committee, however, and continued to take an interest in its work and receive correspondence, reports, and minutes of various meetings until the committee was disbanded in January 1945.[32]

During these same difficult war years, interest in the study of Slavic Europe was again beginning to surface at Canadian universities. As early as 1941, for the first time in any Canadian university, a non-credit course in elementary Ukrainian was offered at the University of Saskatchewan by Dr. T. K. Pavlychenko, a participant in the Ukrainian revolution of 1917 and an agronomist by training.[33] On his return to Saskatchewan, Simpson again became active in university affairs and, in his capacity as chairman of the Committee on Evening Classes, arranged for two new courses to be given in 1943–4: one in elementary Ukrainian, which was taught by Pavlychenko, and one in Russian, which was taught by Irene Siemens.[34]

The new courses at the University of Saskatchewan were not unique. The alliance between the Western democracies and the Soviet Union had increased Canadian and American popular awareness of eastern

Europe and, it seems, legitimized the study of things Slavic. By 1943–4, eight Canadian universities were offering at least non-credit courses in elementary Russian.[35] At Saskatchewan, the new courses were so successful that in 1944–5, a special lecturer, A. Znamensky, was brought in from Harvard to teach Russian language and literature.[36] Moreover, Simpson now thought the time was ripe for the creation of a full-fledged Department of Slavic Studies and submitted a memorandum on the subject to the president of the university, J. S. Thompson.

In his memorandum, Simpson argued that the large number of Slavs in Saskatchewan, their great interest in the study of their ancestral tongues, and, as he put it, the expansion and meeting of Russia and England in North America all favoured the promotion of Slavic Studies. Simpson further argued that, since Saskatchewan still had 81,954 native Ukrainian speakers, 18,771 Polish, 15,875 Russian, and 3,247 Slovak, in all 119,844 Slavic speakers or 13 per cent of the population according to the 1941 census, there existed students for whom the language was still a living tradition. "The English language," he concluded, "is rapidly replacing the mother tongues of immigrants in Canada. It seems clear that if the university is to avail itself of the 'living tradition' it must act with deliberate haste." Simpson ended by noting that, since Ukrainians outnumbered all other Saskatchewan Slavs combined, it would be desirable to employ a Canadian of Ukrainian background who could also teach Russian and Polish.[37]

Simpson already had a candidate in mind. For several years he had known C. H. Andrusyshen, a native Winnipeg Ukrainian who had a long-standing interest in the Slavonic literatures and who held a doctorate in the Romance languages from the University of Toronto.[38] Since 1941, Andrusyshen had taken over as editor of Winnipeg's *Kanadiiskyi farmer* (The Canadian farmer), which was the largest-circulation Ukrainian weekly in Canada. Under Andrusyshen's influence, the paper, which had been edited by an intensely patriotic supporter of Hetman Skoropadsky (who was still resident in Berlin) moved onto a strictly "Canadian" course. The Ukrainian question in Europe receded into the background as more local Canadian issues came forward.[39]

In his memorandum to President Thomson, Simpson had stressed the desirability of getting "someone thoroughly acquainted with Canadian life on the prairies,"[40] and, in the opinion of the ukrainophile history professor, Andrusyshen certainly fit the bill. In 1944, Simpson helped Andrusyshen to get a Rockefeller grant to do further studies at Harvard under the eminent Slavist S. H. Cross. The latter suggested to Andrusyshen the study of Old Slavic, Old Russian, Russian literature, and at least one South Slavic language, "preferably Serbian."[41] As Serbian was far-removed from the ethnic situation on the Canadian prairies, in a private letter to Simpson, Andrusyshen mused that he would have been better off at Columbia studying under Clarence Manning and A. P. Coleman, East Slavic and Polish specialists, respectively, but, on the surface of it, as least, he was quite content to settle down for a year at Harvard as a Research Fellow under Cross. On the completion of his MA at Harvard, Andrusyshen moved to Saskatchewan, where, in 1945, he became chairman of the first full-fledged Department of Slavic Studies in Canada.[42]

It was not only in the academic world that George Simpson made a contribution to Ukrainian life in Canada. During the second half of the war, he continued to advise the various non-Communist organizations that made up the UCC and continued to act as an informal intermediary between the federal government and the Ukrainians. The rightist UNF, in particular, which, since June 1941, had come under fierce Communist attacks and intensive official scrutiny, looked on George Simpson and Watson Kirkconnell as a kind of "protective shield" and would not make a move without first consulting the former.[43] Thus, when the UCC, with the strong support of the UNF, organized a pan-Canadian congress to rally its members and resurrect the issue of a free and independent Ukraine, Simpson and Kysilewskyj were able to channel nationalist passions onto Canadian terrain and redirect most of the discussion towards Canadian issues rather than European ones. Simpson himself was a featured speaker at the historic gathering, which was billed as the "First All-Canadian Congress of Ukrainians in Canada."[44]

Simpson's connections with the UNF and other Ukrainian nationalist organizations did not go unnoticed by the Communists. Shortly after the UCC congress had ended, Progress Books of Toronto published a well-documented propaganda tract titled *This Is Our Land: Ukrainian Canadians Against Hitler* by the experienced Communist propagandist R. A. Davies. In this tract, Davies, whose real name was Rudolf Shohan, praised the ULFTA and its successor, the pro-Communist Ukrainian Association to Aid the Fatherland, and attacked the non-Communists – in particular, the UNF and the Hetman party – as being pro-Fascist and pro-German. Simpson, Kirkconnell, Kysilewskyj, and others were all cited as supporting the idea of a sovereign Ukrainian state in eastern Europe and, by implication, with association with "Fascist" elements. For his part, Simpson was blamed for the suppression of the ULFTA and accused of harbouring Hetmanite sympathies, of having enjoyed "the warm hospitality" of Skoropadsky in Berlin, of later welcoming his son to Saskatoon, and of distorting Ukrainian history in his historical atlas.[45]

Simpson never publicly replied to these allegations. In fact, he was not completely free to do so since he was still connected with the Committee on Cooperation in Canadian Citizenship and, therefore, subject to the general government policy of promoting accord between the feuding Communist and nationalist Ukrainians. Nevertheless, Simpson did react privately and made notes on the errors and distortions that were of direct concern to him. Thus, about the insinuations concerning Hetmanite sympathies and his pre-war trip to Berlin ostensibly to meet Skoropadsky, he commented: "Not true. I went to Berlin for educational purposes not aware that Skoropadsky lived there. Met him incidentally and was invited to afternoon tea. Never at any time discussed political affairs with him." And, concerning his address to the heir apparent, Danylo Skoropadsky, during the latter's Canadian tour of 1937–8, he commented: "Reference is made to allusions to above hospitality but nothing is said regarding the other part of the [welcoming] speech which had to do with our democratic institutions in Canada. My present information is that Danylo is in Great Britain working as a consulting engineer in a British munition factory." Simpson further noted Davies's exaggerations concerning the historical atlas of Ukraine, the fact that he had had no connection whatsoever with the government at the time that the Communist Party of Canada and the ULFTA were suppressed, and that the Communist publication on which Davies had relied for his allegations had already been sued for libel and had been compelled to make retractions. Simpson never did publish these notes and they remained in his private papers after his death.[46]

As the war ended, new issues confronted Simpson and his Ukrainian friends. For example, a new United Nations Organization was being formed to deal with post-war world security and, since the Soviets were occupying all of Ukraine, the Ukrainians in the West wanted to represent their homeland in this body; the UCC asked Simpson how to go about sending a delegation to the upcoming conference in San Francisco. In reply, Simpson advised that the UCC should be cautious and should not claim to represent anybody except a certain segment of Canadian society and that its delegates should stress broad humanitarian principles. "The best one can do," he wrote, "is to assert principles which ultimately will have to be implemented if world security is to be maintained. Against the operation of power politics in its crudest and most cynical form, as directed by dictatorial states must be marshaled public opinion as world-wide in scope as possible." The UCC heeded Simpson's advice, and drew up a memorandum that stressed universal human rights and the necessity for a strong UN security organ that would protect such rights.[47]

Discussions about world peace and human rights were not the only problems the war's end brought to Simpson. The collapse of the Third Reich had left millions of eastern European refugees in the Western Zones of Occupation and in danger of forced repatriation to the Soviet Union. The matter came to Simpson's attention as early as the summer of 1945 when he received a note from his old friend, the historian Dmytro Doroshenko, who was stranded in Augsburg and who wished to move, as he put it, "further west, even across the ocean." "If the Russians lay their hands on Professor Doroshenko," wrote Lazarowich to a UCC leader in Winnipeg, "we will never see him alive again." Simpson, Lazarowich, and others immediately made representations to the minister of immigration and to others in Ottawa, but the bureaucracy would not budge. Like so many other distressed Europeans, Doroshenko was not admissible to Canada under the then-existing regulations.[48] However, Simpson maintained his interest in the refugee question and, in 1946, accepted an invitation to join the New York-based Committee for the Aid of Refugee Ukrainian Scholars.[49] One year later, he responded to a request from Kysilewskyj in Ottawa and brought to Saskatoon from England the young émigré literary scholar George Luckyj, who joined Saskatchewan's Department of English. (Luckyj had done some graduate work on English literature in England during the war and had married an English girl.)[50]

During the post-war years, Simpson continued to interest himself in Ukrainian affairs, which were considerably less stormy than in earlier times. He was active in the newly founded Canadian Association of Slavists and joined the Shevchenko Scientific Society, which was transplanted from Europe by refugee Ukrainian scholars. In 1944, he helped launch the New York-based *Ukrainian Quarterly*, which was edited by Mykola Chubaty, and, in 1951, he contributed a brief essay to the *Slavistica* series published by the newly established Ukrainian Free Academy of Sciences in Winnipeg.[51] Paul Yuzyk found him a "helpful and sympathetic person" and began writing Ukrainian Canadian history under his influence.[52] In the late 1950s, that is, on the eve of Simpson's retirement, the Winnipeg Slavist Jaroslav Rudnyckyj visited Saskatoon and noted the historian's optimism and lively interest in the continued expansion of Slavic Studies, not only in Saskatchewan, but throughout Canada.[53] In 1964, he helped to prepare the brief of the Canadian Association of

Slavists – which argued in favour of the academic cultivation of all languages – to the federal government's Royal Commission on Bilingualism and Biculturalism, and he participated in the early discussions of the novel concept of "multiculturalism," which his former student Paul Yuzyk, whom John Diefenbaker had named to the Senate in 1963, was pioneering. His seeming reluctance to accept fully the new concept, which was apparently based on his fear of disrupting the liberal democratic principle of individual equality before the law, revealed him as a man of the first half of the twentieth century.[54] Simpson's death in 1969 marked the end of an era.

There are several highlights in the history of Simpson's relations with the Prairie Ukrainians. During the 1930s, he pioneered Canadian university studies in Slavic history and was involved in the publication of some of the first English-language scholarly books about Ukraine. In 1939, he explained the Ukrainian case to a curious Canadian radio audience. In 1940, he helped to unite the feuding Ukrainian organizations behind the Canadian war effort and, a year later, was called to head Ottawa's Committee on Cooperation in Canadian Citizenship and do the same for all the country's non-British and non-French minority groups. With the war more than half over, Simpson helped to found the first university-level department of Slavic Studies in Canada. During these same years, moreover, he maintained his close relations with the Ukrainian nationalist leaders and helped to keep them on a steady pro-British course; he endured a certain amount of Communist hostility on account of it. Simpson was active both in public life and in academic life and, in both worlds, proved himself a defender of Canada's Slavs. In his public life, his low-profile approach, patience for the temporary extremism of both right and left, and his general tolerance for a weaker minority were remarkable.

In his academic life, he always remained a firm supporter of Slavic Studies. He was a special friend to the Ukrainians and this was acknowledged in 1947 when the Ukrainian Free University in Munich awarded him an honorary doctor's degree.[55] He was modest, helpful, and never patronizing. In short, George Simpson dared to venture beyond the narrow conventions of English Canadian society of the 1930s and, in doing so, discovered a new world. His country was the better for it.

8 The Post-Secondary Teaching of Ukrainian History in Canada: An Historical Profile

Historia vitae magistra.

During the century and a quarter that have passed since the first Ukrainian settlers arrived in western Canada and inaugurated the formation of what was for a time one of Canada's largest and most high-profile ethnic groups, the sense of history among this cultural minority and the educational institutions that help mould this sense of history have undergone a distinct evolution. This evolution is unique to Canada, and although it has a few characteristics in common with other centres of the Ukrainian emigration, such as that in the United States, it stands in clear contrast to the complex and often tragic situation in the European homeland, which lacks the continuity and sense of progress so evident in the New World.

The history of this evolution must begin with the "pioneer" immigration; that is, the generation of settlers who, before 1914, came to Canada primarily from the provinces of Galicia and Bukovina within the Habsburg Monarchy in eastern Europe. This emigration was overwhelmingly composed of country folk – peasants at most two or three generations removed from serfdom, which had been abolished in 1848 throughout the Austrian Empire. Nevertheless, these hardy settlers from Galicia and Bukovina were not the dregs of society in their eastern European homeland. Rather, it seems, they were predominantly modest landowners and their dependants who left their ancestral homes after the spread of mass literacy across the Galician countryside during the second half of the nineteenth century. Thus, while it cannot be claimed that these immigrants were universally literate, neither can complete accuracy be claimed for the cruel stereotype of the ignorant Galician so common in the English Canadian literature of those days.[1]

Once in the new country, in fact, the former eastern European villagers quickly overcame the initial confusion of life in the New World and began to found religious, social, cultural, and educational institutions to serve their new communities. With regard to educational foundations and academic life, these institutions slowly evolved from *prosvita*, popular education linked to the spread of literacy and knowledge about Ukrainian literature and history, to *nauka*, scientific or scholarly inquiry carried out within the context of clearly recognized institutions of higher learning. As early as 1905, the first Prosvita, or popular enlightenment society, was founded in Winnipeg and, this same year, the first "Ruthenian" bookstore – to use the nomenclature of the day – and a Ruthenian Training School (to prepare teachers for the bilingual English/Ruthenian school system that existed then in Manitoba) were founded.[2] In July 1907, graduates of this school, Canada's first professional Ukrainian schoolteachers, who were the cream of the intelligentsia of the pioneer immigration, held their first convention in Winnipeg and invited a number of prominent Ukrainians in the Old Country to become honorary members of their new organization. The position of honorary president was offered to none other than the distinguished historian and public figure Mykhailo Hrushevsky (1866–1934), who accepted the offer and, in his reply, stressed that he saw the organization of national schools "as the single bastion which will stave off denationalization of the Ukrainian colonies in America."[3] The fact that the first Organization of Ukrainian School Teachers in Canada choose as their honorary president the man who, by 1907, had already become modern Ukraine's foremost historian testifies to the esteem in which Ukrainian history in general, and the person of Mykhailo Hrushevsky in particular, were held by the fledgling Ukrainian intelligentsia of the New Country.

During the following years, small numbers of Ukrainians began to enter western Canadian universities, especially the University of Manitoba, which was located in Winnipeg, where the largest concentration of urban Ukrainian settlers lived. By 1913, the first graduate of Ukrainian origin in Canada, Orest Zherebko, had received his Bachelor of Arts degree from the University of Manitoba, and there was a Ukrainian Students Club in existence at this institution. In the following year, the newly appointed Greek Catholic bishop Nicetas [Nykyta] Budka drew up a memorandum that, among other things, advised the government that it would be in accord with the country's cultural harmony and intellectual betterment to establish what was called at the time higher "Ruthenian" studies at an appropriate Canadian university.[4]

It was not long before others took up the cause of higher Ukrainian education. The Ukrainian schoolteachers were soon in the forefront of the fight. In July 1914, in an article appearing in the Winnipeg newspaper *Ukrainskyi holos*, V. Mihaichuk, a schoolteacher and the secretary of the Organization of Ukrainian School Teachers in Canada, suggested that the Ukrainian language should join German and Icelandic as a subject of instruction at the University of Manitoba; a year later at a convention of Ukrainian schoolteachers, the question was raised again but seems to have come to naught in the atmosphere of war hysteria that then prevailed in Canada.[5]

In fact, war hysteria soon proved to be a major problem for the ethnic minorities from eastern and central Europe who had settled in great numbers throughout the prairies at the turn of the century. All recently arrived immigrants from so-called enemy countries were compelled to register and report regularly to the authorities. Since most of the Ukrainian pioneers had come from the Habsburg Monarchy, with which the British Empire was now at war, they fell into this category and were deemed "enemy aliens." About 7,000 central European labourers and itinerants, principally ethnic Ukrainians, were rounded up and interned in special work camps in Quebec, Ontario, and British Columbia. Popular hostility to the non-British steadily increased and, in 1916, the bilingual educational system was abolished in Manitoba, and Saskatchewan and Alberta took parallel measures. The Ukrainians, of course, fought back. In Manitoba, J. W. Arsenych and a delegation urging retention of the bilingual school system took the idea of a "chair" or department of Ukrainian studies to the Manitoba provincial legislature. However, English Canadian resistance to this idea remained solid.[6]

The closure of the bilingual public educational system forced Ukrainian educators and cultural activists to reorganize. Their tactic was to found private student residences or *bursy*, which were also meant to be institutions for the promotion of the national culture. Such residences were founded in Winnipeg, Saskatoon, and Edmonton, and, to a certain extent, succeeded in preserving the ideal of higher Ukrainian education.[7] Moreover, during the early 1920s, men such as the itinerant schoolteacher Oleksander Gregorovich (1893–1970) travelled the prairies, popularizing the work and selling copies of the books of Hrushevsky and other important Ukrainian authors. In fact, by 1924, Canadian Ukrainians were successful in putting out their own edition of Hrushevsky's

Iliustovanna istoriia Ukrainy (Illustrated history of Ukraine) in a run of several thousand copies. Given the general atmosphere of antagonism towards things Ukrainian, however, university scholarship on Ukrainian subjects, as indeed all Slavic subjects, remained very rare.[8]

Towards the end of the 1920s, the atmosphere improved somewhat. A few curious "English" Canadian scholars were attracted to eastern Europe and its cultures. The young Canadian polyglot Watson Kirkconnell, who was of Scottish ancestry, briefly turned his attention to Polish literature, while the University of Saskatchewan historian George Simpson began to interest himself in Ukrainian history and politics. Among Ukrainian activists, moreover, especially some leading members of the *Soiuz ukraintsiv samostiinykiv* (Ukrainian Self-Reliance League), which largely concentrated its efforts around the *bursy* and the Ukrainian Greek Orthodox Church of Canada, the idea of university studies of Ukrainian history, literature, and language was taken very seriously and a plan was worked out for the compilation of university-level textbooks – grammars and histories – that might be used in prospective university courses. The Edmonton lawyer Peter Lazarowich (1900–1983) and Saskatoon lawyer Julian Stechishin (1895–1971) were especially active in this regard.[9] By 1931, Andrei Hospodyn of the Winnipeg Prosvita Society was once again raising the question of a Ukrainian-language department at the University of Manitoba and, by 1935, Simpson was successful in introducing an elementary course on the history of the Slavic peoples at the University of Saskatchewan. "This was," as the historian later wrote, "the first such course given in any university in Canada."[10]

Towards the end of the 1930s, Lazarowich, Stechishin, and their colleagues intensified their efforts at preparing the ground for university-level studies in Ukrainian affairs. Lazarowich, who had studied both in Canada and in Czechoslovakia, initiated a Canadian tour for the distinguished Ukrainian émigré historian Dmytro Doroshenko, who, during the summer of 1937, lectured on the history of Ukraine at Alberta College in Edmonton and gave public lectures in several major western Canadian cities. The tour was so popular that Doroshenko returned the next summer to lecture on the history of Ukrainian literature.[11] By 1938, the Lazarowich group had arranged to bring out an abridged English translation of Doroshenko's masterful *Survey of Ukrainian History* (*Narys istorii Ukrainy*) and Simpson was busy putting the final touches to the work. The publication of this book the following year meant that an English-language textbook was now available for the use of university students in North America.[12]

While the European political crisis of 1938–39 gripped the attention of the world, Lazarowich and his colleagues lobbied the administration of the University of Alberta for the introduction of a course on Slavic or Ukrainian history. This was expected to parallel the similar course already taught at the University of Saskatchewan. Lazarowich even suggested a suitable instructor, Vladimir Kysilewskyj (1896–1976), a graduate of the East European Institute of the University of Vienna and of the School of Slavonic Studies of the University of London. While in London, Kysilewskyj had also run a non-party Ukrainian Information Bureau to lobby the British government and inform the British press on the Ukrainian question. But Lazarowich's appeals fell on deaf ears. "The prospect of inaugurating a course in Ukrainian history in the summer session of the University of Alberta next year," Lazarowich informed Simpson in March 1938, "has now entirely disappeared."[13] The expansion of university-level Slavic Studies on the Canadian prairies would have to wait. Meanwhile, Europe lumbered steadily into the Second World War.

The outbreak of war in September 1939 raised the profile of the Slavic world among English and French Canadians and, in particular, increased the prestige of the Polish nation, which was now an ally of the British Empire, but it produced no new developments in Canadian Slavic Studies. This paralleled the situation in the United States, where a similar lethargy prevailed.[14]

As the war went on, the situation changed somewhat. In 1940, an Anglo Irish scholar named W. E. D. Allen published a general history of Ukraine, which, while not particularly sympathetic to Ukrainian nationalism, did give a moving synthesis of the history of the country. The following year, partly as a reaction to Allen's work, a group of Ukrainians in the United States put out an English translation of Hrushevsky's popular *Illustrated History of Ukraine*. Both these books would become valuable resources for future university-level students of Ukrainian history.[15]

However, the real breakthrough came in language studies. In 1941, for the first time in any Canadian university, a non-credit course in elementary Ukrainian was offered at the University of Saskatchewan by Dr. Thomas (Tymish) K. Pavlychenko (1892–1958), a participant in the Ukrainian revolution of 1917 and an agronomist by training.[16] In fact, 1941 was a turning point in the history of Slavic Studies in North America. The German surprise attack on the Soviet Union had suddenly turned that country into an ally of the Western democracies, and the prestige of Russian studies, in particular, had never before been so high. In the

United States, the Association of American Teachers of Slavic and East European Languages was organized (1941), while, in Canada, the study of Russian began to seriously increase. By 1943–4, eight Canadian universities were offering courses in elementary Russian and had some four hundred students among them.[17] By 1945, moreover, at the instigation of George Simpson, the first full-fledged Department of Slavic Studies in Canada was founded at the University of Saskatchewan, and C. H. Andrusyshen, a native Winnipeg Ukrainian who had a long-standing interest in the Slavic literatures and who held a doctorate in the Romance languages from the University of Toronto and an MA in Slavics from Harvard, was chosen to head the department.[18] Thereafter, departments of Slavic Studies were founded at the University of British Columbia (1946), where W. J. Rose began teaching, the University of Toronto (1949), and the University of Manitoba (1949).

The conclusion of the war in Europe inaugurated still another phase in the annals of Slavonic Studies and Slavic history in Canada. Canadian veterans of Slavic Studies, such as Simpson, and their Ukrainian scholarly friends, such as Andrusyshen and Kysilewskyj, were joined by a host of émigré scholars fleeing the westward march of the Soviet Army and the destruction caused by the war in western Europe. These scholars helped to staff the new departments of Slavic Studies that were being formed during the post-war years. For example, the philologist J. B. Rudnyckyj quickly made the University of Manitoba a major centre of Ukrainian studies in North America, while the literary scholar George Luckyj pioneered Ukrainian studies at the University of Toronto. Both these men chaired their respective university departments for many long years.[19]

However, for those who were interested in Ukrainian history, as opposed to language and literature, the situation was less fortunate. Students of Ukrainian history either had to content themselves with general "civilization" courses offered by various Slavic Studies departments or to find a place somewhere in the new Russian history courses that had come into existence during the years of the Cold War. The latter were often taught by scholars unfriendly to various Ukrainian views, or, at best, indifferent to them. The only other option for those interested in Ukrainian history was to flee the universities altogether and associate themselves with the new émigré institutions that had sprung up during the post-war years and sponsored research, lectures, and publications of various sorts. In Canada, the most active institution of this type was the *Ukrainska vilna akademiia nauk* (Ukrainian Free Academy of Sciences, or

UVAN), transferred from Germany to Winnipeg under the presidency of Dmytro Doroshenko, who had briefly returned to Canada after the conclusion of the war.

Throughout the 1950s, 1960s, and 1970s, UVAN scholars undertook a number of important historical projects. Dmytro Doroshenko himself briefly turned his attention to Ukrainian Canadian history and edited a handsome and bulky volume on the *Ukrainskyi narodnyi dim* (Ukrainian national home) in Winnipeg; J. B. Rudnyckyj gathered folk and bibliographic materials and edited a series of pamphlets on the history of Ukrainian scholarship in general and the history of Slavic Studies in Canada in particular; and Mykhailo Marunchak published several important volumes on Ukrainian Canadian history. However, the very brief stay of Doroshenko in Canada was not sufficient to put Ukrainian historical studies on a solid base in this country and the history of Ukraine long remained a weak point in UVAN publication ventures.[20]

This did not mean that Ukrainian historians working in Canada were without forums in which to lecture or organs in which to publish. Canadian-based scholars could present papers at various conferences of historians or Slavists, and they could publish in the general English-language journals or in émigré organs such as the proceedings of the Shevchenko Scientific Society (*Zapysky NTSh*) or the journal of the Ukrainian Historical Association (*Ukrainskyi istoryk*). During the early post-war years, moreover, the Ukrainian Free University in Munich served an important function in providing programs and degrees for European scholars whose work had been interrupted by the war.[21]

Although the work of these émigré institutions remained important, it could not replace regular credit courses offered at higher Canadian or American educational institutions. For many years, this lacuna was seriously felt. However, in the late 1960s and early 1970s, the establishment of Ukrainian studies and an endowed professorship in Ukrainian history at Harvard University in the United States raised the profile and prestige of the discipline and had a positive effect on the attitude towards Ukrainian history in Canada.[22] The University of Alberta led the way and, in 1971, initiated regular university instruction in the history of Ukraine. It managed to attract the services of Ivan Lysiak-Rudnytsky, an historian of political thought, who had a talent for explaining in English the central questions of Ukrainian history and politics and for putting these questions within the context of North American conceptualization and academic life.[23] Meanwhile, in 1973, Saint Andrew's College, an Orthodox institution soon to be affiliated with the University of Manitoba, also initiated a course on the history of Ukraine. The University of Manitoba course was pioneered by Oleh Gerus, a Ukrainian political historian who edited and brought out a new edition of Doroshenko's history under the title *A Survey of Ukrainian History*. For many years, this book remained the standard text on the subject.[24] During this same period, another Ukrainian historian, the Rev Oleksander Baran, began teaching a general course on eastern European history at the University of Manitoba. This course had been pioneered some years before by Paul Yuzyk (later appointed to the Senate of Canada by Prime Minister John G. Diefenbaker), who injected into it a considerable amount of Ukrainian content.[25]

Although the history of Ukraine was taught at Canadian universities in the 1970s, Ukrainian historians working in Canada as yet had no research centre affiliated with a Canadian university that could sponsor lectures, organize conferences, and initiate scholarly publications. This breakthrough came only in 1975 with the establishment of the Canadian Institute of Ukrainian Studies at the University of Alberta. The determined political leadership of Albertan Ukrainians not only succeeded in establishing this institute with full university affiliation, but also secured ongoing government funding so that scholarship centred there would not be solely dependent on the consistent generosity of Ukrainian benefactors. The institute immediately initiated a wide-ranging publication program, which included a scholarly journal published twice a year and a monograph series.[26] Works on Ukrainian history appeared in both formats but, whereas the monograph series tended to promote the works of established Ukrainian historians such as Ivan Rudnytsky, the institute's periodical, the *Journal of Ukrainian Studies*, featured the work of younger scholars such as Stephen Velychenko, John-Paul Himka, and Thomas M. Prymak. From its very first years (1976ff.), the *Journal of Ukrainian Studies* tended to attract Ukrainian historians who were primarily concerned with the modern period.

In spite of the immediate success of the Canadian Institute of Ukrainian Studies, the history of Ukraine continued to be taught at very few institutions. As late as 1978, Bohdan Krawchenko, the assistant director of the Canadian Institute of Ukrainian Studies, complained that

> were it not for two institutions, the University of Alberta and Saint Andrew's College of the University of Manitoba, the history and social science study of the Ukraine and of Ukrainians in Canada would be totally unrepresented in Canada. The history of the Ukraine is taught with four courses at Alberta

and two at Saint Andrew's College. Not a single course in Ukrainian history
is offered east of the Prairie Provinces.[27]

Ukrainians in eastern Canada, who, unlike the Prairie Ukrainians, were
mostly of post-war DP background, were acutely aware of this deficiency
and immediately organized to resolve the question.

The effort was centred at Canada's most prestigious university, the
University of Toronto, which holds a position in Canadian society similar
to that of Harvard in the United States. By 1980, studies in Ukrainian
language and literature offered by the Department of Slavic Languages
and Literatures were supplemented by courses in Ukrainian history and
politics offered by a newly created Chair of Ukrainian Studies, which was
located in the departments of history and political economy. The instructor was Paul Robert Magocsi (b. 1945), an historian from New Jersey,
who specialized in the history of Sub-Carpathian Rus'. Magocsi taught
courses, initiated a series of lectures on Ukrainian history, and, for a
time, established a regular seminar series on Ukrainian studies in general. Though the Chair of Ukrainian Studies established no publication
program of its own, during its first years, it did support or attract younger
Ukrainian historians such as Stephen Velychenko, Lubomyr Luciuk,
Stella Hryniuk, and Thomas M. Prymak, and offered them a forum in
which to exhibit their work.[28] The establishment of the Chair of Ukrainian
Studies at the University of Toronto once again raised the profile of
Ukrainian history at Canadian universities and acted as a precedent for
other institutions.

It was not long before other universities also introduced courses in the
history of Ukraine. Shortly after the establishment of the University of
Toronto chair, York University, also located in Toronto, initiated a course
of the history of Ukraine, as well as a new course on eastern Europe, and
appointed another American, Orest Subtelny (b. 1943), a specialist on
Mazepa and the Cossack period, to teach them. Within a few years,
Subtelny distinguished himself by publishing a new general history of
Ukraine with ample bibliographies in English, which could well serve
as a replacement for Gerus's edition of Doroshenko as a textbook in
university-level courses.[29] Meanwhile, the Department of History at the
University of Saskatchewan also briefly introduced a course on the history of Ukraine and brought in Thomas Prymak from Toronto to teach
it. But the course was taught for only one year and there was no attempt
to set up a chair or permanent professorship in Ukrainian history in
Saskatchewan.[30] At the University of Alberta, however, the death of Ivan

Rudnytsky in 1984 did not end studies in Ukrainian history at that institution, and still another scholar of American background, John-Paul Himka (b. 1949), a specialist on nineteenth-century Galicia, was appointed to succeed him. In 1990–1, the centenary of Ukrainian settlement in Canada, the history of Ukraine was offered by Alberta, Manitoba, Toronto, and York universities.

While the 1980s saw a definite expansion in university-level teaching of Ukrainian history in Canada, the end of the decade also saw new developments in the area of pure research. Most significant was the foundation of the Peter Jacyk Centre for Ukrainian Historical Research at the University of Alberta. In 1989, Frank Sysyn, an American specialist on seventeenth-century Ukraine, was appointed its first director. This new centre, designed as a companion institution to the Canadian Institute of Ukrainian Studies, immediately set forth a number of priorities. First among these was the updating and translation into English of Hrushevsky's monumental *History of Ukraine-Rus'*. This project, which had been started but later abandoned by the Shevchenko Scientific Society in the United States – with the cooperation of a number of Canadian scholars including Paul Yuzyk of the University of Ottawa and C. A. Andrusyshen of the University of Saskatchewan, who translated the first volume – was begun anew and prominent Ukrainian historians in Europe were chosen to edit and introduce the various volumes. By early 1990, the project was well underway and the first volume was published in 1997. Several other volumes (on the Cossack period) followed thereafter. The centre also initiated a monograph series in Ukrainian history that envisaged a number of English translations from various European languages.[31] The ambitious program of this well-endowed Centre for Ukrainian Historical Research thus adequately augmented the steady expansion of university-level teaching of Ukrainian history in Canada, and, on the eve of the centenary of Ukrainian settlement in Canada, the teaching and research of Ukrainian history was acknowledged as a specialized discipline in its own right. Since that time, steady progress has been made and numerous books in Ukrainian history published in Canada, and, although no new courses in Ukrainian history were offered in other universities, expansion in related areas such as political studies, Ukrainian Canadian studies, eastern Christian studies, and Ukrainian folklore has taken place.[32] In addition to this, an important new text by Paul Robert Magocsi appeared. His *History of Ukraine* approached the subject with a territorial, non-ethnic, method that took account of all major ethnic groups living on the territory of the Ukrainian state that gained its independence in 1991. This contrasted to

Subtelny's approach, which emphasized the Ukrainian element and the Ukrainian national movement in modern times.[33]

In general, the study of Ukrainian history at Canadian institutions of higher education can be seen as having gone through a definite evolution. This evolution took place in three distinct stages. First, there was the pioneer and interwar period, during which Ukrainian history, as indeed all Slavic history, was generally ignored at Canadian universities. In its early phase, this stage was marked by a struggle on the part of the original Ukrainian settlers for recognition and understanding among educators and academics. Unfortunately, the petitions of Bishop Budka, Arsenych, and others were ignored and the bilingual school system itself was abolished. In its later phase, this stage was distinguished by noble attempts by Simpson, Lazarowich, and others to introduce Ukrainian, or, at least, Slavic, history into the university curriculum of various western Canadian institutions. These attempts were partly successful; a few courses were introduced and a major history textbook published. Second, there was the post-war period, during which departments of Slavic Studies were opened at many Canadian universities and during which Ukrainian studies in language and literature flourished. During this post-war period, however, Ukrainian historians found no places in Canadian universities and students of Ukrainian history had to content themselves with studying Russian history or becoming involved in émigré-style institutions and their publications. The foremost institution of this type in Canada was the Ukrainian Free Academy of Sciences in Winnipeg. Third came the period of fully fledged university study of Ukrainian history. This began in the 1970s with the appointment of Ivan Rudnytsky at the University of Alberta and expanded with the creation of the Edmonton Institute and the foundation of the University of Toronto Chair. Thus, from Budka's first suggestion of a Ukrainian chair in 1914 to the flourishing of Ukrainian history under the auspices of imported scholars of American origin during the 1980s and 1990s, the study of Ukrainian history in Canada has undergone an evolution. It is an evolution marked by continuity and a justified feeling of progress.

9 Ukrainian Scholarship in the West during the "Long Cold War"

I hope to disarm some critics who think it is the highest religion to know nothing of good learning.

Erasmus

The "Long Cold War" between the Soviet Union and the democratic West, which began with the defeat of Nazi Germany in 1945 and ended with the collapse of the USSR in 1991, was fought on many levels: diplomatic, scientific, technological, economic, journalistic, literary, and scholarly. It is with the last of these, the scholarly level, that we are concerned here.

By scholarship (*nauka* in Ukrainian) is usually meant the pursuit of knowledge by means of generally recognized academic disciplines such as history, sociology, language and literature, or political science, within clearly established institutions of higher learning. In central and eastern Europe, various research-oriented academies of sciences supported by government are very important, but in North America, these institutions are generally universities where both research and teaching are carried out, although scholarly societies also play a role.

When the Cold War broke out between the former wartime allies, the USSR and the West, there was very little scholarly research or published material available in the Western countries about Ukraine and Ukrainians. In Soviet Ukraine, independent scholarship had been crushed during the Stalin purges of the 1930s and, with the wartime Soviet annexation of western Ukraine (formerly under Poland, Czechoslovakia, and Romania), independent scholarship in these areas, too, was abruptly curtailed. All the interwar centres of Ukrainian émigré scholarship in central Europe (such as Prague in Czechoslovakia) were in countries now under Soviet occupation, and none of the victorious Western states had any tradition of contact with Ukraine with which to replace them. Moreover, the Ukrainian immigrant communities of North America, which did have a tradition of contact with the Old Country, were overwhelmingly made up of simple workers and farmers, and although individuals within these communities were working hard to gain professional status as medical doctors, lawyers, and teachers, there were still very few true scholars among them. The general situation of Ukrainian scholarship was, thus, very difficult.

Pioneers of Ukrainian Studies in the West

However, the situation of Ukrainian studies was not entirely without hope. Even before the war had ended, in the United States, an historian from western Ukraine, Mykola Chubaty (1889–1975), who had unexpectedly been caught in the West prior to the outbreak of hostilities, launched a journal devoted to Ukrainian affairs titled *The Ukrainian Quarterly*, while, in Canada, the country's first Department of Slavic Studies was founded at the University of Saskatchewan, where the Ukrainian literary scholar and lexicographer Constantine Andrusyshen (1907–1983) held a professorship. Meanwhile, at Columbia University in New York City, the American Slavist Clarence Manning (1893–1972) was already interesting himself in Ukrainian affairs and would produce a whole series of books popularizing Ukrainian history and literature. Moreover, a significant number of accomplished Ukrainian scholars and intellectuals had fled the westward march of the Red Army and were now temporarily resident in various cities and towns in southern Germany, where they immediately began reorganizing themselves.

Interwar Émigrés

During the first years after 1945, the old interwar Ukrainian émigrés continued to be most active. Two of the most important among these were the historians Dmytro Doroshenko (1882–1951) and Ilko Borshchak (1892–1959). Doroshenko, a conservative figure who had worked in Germany, Czechoslovakia, and Poland between the wars, moved to Canada in 1947, where he continued to publish on Ukrainian history. (His *History of the Ukraine* had been published in English in Edmonton as early as 1939.) Borshchak, who was more liberal than Doroshenko, continued to live in France, where he had first immigrated from Ukraine in 1919, and, after 1945, he continued to publish widely in both Ukrainian and French on Ukrainian history, language, and bibliography. In the late 1940s and the early 1950s, he edited an influential monthly journal titled *Ukraina* (Ukraine), which specialized in materials dealing with French Ukrainian relations, although it contained a great deal of material on Ukrainian culture in general.

The DP Emigration

It was, however, with the new émigrés displaced by the Second World War (hence, generally referred to as Displaced Persons, or DPs) that the future lay. These DP scholars had fled to the West with very few possessions, but, occasionally, when it was possible, brought with them papers, documents, manuscripts, or books that they hoped to preserve in emigration. Southern Germany, especially Augsburg and Munich, where many of the DPs lived, soon became active centres of Ukrainian "émigré" scholarship.

The Ukrainian Free Academy of Sciences

The first post-war Ukrainian émigré scholarly society to be founded was the Ukrainian Free Academy of Sciences, later known as the Ukrainian Academy of Arts and Sciences, but usually referred to in common parlance as the UVAN, which was the Ukrainian acronym of the original name (*Ukrainska Vilna Akademiia Nauk*). In November 1945, in Augsburg, some 150 refugee scholars and scientists organized the academy and elected the veteran émigré historian Dmytro Doroshenko as its first president. Early UVAN activities, which included the publication of some new research undertaken before and during the war, were carried out under the difficult conditions of life in refugee camps with the typical shortage of financial and material resources.

During the late 1940s and the early 1950s, when it looked as if war was again about to engulf Europe, most of the Ukrainian DPs, including the scholars, chose to emigrate from devastated Germany and seek their fortunes in the United States, Canada, Australia, or various countries of South America.

In 1949, the UVAN presidium was reconstituted in Winnipeg, in western Canada, where Dmytro Doroshenko and several other UVAN members had resettled. Doroshenko was succeeded as president by the literary scholar Leonid Biletsky (1882–1955) and then by the philologist Jaroslav Rudnyckyj (1910–1997). Throughout the 1950s and 1960s, Winnipeg emerged as a major centre of Ukrainian émigré scholarship, and several important accomplishments by UVAN scholars can be noted: Biletsky's four-volume edition of the poet Taras Shevchenko's collected works or *Kobzar*, which included some very profuse annotation; and Rudnyckyj's etymological dictionary of the Ukrainian language, his studies of Ukrainian Canadian folklore, and his numerous studies of Ukrainian geographical and other names. Somewhat later, Mykhailo Marunchak's prolific studies of Ukrainian Canadian history began to appear, as did various works by Cossack and ecclesiastical historian Oleksander Baran, literary scholar Jaroslav Rozumnyj, and modern Ukrainian historian Oleh Gerus, who, in 1975, published a revised edition of Doroshenko's history for the use of Canadian and American university students.

Not all or even most UVAN scholars relocated to Winnipeg. In 1950, an independent organization, the Ukrainian Academy of Arts and Sciences in the US, was founded in New York. The group of scholars associated with UVAN in the United States included Mykhailo Vetukhiv (who was president from 1950 to 1959), the philologist George Shevelov (1908–2002), the historian Oleksander Ohloblyn (1899–1992), the archivist Volodymyr Miiakovsky (1888–1972), and many others. The American UVAN's most singular accomplishment throughout the years of the Cold War was undoubtedly the publication of the English-language periodical *The Annals of the Ukrainian Academy of Arts and Sciences in the US*. In contrast to many other Ukrainian journals and magazines, including *The Ukrainian Quarterly*, which took actual engagement in the Cold War to be part of their reason for existing, the editors of the *Annals*, which had been founded with the help of the distinguished Columbia University Slavist Philip S. Mosley, strove to remain aloof from active politics and to maintain a dispassionate academic tone. The high standards of scholarship that were maintained and the general respect that the *Annals* soon acquired in the wider non-Ukrainian world are testimony to the success of this policy. Moreover, the very fact that the *Annals* were published in English ensured that they reached a fairly wide public. They were well edited by the young George Luckyj and his English wife Moira, and this, in particular, helped to improve their appearance before an American public that was still unacquainted with the axioms of Ukrainian scholarship. Over the years of the Cold War, UVAN in the US also published in the Ukrainian language several volumes of memoirs and studies dealing

with Ukrainian history and literature, especially concentrating on eastern Ukraine under the Russians. By the end of the Cold War, the UVAN
archives in New York City were one of the main repositories of scholarly
Ucrainica in the Western world.

The Shevchenko Scientific Society

While UVAN in the United States especially attracted émigré scholars
from eastern Ukraine, those from western Ukraine, especially the distinguished geographer Volodymyr Kubiiovych (1900–1985), believed that
the re-establishment of the former Shevchenko Scientific Society, which
had been based in western Ukraine under Poland before 1939, was also
necessary. Numerous members of the society had fled west with the approach of the Red Army and were living in Germany at the war's end.
Thus, in June 1947, the Shevchenko Scientific Society was revived in
Munich and, by 1953, had 126 full members and 226 regular members.
With the dispersion of Ukrainian scholars further westward, new chapters were established in the United States (1947), Canada (1949), and
Australia (1950). In Europe in 1951, the society's executive centre, library, and archives were transferred to Sarcelles near Paris, where members of the hierarchy of the Ukrainian Greek Catholic Church friendly to
the society had obtained facilities. Professor Kubiiovych, who was now
the central figure in the European society, moved to Sarcelles. Meanwhile,
in 1952, the American chapter purchased a building in New York and
established a library and archives there. This library grew steadily and, in
the early 1980s, moved to newer and more spacious facilities. After the
Cold War ended, the catalogue of the society's rich library collection was
computerized and put on-line. Today, it is readily available to researchers
throughout the world.

   During its very first years in Germany, the Shevchenko Scientific
Society concentrated its efforts on publishing a general encyclopedia of
knowledge about Ukraine. Under the direction of Professor Kubiiovych,
this *Entsyklopediia ukrainoznavstva*, as it was titled in Ukrainian, made
steady progress and its first volumes began to appear in the late 1940s.
The encyclopedia, which Kubiiovych strove to make as non-political and
objective as possible, remained the major project of the European society throughout the Long Cold War. At the same time, however, the New
York branch began publishing a wide variety of Ukrainian materials in its
serial entitled the *Zapysky* (Memoirs) of the society. History, literature,
and language were all given space. Moreover, the American Shevchenko

Scientific Society also excelled in publishing special memorial volumes devoted to individual regions and towns in western Ukraine. These volumes often contained valuable information on the social and economic condition of the western Ukrainian lands on the eve of World War II. Most of the society's publications appeared in the Ukrainian language.

The Ukrainian Free University

The one major Ukrainian émigré scholarly institution that remained in Germany after the initial period of the Cold War was the Ukrainian Free University, which had been transferred from Soviet-occupied Prague to American-occupied Munich in 1945. During the early years of the Cold War, the Ukrainian Free University was important in granting academic degrees to émigré scholars whose education and work had been disrupted by the war. It was less active in publishing but did put out a yearbook in German devoted to Ukrainian studies and a series of *Zapysky* and other occasional volumes in the Ukrainian language. By the 1960s and 1970s, the children of the DP emigration provided the bulk of the students of the Ukrainian Free University. A great many of these students travelled from Canada and the United States to take up their studies in Munich. The historian Nataliia Polonska-Vasylenko (1884–1973) was one of the most prominent scholars active at this institution. The Ukrainian Free University flourished especially during the 1950s and 1960s.

During the 1970s and 1980s, however, the emphasis in Ukrainian scholarship shifted from independent émigré-style institutions to institutes affiliated more closely with general public institutions such as publicly funded universities. The 1960s and 1970s saw a significant number of Ukrainian émigré scholars obtain positions in North American universities, and it was in Canada and the United States that a new type of research centre, established within the university context, evolved.

Harvard and Alberta

Two institutions best represent this trend: the Harvard Ukrainian Research Institute (HURI), which was established in 1973, and the Canadian Institute of Ukrainian Studies (CIUS), which was founded in 1975. Because of their close integration into their respective host institutions, Harvard University and the University of Alberta, where studies of Ukrainian language, literature, and history were already being carried out in several departments, neither of these could be labelled an "émi-gré" institution.

Both HURI in Cambridge in the Boston area and CIUS in Edmonton, Alberta, in western Canada, sponsored research and seminars in Ukrainian studies and established full-scale publishing programs including scholarly journals published in English. These journals, the Cambridge-based *Harvard Ukrainian Studies* and the Toronto-based *Journal of Ukrainian Studies*, marked a major shift in Ukrainian studies in the West, which now was carried on primarily in the English language for an English-speaking public. But, whereas HURI scholars and publications, under the influence of founding members such as the orientalist/medievalist Omeljan Pritsak (1919–2006) and the Byzantinist Ihor Shevchenko (1922–2009), tended to emphasize older periods of Ukrainian history and literature, CIUS scholars such as historian Ivan Lysiak-Rudnytsky (1919–1984) and literary scholar George Luckyj (1919–2001) were more interested in modern and contemporary developments. Thus, HURI publications tended to emphasize Kievan Rus' and Cossack Ukraine, whereas CIUS publications stressed nineteenth- and twentieth-century themes. Both HURI and CIUS flourished during the 1980s and, thus, were in a good position to re-establish contact with Ukraine when, in the late 1980s, the Gorbachev reforms in the USSR began to put an end to the Long Cold War.

Other Important Institutions

Of course, the above-mentioned societies and research institutes had no monopoly on the sponsorship of Ukrainian scholarship, and other organizations also existed. For example, from 1954, the Association of Ukrainians in Great Britain began publishing *The Ukrainian Review*, which focused on the national question in Ukraine and in the USSR generally. But *The Ukrainian Review* tended to be overtly political and supported the extremely radical Bandera wing of the Organization of Ukrainian Nationalists. Meanwhile, in the mid-1960s, Ukrainian émigré historians and history enthusiasts established the Ukrainian Historical Association and sponsored a specialist journal titled *Ukrainskyi istoryk* (The Ukrainian historian). Edited by the noted professor of library science at Kent State University, Lubomyr Wynar (b. 1932), this primarily Ukrainian-language journal appeared annually and sometimes twice a year throughout the later 1960s, the 1970s, and the 1980s, and even survived the Cold War to appear throughout the 1990s and into the new century. Wynar strove to keep the journal non-political, but the trend within the Ukrinian Historical Association (at least in its interpretation of twentieth-century events) was toward the Melnyk faction of the Organization of Ukrainian Nationalists, which was the rival of the Bandera wing.

Other institutions such as Saint Clement Ukrainian Catholic University and the religious orders in Rome had their own specialized publication programs. During this period, many important Ukraine-related documents from the Vatican archives were published. Even the Ukrainian Orthodox Church of Canada sponsored a journal, which managed to come out from time to time. The Lypynsky East European Institute in Philadelphia sponsored a number of Ukrainian-language volumes dealing with the conservative Ukrainian political thinker Viacheslav Lypynsky, while the Research Centre of Volyn in Winnipeg sponsored several books and studies on the large and important Ukrainian province of Volhynia. (Metropolitan Ilarion of the Ukrainian Orthodox Church of Canada, whose original name was Ivan Ohienko [1882–1972], and who was a prolific expert in church history, literature, and language, was a major figure in this Research Centre of Volyn.) In 1980, a Chair of Ukrainian Studies was established at the University of Toronto in Canada. This chair, held by the Transcarpathian specialist Paul Robert Magocsi (b. 1945), never grew to become a European-style "chair" or department with lecturers and assistants and a publication program of its own, but remained more or less a regular North American professorship. Magocsi was, nevertheless, a very productive scholar and the establishment of the chair did reflect the shift from the independent émigré scholarship of the 1940s, 1950s, and 1960s to the university-centred scholarship of the 1970s and 1980s. Magocsi's bibliographical guide *Galicia* (1983) and his *Historical Atlas of Ukraine* (1985) both appeared during the last period of the Cold War, on the very eve of the Gorbachev reforms.

Outstanding Scholars

Several important Ukrainian scholars especially stood out during the years of the Cold War. Only the greatest of these scholars can be mentioned here. First, there was the philosopher Dmytro Chyzhevsky (1894–1977), who taught in Heidelberg and elsewhere in Germany after the war but also spent some time at Harvard in the United States. His many studies of the Slavic literatures and philosophy made him one of the most important Slavists in the Western world. His monumental *History of*

Ukrainian Literature first appeared in Ukrainian in the 1950s but was translated into English and republished in the 1970s and again in an updated version in the late 1990s. (Both of these translation projects were organized and carried out under the supervision of George Luckyj of the University of Toronto.) Like Doroshenko and Borshchak, Chyzhevsky had begun his career during the interwar period, but, unlike them, reached full flower during the 1950s and 1960s.

Other important names among Ukrainian émigré scholars of the Cold War include the historians Oleksander Ohloblyn, whose many Ukrainian-language studies of the eighteenth and early nineteenth centuries inspired a whole generation of younger colleagues; Nataliia Polonska-Vasylenko, who authored valuable memoirs and a two-volume synthesis of Ukrainian history; George Shevelov of Columbia University in New York, whose *Historical Phonology of the Ukrainian Language* (1979) stands as a monument of Ukrainian émigré philology; George Luckyj of the University of Toronto, whose many books on Ukrainian literary history were published mainly in English and, thus, reached a wide public; and Volodymyr Kubiiovych, who began his career as a geographer in western Ukraine under the Poles but concluded it in France as chief editor of the monumental *Entsyklopediia ukrainoznavstva*. Kubiiovych's work on the encyclopedia, which eventually reached ten volumes, spanned the entire period of the Cold War and was completed by others only in the 1990s after this conflict had ended. Also in connection with encyclopedia work, the name of Yevhen Onatsky (1894–1979) should be mentioned. Onatsky, like Kubiiovych, was a DP who fled to the West in 1945, but, unlike most Ukrainian scholars, went to South America rather than to the United States or Canada. In Argentina, he single-handedly compiled an impressive *Ukrainska mala entsyklopediia* (Shorter Ukrainian encyclopedia) in four volumes. This work did not compete with that of Kubiiovych and his collaborators but, rather, was overtly ideological and political. It was, however, fairly comprehensive and, as the work of a single individual, was remarkable for its time.

Major Themes of Ukrainian Émigré Scholarship

In the works of the above-named scholars and other contributors to Ukrainian scholarship in the West, a number of themes come to the fore. First, in a world where Ukraine was denied an independent existence and the Russian-dominated scholarship of the USSR constantly downplayed or denied the differences between Ukrainians and Russians,

Ukrainian scholars in the West considered it their task to clearly state the very existence of a separate Ukrainian nation with its own language, literature, and history. They also stressed the continuity of Ukrainian culture over the centuries to modern times. Thus, Ohloblyn's historical studies stressed the patriotism and strivings for independence, or at least autonomy, of the Ukrainian elite of the eighteenth and early nineteenth centuries; Shevelov's phonology demonstrated the continuity of an independent Ukrainian language from Kievan Rus' to modern Ukraine; George Luckyj's literary studies focused on the national awakening of the nineteenth century and the experimental period of the 1920s when Ukrainian writers strove most vigorously to create an independent Ukrainian literature; and Kubiiovych's geographical studies tried to clearly delineate the extent of Ukrainian ethnographic territory and describe demographic changes within this territory in the twentieth century. Kubiiovych's work as an encyclopedist was directed at collecting and preserving knowledge about Ukraine in one great reference work that could not be suppressed by the Soviets but, rather, was freely available to interested readers throughout the Western world.

Major Achievements

The major achievements of Ukrainian scholarship in the West can be inferred from the discussion above. First, of course, must come Kubiiovych's encyclopedia, to which literally hundreds of Ukrainian émigré scholars contributed. Then comes Chyzhevsky's *History of Ukrainian Literature,* Shevelov's *Historical Phonology,* Luckyj's literary studies, and, perhaps, Constantine Andrusyshen's *Ukrainian-English Dictionary* (1955), which is today still a basic handbook for almost every scholar in the English-speaking world working on Ukrainian studies, and Orest Subtelny's *Ukraine: A History* (1988), which was published as the Cold War was ending and which was quickly translated into Ukrainian and reprinted in Kyiv to influence public opinion in Ukraine itself. Shortly later, Paul Robert Magocsi also penned an impressive *History of Ukraine,* but it appeared only in 1996, after the Cold War had already ended.

The Problem of Objectivity during the Cold War

Denounced in Soviet propaganda and unrelentingly criticized by Soviet scholars, publicists, and their sympathizers in the West, Ukrainian émigré scholars (as, indeed, almost anyone then engaged in Ukrainian studies) were often viewed with suspicion by the general academic world as promoting a special political agenda. While Russian specialists, especially Western scholars of Russia, whose work was widely distributed, were more easily seen as "objective" and their works as legitimate, Ukrainian specialists, who always remained a small and little-known minority, were often seen as "subjective" and their works as somewhat illegitimate. Only with the end of the Long Cold War and the emergence of an independent Ukraine, with its accompanying publicity and international recognition, did it become fully apparent that Russian specialists were just as "subjective" as Ukrainian ones, and, moreover, by presenting a previously unacknowledged viewpoint, Ukrainian scholars were enriching the world of learning with new and original ideas that challenged basic assumptions of Western scholarship about eastern Europe. Their work is now acknowledged as forming the basis of present-day Ukrainian studies, which is generally accepted on par with other specialties in the Slavic and East European field. Moreover, in contemporary Ukraine itself, many of these works are now being reprinted for the benefit of today's Ukrainian reader and are enriching the national culture by what contemporary Ukrainians see as their freshness and courage. The Ukrainian scholars of the Cold War worked long and hard and under some very difficult conditions to preserve and enrich their culture and make their ancestral homeland better known to the world of learning and the general Western public. We may conclude modestly by saying that their efforts were not entirely in vain.

Bibliographical Note

No history of Ukrainian scholarship during the twentieth century or during the Cold War, in particular, has yet been written, and much of the material in the present essay is based on personal experience working in the field. For the period up to 1945, however, there is an extensive treatment in *Ukraine: A Concise Encyclopedia* (Toronto: University of Toronto Press, 1971), 232–90. The early DP period is covered by Lubomyr Wynar, "Ukrainian Scholarship in Exile: The DP Period 1945–1952," *Ethnic Forum* 8, no. 1 (1988): 40–72. There is also some material on Ukrainian issues in Clarence A. Manning, *History of Slavic Studies in the United States* (Milwaukee: Marquette University Press, 1957), and much more in Volodymyr Zhyla, *Z istorii ukrainoznavstva i slavistyky v Kanadi* (Winnipeg: UVAN, 1961).

On individual Ukrainian institutions, especially émigré institutions, see the relevant articles in the alphabetical five-volume *Encyclopedia of Ukraine* (Toronto: University of Toronto Press, 1984–93). This valuable reference work is presently being put on-line. See www.encyclopedia ofukraine.com. It is an updated and revised edition and translation of Kubiiovych's great encyclopedia. The first volume of the translation was published in Toronto in 1983, just before the Cold War ended. There is some material on the history of the New York UVAN in *Visti UVAN* 3 (2004), though a general history of the institution remains to be written. On the Winnipeg UVAN, see Jaroslav Rozumnyj, "UVAN in Canada: Fifty Years of Service," in his *Yesterday Today Tomorrow: The Ukrainian Community in Canada* (Winnipeg: UVAN, 2004), 117–54. There is as yet no general history of the Shevchenko Scientific Society during its émigré period.

There are a number of shorter works on individual scholars. Kubiiovych and Chyzhevsky have justly received the most attention. On the former, see O. I. Shablii, *Volodymyr Kubiiovych: Entsyklopediia zhyttia i tvorennia* (Paris, Lviv: NTSh, 1996), *idem, Mandrivky Volodymyra Kubiiovycha* (Lviv: NTSh, 2000), and Vasyl Markus, *Budivnychi NTSh i EUD Volodymyr Kubiiovych (1900–1985) Atanas Figol (1908–1993): Naukovyi zbirnyk* (Kyiv: Oberehy, 1998), and, on the latter, see Yevhen Pyziur, *Dmytro Ivanovych Chyzhevsky (Do 60-ty litnoho iuvileiu)* (n.p., 1955), and Jurij Bojko-Blochyn, *Dmytro Ivanovyc Cyzevsky* (Heidelberg: C. Winter, 1988), in German. There is also an entire issue of the *Journal of Ukrainian Studies* 32, no. 2 (Winter 2007), devoted to Chyzhevsky. On Doroshenko, see Lubomyr Wynar, "Dmytro Ivanovych Doroshenko: Zhyttia i diialnist (u 50 littia smerty)," *Ukrainskyi istoryk* 38, nos. 1–4 (2001): 9–67. On Borshchak, see the essay by Iaroslav Dashkevych in his *Postati: Narysy pro diiachiv istorii, polityky, kultury*, 2nd ed. (Lviv: Piramida, 2007), 461–71. On Chubaty, see the pamphlet by Iaroslav Padokh, *Mykola Chubaty (1889–1975)* (New York, Toronto, Munch: NTSh, 1976). On Rudnyckyj, see *Scripta Manent: A Bio-bibliography of J. B. Rudnyckyj* (Winnipeg, Ottawa: UVAN, 1975), which contains a biographical sketch by Olha Woycenko. On the two principal émigré historians, see Lubomyr Wynar, *Oleksander Petrovych Ohloblyn 1899–1992: Biohrafichna studiia* (New York: Ukrainske istorychne tovarystvo, 1994), and the numerous commemorative pieces scattered through various numbers of *Ukrainskyi istoryk*, and Iraida Gerus-Tarnawecky, *Nataliia Polonska: Biohrafichnyi narys* (Winnipeg: UVAN and Institut doslidiv Volyni, 1974). This latter sketch is also available in German in *Jahrbuch der Ukrainekunde* 24 (1987): 78–97. On the Ukrainian Canadian lexicographer, see June Dutka, *The Grace of Passing: Constantine H. Andrusyshen, the Odyssey of a Slavist* (Edmonton, Toronto: CIUS, 2000). On the intellectual historian Ivan Rudnytsky, see the substantial study by Iaroslav Hrytsak, "Ivan Lysiak-Rudnytsky (Narys intelektualnoi biohrafii)," *Suchasnist* 11 (1994): 73–96. On Pritsak, see Edward L. Keenan, "Omeljan Pritsak (1919–2006)," *Kritika: Explorations in Russian and Eurasian History* 6, no. 4 (2006): 931–36; and Oleksander Dombrovsky, "Pamiati Omeliana Pritsaka (Spohady)," *Ukrainskyi istoryk* 43, nos. 1–3 (2006): 228–37. George Shevelov and George Luckyj remain untreated for the moment, but both of them have written voluminous memoirs. Shevelov's are titled *Ia-meme-meni..(i dovkruhy): Spohady*, 2 vols. (Kharkiv, New York: Berezil'-Kots', 2001); Luckyj's volume dealing with his career in the West is titled *Na storozhi* (Kyiv: Krytyka, 2000). For a brief overview of Ukrainian studies in the West during the middle of our period, see Omeljan Pritsak, "The Present State of Ukrainian Studies," *Canadian Slavonic Papers* 14, no. 2 (1972): 139–52.

10 Lubomyr Wynar and the Ukrainian Historical Association in the United States and Canada

It is striking how history, when resting on the memory of men, always touches the bounds of mythology.

Leopold von Ranke

The past is never dead; it is not even past.

William Faulkner, quoted in *Newsweek*

Liudmyla Sakada, *Ukrainskyi istoryk: Heneza Tematyka Postati* (New York, Kyiv: Ukrainske Istorychne Tovarystvo, 2003).
Liubomyr Wynar, *Ukrainskyi istoryk: 40 rokiv sluzhinnia nautsi 1963–2003* (New York, Ostrih: Ukrainske Istorychne Tovarystvo, 2003).

Lubomyr Wynar (b. 1932) has been a controversial and influential figure within the circles of Ukrainian émigré scholarship since his first appearance on the scene in the late 1950s. Of Ukrainian "Displaced Person" or "DP" background – that is, as a youthful member of that political emigration of Ukrainians who were "displaced" and fled the westward march of the Red Army towards the end of the Second World War – he is an extremely prolific author and well known as an eminent professor of library science at Kent State University in Ohio and a professor of history at the Ukrainian Free University in Munich. He was also the founding editor of the émigré historical journal *Ukrainskyi istoryk* (The Ukrainian historian), a specialist on the life and work of the dean of Ukrainian historians Mykhailo Hrushevsky (1866–1934), a prolific writer on the history of the Ukrainian Cossacks, and a critic of Soviet Ukrainian and Russian historical scholarship throughout the period of the Long Cold War. Moreover, throughout his long career as a bibliographer and historian, Wynar was also very active in American ethnic studies and penned a number of important bibliographies and guidebooks in that field; for many years, he edited the Ohio bibliographical journal *Ethnic Forum*. Within Ukrainian scholarship, however, it is as head of the Ukrainske Istorychne Tovarystvo (Ukrainian Historical Association) and editor of its journal *Ukrainskyi istoryk* that he is best known.

The two books to be discussed here give a good idea of the scope and importance of Wynar's work as the association's head and the editor of its journal. The volume by Liudmyla Sakada, *Ukrainskyi istoryk: Heneza Tematyka Postati,* outlines the history of the journal, gives us much information about its major themes and philosophical principles (not to say ideology), and tells us something about the central figures of its sponsoring organization, the Ukrainian Historical Association. The second volume, *Ukrainskyi istoryk: 40 rokiv sluzhinnia nautsi 1963–2003,* is a collection of Wynar's programmatic articles published in the journal from its founding in 1963 to a few years after the beginning of the new century in 2003. Both these were published on the fortieth anniversary of the first publication of the journal in 1963 and are commemorative volumes of a sort.

The idea of a professional historical journal published in the West in the Ukrainian language (an idea that was simply inconceivable before the emigration of the DPs, among whom there was a relatively high proportion of educated people and cultural activists), was, in fact, conceived and brought into being by Wynar himself. At the time that Wynar launched the journal, at a very young thirty-one years of age, he was already a fairly well-known figure in Ukrainian historical scholarship; he was the author of two brief but highly specialized Ukrainian-language books on major personalities of the Cossack era, and a short monograph in English connected to his work as a librarian and bibliographer, the *History of Early Ukrainian Printing* (1962). He was assisted in his journal endeavours by his former mentor in Ukrainian history at the Ukrainian Free University in Munich, Oleksander Ohloblyn (1899–1992), who, before the Second World War, had been a professor of Ukrainian history at Kyiv University. Ohloblyn, who, in emigration, became a leading historian of the Mazepa era and eighteenth- and early nineteenth-century Ukraine, advised Wynar on the organization and content of the projected journal and wrote a number of important articles for some of its first numbers. In the very first issue appeared Ohloblyn's programmatic piece "The Tasks of Ukrainian Historiography in Emigration." This article stressed that that journal should try to preserve the best traditions of Ukrainian national historiography developed in the nineteenth and early twentieth centuries and act as a "supplement" and "corrective" to the work that Soviet Ukrainian historians were then cautiously doing in the oppressed European homeland. Other early supporters of, and contributors to, *Ukrainskyi istoryk* included the second major Ukrainian émigré historian of the Cold War era, Nataliia Polonska-Vasylenko (1884–1973), a specialist on Kyivan Rus' and the eighteenth-century settlement of southern Ukraine, who contributed memoir materials as well as scholarly articles; Marko Antonovych (1916–2005), who specialized in the national movement of the nineteenth century; Vasyl Dubrovsky (1897–1966), who was an orientalist and specialist on the Turkic peoples of the steppes and the Caucasus; Roman Klymkevych, who was primarily a genealogist; Mykhailo Zhdan, who specialized in the earlier periods of Ukrainian history; and Lubomyr's brother Bohdan Wynar, who was interested in bibliography and economic history. Aside from ordinary research articles on the various periods of Ukrainian history, from the very beginning, criticism of Soviet scholarship and biographical materials about various Ukrainian historians, both pre-revolution historians and also Ukrainian historians surviving in the West, took up much space in the journal. For example, in the very first issue was an obituary of the famous Ukrainian bibliographer and librarian Volodymyr Doroshenko (1879–1963), who, towards the end of his life, published a whole series of articles on the life and work of Hrushevsky. Bibliography and historiography, especially works on Hrushevsky, were to remain strong points in the journal's profile throughout the period of the Cold War.

At the time that *Ukrainskyi istoryk* was founded, many voices in the Ukrainian emigration expressed doubts as to whether an émigré and immigrant community such as the Ukrainian one (which, despite the arrival of the DPs, still contained a relatively small number of professional historians) could support a truly scholarly journal. For example, the historian of political thought Ivan Lysiak-Rudnytsky (1919–1984) believed that occasional collective volumes or *zbirnyky* published by the *Ukrainska Vilna Akademiia Nauk* (Ukrainian Academy of Arts and Sciences in the US, or UVAN) would adequately fill the needs of Ukrainian historians in the West. But Wynar persisted, arguing that a regularly appearing independent journal, complete with full research articles, reviews, and scholarly obituaries, and not linked to either the UVAN or its rival, the *Naukove Tovarystvo im. Shevchenka* (Shevchenko Scientific Society, or NTSh) would be irreplaceable.

On a somewhat different level, there was also a danger that Wynar's background, close to the Melnyk faction of the *Orhanizatsiia Ukrainskykh Natsionalistiv* (Organization of Ukrainian Nationalists, or OUN) would give the journal too much of a nationalist "party" character. But with Ohloblyn's help and that of several other contributors who did not entirely support the OUN (both Ohloblyn and Polonska-Vasylenko were inclined towards the monarchist or Hetmanite movement), this danger was avoided to some extent and *Ukrainskyi istoryk* never became a "party" organ in the narrow sense of the term.

Following the example of Hrushevsky, who was his model, in his various programmatic articles published in *Ukrainskyi istoryk*, Wynar clearly distinguished between "national" historiography, which he strongly supported, and "nationalistic" historiography, which he ostensibly rejected. The general idea here was that Ukrainian historians in the West should reject both the "party-minded" history then being promoted in the USSR and also the nationalist extremism of certain cultural and political figures then active in the West.

Of these two dangers to independent Ukrainian historical scholarship, the Soviet Russian one was obviously most pressing. Thus, the basic thrust of *Ukrainskyi istoryk* was usually directed against the official type of Communist histories then being produced in the USSR. As was argued at the time, Ukrainian history, as it was taught and studied in Soviet Ukraine, was not free to describe accurately the historical experience of the Ukrainian people. It largely ignored the national aspects of this experience and simply could not develop as a healthy and independent discipline that would both serve the national interests of the Ukrainian people and remain true to basic historical facts. This task could be accomplished in the Western world only by émigré historians working free of party control and government censorship.

With regard to his general philosophical position, moreover, "fact" played an important part in Wynar's historical methodology. From his early years, it seems, Wynar was always committed to a "Rankean" historical methodology in which, so he believed, the careful collection of both well-established and newly discovered "facts," and their dispassionate arrangement in an historical narrative, naturally led to objectivity and to the progress of "historical science" (*istorychna nauka*). This ostensibly great faith in "objectivity," progress, and science exudes from much of Wynar's discourse, both written and spoken, and formed a key element in the *raison d'être* of the journal. It was, in fact, a patent rejection of both Soviet ideology with its exclusivist claims to "science" and of the usual

Western, russo-centric criticism of Ukrainian scholarship as being nationally "biased."

During its early years, a pattern was established in *Ukrainskyi istoryk* that was to characterize the journal for a very long time. In particular, certain themes received more attention than others. Of course, this was mostly due to the limited pool of contributors upon which the editor could rely. Thus, ancient Ukraine of the Scythians received much attention because of the contributions of Oleksander Dombrovsky (b. 1914), a specialist in ancient Greek; the Cossack period was examined thanks to the articles of Wynar himself, Ohloblyn, the Rev Oleksander Baran (1926–2005), and others; and the era of Hetman Mazepa was explored by both Ohloblyn and Theodore Mackiw (b. 1918). Moreover, the Rev I. Nazarko made contributions on church history, and Wynar himself, as well as others, examined various Ukrainian historians of the nineteenth and twentieth centuries, especially the life and works of Hrushevsky. Wynar also recruited some of his colleagues in library science into the work of the Ukrainian Historical Association. Thus, librarians and bibliographers such as Lev Bykovsky (b. 1895) from the oldest generation of Ukrainian Historical Association supporters, and Dmytro Shtohryn (b. 1923) from the next generation, contributed extensively to the journal. (Bykovsky was especially important with regard to the publication of memoir materials and obituaries of prominent members of the generation of 1917.) In addition to this, a score of other prominent veterans of the national movement or of public life in the Old Country told of their experiences and acquaintances in a special section devoted to memoirs, with the revolutionary period being well represented, while another section was reserved for previously unpublished documents and letters, especially those of prominent Ukrainian historians. Occasionally, the heads of some of the more prominent Ukrainian academic institutions also contributed to the journal. Thus, Omeljan Pritsak (1919–2006) of the Harvard Ukrainian Research Institute, Volodymyr Kubiiovych (1900–1985) of the European branch of the NTSh, and George Luckyj (1919–2002) of the New York UVAN and the Canadian Institute of Ukrainian Studies all contributed at one time or another.

With regard to the geographic origins of the various contributors, the following may be said: the origins of the contributors largely reflected the geographic dispersion of the DP emigration during the post-war period. The largest centres of this emigration produced the largest numbers of contributions. Thus, the United States, where the Ukrainian Historical Association was primarily based, produced the largest number of contributions, with a great many originating in New York, New England, and the Midwest.

During the early years, there was also a significant number of contributions from Colorado, where several important Ukrainian intellectuals, including Bykovsky and Wynar's brother Bohdan, had settled and a branch of the UVAN existed for a while. (Lubomyr Wynar himself had lived in Colorado for a time.) Many other contributions came from Canada, where Wynar's close collaborator and fellow supporter of the Melnyk branch of the OUN, Marko Antonovych, lived. Antonovych was resident in Montreal in the East, but, over the course of many years, contributions also came from Ottawa and Winnipeg. Through to the 1970s, the latter city was known as the unofficial capital of Ukrainian Canada and was the home of the Canadian branch of the UVAN, founded by Dmytro Doroshenko (1882–1951), the distinguished émigré historian who had flourished during the interwar period. Several Winnipeg UVAN members, including Oleksander Baran, Oleh Gerus, and others, made more than one contribution to the journal.

In connection with Canada, it should be noted that a very large Ukrainian immigrant community had existed in this country since the 1890s, and certain representatives of this old economic emigration, such as Vladimir Kaye-Kysilewskyj, who had begun his academic career in the 1930s, and Paul Yuzyk, who flourished during the 1950s and 1960s, participated in the work of the Ukrainian Historical Association. This phenomenon had no exact counterpart in the United States, where certain historians, leading lights of the older economic emigration such as Wasyl Halich, who, like Kysilewskyj, had begun his career in the 1930s, and John Reshetar, who, like Yuzyk, published his best work in the 1950s and the 1960s, took no part in building the Ukrainian Historical Association.

As for Europe, contributions were more plentiful during the earlier period but declined thereafter as the centres of Ukrainian émigré intellectual life moved steadily westward to North America. (There were some exceptions to this trend. For example, in France, the specialist in Bukovinian history Arkadii Zhukovsky [b. 1922], over the course of many years, proved a devoted and repeated contributor to the journal.) From South America, in particular, Argentina, Wynar received some support from the encyclopedist and Melnyk political activist Yevhen Onatsky (1894–1979), but little else. Australia and other parts of the world took very little part in the work of the Ukrainian Historical Association and *Ukrainskyi istoryk.*

It seems that the existence of the Ukrainian Historical Association and its journal did have some effect on the situation of Ukrainian historians working in the USSR. This appears to have been the case even during the journal's early years. The appearance of *Ukrainskyi istoryk* in the West in the early 1960s was immediately noted by Ukrainian historians working in Soviet Ukraine. Of course, under Soviet conditions of censorship and control of scholarship, most Soviet Ukrainian historians had no possibility of examining at first hand the work of their ostensible "rivals" in the West, but, as Sakada points out (49), as early as 1966, a leading Soviet Ukrainian historian, Fedir Shevchenko (1914–1995), bravely remarked on the existence of *Ukrainskyi istoryk* on the pages of the leading Soviet Ukrainian historical organ, the Kyiv-based *Ukrainskyi istorychnyi zhurnal* (Ukrainian historical journal), and thus let a wide circle of his sheltered colleagues know that their compatriots in the West were indeed still active. This must have had some small effect on the morale of these hard-pressed Soviet Ukrainian scholars.

However, political conditions in Ukraine took a definite turn for the worse in the early 1970s. After 1972, a series of purges and dismissals brought an end to the fragile cultural flowering that had occurred under the protection of the First Secretary of the Communist Party of the Ukrainian SSR, Petro Shelest. With the fall of Shelest, two of the three major Soviet Ukrainian historical journals were closed down completely and Kyiv's surviving *Ukrainskyi istorychnyi zhurnal* filled its pages with dreary articles on Party history and the achievements of the Soviet system. Thus, by 1978, in a second important programmatic article published in *Ukrainskyi istoryk*, Ohloblyn felt compelled to state that his original program had to be amended and Ukrainian historians in the West now had to go beyond "supplementing" and "correcting" the work of their Soviet colleagues and take on the whole burden of preserving the traditions of Ukrainian national historiography by themselves. Indeed, it was generally believed that only the embarrassing existence of *Ukrainskyi istoryk* in the West induced the Communists to allow the continued publication of the Ukrainian-language *Ukrainskyi istorychnyi zhurnal*, and this at a time when most other Ukrainian-language scholarly journals were either being suppressed or completely russified.

While Ukrainian historians living under Soviet rule were suffering these very severe blows, their colleagues in the Ukrainian Historical Association were also coming under new pressures. By the 1970s, the generation of 1917, many of whom had contributed greatly to *Ukrainskyi istoryk* during the late 1960s, was in the course of passing away. In spite of Wynar's best efforts, the pool of prospective memoirists and contributors was growing ever smaller. The numbers of younger scholars in the West interested in writing Ukrainian history were also small, and many of them could not write fluently in Ukrainian. Thus, the Ukrainian Historical Association faced a severe generational crisis.

At this time, Wynar did his best to recruit new contributors to the journal. Although the original emphasis on Ukrainian-language material was maintained, occasional articles and reviews in English were welcomed. A new generation of historians began to contribute to *Ukrainskyi istoryk*. The late 1970s and the 1980s saw the first contributions of younger historians such as Oleh Gerus of the University of Manitoba, John-Paul Himka, who eventually joined the University of Alberta, and the author of these lines, who was a product of the University of Toronto. Certain other members of this generation, such as Alexander Sydorenko of Arkansas State University, eventually took a prominent role in the further development of the journal. Moreover, in the early 1980s, Wynar tried to expand *Ukrainskyi istoryk* thematically and the journal began to advertise itself not only as an historical periodical but also as a general journal of Ukrainian studies, including literature, language, and politics within its mandate. The results were mixed. Although, after 1983, a few articles on literature did appear in *Ukrainskyi istoryk*, the journal always retained its original emphasis on history.

It was at this same time that *Ukrainskyi istoryk* celebrated the twentieth anniversary of its founding. In connection with this anniversary, Wynar published another programmatic article listing the practical tasks of the Ukrainian Historical Association and Ukrainian historians in the West. These he enumerated as follows. The first task was to research the central themes of Ukrainian history that are directly related to world history. The second task was to propagate in world historiography Hrushevsky's national scheme of Ukrainian history, which clearly distinguished between Ukrainian and Russian spheres and claimed Kyivan Rus' for Ukraine alone. Doing this, Wynar believed, would dissipate any Ukrainian "inferiority complex" towards Russian historiography, a phenomenon that he believed was being promoted by Russian émigré historians who freely advanced the Russian scheme of eastern European history in their various writings. (In this regard, it should be noted that several of the leading Russian émigré historians working in the United States since the 1930s actually traced their origins to Ukraine. This was true of three of the most influential: George Vernadsky of Yale, Michael Florinsky of Columbia, and Anatol Mazour of Stanford.)

The third task was to actively combat Soviet falsifications of Ukrainian history; the fourth was to seek out and publish new archival materials available in the West; the fifth was to cooperate with various professional historical and Slavistic associations in Europe and the United States; the sixth was to aid various Ukrainian émigré scholarly institutions active in the West; and the seventh task was to promote Ukrainian history courses at universities in countries where there were large Ukrainian immigrant populations (Wynar, pp. 203–4). This program was extremely ambitious and, to the end of the 1980s, remained only in very small part fulfilled.

However, thanks to political changes in eastern Europe, the late 1980s and early 1990s opened a new stage in the history of the Ukrainian Historical Association and *Ukrainskyi istoryk*. The progress of "restructuring" and "openness" in Soviet Ukraine soon led to new contacts between Ukrainian historians in the West and those in the European homeland. By 1990, a number of new contributors from Ukraine began publishing on the pages of *Ukrainskyi istoryk*. Some of the first were Viktor Zaruba, who was interested in historiography and the biographies of important historians; Serhii Bilokin, who was researching Soviet Ukrainian history, especially the purges and the famine of 1932–33; and Ya. Dzyra and V. Serhiichuk, who had a wider variety of interests including Cossack history. Later on, the Kyiv-based historian Ihor Hyrych, who shared many of Wynar's methodological approaches and intellectual interests, especially his interest in Hrushevsky, became one of the most frequent contributors to the journal.

The collapse of the USSR and the emergence of an independent Ukraine led to even closer contacts and more contributions from the European homeland. By the mid-1990s, *Ukrainskyi istoryk*, which, for many years, had come out in only one or two rather thin issues a year, turned into a truly thick journal with many different kinds of contributors and articles. Historiography remained a central theme, with much attention devoted to Hrushevsky, but new themes such as the Ukrainian experience under the Soviets began to be explored in detail. Eventually, prominent Ukrainian historians, such as the eminent archaeologist and specialist on Kyivan Rus' Mykhailo Braichevsky (1924–2001), and the specialist in "source studies" (*dzhereloznavstvo*) Mykola Kovalsky, joined the editorial board. New centres of the Ukrainian Historical Association were founded in various parts of Ukraine, especially the western and central parts of the country, and the journal became much more available there. By 2004, the Ostroh-based historian Alla Atamenenko, who was very interested in Ukrainian émigré historiography, joined as a co-editor and Wynar began the process of transferring the editorial offices to the Ostroh Academy in Volhynia. The hope was that the traditions carried on for so many years by Ukrainian historians in the West would now be fully taken up by historians in Ukraine and that they would thrive and expand there to influence future generations of Ukrainians.

The volumes of Liudmyla Sakada and Lubomyr Wynar contribute greatly to the elucidation of this story. They document its various phases, point out the obstacles to be overcome, and, in part, show how the members of the Ukrainian Historical Association fared in this task. Of course, there were some defeats. During the most difficult days of the Cold War, social and economic history were largely missing from the pages of *Ukrainskyi istoryk*, the histories of the Ukrainian communities in the Americas were hardly touched upon, and, except for certain polemics, the history of Soviet Ukraine was largely ignored. It is notable, for example, that before the expansion of the journal in the 1990s due to the contributions of new historians from independent Ukraine, not a single article was devoted to the history of the Great Famine of 1932–33, arguably one of the most important events in the history of the Ukrainian people in modern times.

At the same time, it should be noted that several of the most important and most influential Ukrainian historians working in the West during the Cold War contributed little or nothing to the pages of *Ukrainskyi istoryk*. Thus, for example, Ivan Lysiak-Rudnytsky of the University of Alberta, Omeljan Pritsak, who held the Hrushevsky Chair of Ukrainian History at Harvard, and Roman Szporluk, who succeeded Pritsak in this position, all had very little contact with the journal. (Pritsak, in particular, in spite of his academic title, was somewhat unfriendly to the full promotion of the Hrushevsky legacy that Wynar was so prominent in advancing, and was even the target of some criticism by Wynar because of what Wynar believed was his unconscionably accommodating position on Jewish–Ukrainian relations.) Also, during the early years of the journal's existence, many of the surviving veterans of the Ukrainian democratic socialist movement, scholars like the former Galician Radical Matvii Stakhiv (1895–1978), who were the logical heirs of the Hrushevsky tradition, declined to contribute to Wynar's journal, which, in spite of its editor's best efforts, continued to breathe a fairly conservative and even "nationalist" *derzhavnyk* or "pro-state" interpretation of Hrushevsky's legacy and other issues. Later on, younger heirs of this ideologically left-wing tradition, such as the specialist in Galician history John-Paul Himka, and the political scientist with historical interests Bohdan Krawchenko, contributed very little or nothing at all to the journal. Somewhat more surprisingly, other historians of this younger generation, who lacked this left-wing tilt – in particular, Orest Subtelny (b. 1943), who published his well-received "national" survey, *Ukraine: A History*, in 1988, and Paul Magocsi (b. 1945), who finished his rival "territorialist" *History of Ukraine* in 1996 – refrained from contributing even a single article to *Ukrainskyi istoryk*. Similarly, Zenon Kohut, who specialized on the later Hetmanate, and Frank Sysyn (b. 1946), who concentrated on the Khmelnytsky revolution, both of whom were associated with Harvard during the Pritsak era and then later found employment with the Canadian Institute of Ukrainian Studies, for many years declined to publish in the journal. Finally, appearing as they did mostly in the Ukrainian language, the achievements of Wynar and his collaborators were largely restricted to the narrow circle of Western scholars who could read and understand Ukrainian. Thus, during most of the Cold War, the effect of *Ukrainskyi istoryk* on the wider community of Western scholars engaged in the study of eastern Europe was slight.

The true legacy of the Ukrainian Historical Association became clear only after the events of 1991. With the emergence of new intellectual freedoms at that time, Ukrainians in the homeland who still were unfamiliar with Western languages could easily read *Ukrainskyi istoryk* and the other Ukrainian-language publications of the Ukrainian Historical Association, which now became freely available to them. They were clearly impressed with these (for them) "new" interpretations and began to enthusiastically support Wynar's "national" program for Ukrainian historical scholarship. This process grew for at least fifteen years and even in the early twenty-first century still showed no sign of letting up.

Thus, it seems clear that over the course of some forty years, the Ukrainian Historical Association and its journal went through a number of stages. It began as a tentative project, a mere bulletin of sorts, with a limited number of contributors, many of whom were already elderly. But these pioneers persevered and produced a steady stream of new documentation and historical literature about Ukraine. From almost the beginning, it proved impossible to put out a real quarterly, and *Ukrainskyi istoryk* usually consisted of only one or two issues per year. Nevertheless, it came out regularly and maintained a regular journal format with articles, memoirs and letters, reviews, and important obituaries in almost every issue. As early as the late 1960s, very valuable and substantial special issues were devoted to the life and work of Hrushevsky (1966) and to the Ukrainian revolution (1967). As well, the Ukrainian Historical Association occasionally published historical titles under separate cover, sometimes reprinting longer articles from *Ukrainskyi istoryk*. (This did not always add to the fundamental body of research on Ukrainian history, but did have the advantage of the material's appearing separately in the university library catalogues.) Works by Wynar, Ohloblyn, Mackiw, Bykovsky, and the archaeologist Yaroslav Pasternak (1892–1969) all appeared in this format. Two of the most notable titles were the full-colour *Istorychnyi atlas Ukrainy* (Historical atlas of Ukraine) by I. Teslia and E. Tiutko (1980), which was an original work of scholarship, and the Wynar-edited *Mykhailo Hrushevskyi: Bibliographic Sources 1866–1934* (1985), which was a reprint of some very rare bibliographies of Hrushevsky's works as well as a bibliography of works about him. In later years, Wynar also made a serious effort to collect and reprint Ohloblyn's more important works. This effort began in 1995 with the publication of that historian's *Studii z istorii Ukrainy: Statti i dzherelni materiialy* (Studies in Ukrainian history: Articles and source materials).

The association and the journal survived the difficult transition to the 1980s with new publications as well as the addition of a new generation of contributors. Moreover, it greatly expanded after 1989, due to the favourable political changes in eastern Europe. Thereafter, three, very bulky, commemorative volumes, which contained many new contributions from Ukraine, were devoted to Hrushevsky, and the treatment of Soviet–Ukrainian history was becoming more extensive. The sections on other periods of Ukrainian history were also making some progress, and work on émigré historiography and historians continued to expand.

By 2004, it was clear that Wynar and his colleagues had remained true to their original purposes and the association and the journal had made a fairly successful transition to work in Ukraine itself. The dedicated labours of that small band of Ukrainian émigré historians, those former DPs, who, in the early 1960s, bravely set out to thwart the oppressive academic and propaganda apparatus of the Soviet state, as well as the prejudices of Western scholarship, and to set Ukrainian national historical scholarship on a firmer footing, were not entirely in vain. Their legacy continues to flower in today's Ukraine, where Alla Atamanenko of the Ostroh Academy in Volhynia has taken up the editing of the journal (now formally transferred to Ukraine) and even written a detailed history of the Ukrainian Historical Association. This gives considerable hope for the future.

11 In the Shadow of a Political Assassination: Gabrielle Roy's "Stephen" and the Ukrainian Canadians

Plaisir d'amour ne dure qu'un moment.
Chagrin d'amour dure toute la vie.

Jean de Florian, "Célestine"

Quis, quid, ubi, quibus auxiliis, cur, quomodo, quando?
(Who, what, where, by what means, why, how, and when?)

Traditional Latin hexameter line, setting out lines of analysis.
Nicholas Ostler, Ad Infinitum: A Biography of Latin

Gabrielle Roy (1909–1983) was one of the most outstanding and beloved French Canadian writers of the twentieth century. Her early work as a journalist displayed an eye for the relevant and important, and a sensitivity for her subjects that was immediately noticed by her readers; her path-breaking novels marked a turn in French Canadian literature from the traditional, rural, and romantic to the modern, urban, and realistic; and her moving autobiography, written towards the end of her life and published posthumously, revealed a psychological depth and honesty to a younger generation that already knew her as a Canadian and Quebec literary icon. She won the Governor General's Award for literature three times during her long career as a writer, was the first woman inducted into the Royal Society of Canada, and, in her lifetime, was translated into many languages across the world. All her major works have been translated into English and they have been widely read by English-speaking Canadians of many different backgrounds. Some of these works in the original French are also studied in the school curricula of more than one Canadian province, beginning in Manitoba and ending in Quebec.

A quote from Gabrielle Roy in both French and English appeared on the obverse of every twenty-dollar bill issued in Canada at the beginning of the twenty-first century.[1]

The fact that Roy is quoted on the Canadian national currency is not all that surprising, for her works go well beyond the province of Quebec, where she lived most of her adult life, to also encompass Prairie Canada, especially Manitoba and the cities of Saint Boniface and Winnipeg, where she was born and raised. Although her first novel *Bonheur d'occasion*, translated into English as *The Tin Flute*, appeared to be politically engaged, hostile to the reactionary *duplessisme* that controlled Quebec in the 1940s, and sympathetic to the trade union movement, in general, Roy kept a certain distance from politics and remained quietly federalist during the stormy years of the late 1960s. The one exception to this position was in 1967 when she could not control her anger at General de Gaulle's speech on the balcony of the Montreal City Hall where he called out for a "free Quebec": "*Vive le Québec! Vive le Québec libre!*" Roy publicly responded: "*Je proteste contre la leçon que le General de Gaulle prétend donner à notre pays.*" In general, she rejected Quebec nationalism and sovereignty and remained quietly cosmopolitan and committed to both parts of the Canada she knew best: Quebec and the Prairie West.[2]

Roy's various works are known for their honesty, sensitivity, and sympathy for their subjects. She sometimes describes the inequalities between French and English in Canada but never reveals any hostility to the English. Indeed, from a very early age, she knew that Canada went beyond even French and English to include the many different peoples who had settled the West and made up the polyethnic mosaic that was the Manitoba in which she was raised. Her father Léon Roy was a federal civil servant, a settlement agent, who placed skilled immigrant farmers from all over Europe, as well as smaller numbers of his ethnic confreres from Quebec, on the free lands that had suddenly become available on the Prairies after the completion of the CPR and the suppression of the Metis resistance movement of 1885. Léon developed a deep affection for his immigrant charges, Ukrainians and many others, and told stories about them when he returned to his family from work. Thus, from her very first years, Gabrielle became aware of the existence, and sympathetic to the situation, of ethnic Canada. The fact that ethnic Canadians were then often called "foreigners" by the English, and perhaps also by the French, even though most of them had been born in this country, did not escape her notice, and, years later, she shook with emotion as she recalled this "insult to humanity," as she called it.[3] And among these early prairie homesteaders, the Ukrainians, or "Ruthenians," as they were at first sometimes known, did not take second place. For example, in her auto-fictional account "Les puits de Dunrea" ("The Well of Dunrea") in one of her most important Manitoba books, *Rue Deschambault* (*Street of Riches*), Roy recounts of the Ukrainians/Ruthenians:

> At the time in question, Papa was especially well pleased with the colony of White Russians or Ruthenians [*la colonie des Blancs-Russiens ou Ruthènes*] established at Dunrea. For a reason unknown to us he called them his 'Little Ruthenians' [*Petits-Ruthènes*]. Of all the groups he had settled this one prospered best. It had not yet been established for a full decade; a short enough time in which to build a happy settlement out of a handful of suspicious and illiterate immigrants, let alone clear the land, build houses, and even make God at home with icons and votive candles. Yet all this and much more had the Little Ruthenians accomplished. They were not a people absorbed in vexations, like the Doukhobors. Agnes seemed to remember that they, likewise, were Slavs, probably from Bukovina. Certainly the past counted for something in their lives – a past deeply wretched – but it was in the future, a wonderful and well-founded future, that the Little Ruthenians above all had faith when they came to Canada. And that was the sort of settler Papa liked: people facing forward, and not everlastingly whining over what they had had to leave behind.[4]

Ukrainians also pop up elsewhere in Roy's corpus, as, for example, in the character Nick Sluzick, the morose and unsociable postman in her recollection of her time as a rural schoolteacher, *La petite poule d'eau* (*Where Nests the Water Hen*), who sits uncomfortably in church while the talented priest Father Joseph-Marie, who switches from language to language for his multilingual congregation, lectures about the wonderful variety of birds in this world that must fly free and about the need to uncage people, particularly women.[5] In this scene, not only Nick Sluzick but even the priest has an historical basis, for several French Canadian and Belgian priests had learned the Ukrainian language and transferred to the Eastern Rite to serve the numerous and pious Greek Catholic Ukrainians of western Canada who, for many years, lacked sufficient clergy of their own.[6] Similarly, there is the character Nil, the little boy in another of Roy's autobiographical accounts of her time as a schoolteacher in rural Manitoba, *Ces enfants de ma vie* (*Children of My Heart*), who sings so naturally and beautifully, including various Ukrainian songs. It may be that Roy's later experience with a particularly talented

Ukrainian baritone in England in 1938 brought Nil to life for her again after so very many years.[7]

In fact, during the early 1930s, when Roy first gained primary experience with them, the Ukrainians were one of Canada's most prominent ethnolinguistic groups; at that time, they constituted the fourth-largest ethnic group in the Dominion after the British groups, the French, and the Germans. On the Prairies, they even outnumbered the French, thus making up the third-largest group after the British groups and the Germans. The Canadian census of 1931 counted some 225,113 Ukrainians in the country and the census of 1941 counted 303,929, which constituted just short of 3 per cent of the total population of the Dominion. For a long time, they were known under various regional or other names such as "Galicians," "Bukovinians," or "Ruthenians," but, by 1931, these names had decreased in use and in the 1936 census, only "Ukrainian" was reported. Thus, the fact that Léon Roy had earlier called them "Little Ruthenians" is not surprising; it can even be seen as a positive thing, since the frequently used alternate term "Galicians" was increasingly considered by those named such as a derogatory label that denied their nationality, for many Poles and others on the Prairies also originated from the old Austrian Crown Land of Galicia from which most of the Ukrainians had come.[8]

The Ukrainians were particularly numerous in Manitoba, where, by 1941, they made up some 12.5 per cent of the total population. Winnipeg was their metropolitan centre and both the Ruthenian Greek Catholic Church (as it was still officially called) and the Ukrainian Greek Orthodox Church were headquartered in that city. Winnipeg also possessed many Ukrainian cultural organizations such as the *Ukrainskyi narodnyi dim* (Ukrainian National Home) and the *Prosvita* (Enlightenment) Society. Some of Gabrielle's Ukrainian friends, in particular the musicians of the Hubicki family, were active in these institutions.

Ukrainian politics were also very intense in Winnipeg with the pro-Communist *Tovarystvo Ukrainskyi Robitnycho-Farmerskyi Dim* (Ukrainian Labour Farmer Temple Association, or ULFTA) having a very large presence. Although they made up the largest Ukrainian Canadian secular organization, the labour temples held the firm loyalty of only about 10 per cent of all Ukrainian Canadians. Most of the others were either totally non-political or split among the populist liberal-leaning *Soiuz Ukraintsiv Samostiinykiv* (Ukrainian Self-Reliance League), which was affiliated with the Orthodox Church, or the newly formed and much smaller *Ukrainske Natsionalne Obiednannia* (Ukrainian National Federation, or UNF), a rightist organization whose members tended to support revolutionary-style radical nationalism in Europe (where various foreign authoritarian regimes ruled Ukrainian-inhabited lands), but to vote conservative within the Canadian political spectrum. There was also the monarchist *Soiuz Hetmantsiv Derzhavnykiv* (United Hetman Organization), another rightist organization, which was also conservative when it came to Canadian politics and, in Europe, rejected the "revolutionary" nationalism of the UNF. But the leader of the Hetmanite movement, Pavlo Skoropadsky, who claimed the title of "Hetman of Ukraine," was resident in Berlin throughout the interwar period. Each of these varied Ukrainian political organizations tried to influence Canadian and British politics in favour of their own interpretation of the burning "Ukrainian question" of the 1930s. The essence of this question was the national self-determination of the Ukrainian people in Europe then living under mostly Soviet and Polish, but also partly under Czech and Romanian, rule. It should be noted that throughout most of the twentieth century, the approximately forty million-strong Ukrainians formed the largest distinct people in Europe who remained without their own national state to represent their interests.[9]

In the late 1930s, when Gabrielle Roy first left Manitoba and went to Europe to study drama and get a wider world view, there were already several Ukrainian Canadians in London, which most Canadians still looked to as the cultural as well as the political capital of the still-powerful British Empire. Foremost among these was Vladimir Kysilewskyj (1896–1976), the former editor of Edmonton's Catholic Ukrainian-language newspaper *Zakhidni visti* (The western news), who, in the early 1930s, went to England to run a "Ukrainian Bureau" in the empire's capital. This bureau was financed by the idiosyncratic Ukrainian American millionaire Jacob Makohin. Throughout the 1930s, Kysilewskyj ran this non-partisan Ukrainian information bureau, made contacts with the British Foreign Office, and distributed information to various British newspapers. At the same time, he enrolled in doctoral studies at London's School of Slavonic and East European Studies, where he studied under the famous British Slavist R. W. Seton-Watson, who had played a modest role in the emergence of an independent Czechoslovakia and whom Kysilewskyj hoped would also look favourably on Ukrainian national aspirations. R. W. Seton-Watson certainly had contacts in the government circles Kysilewskyj wished to influence. It helped, moreover, that Kysilewskyj's mother Olena was a member of the Polish Senate from a moderate democratic party committed to parliamentary methods, and, insofar as its interest could be aroused, the British Foreign Office was able to appreciate Kysilewskyj's reasoned approach and democratic background. Kysilewskyj's activities were also reported in the mainstream Ukrainian Canadian press, such as Winnipeg's *Ukrainskyi holos* (Ukrainian voice), which was the tribune of the liberal-leaning Self-Reliance League.[10]

Other Ukrainian Canadians then in London included Stephen and Olga Pawluk from Toronto. Stephen was originally from Vegreville, Alberta, but had organized the UNF youth wing's Ukrainian Radio Telegraphy School in Toronto before he and his co-instructor John Strogin left for England at the end of 1937 to join Marconi International Services. Stephen's wife Olga, whom he had married just before leaving for England, was an interwar immigrant to Canada from Soviet-ruled Ukraine who translated Ukrainian- and Russian-language materials for the handful of British scholars and publicists who were interested in the Ukrainian question.[11]

Also in London in the 1920s and the 1930s were the Hubicki brothers, the solo violinists Taras and Bohdan, from Winnipeg. Taras went to London in the 1920s to study at the Royal Academy of Music but returned to North America and moved to Detroit in 1937, where he joined the Detroit Symphony Orchestra. His younger brother Bohdan followed his example and went to London in the late 1930s, similarly to study at the Royal Academy. In early 1938, their younger sister Honoré, a pianist, was supposed to join Bohdan in England. Bohdan seems to have known Gabrielle Roy from Winnipeg, as he met her when she arrived from Paris in early 1938 and helped to find her appropriate living quarters in the city. In fact, he seems to have found her a room in the same house as Stephen and Olga Pawluk, and the two women, a French Canadian and a Ukrainian Canadian, often went out shopping and to the cinema together.[12]

One further Ukrainian Canadian must be mentioned: Stephen Davidovich (1913–1987), who, like Stephen Pawluk, was from Alberta. He did not come directly from Canada to England, however, but from the USA, where he had been studying economics at various American universities including Fordham and New York University. In Passaic, New Jersey, Davidovich became involved in the *Orhanizatsiia Derzhavnoho Vidrodzhennia Ukrainy* (Organization for the Rebirth of Ukraine, or ORU), which, like the UNF in Canada, supported the radical underground movement in Europe called the *Orhanizatsiia Ukrainskykh Natsinalistiv* (Organization of Ukrainian Nationalists, or OUN). Davidovich was a talented vocalist with a beautiful baritone voice and was most active

in the ORU choir, but undoubtedly he was also aware of the armed struggle and political violence carried out by OUN members in what they
considered to be Polish-occupied "Western Ukraine" (formerly eastern
Galicia).[13] The underground OUN also tried to penetrate the Soviet
Union and influence events in Soviet Ukraine, where there were fresh
memories of the ferocious political purges and the Great Famine of
1932–3, which was caused not by natural disasters but, rather, by Soviet
leader Joseph Stalin's campaign of rapid collectivization and forced grain
requisitioning from the defenceless peasantry. However, the comprehensive security presence in the Soviet police state made this very difficult.

In view of the ruthless nature of its enemies, the OUN was from the
start frankly militarist and its doctrines consisted of direct action, strength
on one's own, the cult of the charismatic leader, national revolution, and
especially national liberation. It was a conspiratorial terrorist organization, which, in 1933, as a sign of protest against the Great Famine, assassinated a Soviet consular official in Lwów (Lviv in Ukrainian), the major
city in the Ukrainian-inhabited part of interwar Poland (the eastern part
of old Galicia). Some time later, in Warsaw, OUN member H. Matseiko
assassinated Bronisław Pieracki, the Polish interior minister who had
been responsible for much of the government oppression of the Ukrainians in this region, tendentiously called "Eastern Little Poland" by the
interwar Polish government.

The OUN supporters generally believed that direct action and militant
doctrines were justified in a Europe where the general malaise and re-
treat of parliamentary democracy stood in self-evident contrast to the success of the Nazi and Communist party organizations with their military
discipline, absolute leadership, and party monopoly of power. The OUN's
chief opponents were, of course, the authoritarian Piłsudski-ite regime
in Poland (by the late 1930s already headed in a quasi-Fascist direction)
and Stalin's USSR (at that time experiencing the Great Purges, the so-
called "Great Terror" carried out by the regime's dreaded secret police,
the NKVD, formerly the OGPU, which was commemorating the twentieth
anniversary of its founding). These repressive regimes were hardly less
violent or extreme than their Ukrainian nationalist opponents.

But, in North America, the situation was completely different. In
Canada, parliamentary democracy was strong, and in the USA, liberal
values and the ideals of political freedom were hardly questioned.
Therefore, in North America, the Canadian UNF and the American ORU
voiced no objections to democratic institutions and liberal democracy
on this continent and in every way tried to work for the Ukrainian cause

within the given system. In Canada, in particular, most UNF members tended to support the Conservative Party of Canada, although some also eventually supported Social Credit in Alberta. The OUN leader or *Vozhd* was Colonel Yevhen or "Eugene" Konovalets, a former military commander during the Ukrainian struggle for independence from 1917 to 1921, who seems to have been flexible enough to see that various OUN-supporting organizations in different countries with different political systems had to use different tactics and methods, although the ultimate goal of a completely independent Ukraine freed of Polish and Russian rule was shared by all. In the 1930s and in later years as well, it was often said by the OUN's critics, Communist and non-Communist alike, that it entertained close relations with Nazi Germany and Fascist Italy and that it was anti-Semitic and Fascist, but the OUN itself never accepted the Fascist label, tried to play an independent role in international affairs, and would have welcomed support from London and Paris as well as Berlin and Rome. (The fact that the OUN's major newspaper *Ukrainske slovo* [The Ukrainian word] was published in Paris rather than in Berlin or Rome is testimony to this.) The national liberation of the Ukrainian people living under foreign rule, rather than the future form of the Ukrainian state, occupied most of the OUN's attention.[14]

Sometime in mid-1937, the OUN leadership in Europe sent a request to the ORU leadership in the USA to find an appropriately educated English-speaking member who could be sent to London to work on behalf of the Ukrainian nationalist cause in the British capital. Attention was soon focused on Davidovich, who not only had a university education and spoke fluent English and Ukrainian, as well as some other languages including French, but was also a Canadian citizen and, therefore, a British subject. Davidovich, it seems, hesitated about giving up what might be several years of his life and career for the sake of an unpaid secret mission abroad, but, at the urging of the ORU leaders and possibly a personal letter from the *Vozhd* in Europe, Konovalets himself, finally agreed to take up the task. In the fall of 1937, Davidovich took leave of his Ukrainian friends in New York and boarded a ship for Europe.[15]

Once in Europe, the young and inexperienced emissary from America had to orient himself to the current political situation and undergo some training. He visited Germany, Austria, and France, where the OUN published its major newspaper *Ukrainske slovo*, as well as Italy, where he met Konovalets and several other important OUN leaders. During this time, he also seems to have undergone a certain kind of training for his future assignments, supposedly overseen by Konovalets himself. By early 1938,

Davidovich was already in London, where he met Kysilewskyj and stayed with him in his house. For two months, Davidovich and Kysilewskyj were very close. The director of the Ukrainian Bureau introduced the young-er man to various British contacts who were sympathetic to the Ukrainian cause, including Colonel Cecil Malone, a labourite who worked closely with the bureau, and Lancelot Lawton, a right-winger who edited a jour-nal called *Contemporary Russia* and whose wife was Ukrainian or, at least, a pro-Ukrainian Russian. Kysilewskyj did his best to co-opt the younger man into the work of the bureau and encouraged him to help with trans-lations, press releases, and the preparation of articles for the press. He also helped him to apply for admission to the semi-official Royal Institute of International Affairs (Chatham House) where the famous historian Arnold Toynbee was director. At the same time, Davidovich applied for admission to the School of Slavonic and East European Studies at the University of London, where he undertook to do graduate work in his chosen field; this student identity served both as a cover for his secret mission on behalf of the OUN and as a "useful" preparation, as he later put it, for a future academic career.[16] It was at this point, only about two months after arriving in London, that the twenty-four-year-old Stephen Davidovich met the twenty-eight-year-old Gabrielle Roy.

Gabrielle was still associating with the Pawluks and Bohdan Hubicki when she met Stephen. Bohdan, her most trustworthy protector, had introduced her to a circle of rich and influential people who regularly gathered at the house of Lady Frances Ryder on Cadogan Gardens in South Kensington. "This generous lady," as Gabrielle later described her, "used to open her London apartment every day at tea-time to students, regardless of colour, from every corner of the Empire." As a rare French Canadian visitor, Gabrielle was especially welcomed. One day, a certain Lady Wells, who was often hostess in place of Lady Frances, rushed to Gabrielle, holding out both hands. "Dear," she said, "I've someone really special for you to meet." Gabrielle's eyes turned across the hundred or so people in the room and only one pair of eyes, "dark, burning," drew her attention. They belonged to a handsome young man of medium stature with dark hair. Lady Wells introduced the two Canadians to each other and they immediately seemed transfixed. For a long time, they simply sat together looking into each other's eyes. It was quite literally love at first sight. The young couple was amazed to find each other after coming halfway across the globe. Stephen, it turned out, was a friend of Bohdan Hubicki's, and Bohdan had already wanted to introduce Stephen and Gabrielle, saying to the young woman: "He's a funny fellow, fascinating in a way that bothers me a bit because you'd say he's trying to make you forget you know practically nothing about him. I don't really know what to think of him. He could be a fine person, however ... And yet ..."[17]

The two young people, the hopeful French Canadian drama student and the secret OUN emissary posing as a student of eastern Europe, were soon going out together. One of their first dates was at the opera, where they heard Boris Godunov. At one point, Stephen, premier vocalist that he was, sang for his new girlfriend a few bars of the monk Pimen's "Great Song of Destiny." It was not long before the couple became lovers, and the following weeks of that winter and spring of 1938 became among the most memorable of Gabrielle Roy's entire life. The story of this love affair, Gabrielle's first, is told with great sensitivity and artistic skill in the young writer's autobiography, written some forty years later; it is today considered to be a classic of the genre in Canadian literature.[18]

At this same time, Stephen made some of his first reports to Colonel Konovalets on his activities in London. They are brief and direct, written in a cursive Cyrillic handwriting. In a letter of 31 March 1938, he described the general political climate in England for the colonel, who seems to have known very little about that country. Stephen told Konovalets that, aside from the small circle of people in contact with the Ukrainian bureau, the English knew nothing of Ukraine. The English public was generally in favour of peace, and Winston Churchill, so Stephen wrote, led the forces that wanted to see close ties between England, France, and Russia. Stephen wrote that he had prepared an article on Ukrainian affairs for the *Fortnightly Review* but did not yet know if it would be accepted. He told Konovalets that he had become a member of the Royal Institute of Foreign Affairs and informed him of people whom he had met there and through his activities as a student. These included a certain "Dr Segal, a Jew," whom he thought represented a Russian viewpoint, Professor Rose, whom he mistakenly thought was a "Canadian Pole," R. W. Seton-Watson, who headed the School of Slavonic Studies, and Colonel Malone, who worked most closely with Kysilewskyj's bureau.

In this same letter, Stephen informed Konovalets that the best opportunities for promoting the Ukrainian cause were provided by the informal clubs of the British gentry for overseas British (*zamorski Britiitsi*), especially the Lady Frances Club. He noted that as soon as he gave his Slavic-sounding name at parties there, he always was requested to say something explaining his background (*davaty korotkyi narys pro ukraintsiv*). Remembering Bohdan Hubicki, it seems, he also noted the possibilities that the group of Ukrainian Canadian musicians in London had for spreading information about Ukraine.[19]

On 25 April, Stephen wrote his second report to Konovalets. In this letter, he praised the work that Kysilewskyj was doing, though he noted that Kysilewskyj's patron Makohin seemed to have had personal ambitions of some sort. He also noted that Kysilewskyj had asked him to help draw up a memorandum for the Foreign Office and that Kysilewskyj's contact, a man who had just returned from Turkey, had taken this document and presented it to the British foreign minister, Lord Halifax; he was told that the two men spent a half-hour discussing the Ukrainian question together. This mysterious man from Turkey, it turned out, was the famous British spy Tracy Philipps, whom Stephen got to know well and who was sent to Canada after the outbreak of war to lecture on British war aims; at that time, he also undertook serious work helping to get non-British Canadian citizens onside for the war effort. (Philipps later married Lubka Kolessa, a prominent pianist of Ukrainian background.) Stephen ended his letter to Konovalets by noting that in England, Lancelot Lawton, the editor of the journal *Contemporary Russia*, was "the greatest knower and friend of things Ukrainian." Four days later, on 29 April, Stephen sent another brief letter to Konovalets in which he informed him that he had found a printing house capable of printing Ukrainian-language materials. This note was to be Stephen's last communication with the *Vozhd*. It is notable, though hardly surprising, that in none of these letters to Konovalets does Stephen say anything about his personal affairs or mention his relationship with Gabrielle Roy.[20]

Throughout April and May of 1938, Gabrielle and Stephen saw each other almost every day. Their affair was intense and passionate, and Gabrielle, in particular, was growing very dependent on Stephen. Then, suddenly one day towards the end of May, Stephen simply disappeared. Gabrielle, of course, was deeply disturbed. She called his home, frequented places they had been together, and made inquiries about him. But all to no avail. It was at this point that she realized how very little she actually knew about him. Certainly, he was young, handsome, well spoken, educated, and, of course, a fellow Prairie Canadian, but she knew little more. When she thought about it, she discovered a good many allusions to cities he apparently knew: Paris, Prague, Munich, Vienna, and others, though he had never actually told her he had been in any of them. Slowly, a feeling of distrust and resentment against Stephen began to build up inside the anxious Gabrielle. Who exactly was this man to whom she had so freely given her heart? Where had he so suddenly disappeared to, and why did he not even stop to say goodbye or even telephone her? The days and then the weeks went by and still no word from Stephen. Greatly disturbed, Gabrielle fell into a very deep pit of depression.[21]

Gabrielle and Stephen's fate was sealed on 23 May 1938, when a bomb exploded on a Rotterdam street, instantly killing Eugene Konovalets. The OUN leader had had a secret luncheon meeting with one of his many agents in eastern Europe, a man who went by the name of Valiukh, who was working underground in Stalin's USSR. But this particular agent turned out to be an assassin, not a nationalist but an NKVD agent whose real name was Pavel Sudoplatov, sent by Stalin, who had personally ordered the murder of Konovalets. Stalin was expecting a new war to break out in Europe, knew much about the OUN and its ties to German intelligence, and thought Konovalets and his organization to be preparing to overthrow Soviet rule in Ukraine with the help of Moscow's enemies. Sudoplatov himself had even heard, incorrectly as it turned out, that Konovalets had met with Hitler twice to prepare the ground for such an eventuality. With the help of an NKVD special department, a bomb had been placed in a box of chocolates that Sudoplatov gave to Konovalets on that fateful 23 May. (Sudoplatov knew that Konovalets loved chocolates.) The bomb was set to explode thirty minutes after its box was set from vertical to horizontal. Sudoplatov met briefly with Konovalets in a Rotterdam café, gave him the chocolates, and then made an excuse to leave. As he was escaping down the street, he heard the bomb explode. Konovalets was instantly killed.[22]

The entire Ukrainian world outside the Soviet Union was shaken by the murder of Konovalets. In Paris, Rome, the United States, and Canada, as well as western Ukraine under the Poles, the news spread like wildfire. "This sorrowful news," UNF activist Michael Sharik later recalled, "which the UNF Dominion Executive distributed by telegram across all Canada aroused the membership of our entire organization and stimulated a strong anti-Moscow reaction. As early as Saturday morning on 25 May 1938, great black flags were hung on our National Homes from Montreal to Vancouver letting both our own people and others know about the terrible murder carried out by Moscow in Rotterdam."[23] On 31 May, the front page of the UNF's official newspaper, *Novyi shliakh/The New Pathway*, exclaimed: "The OUN Leader has been murdered!" This was accompanied by a large picture of Konovalets framed in black. A statement below exclaimed: "Ukrainians! Nationalists! Our Leader [*Vozhd*] and the Guide [*Providnyk*] of the Ukrainian nation has fallen in bloody heroic struggle for freedom and state by the bandit hand of our mortal foe, Red Moscow!" The statement ended: "Glory to the leader, Eugene Konovalets of glorious memory! Long live the OUN! Long live the National Revolution! Death to the enemies of Ukraine! Glory to Ukraine [*Slava Ukraini!*]."[24]

Meanwhile, in London, the young OUN emissary Stephen Davidovich was immediately called away to do work on the continent. He went to Rotterdam and, posing as a British journalist, spoke with Dutch police and made inquiries as to the circumstances of Konovalets's death. On this trip, he also seems to have delivered a sum of money to Konovalets's widow and to have made certain arrangements for her. Shortly afterwards, he made a second trip to Rotterdam and spoke with police and justice officials again and met with Konovalets's secretary Volodymyr Baranovsky. He may have also undertaken other assignments at this time, about which we do not know.[25]

It was nearly a month before Stephen got in touch with Gabrielle. He called her and they arranged to meet. But it was not the same. They were both changed people. Gabrielle, who had known nothing but her own loneliness and misery for the last month, noticed a change in her boyfriend as well. She later wrote:

> When he came into view he was still quite far away and in the light of the streetlamp I thought his face looked thin and drawn, prematurely showing the wear and tear age would bring, he who was so young and vigorous ... We had come to a kind of little square with a bench, some trees, perhaps a fountain. We sat on the bench. Stephen looked straight ahead. He seemed so miserable, so much at a loss that I felt for him, thinking he was about to give me a plausible and convincing explanation for his behaviour and I was going to be ashamed of my suspicions. He took a deep breath and began to tell me a story which even today I wonder if I really heard from his lips.

It was then that Stephen told Gabrielle something of his secret work for the OUN, though seemingly he did not name that organization. He cautioned his French Canadian girlfriend that everything he was about to say must be kept in the strictest possible secrecy. He then told her of the underground struggle for an independent Ukraine and of the crimes of Stalin, mentioning the Great Famine, but, probably wishing to spare her unnecessary anxiety, said nothing about the recent murder of Konovalets. He told her he had been to the continent and had been trailed by the Soviet secret police, the NKVD. He said that his life was in danger and that by consorting with her, he was probably putting her in danger as well. Still, he seemed to think that their relationship was not yet doomed. Having told her something of the secret burden he was carrying, he felt relieved and talked of things they could do together in the future. But, for Gabrielle, things would never be the same again. Never again would she give her heart to Stephen as she had done when they first met; never again would she trust him so completely, or so, at least, she later claimed in her autobiography.[26]

The two young Prairie Canadians continued to see each other, but the pure elation of those first weeks together was gone. Towards the end of June, it seems, Stephen was called away again on one of his secret missions, this time "to one of the Balkan countries," says Gabrielle in her autobiography, but more likely to central Europe. There were no telephone calls or letters, only a note slipped under her door apologizing for not being able to give her any news. The less she knew about his activities, the better for her own safety, he told her. "Perhaps he was right," she concluded.[27]

Deeply confused by her steadily more complex relationship with Stephen, Gabrielle retreated to the English countryside. There in the village of Upshire in the county of Essex, just outside London to the northeast edge of Epping Forest, she happened upon the house of Esther Perfect and her father William in the course of a bus trip. The Perfects took her in and refreshed her with their warm house and calm, reassuring manners. It was there at the Perfects', still reeling from her experience with Stephen, that Gabrielle finally decided to become a writer rather than an actress. Oblivious to the gathering war clouds on the continent, she would return to the house of the Perfects several times before she returned to Canada, and again after the war had ended. During the summer and fall of 1938, she also continued to see Stephen. At one point, she went on a double date with him and Stephen and Olga Pawluk. Stephen Pawluk later recalled that she was a small and somewhat delicate woman who was always writing something down in her free moments.[28] On another occasion, she even accompanied Stephen to a reception at the Kysilewskyjs', as we know from an entry in the latter's London diary from 2 October 1938.[29] In these anxious days following the Munich Pact, which partitioned Czechoslovakia and gave the Sudetenland to Hitler, it would have been impossible to mix with such politically active Ukrainians without discussing politics and the possibility of a new war in Europe, and Gabrielle most certainly would have been aware of how excited they were about the fate of the most easterly region of Czechoslovakia, the province called Subcarpathian Ruthenia, which was then becoming known as "Carpathian Ukraine." Hitler had held out hopes to the Ukrainians, and many of them, especially OUN members and supporters like Stephen, already believed that an autonomous Carpatho-Ukraine might become the kernel of a new independent Ukrainian national state.

In fact, it was not long before an autonomous Carpatho-Ukrainian government was formed, complete with its own defence force, the so-called Carpathian Sich.[30]

This same autumn, Gabrielle retreated again to the calm of the Perfects' house in the countryside and was surprised when, shortly later, Stephen unexpectedly showed up at the door. Somehow, he had tracked her down through the registry at Canada House, the home of the Canadian High Commission (embassy) in London. This meeting at the Perfects' was as intimate and complex as their previous meeting in the spring at the time of the Konovalets assassination, after Stephen had first so unexpectedly disappeared: tender feelings; dark foreboding in the background. Stephen immediately charmed the Perfects with his bright face and easy manner. He sang and played the harmonium for them. Later, when the elderly William Perfect brought up his fears about the outbreak of a new war in Europe, Stephen became somewhat disconcerted but tried to reassure the old man that everything would be all right in the end. Before leaving, Stephen urged Gabrielle to leave England and go back to Canada as soon as possible. He told her: "I didn't want to talk about it seriously in front of Esther and the old man, he's so emotional, but I don't see how we're going to avoid war. It's almost certain, and it will be very soon." Gabrielle then asked Stephen about himself and he replied that he would probably end up in the Canadian army, but that he thought Stalin was a worse enemy than the Nazis, who had held out hopes to the Ukrainians about liberating them from the Communists.

"You'd trust Hitler?" Gabrielle asked in disbelief.

"For a while at any rate – or I'd pretend to. He'll arm us against the Russians. It's already begun, in fact. Then we'll use those arms to free ourselves from the Nazis."

"You might even stoop to terrorism, I suppose?" Gabrielle asked.

His eyes flashed briefly but fiercely. "If I had to ... perhaps ... yes. My people have suffered far too much over the centuries."

In Gabrielle's account, which almost certainly collapses several different conversations in different places and at different times into this last meeting, this was the point at which she finally turned against Stephen. She let him leave with a bitter feeling in her heart. They would never meet again. Still, she would never forget him.[31]

About a month after the evening party at the Kysilewskyjs' that Gabrielle attended with Stephen, new developments occurred in Czechoslovakia. Some territory in Slovakia and Carpatho-Ukraine was ceded to Hitler's ally, Hungary, and the Carpatho-Ukrainian government transferred its capital to the town of Khust in what remained of its autonomous country. This small polity was already beginning to take on the characteristics of an independent state. The defence force grew, a kind of foreign ministry was formed, and Ukrainian nationalists from all over Europe, but especially from Polish-ruled Galicia, poured into the country to help. In February 1939, elections to a local parliament were held. About this time, it seems, Stephen Davidovich also went briefly to Khust. On his return to England, he published an enthusiastic article in Lawton's journal *Contemporary Russia* about the tiny new state; this article clearly pointed out its national significance, its stimulating effect on Ukrainians living in Poland, Romania, and even the Soviet Union. He pointedly warned the Poles, in particular, that they would meet the same fate as the Czechs if they, too, did not make substantial concessions to their numerous and defiant Ukrainian minority in eastern Galicia. In general, Davidovich was optimistic, perhaps unrealistically so, about the future economic and political success of the new Carpatho-Ukrainian entity.[32]

At this time, as well, on instructions from the OUN leadership and with the financial support of the ORU and the UNF, Davidovich "broke" with Kysilewskyj and set up his own Ukrainian National Information Service. Kysilewskyj was, of course, deeply disappointed with this development, for he had never ceased trying to co-opt Davidovich into his own bureau. Doubtless, to some extent, it was tension over Carpatho-Ukraine and the proper Ukrainian attitude to take towards Hitler that spurred the break. At any rate, despite their political differences, Kysilewskyj and Davidovich remained on relatively good terms; they continued to cooperate in ways, exchanged information, and took care to avoid duplication and mutual criticism in their publications. The two men were destined to work together again in the future.[33]

By February 1939, it became evident that Hitler's "promises" to the Ukrainians, if they were that, about an independent Carpatho-Ukraine were empty and he was preparing to give this territory in its entirety over to the Hungarians. In March, with Hitler's blessing, the Hungarians invaded and annexed Carpatho-Ukraine, which symbolically but belatedly declared its independence. The small Carpatho-Ukrainian defence force was overwhelmed by the Hungarians and many people were killed. At this point, many Ukrainians, especially Ukrainian Canadians, including, perhaps, some moderate nationalists like Davidovich, became thoroughly disillusioned with Hitler. In June and July, Wladimir Kossar, the head of the Canadian UNF, made a fact-finding trip to Europe to discover the position that his organization should take if a general war should break out in Europe. In London, he visited Canadian High Commissioner Vincent Massey and, with his help, had an interview with the British Foreign Office. At this time, he also visited the office of Davidovich and his Ukrainian National Information Service, which, as he later told the RCMP, was funded by the UNF's "Penny Fund" collected for it from the Ukrainian Canadians. On his return to Canada, Kossar reported on his trip to Norman Robertson, Canadian Undersecretary of External Affairs.[34]

Meanwhile, the European OUN was adjusting to the new political situation in the continent. On 27 August 1939, only three days after the conclusion of the Molotov–Ribbentrop Non-Aggression Pact between Germany and the USSR, and most likely before its full significance could be appreciated, and only four days before the outbreak of the Second World War, the OUN held a general assembly of its leading members in Rome. At this meeting, Colonel Andrii Melnyk was formally chosen as successor to Konovalets and certain other changes were made to the organization. Stephen Davidovich attended this meeting as a Canadian representative under the somewhat transparent pseudonym "Davyd."[35]

While Europe and the Ukrainian Canadians were experiencing these vicissitudes of international politics, Gabrielle went her own way. She had been suffering health problems, including a throat ailment, for some time, and in early 1939, her illness translated into a fateful prognosis: she must surrender for good all hope of becoming an actress, for her throat could never endure a stage career. This strengthened her resolve to become a writer. In the winter and early spring of 1939, before returning to Canada, she made one last trip to France to see the south of that country. At that time, the Spanish Civil War was just ending and thousands of republican refugees were crowding across the border into France. Gabrielle witnessed the misery of these refugees from Franco's nationalists, and this probably helped to clarify her political ideas. After three months in France, Gabrielle returned to London and then, finally taking Stephen's advice, set sail for Canada. But she did not return to Manitoba; rather, she settled in Montreal, where she determined to make a living by writing, primarily through journalism. When, in September 1939, war broke out in Europe, Gabrielle was already preparing for her career in journalism, but she never wrote directly about the war, though she was already acquainted with some of its terrors through what she had seen in southern France. Rather, she sat down to chronicle its indirect, sometimes bitterly ironic, and always destructive consequences for the poor inhabitants of Montreal in her stunningly successful first novel *Bonheur d'occasion* (*The Tin Flute*). But this book was published only after the war had ended. During its course, her main job was journalism and one of her most important assignments was to report on the various "Peoples of Canada" for the Quebec magazine *Le bulletin des agriculteurs* (The farmers' bulletin). In this series, she described the variety of peoples who had settled the West, including the Hutterites, the Doukhobors, the Mennonites, some Jewish farmers in Saskatchewan, some Sudeten refugees, and, last but not least, the Ukrainians.[36]

Perhaps with some memories of her father in mind, Gabrielle titled this April 1943 piece "Petite Ukraine" (Little Ukraine). In it, she described the Ukrainian communities scattered across the northern edge of the prairie, the so-called poplar belt, from Mundare in Alberta, through Edmonton, North Battleford, and Canora to the Manitoba border. She described the physical appearance of these Ukrainian communities, with their oriental-style domed churches rising clearly above the broad prairie skyline, but she concentrated on what she believed to be the Ukrainian Canadian national character. With their community deeply divided along both political and religious lines, she called the Ukrainians "the Irish of the continent." She painted a colourful picture of their virtues and faults, their picturesque qualities and their mundane side, their generosity and their stinginess, their neat thatched and whitewashed cottages, but also their plain interiors and dirt floors. She did not omit their peculiar situation between the new country and the old: "Broadminded and tolerant in Canadian affairs," she wrote, "they remain fanatical about things that are buried in their national past." She concluded with this perceptive observation of their 1940s character:

> The Ukrainians supposedly remain peasants, but they are peasants with a taste for learning. And when they are educated they gravitate toward the liberal professions, toward teaching in universities and schools, toward music and politics. They also invade the agricultural colleges, high schools and universities of Saskatchewan and Alberta. These are farmers who transform themselves completely in less than two generations.
>
> The Ukrainian population of Canada – next largest to that of the French Canadians – [*Le groupment ukrainien au Canada, le plus important après le bloc français*] is no longer tied to the land. It is no longer even a minority in the strict sense of the word. It too is involved in our national life. It has participated too intimately in Canada's self-expression to merit this description. A strange thing: this people, so fiercely nationalist, the one which could most easily have resisted assimilation, is in fact the one which has most completely adapted to the country [*Étrange chose: ce peuple le plus féru de nationalisme,*

celui qui aurait le plus facilement résister à l'assimilation, est quant même celui qui c'est le plus completement adapté au pays ...] and not only adapted but contributed to fashioning the features of Canada's West. Its traditions have passed into our national heritage. Its dances, costumes and songs have become our own.

Her final sentence reads: "One cannot imagine this country without them, for they have contributed an indefinable touch of roughness and extreme gentleness, of violent gaiety and violent protest, the profound characteristics, no doubt, of this people, excessive in all things, in all things impulsive."[37] Doubtless, Gabrielle's passionate affair with the young and committed OUN emissary in London, Stephen Davidovich, coloured her judgment considerably.

The end of the war brought a new phase in the lives of Gabrielle and Stephen as well as their Ukrainian Canadian friends in London. In 1945 and after, of course, Gabrielle published her Montreal novel *Bonheur d'occasion* to general acclaim, won the Governor General's Award for literature and the Prix fémina in Paris, and gained some world fame. In 1947, she fell in love with and married a Manitoba physician, Marcel Carbotte; at first, they were happy together, but the good doctor, it seems, turned out to have some homosexual tendencies and the marriage had its problems, at least in later years.

As to Stephen, from 1939 to 1941, he continued to run the Ukrainian National Information Service in London; he continued to write news releases and articles for the press and to make useful contacts in British society. He distributed a monthly bulletin on Ukrainian affairs not only to the press but also to every British MP and member of the House of Lords. The fact that from September 1939, when war broke out, to June 1941, when Hitler launched his surprise attack against the USSR, these two anti-democratic powers had partitioned Poland, as well as most of eastern Europe, between themselves and were de facto allies made Stephen's work easier; his anti-Soviet position was also "objectively" anti-Nazi, and, of course, it was the Nazis with whom the British were at war. It was at this time that Stephen published what was probably his most influential article in the British press, his essay on "the Ukrainian Problem," which appeared in December 1939 in the British journal *The Nineteenth Century and After.* In this article, Stephen pointed out the weakness of both Poland and Czechoslovakia, which had fallen to Germany so very easily, and he argued in favour of a Ukrainian national state in eastern Europe, which, together with Poland and Czechoslovakia, could stand as a strong independent power or block and, by implication, a possible ally of Britain against both German and Soviet "imperialism." Stephen argued that since Ukraine was large enough in size, economy, and population, with a distinct population in terms of anthropological, linguistic, and cultural characteristics, and also had a firm desire for unity and independence, it deserved this unity and independence.[38]

At the same time, Stephen continued to lobby influential Britons and cultivate contacts in British society. One of the most important of these contacts was Charles Milnes Gaskell, a well-placed English aristocrat who had travelled in eastern Europe and, about this time, completed a deeply sympathetic history of Ukraine. Stephen spent many long hours discussing politics and history with him, and, among the Ukrainian Canadians, including Stephen, it was thought that Milnes Gaskell might have been working with British intelligence; this was not improbable, as he was very well informed and certainly had many contacts in government. Given this relationship with Milnes Gaskell, as well as with Tracy Philipps, it can be said that at various times the OUN probably had contact with British as well as German intelligence.[39] On another level, just before the war broke out, Stephen had a personal confrontation with Ivan Maisky, Stalin's ambassador to Great Britain, which took place at the Royal Institute of International Affairs. This altercation must have been significant, because Stephen recalled it quite clearly some forty years later.[40] At any rate, in 1941, Hitler's surprise attack on the USSR and its new status as Britain's senior ally (replacing Canada in this position) made Stephen's continued political work impossible. He was forced to close down his office and cease his criticism of the USSR. He was suddenly "pressed" by certain officials, as he later put it, to join the Britiash army, but he preferred to join the Canadian army stationed in Britain, and he spent the rest of the war in Canadian service, where he attained the rank of captain. When the war ended, he taught at first at the Canadian overseas university for servicemen in England; then, in 1946, he returned to Canada and (with Kysilewskyj's help) joined the Citizenship Branch of the federal government in Ottawa, where he played a modest role in the drafting of the new Citizenship Act (1947), which, for the first time created a Canadian citizenship separate from British. Afterwards, he transferred to the Ontario government, where he worked in the Department of Education on citizenship matters, then in the administration of the civil service. He married twice (the first time to an English woman; the second time to a Ukrainian woman) and eventually joined Atkinson College of York University, where, for several years, he taught evening courses in public administration. He was also very active in the 1950s and again in the 1970s in the movement in the Toronto Ukrainian community to establish a Chair of Ukrainian Studies in the history department at the University of Toronto.[41]

The other Ukrainian Canadians from London had different fates. Kysilewskyj closed his bureau and returned to Canada shortly after the war began, and, after being compelled to change his name to Kaye, was taken on by the federal government as the main employee of the new Nationalities Branch, which monitored opinion among ethnic Canadians during the war and strove to rally them behind the effort. This was a fitting position for a multilingual representative of the largest Canadian ethnic group after the British, the French, and the Germans. This Nationalities Branch was the forerunner of the Citizenship Branch, which Stephen later joined and which, in the 1970s, was transformed into the Multiculturalism Directorate. Kysilewskyj ended as a professor of Slavic Studies at the University of Ottawa and published some seminal works on Ukrainian Canadian history of the pioneer period.[42]

Gabrielle's closest friend, Bohdan Hubicki, married an English woman in 1940, also a musician, but he was killed in an air raid three months later.[43] During the war, Stephen Pawluk worked for the British in top-secret radar installations; he and Olga Pawluk returned to Toronto after the war, where Stephen founded a Ukrainian branch (number 360) of the Canadian Legion. He remained a trusted though not particularly close friend of Gabrielle's Stephen and was active in funding scholarly books about the Ukrainian Canadians; in fact, he saw Kysilewskyj's master work on the pioneer immigration through to press.[44] Thus, Gabrielle's remark about the attraction of the liberal arts and the academy to professionally minded Ukrainian Canadians was not entirely off the mark, at least with regard to those whom she knew best.

The story of Gabrielle's amorous affair with Stephen became public knowledge in 1984 when her autobiography was first published, but in this autobiography she gave only Stephen's first name; for most students of her life, his surname remained a mystery. As late as 1996, her best-informed biographer, François Ricard, had no idea who "Stephen" was or to what secret organization he belonged, never mind what important business he had been called away to at the end of May 1938. But some of these things were well known to certain individuals in the Ukrainian community in Toronto, where Stephen lived until 1987. Also, much was known about the assassination of OUN leader Eugene Konovalets as early as 1938, when it occurred. (Stephen himself made some of the first inquiries about it.) Only some further details, albeit very interesting, and the real name of the assassin first became public with the publication of Sudoplatov's book in the 1990s. It is the conjunction of Gabrielle and Stephen's affair and the Konovalets assassination, a conjunction that was unknown to Gabrielle herself, but the effects of which shook her confidence in her love and firmly turned her towards becoming a writer, together with the approaching war in Europe and, in particular, the 1938–39 Carpatho-Ukraine crisis, that is the central point of this story. It is a story that forever changed the course of Canadian and Quebec literature and that says much, as well, about Ukrainian Canadian history of the mid-twentieth century.

Library Studies and Reference Works

12 Inveterate Voyager: J. B. Rudnyckyj on Ukrainian Culture, Books, and Libraries in the West during the "Long Cold War"

Littera scripta manet, verbum imbelle perit.
(Napysana bukva zalyshaietsia, bezsilne slovo znykaie.)
(The spoken word perishes, but the written word remains.)

Iu. V. Tsymbaliuk, Latynski pryslivia i prykazky

Jaroslav B. Rudnyckyj (1910–1995) was a leading Ukrainian émigré scholar during the period of the Long Cold War, which began with the defeat of Nazi Germany in 1945 and ended in 1991 with the collapse of the Soviet Union. A philologist and linguist by training, he made significant contributions to Ukrainian scholarship in many areas, including Ukrainian dialectology, lexicography, etymology, onomastics, folklore studies, and library science and bibliography. Although he is mainly known in scholarship for his important but unfinished two-volume *Etymological Dictionary of the Ukrainian Language*, his Ukrainian-German dictionary, and his extensive study of the term and name "Ukraine,"[1] he also penned several travel books, as well as surveys of Ukrainian libraries and library collections that deserve attention on their own account. These works on his academic travelling and on bibliography and library science are the subjects of the present chapter.[2]

J. B. Rudnyckyj was, in many ways, a typical Ukrainian émigré scholar of the so-called DP (Displaced Persons) emigration that fled to the West before the advance of the Soviet Army during the final phase of the Second World War. He was born and spent his early childhood in the town of Przemyśl (Peremyshl in Ukrainian) in Habsburg Galicia and received his university education in Slavistics at the University of Lwów (Lviv in Ukrainian) in what was then an eastern, largely Ukrainian-inhabited province of interwar Poland. His doctoral thesis supervisor was the Polish scholar Witold Taszycki, a specialist in the study of Slavic names, and Rudnyckyj inherited this interest from his supervisor, whom he greatly admired. After receiving his doctorate in Lviv in 1937, with the blessing of his Polish supervisor, Rudnyckyj went to Berlin to work on an ambitious Ukrainian-German dictionary at the Ukrainian Scientific Institute in that city. (The Ukrainian Scientific Institute in Berlin had been established by the conservative Ukrainian Hetman, or monarchist organization, but Rudnyckyj's association with it was purely academic.) At the outbreak of war in 1939, Rudnyckyj (still a Polish citizen) was briefly arrested by the Gestapo, but managed to be shortly released and, in 1940, completed his "*Habilitation*" (which was required for university teaching) at the Ukrainian Free University in Prague (*Ukrains'kyi vil'nyi universytet u Prazi*). He remained in Prague for the rest of the war, married Maryna Antonovych, a girl from a very distinguished Ukrainian émigré family, and was resident there when his big Ukrainian-German dictionary was published. At war's end in 1945, with the Soviet Army approaching the city, he moved to the American zone of occupation in western Germany. In Germany, Rudnyckyj taught Slavistics, including Church Slavonic, at various institutions including the Ukrainian Free University, which had been transferred to Munich, and at the University of Heidelberg. At this time, rumours of a new war between the West and the Soviet Union were ripe and Rudnyckyj, like most of the eastern European Displaced Persons living in Germany, very much wanted to move further west. About this same time, Canadian immigration policy became more open. In 1949, having been offered temporary work by the Ukrainian Cultural and Educational Centre in Winnipeg (*Oseredok ukrainskoi kultury i osvity*), which had been established a few years previously by the Ukrainian National Federation of Canada (UNF), he emigrated to the North American Dominion and settled in Winnipeg. (The Ukrainian Canadian schoolteacher and UNF activist Oleksander Gregorovich had been instrumental in this.) Later that same year, Rudnyckyj founded the Department of Slavic Studies at the University of Manitoba.

In Canada, Rudnyckyj settled down very quickly and soon became one of Winnipeg's most prominent Ukrainians. At this time, he was very active in the émigré Ukrainian Free Academy of Sciences in Canada (*Ukrainska vil'na akademiia nauk v Kanadi,* or UVAN), which he had helped to transfer to Canada from Munich and was headquartered in Winnipeg. In Canada, Rudnyckyj continued work on his *Etymological Dictionary of the Ukrainian Language,* which he had begun in Prague during the war, and the first fascicule was published in 1962. In 1963, Prime Minister Lester

B. Pearson invited Rudnyckyj to serve on the Royal Commission on Bilingualism and Biculturalism and Rudnyckyj accepted, becoming a main spokesman for the country's non-English and non-French ethnic groups. As such, he was a principal author of the fourth book of the Royal Commission, which dealt with the contributions of "Other Ethnic Groups" and was the basis for the new federal policy of multiculturalism proclaimed in the early 1970s. It was also during his Winnipeg period that Rudnyckyj, who, as a graduate student in Lviv, had had some basic training in librarianship, published several of his most important contributions to Ukrainian and Slavic bibliography and library studies. These included several substantial booklets of travel journals published by the Winnipeg Ukrainian printer Ivan Tyktor, who was also a political refugee from Lviv, which, as the major city of "Western Ukraine" (largely the eastern half of old Galicia) was finally annexed to the Ukrainian SSR in 1944. Throughout his Winnipeg period, Rudnyckyj publicized these and other works in general articles for the public-at-large in the Ukrainian- and English-language press. He published these articles in a variety of Ukrainian newspapers affiliated with several different political organizations, both traditionally conservative and more radically nationalist as well as liberal democratic. None of them, however, was pro-Communist. In 1976, Rudnyckyj retired from the University of Manitoba and moved to Montreal, from which he frequently commuted to Ottawa to work in the National Archives and the National Library and teach part-time at the University of Ottawa. During this period, apparently for the first time in his life, he became openly active in Ukrainian party politics and joined the government of the liberal democratic Ukrainian National Republic in exile. He returned to his native Ukraine only after the collapse of the USSR and the proclamation of Ukrainian independence in 1991. He never completed his visionary etymological dictionary and died in Montreal in 1995.[3]

Rudnyckyj's contributions to the general history of Ukrainian studies in the West and to Ukrainian bibliography and library studies can be divided into three categories: 1) his travel writings in which he described his visits to various Ukrainian libraries, archives, and museums in the West and briefly described their most important holdings; 2) his formal descriptions of individual libraries in which he again listed their most important holdings; and 3) his annual bibliographies of Ukrainian and Slavic literature published in Canada.

Rudnyckyj's travel writings consist of five substantial booklets and several smaller pamphlets describing his travels to various parts of the

Western world. These writings were limited to the Western world because Rudnyckyj was an émigré scholar forbidden entry to the Soviet Bloc where his major cultural and academic interests lay. Thus, he actively sought out and publicized Ukrainian and Slavic culture wherever he could find them in the countries that were open to him. These included Canada, the USA, and the countries of western Europe. Being an untiring traveller, Rudnyckyj also visited and wrote about other parts of the world, but, since Ukrainian and Slavic culture played a lesser role in those countries, they will not be treated in depth in this chapter. In general, it should be stressed that Jaroslav Rudnyckyj was very conscious of his status as an exile or émigré scholar who, because of the Communist dictatorship and its tight ideological control of all culture, could not return to his native land. His travel writings, therefore, have a certain sense of urgency about them. He was determined to describe, collect, and preserve as much of his native culture as he could, believing that it was under great threat in his occupied and "enslaved" homeland.[4]

The first of Rudnyckyj's major travel booklets and the one that served as a model for several others was his *Z podorozhi navkolo pivsvitu* (Travels across half the world). In this booklet, the Winnipeg professor described a trip to Europe he made in 1955 to attend a conference on onomastic science in Salamanca, Spain; he used the opportunity to visit several other European countries as well, including Switzerland, Germany, Belgium, France, England, and Holland. In each of these countries, Rudnyckyj sought out Ukrainian émigré contacts and visited libraries and museums in the hope of gathering material on Ukrainian culture "in exile."[5]

After a brief introduction consisting of previously published newspaper reports on his travels, Rudnyckyj begins by describing the onomastics conference in Salamanca, mentions the names of the three Ukrainians who participated, and gives the titles of the two papers he delivered: "Toponymic Neologisms in Canada" and "Spanish Names in the Ukrainian Version of Don Juan." He then describes the contents of these papers before going on to other matters. These latter concerned the Ukrainian collection of the Centre for Oriental Studies in Madrid, his visit to the famed Alcazar (High Castle) in Toledo, which reminded him of the Ukrainian poem on this theme by the interwar western Ukrainian poet B. I. Antonych, and his stay in Barcelona, where he noted the paucity of Ucrainica in the local libraries but refrained from discussing the local language or Catalan nationalism, which, in fact, had many parallels to Ukrainian nationalism. In general, Rudnyckyj was most impressed by the library of the Centre for Oriental Studies in Madrid, which, despite its geographical and cultural distance from Ukraine, had about a thousand titles devoted to the country. He made no comments on the Franco dictatorship but made it clear that, with Antonych and most western Ukrainian intellectuals, he sympathized with the Royalists and not the Republicans during the Spanish Civil War. Perhaps his ostensible lack of interest in the Catalans can be explained in part by this political stance, for the Catalans had been among the strongest supporters of the republic, the Republican cause being dominated by the Communists just as the Royalist cause was dominated by the Fascists.[6]

From Spain, Rudnyckyj went to Switzerland, which he described as "the land of well-ordered details." The city that most interested him in this country was Geneva, the home of what Rudnyckyj called "the bankrupt" League of Nations and the place where, during the First World War, a small group of exiled Ukrainians, whose history went back to the 1880s when the famous folklorist and political activist Mykhailo Drahomanov went into exile, published *La revue ukrainienne*. This pioneering journal had been a strong supporter of Ukrainian independence, and Rudnyckyj mentioned in passing that he and his generation, in general, shared the newer independentist goals of the journal rather than the older federalist ideals of Drahomanov. Rudnyckyj also visited Lausanne, where he noted that all Ukrainian materials in the libraries were lumped together under the classification "Russia."[7]

From Switzerland, Rudnyckyj went on to Germany, Belgium, France, England, and Holland, in each country visiting local Ukrainian contacts, libraries, archives, and museums. In Germany, where he had previously lived for several years, he was especially attracted to Heidelberg with its great university where he had once taught, Munich, where so many eastern European émigrés had been based after the war, and Marburg, which was the home of "Canadian Studies" in Germany and the "Canadian Library," which contained several series of UVAN publications from Winnipeg.[8] In France, he visited the Petliura Library in Paris, which had been founded by Ukrainian émigrés in the 1920s, confiscated by the Germans during the war, and with great difficulty started anew after 1945.[9] In England, he visited the library of the British Museum and discussed the terminological, transliteration, and classification problems of the Ukrainian books stored there. He noted that the British Museum held a large collection of valuable Ukrainian materials from the nineteenth century, including seminal works by Mykhailo Maksymovych, Taras Shevchenko, and Mykola Kostomarov. It also subscribed to the newspapers *Ukrainskyi holos* (Ukrainian voice) and *Kanadiiskyi farmer* (The Canadian farmer) from Winnipeg. (At the time, these were the largest-circulation Ukrainian newspapers in Canada.) Also in England, Rudnyckyj visited the School of Slavonic Studies of the University of London, which published the prestigious *Slavonic and East European Review*, and Oxford University, where he examined the books and manuscripts of the pioneering nineteenth-century British Slavist W. K. Morfill, who paid some attention to Ukraine. His notes on Belgium and Holland were less extensive than those on France, Germany, and England, but everywhere the Winnipeg professor went, he managed to find connections to Ukraine and Ukrainian books.[10]

The structure of *Z podorozhi navkolo pivsvitu* also deserves some attention. This book is very much a travel journal rather than a memoir. It was pieced together from notes and articles, some of them already published, made in 1955 during the actual voyage itself. It contains very little in the way of an introduction or conclusion, and its main value lies in its brief vignettes of Ukrainian culture and the Ukrainian collections that existed in western Europe on the eve of the events of 1957, especially the launching of Sputnik, which revolutionized Western, especially American, views of the Soviet Union, Soviet education and science, and Slavic culture. The western European Ukrainian collections of 1955 were substantial, but they had been built up very gradually over the course of the nineteenth century, and there was no sense of great progress or movement in the contemporary collection of these materials. This was quickly to change after Sputnik and the Soviet launch of the first man in space.[11]

On a different level, it should be noted that Rudnyckyj's booklet did not go into detail about how the various Ukrainian collections in western Europe had been acquired, nor did it tell why Rudnyckyj chose to describe some libraries and not others. Aside from his special interest in philology, dictionaries, and grammar books, Rudnyckyj was seemingly simply attracted to whatever Ukrainian materials were at hand: the larger the collection, the more the scholar was attracted to it.

Nevertheless, Rudnyckyj's first travel book must have enjoyed some success, for, in quick succession, he published a number of additional volumes in the same format and on similar themes. One of the most important of these was his *Z podorozhei po Kanadi 1949–1959* (Travels across Canada 1949–1959).[12]

This travel book about Canada was somewhat more reflective than Rudnyckyj's book on Europe in 1955. It contained fewer notes made during his voyages and more detail on the cities and libraries he visited. The book begins auspiciously with a discussion of Rudnyckyj's home in

Canada, Winnipeg, the "Ukrainian capital of Canada" right through to the 1970s. In these years, among Canadian cities, Winnipeg had by far the largest population of Ukrainian origin and had a great number of Ukrainian cultural institutions, including libraries.

First, Rudnyckyj, etymologist that he was, discussed the origin of the name "Winnipeg," deriving it from a Cree phrase meaning "muddy waters." He then turned to the orthography of the name and noted that in Ukrainian it was variously spelled "Vinnipeg," "Vynnipeg," "Vynypeg," and "Vynipeg." This orthographic confusion was even further complicated by the fact that in Soviet Ukraine, the letter "g" was banned after the 1920s, and that, therefore, in the USSR, it was also spelled with a final "h," thus rendering "Vynnipeh" and so on.[13]

Rudnyckyj then noted that approximately 10 per cent of Winnipeg's population was of Ukrainian origin and the city hosted a plethora of Ukrainian institutions. These included the umbrella Ukrainian Canadian organization called the Ukrainian Canadian Committee, the UVAN, in which the professor was a major figure; the Ukrainian Cultural and Educational Centre (*Oseredok ukrainskoi kultury i osvity* in Ukrainian, or Oseredok), where Rudnyckyj had worked during his first months in Canada; the Prosvita or "Enlightenment" Institute, which was a general social and cultural centre; the separate Prosvita Reading Society (*Prosvita Chytalna* in Ukrainian), which was basically a book club; the Ukrainian National Home (*Ukrainskyi narodnyi dim* in Ukrainian); and the Ukrainian collections in the libraries of the University of Manitoba and Saint Andrew's College, the latter a post-secondary institution and Orthodox seminary that, much later, in 1981, affiliated with the University of Manitoba. Winnipeg Ukrainians also played a pioneering and leading role in Canadian politics. It was one of the first major Canadian cities to have a mayor of Ukrainian origin (Steven Juba, 1914–1993) and also it was the home of one of the first federal senators of Ukrainian origin (Paul Yuzyk, 1913–1986).

Rudnyckyj then mentioned various local art and dancing schools and discussed Oseredok and its talented curator Tetiana Koshyts (1892–1966) before turning to his first love, Ukrainian books. He devoted an entire section to the Winnipeg Public Library and its Ukrainian collection. Remarkably, this library had contained no Ukrainian books at all prior to Rudnyckyj's arrival in Winnipeg in 1949. Local Ukrainians had patronized the libraries of the Ukrainian National Home, the Prosvita Reading Society, and Oseredok, but had neglected to demand a share of the activity at the public library. This changed with the professor's arrival;

he stimulated interest in Ukrainian affairs among the library's administration, helped with the acquisition of Ukrainian books, advised on the cataloguing of the collection, and interpreted Ukrainian orthography for the institution. Although, in 1959, the collection remained very small indeed (about 100 books), at least it had finally been initiated.[14]

From Winnipeg, Rudnyckyj passed on to other Canadian cities and in turn discussed Ottawa, Montreal, Regina, Moose Jaw, Saskatoon, the town of Mundare, Edmonton, Calgary, and Vancouver. In the nation's capital, he was greatly impressed by the young Ukrainian collection at the University of Ottawa and described his meetings with local Ukrainian scholars such as Vladimir Kaye-Kysilewskyj, Constantine Bida, Ivan Teslia, and Bohdan Kazymyra. The literary scholar Constantine Bida (1916–1979), in particular, was presiding at that time over a rapid expansion of Ukrainian studies at the university, whose library already contained over 2,500 volumes of Ucrainica.[15] In Montreal, which Rudnyckyj considered to be Canada's major city, he was impressed by the Ukrainian art collection of Ie. Dovhan, and, in Toronto, by local efforts at expanding the Ukrainian-language educational system. Strangely, however, he said nothing about the French-language University of Montreal, where, from 1949 to 1952, the famous ideologist of militant Ukrainian nationalism Dmytro Dontsov lectured on Ukrainian literature, or about the University of Toronto, where the teaching of Ukrainian literature was being pioneered by George Luckyj (chairman of the Slavic Department since 1957), and which already possessed a significant collection of Slavic books.[16] In general, however, it was the prairie provinces and their cities that seemed to impress Rudnyckyj most with their enormous populations of Ukrainian background – 12 per cent in Manitoba, and 10 per cent in both Saskatchewan and Alberta. Saskatoon and its university, he remarked, had hosted the first university-level course in the Ukrainian language and was home to the historian George Simpson, who was very interested in Ukraine, and the lexicographer Constantine Andrusyshen (1907–1983), who headed the first fully fledged Department of Slavic Studies in Canada. Other local Ukrainians such as the agronomist T. K. Pavlychenko (1892–1958) and the lawyer/grammarian Julian Stechishin (1895–1971) played an important role in Prairie Ukrainian culture. Saskatoon was also home to two, important, private student residences, each with its own library: the Petro Mohyla Institute, which was a very active Orthodox institution, and the Sheptytsky Institute, which was Ukrainian Catholic.[17] Finally, in Edmonton, Alberta, Rudnyckyj was impressed by the R. Gonsett Ukrainian Collection housed separately in the University of Alberta

Library. He devoted several pages to describing the holdings of this library, which possessed one of the richest Ukrainian collections in the country. In Alberta, he also visited the Ukrainian Catholic Basilian Monastery in Mundare, the library of which held a very rich collection of old Ukrainian books, especially religious books including some very rare items from the seventeenth century. (Although Rudnyckyj did not explicitly state it, many of these books had seemingly been brought to Canada from western Ukraine during the interwar period.) Finally, in Vancouver, he described the efforts of local Ukrainians, especially his fellow "onomast" Forvyn Bohdan, to build a Ukrainian collection at the University of British Columbia.[18] The book concludes with a comparison of the 1936 *Encyclopedia of Canada* (which treated "Galicians" in Canada, as Rudnyckyj put it, "incorrectly, insultingly, and tendentiously" [p. 123]) with the projected *Encyclopedia Canadiana,* to which Rudnyckyj, Simpson, Yuzyk, and Kaye-Kysilewskyj had all been invited, at Rudnyckyj's suggestion, to contribute. Rudnyckyj looked forward to seeing a very clear and respectable Ukrainian presence in this new encyclopedia.[19] In general, in spite of its undervaluing of the universities of Toronto and Montreal, Rudnyckyj's *Z podorozhei po Kanadi 1949–1959* gave a relatively good overview of Ukrainian scholarly life in Canada during the 1950s, which, of course, was one of the most intense periods of the Cold War. The fact that Ukrainian national culture could survive and even thrive in Canada during these years shines from every page of Rudnyckyj's work.[20]

Just as he produced travel booklets on Europe and Canada, so, too, did Rudnyckyj produce one on the United States. *Z podorozhi po Amerytsi 1956* (Travels across America 1956) paralleled Rudnyckyj's other travel writings both in form and content.[21] In it, he described a trip he made in 1956. He wrote about the various Ukrainian scholars and cultural activists whom he met and outlined the qualities of the various Ukrainian collections in the libraries he visited. During this voyage, Rudnyckyj was unable to visit the western USA, including California, but he did visit both the Midwest and the East. He started in Manitoba's neighbour, North Dakota, where a sizable colony of Protestants from central Ukraine had settled before the First World War, and then he passed on to Minneapolis, Madison, Detroit, Chicago, and then Washington, DC, which was one of his main destinations because it was the location of the Library of Congress (LC), which Rudnyckyj quite rightly called "the American National Library." From Washington, our professor went to New York, Boston, and through Ohio to Niagara, where he crossed over to Canada.

Rudnyckyj's American trip had many notable highlights. First, in Minneapolis, he visited the University of Minnesota, where there was considerable interest in American ethnic history, especially the history of the Great Economic Immigration that had occurred before the First World War. (About this time, Paul Yuzyk was doing his doctorate there on the history of the Ukrainian Greek Orthodox Church of Canada.) Eventually, an Immigration History Research Center was founded there and, by the 1970s, grew to become one of the foremost centres of American ethnic history in the United States. Rudnyckyj described the Ukrainian holdings of the university library, which included many rare items such as a Swedish biography (1909) of the early eighteenth-century Ukrainian Cossack Hetman or ruler Ivan Mazepa. He also surveyed the Minneapolis Public Library and described an affectionate meeting with Professor Oleksander Granovsky (1887–1976), a biologist with a specialty in insects who was a veteran of the Ukrainian American political scene and who had unofficially represented the Ukrainians of North America at the 1945 San Francisco conference where the United Nations was founded.[22] In Madison, Rudnyckyj surveyed the University of Wisconsin Library, and, in Chicago, he was most impressed by the Newberry Library, a public library that held a number of very rare nineteenth-century grammars of the Ukrainian language. The library had acquired these from the collection of the French prince Louis Bonaparte, who had been an amateur linguist and enthusiastic bibliophile. In Detroit, in which a significant Ukrainian community lived, Rudnyckyj was also impressed by the Ukrainian collection of the public library, but, of course, it was Washington's Library of Congress (LC) that drew his greatest admiration. At this time, Rudnyckyj did not yet know it, but the library's oldest Ukrainian titles – some eighteenth-century imprints in French – had been acquired from the private collection of Thomas Jefferson at the beginning of the nineteenth century and sporadically added to ever since. Rudnyckyj noted that not only was the library very rich in nineteenth-century titles from Russian Ukraine, but also subscribed to most émigré serials including those of UVAN and Oseredok in Winnipeg, and the very active Shevchenko Scientific Society (*Naukove tovarystvo im. Shevchenka*) in New York and Europe.[23] While in Washington, Rudnyckyj organized an exhibit of Ukrainian books, and arrangements were made for him to do a more formal survey of the library's Ukrainian holdings for the use of its employees and patrons. Rudnyckyj also noted that the valuable collection of the defunct embassy of the Ukrainian National Republic of 1918 to 1921 had been acquired by the library after the fall of the republic to the Bolsheviks.[24]

New York was Rudnyckyj's second major destination in the United States. Not only was the New York Public Library a major holder of Slavic materials in North America, but New York's Columbia University Library also possessed a sizable Slavic collection, and private Ukrainian libraries like that of the New York branch of the UVAN were also important. Rudnyckyj visited all these libraries and stated that, in his opinion, the New York Public Library was definitely the second-greatest centre of Ukrainian materials in North America after the Library of Congress. At that time as well, Columbia was a major centre of Ukrainian studies and scholars such as the literary historian Clarence Manning and the linguist Yury Shevelov (1908–2005) were working there. Moreover, the New York UVAN possessed an especially large collection of post-war printed materials from the DP camps in Germany, and the Ukrainian archivist Volodymyr Miiakovsky (1888–1972) was active in arranging and preserving these materials. Rudnyckyj met with as many of these people as he could and also participated in a centennial commemorative gathering in honour of the western Ukrainian writer Ivan Franko (1856–1916). An exhibition of Franko's numerous published works was part of this commemoration.[25] Finally, Rudnyckyj visited Yale University in New Haven, Connecticut, and Harvard University in the Boston area. Yale was the home of the famous Russian historian of Ukrainian origin George Vernadsky (1897–1972), and held some important titles in Ukrainian history, including works by Dmytro Bantysh-Kamensky, Kostomarov, Iavornytsky, Doroshenko, and others, while Harvard was at that time the North American home of the philosopher Dmytro Chyzhevsky (1894–1977) and the Byzantinist Ihor Shevchenko [Ševčenko] (1922–2009). The latter was later (in the 1970s) to be a founding member of the prestigious Harvard Ukrainian Research Institute, but at the time that Rudnyckyj was writing, Harvard was still very far from being an important centre for Ukrainian studies.[26] At the very end of his book, Rudnyckyj mentioned some important private Ukrainian libraries in the United States. One of the most notable of these was the personal library of Oleksander Sushko (1880–1966) of Chicago, formerly of Winnipeg, whose collection of nineteenth-century Galician Ukrainian publications (probably mostly acquired during his youth in Galicia and his Winnipeg period before 1914) was extensive.[27]

In general, Rudnyckyj's book on the United States closely paralleled his books on Europe in 1955 and on Canada from 1949 to 1959. However, it went into somewhat greater detail on the descriptions of the various library holdings. Moreover, the Winnipeg professor's enthusiasm for the Library of Congress and the New York Public Library was evident.

Rudnyckyj produced two further substantial titles in this same genre: *Z podorozhi po Italii* (Travels across Italy) and *Z podorozhi po Skandynavii* (Travels across Scandinavia).[28] In both these booklets he followed the same procedure as in his books on Europe, Canada, and the United States. In Italy, he visited the major sights in Rome and elsewhere, following the steps of predecessors like the Ukrainian poet Lesia Ukrainka (1871–1913) and others, but, unfortunately, said very little about Ukrainian books. In Scandinavia, he visited both Stockholm and Helsinki, where there were some very interesting Ukrainian materials. The latter was especially important as a Russian Imperial Deposit Library and held almost all major titles, both periodicals and individual books, published within the Russian Empire in the nineteenth century. In his later years, Rudnyckyj penned some further travelogues, most of which he published on his own, but none of these were as extensive as those published by Ivan Tyktor in the 1950s or early 1960s. However, even in countries very far removed from Ukraine, which Rudnyckyj visited later on, surprising things sometimes turned up and he was able to describe them. For example, in his brief description of the island of Malta, in the middle of the Mediterranean, he did note that the Royal Library in Valetta, the capital, had a rare copy of the Ostroh Psalter published in 1580, and that in the Church of Saint Florian, the cathedral church of the Knights of St John, beneath an old monument to one of the Grand Masters of the order, were depicted a conquered moor and a subjected Zaporozhian Cossack.[29]

In addition to this travel literature describing his visits to various libraries, Rudnyckyj also wrote several more formal surveys of individual libraries in Canada and the USA that he thought particularly important. These included both Ukrainian libraries in Winnipeg and elsewhere in Canada,[30] as well as his most favoured library, the Library of Congress in Washington. Three books sum up these various reports: 1) *Ukrainski biblioteky v Kanadi* (Ukrainian libraries in Canada); 2) "Ukrainica Congressiana: A Survey of Ukrainian Holdings at the Library of Congress"; and 3) "The Pre-1950 Ukrainica in the National Library of Canada."[31] The second of these three, although merely a mimeographed book distributed by the author to a few select libraries, was substantial and was by far the professor's most important contribution to library science.

Rudnyckyj's smaller book on Ukrainian libraries in Canada was divided into three parts: 1) church libraries affiliated with one of the two major Christian confessions among the Ukrainian Canadians, the Ukrainian Greek Catholic Church of Canada and the Ukrainian Greek Orthodox

Church of Canada; 2) secular libraries including both the libraries of various Ukrainian institutions in Canada and those of Canadian universities with Ukrainian studies programs; and 3) private collections of certain individuals, including scholars, clergy, and others.

Among the church libraries surveyed by Rudnyckyj in the 1950s, the Redemptorist Fathers' Library in Yorkton, Saskatchewan, stands out as the largest. It contained over six thousand volumes. But the Ukrainian Greek Catholic Archbishop's Library in Winnipeg, with some three thousand volumes, came in as an important second place, and the Basilian Fathers' Library in Mundare was very important because of its valuable collection of older imprints. These included the famous *Apostol* of 1563–64 and Ivan Fedorovich's pioneering Slavonic *Ostrozka Biblia* (Ostroh Bible) of 1581. (This latter work was photo-reprinted in Winnipeg in 1983.)[32] All these libraries were affiliated with the Ukrainian Greek Catholic Church, but the Orthodox were also represented, the libraries of the Petro Mohyla Institute in Saskatoon and the library of Saint Andrew's College in Winnipeg being the most important. The only church library in eastern Canada discussed by Rudnyckyj was that of Saint Nicholas Monastery (Orthodox) in Grimsby, Ontario.[33]

Rudnyckyj's treatment of Ukrainian secular libraries in Canada was more detailed than his treatment of church libraries. Among these, the single most important was undoubtedly the library of the Ukrainian National Home in Winnipeg. Founded before the First World War, it was certainly one of the oldest Ukrainian libraries in Canada, with extensive holdings in both fiction and the humanities, and its books were well arranged and attractively stored. Other important Winnipeg Ukrainian libraries included the library of Oseredok (founded in 1944), the library of the Prosvita Institute (founded 1918), the library of the Prosvita Reading Society (founded 1915), the UVAN library (founded 1949), and the Ukrainian department of the library of the University of Manitoba (also founded in 1949). The last-named library possessed the oldest Ukrainian book in Canada, the *Horodytskyi pomianyk* of 1484–1737. This is a bulky volume of 548 pages that lists the names of persons commemorated over the centuries at remembrance services in the church of Horodyshche, a village in Volhynia. As the oldest Cyrillic manuscript book on the North American continent, it was, of course, of enormous interest to Rudnyckyj, with his specialty in names.[34] The two Prosvita libraries were especially rich in *belles lettres*, including translations of western authors into Ukrainian, and the smaller UVAN library was basically a humanities scholarly collection. Although Rudnyckyj did not explicitly say it, the great bulk of these collections had obviously been acquired in western Ukraine before 1939 or was made up of North American imprints.[35]

Beyond Winnipeg, the most important Ukrainian collections in the country belonged to the Gonsett Collection of the University of Alberta and the library of the Ukrainian National Home in Toronto. The latter had been founded in 1917 and continuously added to since, while the former, already quite rich, was currently growing at a rapid rate. The third major university library collection of Ukrainian materials was housed at the University of Ottawa. Several other university libraries, such as those of the universities of British Columbia, Saskatchewan, and Toronto, had begun collection of Ukrainian materials but, in the 1950s, when Rudnyckyj did his survey, none approached the extent of the universities of Manitoba, Alberta, or Ottawa.[36]

Finally, Rudnyckyj listed some ninety-nine individuals, primarily scholars, who possessed large personal libraries and he gave their specialties: history, literature, philology, and so on. Rudnyckyj's book contained a bibliography (of mostly newspaper articles describing individual libraries) but no general conclusions. Also, most probably because of the political difficulties involved, Rudnyckyj took no account of the libraries of the pro-Communist organizations, the labour temples. (These organizations had substantial libraries in both Winnipeg and Toronto, including very full runs of much of the pro-Communist Ukrainian Canadian press and many rare items from Soviet Ukraine in the 1920s and 1930s.) Nevertheless, commenting on Rudnyckyj's volume several years later, the Toronto bibliophile Bohdan Budurowycz praised his "pioneering" effort at describing the various Ukrainian libraries of Canada.[37]

Rudnyckyj's more extensive and detailed, but unpublished, book on the Library of Congress (LC) was divided into several major parts: introduction, library policies about Ukrainian materials, an evaluative survey, a section on rare and valuable editions, and, of course, conclusions and appendices. It contained a brief history of the holdings of the library, a detailed description of them with indication of their strengths and weaknesses, a discussion of the very rarest books in the library, and recommendations as to possible improvements to the collection.

Rudnyckyj noted that Ukrainian materials had traditionally not been well distinguished from Russian and Polish materials in the library and that it was not until 1902 that a Slavic specialist had been engaged to work in the library. In 1907, this specialist, A. V. Babine, was instrumental in bringing the Genadii V. Yudin Collection from Russia to the library.[38] This collection was made up of many thousands of nineteenth-century titles from the Russian Empire, including many important Ukrainian titles. All these volumes, however, were accessed as "Russian" titles, and no attempt was made to distinguish Ukrainian materials from Russian. Indeed, the very name "Ukraine" was itself little known. On the other hand, for subsequent periods, our professor noticed steady progress in the handling of Ukrainian materials. The name "Ukraine" was introduced after 1914 and "a firm identification" of Ukrainian titles emerged after the Second World War. He noted, however, that, in spite of this progress, the Ukrainian community in the United States remained suspicious of the library for its believed "Russophile" tendencies in Ukrainian matters and this had impeded cooperation between local Ukrainians and the library in the acquisition of new Ukrainian materials. Many Ukrainian émigré authors and publishers simply did not send the library examples of their imprints.[39]

Rudnyckyj then noted that Ukrainian materials in the library actually antedated the acquisition of the Yudin Collection by almost a century. As mentioned above, some Ukrainian material in French had been acquired by the library in 1815 when it purchased the private library of Thomas Jefferson. These titles contained geographical works by the Polish count Jan Potocki (1761–1815), whose family held large estates in Ukraine, especially the large and important province of Podolia. Another early accession was a book on languages, *Sravnitelnye slovari vsekh 'iazykov' i narechii po azbuchnomu poriadku razpolozhennye/Linguarum Totius Orbis Vocabularia Comparativa*, by Peter Simon Pallas (1741–1811), who included a section on the "Little Russian dialect" in his volume. Rudnyckyj noted in passing that Pallas's description of the Ukrainian language as a Russian dialect influenced by Polish is not accepted by contemporary linguists, who consider the Ukrainian language to be close to Russian but nevertheless an independent tongue. Rudnyckyj then noted that the oldest Ukrainian book in the library was a copy of the Ostroh Bible of 1581, which had been acquired in 1958. At the time, only two other examples were known by him to exist in North America, one in Mundare, the other in Winnipeg.[40]

Having outlined the history of the Ukrainian collection, Rudnyckyj passed on to classification problems. These, he believed, were of great importance because many North American libraries followed the LC system very closely and, therefore, any error in its system was automatically copied to libraries throughout the continent.

Rudnyckyj believed that the main problem with the LC system was that it originated during the nineteenth century when almost all of eastern

Europe was politically divided among the Russian, Austrian, German, and Ottoman empires. The territory of today's Ukraine fell to the Russian and Austrian empires, and, therefore, Ukrainian materials in the library were classed as either Russian or Austrian regional materials (for historical titles, for example, either DK or DB). But throughout the twentieth century, momentous political changes had occurred in eastern Europe; the old empires had all collapsed and new states arisen. After 1945, almost all Ukrainian ethnic territory was united in the Ukrainian SSR, but the old LC regional classification system remained and did not reflect the new political situation. (Needless to say, the emergence of an independent Ukraine in 1991 even further displayed the inadequacies of the old LC regional system.) Rudnyckyj quoted extensively from the Toronto librarian Wasyl Veryha on how to remedy these shortcomings.[41]

Rudnyckyj then passed on to a statistical analysis of the Ukrainian collection. He quoted an internal LC audit by Basil Nadraga to the effect that, in 1978, the library contained some 39,250 Ukrainian volumes, of which 325 titles were stored in the rare book section. The collection was strongest in history, language, and literature, and then the physical sciences.[42]

The next section of Rudnyckyj's book dealt with transliteration problems, a subject on which he was expert. As is evident from the way he spelled his name, Rudnyckyj favoured the European or international system of transliteration over that of the LC. He admitted, however, that the international system with its many diacritical marks was inconvenient for non-linguists. He discussed a number of possible modifications to the LC system, but in the end made no insistent recommendations and left the entire question open.[43]

The following section of Rudnyckyj's book consisted of an evaluative survey of LC holdings of Ucrainica. Of these, he thought reference materials, encyclopedias, and bibliographies to be well represented, "rich, strong, and varied" (p. 221), language and literature to be especially strong, especially in materials from nineteenth-century Russia, but, ironically, weak in Ukrainian materials from Canada and the USA; folklore was modestly represented, the fine arts, especially from the post-Second World War period, somewhat better represented; as to the history collection, it was positively "rich," again in the nineteenth-century matter largely originating from the Yudin Collection. Geography was somewhat weaker, as were economics and law, with religion weakest of all. Rudnyckyj also surveyed the physical sciences and technology (especially interesting to Americans after the launching of Sputnik), and also health, but was modest in his recommendations in these areas. He did note, however, that Ukrainian materials printed in the West were a weakness in the collection.[44]

Rudnyckyj concluded his book with a series of recommendations for the library. He suggested that it expand its acquisition program through greater use of Ukrainian bookstores in North America and intensification of its exchange programs with scholarly institutions, that it publicize its activities better among North American Ukrainians, that more care be taken in the classification of materials; that many books be transferred to the rare book collection; that the valuable Cyrillic Union Catalogue be continued "under any circumstances"; and that a complete bibliography of Ukrainian materials in the collection be undertaken. However, he did not say anything about the acquisition of new "Samizdat" or "self-published" materials then being smuggled out of the Eastern Bloc. In general, there is no doubt about Rudnyckyj's high estimation of the LC collection of Ukrainian materials. His report strove to underline its importance and clearly mark it off as an independent field that would eventually affect the operation of other North American libraries and attract the positive attention of the Ukrainian reading public. Thus, he was greatly disappointed when the library declined to publish this report. As a result, he published a summary of his findings on his own, a summary in which some of his criticisms of LC practices and traditions were considerably blunter, or, at least more succinct, than in the original report.[45]

Finally, after completing his major report on the LC, Rudnyckyj turned to the National Library of Canada in Ottawa (NLC), where, after his retirement from the University of Manitoba, he was a part-time resident. He produced a parallel report on this library that made some useful comparisons between the Washington and Ottawa libraries. In general, he noted that while the LC had a huge collection of Slavica published abroad, but was weak in Canadian and even American materials, the NLC had a much weaker collection of European Slavica but was stronger in materials published in Canada. Rudnyckyj seemed to believe that this was due to the much stronger emphasis on ethnic studies and multiculturalism in Canada. He noted that about 3,000 Ukrainian language titles had been published in Canada from 1903 to 1949 but that the library held only about a quarter of them. It was very much stronger in titles published from the early 1950s when the NLC became a national deposit library, which, by law, received two copies of all titles published in Canada. The main recommendation of Rudnyckyj's report was that the library undertake strenuous efforts to fill in the lacunae in its pre-1950 collection of Canadian Ucrainica. Subsidiary recommendations concerned the necessity of similar reports to be done on Slavic materials in general and on materials concerning other Canadian ethnic groups, including Russians, Poles, Icelanders, and many others. Like his report on the LC, his report on the NLC was never published as a printed book and is preserved only in typescript and photocopies.[46]

Rudnyckyj's third major contribution to Ukrainian library science and bibliography was quite different from his description of the holdings of the LC and his works on other individual libraries, or from his travel books. His third contribution was systematic, yearly bibliographies of Ucrainica and Slavica published in Canada. In fact, Rudnyckyj published two separate series, one devoted to each of these subjects.

The first serial was *Slavica Canadiana*.[47] Titles in the volumes of this series were listed according to subject – language, literature, history, and so on – and Cyrillic ones given also in Latin transliteration with an English translation. Although most of the titles were in Ukrainian, there were also many in English and some in other Slavic languages including Polish, Russian, Slovak, and even Belarusan. There was also the occasional title by Rudnyckyj himself, amazingly, in German, on a Slavic subject, published in Canada. After a while, Rudnyckyj also added a section of book reviews in which important titles in Canadian Slavonic studies were reviewed by expert reviewers. Contributors included Victor Buyniak, Vladimir Kaye-Kysilewskyj, and others for Ukrainian materials, J. M. Kirschbaum for Slovak materials, and Benedykt Heydenkorn for Polish materials. Rudnyckyj continued this annual bibliography from 1951 to 1971.

Rudnyckyj's second serial on bibliography was his *Ukrainica Canadiana*, which began publication in 1953.[48] The listings were again divided by subject, and the Ukrainian language listings, which were the bulk of the material, given not only in Cyrillic but also in both Latin transliteration and English translation. Although it was quite detailed, Rudnyckyj's bibliography listed only books and pamphlets appearing under separate cover. No journal or newspaper articles were included. Rudnyckyj had some help with this publication, individual volumes or parts of individual volumes being compiled by Olha Woycenko, S. Sokulsky, and others. *Ukrainica Canadiana* and *Slavica Canadiana* generally covered a period of great growth in Slavic studies and Slavic literature in Canada. When, in the early 1970s, they ceased publication, other bibliographers took up the task and an annual bibliography of Canadian Slavic Studies began appearing in *Canadian Slavonic Papers*, the professional journal of the Canadian Association of Slavists.[49]

Rudnyckyj's annual bibliographies of Ukrainian and Slavic materials appearing in Canada, like his surveys of Ukrainian libraries in Canada and his survey of the LC, as well as his prolific travel writings, when taken together, form a composite picture of Ukrainian and Slavonic studies in the West during the Cold War. Although Rudnyckyj himself was always concerned with the immediate and the particular, and, in the works considered here, made very few generalizations about Ukrainian and Slavic culture in the West and refrained from evaluating new materials emanating from the Soviet Bloc, or, indeed, even Ukrainian Communist and pro-Communist materials published in North America, these works of Rudnyckyj do reflect the general contours of the history of non-Communist Slavonic and Ukrainian studies. First, Ukrainian culture in the West was cut off from its sources in eastern Europe by the existence of the Iron Curtain; Ukrainians in Canada and elsewhere in the West were on their own and had to make do with whatever cultural resources were at hand. Rudnyckyj, an émigré professor, was deeply aware of this problem but adapted himself well to his new environment in Canada. He researched the Ukrainian community that had been established in Canada prior to 1914, described its cultural – especially library – resources, and made possible their later evaluation by others. Second, Rudnyckyj approached major public institutions such as the Winnipeg Public Library, the NLC, and the LC, described their treasures, and urged them to open up to the Ukrainian communities in Canada and the United States; similarly, he urged Ukrainians to make better use of these facilities. Third, Rudnyckyj provided clear documentation for the history of Slavonic studies in Canada and the West so that, in future, their histories might be accurately written. In Canada, of course, he saw the University of Manitoba, the University of Alberta, and the University of Ottawa as the main centres of Ukrainian studies in his time; in the United States, he was particularly impressed by Washington and New York and their research institutions.

Of course, these general observations and conclusions of Rudnyckyj's, and his work taken as a whole, represent a certain stage in the history of Slavonic library studies and bibliography in North America. Certain defects might be mentioned. First, Rudnyckyj was very much an "engaged" scholar; that is, he was firmly committed to the very idea of "Ukrainian studies" and the existence of an independent Ukrainian tradition in books and culture that stretched back through the centuries. This alone explains his criticisms of libraries and librarians, including the LC and some of its employees, who, out of ignorance or convention, were reluctant to recognize any independent Ukrainian political or cultural tradition. Today, when the concept of the Ukrainian national awakening of the nineteenth century is more widely known, Ukraine is a fully independent country, and nationalisms of all sorts generally explained in terms of "invented traditions" and "imagined communities," his accusations of bias against those who, in his time, did not recognize the uniqueness of the Ukrainian book tradition seem somewhat dated; that is, it was largely indifference, convention, and inertia, not nationalist bias on the part of current librarians, that kept Ukraine from getting its own letters in the LC classification system. Second, and on a different level, in his travel books, Rudnyckyj omitted discussing, or even mentioning, many important people and institutions: in Canada, Dmytro Dontsov at Montreal, or George Luckyj and the University of Toronto Library are examples; similarly, in the United States, he did not foresee the future development of Ukrainian studies at Harvard, though there were signs of such developments as early as the late 1960s. Such omissions reveal that his surveys of various libraries and institutions were less thorough than they could have been. Third, and on a still different level, Rudnyckyj was a professional Slavist and philologist, but, as a librarian and bibliographer, he was somewhat of an amateur, though a dedicated, prolific, and very talented one. As was necessary for a path-breaker in this field, his travels were extensive and his surveys very general. Some might even call his travel writings somewhat superficial. Certainly, his tendency to publish his various writings on his own when he seemingly could not get reputable academic presses or prestigious institutions to publish them can be seen as a defect as well as a virtue. His fellow linguist Yury Shevelov, in a memoir replete with *ad hominem* remarks, called him energetic but "undiscriminating, a bit of a wandering rogue, and very much overly insistent."[50] Nevertheless, he was very successful in attracting a number of admiring students, friends, and supporters to his cause; moreover, his travel journals were widely read and his library surveys laid the basis for more specialist studies that would come later. Suffice it to say that later librarians and bibliographers, scholars of the next generation, such as Lubomyr and Bohdan Wynar in the United States, and Andrew Gregorovich and Bohdan Budurowycz in Canada, who all were to compile important bibliographies or guides in the field, represented the next stage in Ukrainian and Slavonic bibliography on this continent. All these scholars flourished during the latter half of the Cold War and leaned on work done in the 1950s and 1960s by Rudnyckyj; all of them knew him personally and respected his various talents; like him, they travelled extensively throughout the West, and, again like him, made use of pre-computer-age methodology.

Behind all this, of course, stood certain inescapable political realities of the Long Cold War; Rudnyckyj himself, in fact, was keenly aware of being an émigré scholar whose work was to question the predominance of ideas and things Russian in the Slavic field as well as the axioms of Soviet scholarship and Communist propaganda. His job, as he seems to have seen it, was to discover, catalogue, and preserve as much of his native culture as possible where this could be safely done; indeed, to preserve it for a time when, perhaps, it could once again be properly appreciated in the European homeland. In this, we may modestly conclude, he was not entirely unsuccessful.

13 Scholarship on Mykhailo Hrushevsky during the Early 1980s: Ukrainian Books and Libraries in Canada and the United States

Der Historiker ist ein rückwärts gekehrter Prophet.
(The historian is a prophet looking backwards.)

Friedrich Schlegel, *Athenaeum*

I have always been interested in history and, even during my first years in graduate school at the University of Manitoba, I paid some attention to my eastern European background, doing several essays on Russian subjects for a general course on nineteenth-century Europe under Professor Michael Kinnear at the Fort Garry campus of the university. But it was only after the completion of my MA thesis on the medieval Crusades to the Holy Land, which I wrote under the wise supervision of L. A. Desmond, a conservative Catholic of Irish Canadian background, that I firmly decided to turn to the Slavic world and take up the serious study of eastern Europe.[1]

The question immediately arose: if I were to do a PhD in Russian or Ukrainian history, where was the best place to study? At that time, Ukrainian history was still widely regarded in the West as a subdiscipline of Russian and Soviet history, and specialists in Ukrainian history, which, for the most part, was my particular interest, were few and far between. The principal centres for the study of Ukrainian history in North America were then Harvard University in the United States, where a medievalist with oriental interests, Omeljan Pritsak (1919–2006), held the Mykhailo Hrushevsky Chair of Ukrainian History, and the University of Alberta in Edmonton in western Canada, where Ivan Lysiak-Rudnytsky (1919–1984), an historian of political thought, was teaching. At my alma mater, the University of Manitoba, there were two Ukrainian historians on staff, Oleh

Gerus (b. 1939), only recently hired, who specialized in the modern period, and the Rev. Oleksander Baran (1926–2004), who did the Cossack era; but I had already received two degrees from that university and thought it necessary to expand my horizons somewhat by studying elsewhere for my next degree. At the University of Toronto, Canada's most prestigious university, where I had already done some work towards a PhD in medieval history, there was a respectable contingent of Russian historians (John Keep, Harvey Dyck, and Andrew Rossos) and also a well-respected Polish historian (Peter Brock), but no specialist in Ukrainian history. Nevertheless, I had family contacts in Toronto and had already had some experience with the university there, and I decided to retrain myself as a Slavist and Russian historian at that institution. In 1975, I enrolled as a special student in East European studies and, in 1977, as a PhD student in Russian and East European history at the University of Toronto.

By 1980, I had completed my coursework and passed my comprehensive examinations and was considering various topics upon which to write a thesis. The choice of a thesis topic would also determine who my faculty advisor would be, as Dyck handled Muscovy and eighteenth-century Russia, Keep handled nineteenth-century and Soviet Russia, Rossos did Russian foreign policy and the Balkans, and Brock covered all of eastern Europe north of the Balkans. For some time, I considered doing something on older Ukraine, perhaps the Cossacks, with Dyck as my supervisor, but, for certain reasons having to do with divergent views on history and politics, especially as concerned Ukraine, found this to be impractical. Thereafter, the choice of writing on the great Ukrainian historian and political leader Mykhailo Hrushevsky (1866–1934) came quite easily.

I wanted to work on an important subject and I had always been interested in biography. Of the people who were then considered to have been the three greatest figures of modern Ukraine – the poet Taras Shevchenko, the historian Hrushevsky, and the western Ukrainian leader Ivan Franko – Shevchenko was already the subject of a first-rate biography written by Pavlo Zaitsev in interwar Poland and published in the West in 1955, and Franko, like Shevchenko before him, was more important as a literary than a historical figure. I was not a literary scholar. This left Hrushevsky, an outstanding historian and an important political figure. He might be, I hoped, a man whom I could understand. Moreover, there was at that time almost no full-length book on him in any language, including Ukrainian, and rumours and accusations of various kinds swirled about him. My choice was self-evident. I set about to write a political biography of Mykhailo Hrushevsky.

I was concerned, however, that I would not be able to find sufficient primary materials about Hrushevsky in Western libraries, archives, and repositories. Soviet assistance on such a politically sensitive subject was inconceivable, as Hrushevsky, who in the West symbolized Ukrainian national independence, was definitely a *persona non grata* in the USSR. With this question in mind, I wrote to Ivan Lysiak-Rudnytsky and asked him about the feasibility of undertaking such a study. He replied that he was certain that a book such as the one I had in mind was entirely possible, and that, in fact, it was simply a scholarly scandal (*naukovyi skandal*) that nothing of significance had already been published about Hrushevsky, who had led Ukraine to political independence during the revolution of 1917–18 and died under mysterious circumstances in Stalin's Soviet Union. Professor Brock, who had done a bit of work on the Ukrainians in old Austrian Galicia (on the early nineteenth-century Ruthenian national awakener Ivan Vahylevych, to be exact) happily agreed to supervise a thesis on Hrushevsky and I immediately set to work.

I began by gathering and examining the scattered bits and pieces, interpretive essays and synthetic treatments, that had been published in Western countries in the decades after the Second World War. Curiously enough, the first such essay that I read was Omeljan Pritsak's commemoration piece entitled "On the Centenary of the Birth of M. Hrushevsky."[2] This highly controversial essay was very critical of Hrushevsky and attacked his "populist-socialist" approach to both politics and history from a very conservative Hetmanite point of view. (The Hetman, or monarch, Pavlo Skoropadsky had overthrown Hrushevsky's socialist Central Rada government in a coup d'état during the revolution of 1917–18.) It was surprising to me that such an attack on Hrushevsky could even be published as a commemorative work. I could not understand how the holder of the Mykhailo Hrushevsky Chair of Ukrainian History at Harvard could entertain such a critical position on the great historian. On the other hand, I was relieved and delighted that Hrushevsky was turning out to be a socialist and a radical democrat rather than a rightist nationalist, as this corresponded to some degree with my own political convictions of the time. In my opinion, this made him a much easier man to study.

After examining Pritsak's rather startling introduction to the great historian's life, I picked up the small but important collection of Hrushevsky's political writings published by Mykola Halii and a group of émigré Ukrainian socialists in New York in 1960.[3] This collection contained many of the historian's political tracts produced during the revolution of 1917 to 1921. These included his influential essay *Iakoi my khochemo avtonomii i federatsii* (What kind of autonomy and federation we want) and parts of the collection titled *Vilna Ukraina* (Free Ukraine), which set forth his idea that at that time the best geopolitical arrangement for Ukraine would be a wide national autonomy approaching complete independence; the Halii collection also included his thorough tract *Na porozi novoi Ukrainy* (On the threshold of a new Ukraine), which went beyond autonomy and considered the ideal principles and structure of the independent and democratic Ukraine that had actually emerged out of the chaos of the revolution. The slogan "*Vilna Ukraina*" was a leitmotif of the early, most hopeful, stage of the Ukrainian revolution, but Hrushevsky, for a time at least, considered the latter essay to be what he called his "political testament" to later generations of Ukrainians.[4] I immediately became an admirer of the "*Vilna Ukraina*" mentality and thereafter always preferred it to the "*Slava Ukraini*" (Glory to Ukraine) slogan that arose later on and became the cry of the 1940s nationalists. Moreover, I found that the general introduction to Halii's volume by Volodymyr Doroshenko (1879–1963), a former member of the Ukrainian Social Democratic Workers' Party (SDs), a librarian at the Shevchenko Scientific Society in Lviv between the wars, and thereafter an émigré in New York, was particularly sympathetic and valuable. Volodymyr Doroshenko had known Hrushevsky personally and was politically close to him. I later discovered that in the 1950s, this same Doroshenko had published a whole series of biographical articles on Hrushevsky in the American Ukrainian-language magazine *Ovyd* (Ovid).[5] These articles were of special help to me in piecing together the various parts of Hrushevsky's long and very productive political career as well as his enormous contribution to Ukrainian scholarship. Once again, Hrushevsky's position as a democratic socialist and a radical democrat came out very clearly in Volodymyr Doroshenko's interpretation of the great historian.

Once I had put together a general outline of Hrushevsky's scholarly and political career, I turned to the journal of the Ukrainian Historical Association, *Ukrainskyi istoryk* (The Ukrainian historian). This journal, which was edited by Lubomyr Wynar (b. 1932) of Kent State University in Ohio, contained a great variety of materials about Hrushevsky. Wynar and his associates had made a special point of publishing primary documentation, autobiographical notes, letters, memoirs, and research articles by or about Hrushevsky. All this was geared to provide primary material for some future biographer. The work had been progressing steadily since 1966 on the occasion of the centenary of the historian's birth, when an entire issue of the journal had been devoted to him.

This centenary volume contained articles and materials by Ukrainian émigré authors from all over the Western world; besides Wynar, other contributors included Oleksander Ohloblyn, Illia Vytanovych, Oleksander Dombrovsky, Mykhailo Zhdan, Borys Martos, Roman Klymkevych, and Vasyl Dubrovsky.[6] Some of these authors had met Hrushevsky earlier in their careers and Borys Martos had actually been a member of the Ukrainian Central Rada during the revolution. In contrast to Mykola Halii's group of Ukrainian socialists in New York, however, the contributors to *Ukrainskyi istoryk*, especially Wynar himself, breathed a considerably more conservative, or perhaps one should say "nationalist," spirit and usually stressed what they believed to have been the historian's contributions to Ukrainian "state building." From Wynar's point of view, this was progress, since the more extreme 1930s nationalists had usually completely rejected Hrushevsky as a soft "humanitarian socialist" and even a "pacifist" who, they claimed, disbanded the Ukrainian army when it was most needed during the revolution. But Wynar and his colleagues, in their attempt to make Hrushevsky more acceptable to the "nationalist" viewpoint (or "national" viewpoint, to use Wynar's own terminology), tended to downplay his convictions as a radical democrat and a socialist. Thus, in general, I was quickly finding that materials by and about Hrushevsky, although scattered and contradictory, were abundant indeed!

This discovery was confirmed when Andrew Gregorovich, a librarian at the University of Toronto who had a long-standing interest in Hrushevsky (his father had corresponded with him in the 1920s), put his personal file of Hrushevsky materials at my disposal. This substantial file contained news clippings, journal articles, photographs, and Hrushevsky's unpublished correspondence with Gregorovich's father. It also contained Gregorovich's own reprint of Hrushevsky's brief but valuable autobiography, which had first been published in Lviv in 1906. Gregorovich had personally run this booklet off a printing machine while he had been a student and he published it in 1965 under the auspices of the Ukrainian Canadian University Students' Union (SUSK), of which he had been an active member. My work was making swift and steady progress.[7]

At this point, Roman Senkus, the editor of the Toronto-based *Journal of Ukrainian Studies*, asked me to review a new commemorative volume devoted to Hrushevsky that had just been published by the Shevchenko Scientific Society in New York City. This volume, which was largely devoted to Hrushevsky's last years in Soviet Ukraine (1924 to 1934), was edited by Matvii Stakhiv (1895–1978), a democratic socialist and a former member of the Radical Party in interwar Galicia who emigrated to the United States after the Second World War and, for many years, edited the labour-oriented newspaper *Narodna volia* (The people's will) in Scranton, Pennsylvania, where a large number of Ukrainian Americans of the older economic immigration still lived.[8] I used this opportunity to synthesize my thoughts and current research on Hrushevsky and to outline the historiographical debate among Ukrainian scholars concerning his person. This debate revolved around the question of whether Hrushevsky had remained a populist (*narodnyk*) with federalist ideals throughout his life – a position taken by conservatives and radical nationalists who accused him of writing biased history and ruining the chances for the survival of an independent Ukrainian state during the revolution – or whether he had evolved into a true partisan of independent statehood (*derzhavnyk*) who had written inspired history and had guided the Ukrainian People's Republic wisely during the brief period of its existence, a position held by his democratic socialist admirers. I saw some merit to both points of view.[9]

The Robarts Library at the University of Toronto

Most of my work on Mykhailo Hrushevsky's biography was carried out at the Robarts Library of the University of Toronto, the main humanities research library at that university and the primary university research library in Canada. (The building that houses this institution is some fourteen storeys tall!) There is no doubt whatsoever that in the 1980s, this library held the largest collection of Ucrainica in the country and, with the possible exception of the University of Alberta library in Edmonton (which is home to the Canadian Institute of Ukrainian Studies), at that time was the best place in Canada to carry on advanced research in this field. A detailed catalogue of its Ukrainian holdings published in the mid-1980s fills two very stout volumes.[10]

The University of Toronto collection of Ukrainian materials was built up almost entirely after the Second World War. The compilation of this collection had followed the establishment of a Department of Slavic Studies at the university in 1949 and progressed rapidly. The contributions of Ukrainian librarians on the Robarts Library staff, such as Bohdan Budurowycz, Wasyl Veryha, Andrew Gregorovich, and Luba Pendzey, were particularly notable. A librarian of Russian Doukhobor ancestry, Mary Stevens, also made a significant contribution to the field. Later on, the establishment of a Chair of Ukrainian Studies in the departments of history and political economy (1980) and the appointment of Professor

Paul Robert Magocsi to hold this chair further improved the situation, but my work at the university was already well progressed by the time that this chair was starting its activities and I remained under the supervision of Peter Brock, under whom I had started my project.

Soviet Ukrainian publications of the 1920s, when Hrushevsky was active in Kyiv, were important for the completion of my project. In the early 1980s, the Robarts Library already had a very full collection of serial publications of the 1920s All-Ukrainian Academy of Sciences, where Hrushevsky was so important a figure. Most of these journals and periodicals were actually in the original hard-cover book editions rather than microform copies, which is more common in North American university libraries. The journal *Ukraina*, which was edited in Kyiv by Hrushevsky himself until his exile from Ukraine in 1931, was of particular interest to me, and I was able to use a few volumes in hard cover and the rest in microform. Other important materials from Kyiv that I used in microform included the *Zapysky* (Notes) of the Kyiv-based pre-revolution Ukrainian Scientific Society (*Ukrainske Naukove Tovarystvo*). This journal contained a rather full memoir by Hrushevsky about his scholarly mentor Volodymyr Antonovych.[11] Similarly, the Robarts Library possessed full collections in microform or hard copy of the major Ukrainian periodicals from pre-World War I Lviv, including publications established or built up by Hrushevsky himself, such as the scholarly *Zapysky* (Notes) of the Shevchenko Scientific Society and the literary review *Literaturnonaukovyi vistnyk* (Literary-scientific herald) in which the historian published extensively; I also made good use of the important Lviv daily newspaper *Dilo* (Action). The collection of pre-1914 Galician Ukrainian periodicals in microform in the Robarts Library is at present almost complete, since, in 1983, when I was completing my work on Hrushevsky, the Chair of Ukrainian Studies acquired full or nearly complete runs of some 175 newspapers and journals of western Ukrainian origin. These were obtained from the Austrian National Library in Vienna.[12] Most of my work on Hrushevsky, however, was done on the basis of *Dilo* and other periodicals that the library had possessed prior to 1983.

Somewhat more typically, the Robarts Library also had a very full collection of Ukrainian émigré journals and magazines published in the West since 1945. These included the journal *Suchasnist* (The present), which was particularly disliked by the Soviets. A very important article by Volodymyr Doroshenko on the mutual relations between Hrushevsky and Ivan Franko had appeared in the early 1960s in *Suchasnist*, and an article by Lubomyr Wynar on the bibliographical problems of working on Hrushevsky had appeared in it in the jubilee year, 1966.[13] (Almost twenty years later, well after the completion of my research but only shortly before the collapse of Communism in eastern Europe, Wynar published an interesting synthesis of his work on Hrushevsky in this same journal.)[14] For many years, in fact, *Suchasnist* had the reputation of being the most substantial and varied Ukrainian periodical published in the West. Its prestige was firmly established outside Ukrainian circles by the fact that it usually reflected a general democratic point of view, while including various shades of opinion from liberal to conservative within its circle of contributors. It was widely rumoured at the time that the CIA secretly funded *Suchasnist*, though I was unaware of this when I began to use the journal.

Other important Ukrainian émigré journals in the Robarts Library included *Kyiv*, published in Philadelphia, and *Lysty do pryiateliv* (Letters to friends), published in New York City. Both these journals were more or less non-partisan, criticized the Ukrainian émigré establishment, and flourished during the early 1960s. Even more important for research on Hrushevsky was *Novi dni* (New days), a non-partisan monthly magazine published in Toronto by émigrés from eastern Ukraine. This magazine contained an important memoir by Ievhenia Krychevska on the bombardment and destruction of Hrushevsky's great house and private library in Kyiv during the revolution, and some smaller polemical articles on Hrushevsky's place in Ukrainian history.[15] Unlike *Kyiv* and *Lysty do pryiateliv*, however, *Novi dni* continued to appear throughout the 1970s and 1980s. It ceased publication only in the late 1990s, some time after Communism collapsed and Ukraine became an independent state.

At that time as well, the Robarts Library also had very full collections of two important western European Ukrainian journals that contained materials on Hrushevsky. First, there was *Ukraina*, published in Paris by the émigré Ukrainian socialist Ilko Borshchak (1892–1959), who had personally known and corresponded with the historian. This modest magazine, which flourished during the 1940s and 1950s, represented a francophile liberal democratic viewpoint, but also contained materials from other viewpoints. Most interesting for my purposes were the memoiristic accounts by Nataliia Polonska-Vasylenko (1884–1973), which described in detail the conflict between Hrushevsky and the orientalist academician Ahatanhel Krymsky (1871–1942), at the All-Ukrainian Academy of Sciences in Kyiv during the 1920s.[16] Second, the Robarts Library had a full collection of the journal *Vyzvolnyi shliakh* (The liberation path), published in London, England, from the later 1940s. This

latter journal, which reflected the rightist opinions of the Bandera faction of the Organization of Ukrainian Nationalists, was not sympathetic
to Hrushevsky's liberal humanitarian ideas, but, in 1967, did publish a
significant article by Bohdan Budurowycz (1921–2007) about the interpretation of Hrushevsky found in Western reference works and encyclopedias. Budurowycz then taught in the Department of Slavic Languages
and Literatures at the University of Toronto and eventually sat on my
thesis examination committee.[17]

At this point, mention should be made of the most important memoir
literature about Hrushevsky. Even then, most of this literature was easily
accessible in the Robarts Library or in any important Ukrainian collection in the West. For the early years, prior to Hrushevsky's move to Lviv
and before the revolution, the voluminous memoirs of Oleksander
Lototsky (1870–1939) are very important. Lototsky, an Orthodox theological student, knew Hrushevsky as a fellow student in Kyiv in the 1890s
and was present at his master's thesis defence. He also shared many of
his liberal democratic ideals. He lived and worked as an émigré scholar
in Poland between the wars.[18]

After Hrushevsky moved from Kyiv in the Russian Empire to Lviv in
Austrian Galicia, certain other memoirists become very important. Of
these, the most significant is probably Ivan Makukh (1872–1946), a
Galician Radical who personally knew Ivan Franko, lived through the
period of political party formation in Galicia in the 1890s, and was able
to recall and explain Hrushevsky's place in this process. The editorial
notes (by Matvii Stakhiv) to this substantial volume were, as well, quite
useful to me.[19]

Also important for the early years are the memoirs of Dmytro
Doroshenko (1882–1951) (no relation to Volodymyr Doroshenko), later
the dean of Ukrainian émigré historians, whose testimony is very valuable for the period of the revolution of 1905 and Hrushevsky's visits from
Galicia to Saint Petersburg during the Duma period.[20] Although this
Doroshenko, unlike Volodymyr, was to accept a conservative Hetmanite
or monarchist position during the revolution, his memoirs are open-
minded and acknowledge that Hrushevsky was universally respected
among Ukrainian activists and sympathizers before 1917. It was only during the course of the revolution itself, when Hrushevsky's radical opinions became more evident, that more conservative Ukrainians began to
turn against him.

For the period of the 1917 revolution itself, Dmytro Doroshenko is once
again one of our principal informants. His memoirs and his general

history of this period are both particularly well informed, although his conservative viewpoint emerges more clearly as the years pass. To the end of his life, Dmytro Doroshenko retained respect for Hrushevsky and never cut off relations with his more liberal democratic colleagues.[21] Of equal importance for the revolutionary period are the memoirs of the Socialist Revolutionaries (SRs) Mykola Kovalevsky (1892–1957) and Nykyfor Hryhoriiv (1883–1953), both of whom were well informed as to the events and manoeuvrings within the democratic socialist camp and Hrushevsky's place within these manoeuvrings.[22]

For the years that Hrushevsky spent in emigration, no single memoirist stands out. However, for the following period from 1924 to 1934, which he spent in the Soviet Union, it is necessary to mention the highly personal history of the Ukrainian Academy of Sciences, written by the Ukrainian émigré historian working at the Ukrainian Free University in Germany, Nataliia Polonska-Vasylenko. Hrushevsky plays a very important role in the first volume of this history, but Polonska-Vasylenko's treatment of him is marred by her obvious antipathy to his person. During the revolution, her husband Mykola Vasylenko had supported the conservative Hetman, and, later on, during the 1920s, she herself supported Krymsky's rival faction against Hrushevsky's within the academy.[23]

Other Ukrainian Collections in Toronto

Although the Robarts Library at the University of Toronto held the largest collection of Ucrainica in the city, several other collections were of considerable use to me. In the order of their value to me, these were the following: 1) the Saint Vladimir Institute Library, which was established by supporters of the Ukrainian Greek Orthodox Church of Canada; 2) the Ukrainian National Federation Library, which was linked to the rightist nationalists in Europe from the 1930s; and 3) the Library of the Ukrainian National Home, which had been founded during or shortly after the First World War and became associated with the Petliurist movement during the interwar period.

Although it is the youngest in age (established only in the 1970s), the Saint Vladimir Institute Library was the most valuable to me of the three above-named institutions. The fact that it was located very close to the University of Toronto campus was significant. Not only was I able to borrow books and journals from this library for extended periods of time and on more flexible terms than from the university, but I was also able to exchange duplicates with this institution and thus build up my own personal collection of Hrushevsky materials. This was of considerable practical help to me. It was usually in copies from the Saint Vladimir Library on my home library shelf that I examined the many articles, memoirs, and reviews concerning Hrushevsky that I discovered scattered through the various volumes of *Ukrainskyi istoryk*. I turned to this material time and time again during the course of my research. However, the Saint Vladimir Library also contained much material that the Robarts Library at that time did not have, and some of this material was invaluable to me in my work on Hrushevsky. The single most important item of this nature in the Saint Vladimir collection was the journal *Vilna Ukraina*, published in the United States by a group of Ukrainian democratic socialists, former SRs and SDs from revolutionary Ukraine, who, as the title of their journal clearly revealed, greatly admired the life and ideals of Mykhailo Hrushevsky. This group, which included Mykola Halii, who had edited the collection of Hrushevsky's political writings in the 1960s, was very prolific in its treatment of Hrushevsky and the Central Rada period of Ukrainian history, and criticized both the Bolsheviks and conservatives such as Polonska-Vasylenko and Dmytro Doroshenko for what they believed to be their slanted interpretation of these topics. *Vilna Ukraina* flourished during the 1950s and 1960s but declined thereafter as the veterans of the revolution slowly died off.[24]

The Saint Vladimir Library contained other rare Ukrainian materials I was able to use. On the one hand, there were periodicals such as the serial *Za derzhavnist* published by the Ukrainian Military History Institute in Toronto. Edited by General M. Sadovsky, this serial was an important source for information about the military struggle for Ukraine's independence and contained considerable material on Hrushevsky and the Central Rada. On the other hand, there were many booklets and pamphlets, such as the memoir of Ivan Franko's daughter Anna Franko-Kliuchko, who gave a picture of the relations between these two great figures of modern Ukraine. Franko-Kliuchko, who lived in Toronto during the post-war period, had a negative animus towards the historian and stressed the negative features of his personality. She claimed that Hrushevsky had overworked and greatly oppressed her father. Her story was later critically analyzed and corrected by Volodymyr Doroshenko in his article on the two men.[25]

The library of the Ukrainian National Federation of Canada (*Ukrainske Natsionalne Obiednannia Kanady*) was the second important private Ukrainian library in Toronto of which I made extensive use. This library was considerably older than the Saint Vladimir Library and dated back to the period between the two world wars when its sponsoring organization, the Ukrainian National Federation (UNF), which was affiliated with the Organization of Ukrainian Nationalists (OUN) in Europe, was vigorous. The UNF library owned materials from between the wars that neither Robarts nor Saint Vladimir possessed, and much of this material had no ideological connection to the UNF. For example, the UNF library had a very full collection of the serial entitled *Istorychnyi Kalendar-almanakh Chervonoi Kalyny* (The historical calendar-almanac of the red cranberry), which was published annually in Lviv during the 1930s. This almanac contained several articles of value to me in my work on Hrushevsky and from its pages I reproduced two interesting pictures of events during the revolution of 1917–18. (One of them was the photograph taken of Hrushevsky's house in Kyiv after its destruction by Muravev.) Another interesting serial in the UNF library was *Vilna spilka*, a periodical published by Hrushevsky's socialist colleagues in Prague during the emigration period. In this serial, Mykyta Shapoval (1882–1932) published a valuable synthesis of the history of the Ukrainian Socialist Revolutionary movement during the revolution and paid considerable attention to his rival, Hrushevsky.[26] It was also in the UNF library that I used the American magazine *Ovyd* in which Volodymyr Doroshenko's valuable literary portrait of Hrushevsky had appeared.

Aside from rare periodicals, I was able to use several unique copies of rare books in the UNF library. Of these, the most important item was Symon Narizhny's encyclopedic history of the Ukrainian political emigration in central Europe between the wars.[27] This book was richly illustrated and I reproduced several rare photographs from it in my own book. One of these rare pictures was that of Hrushevsky, D. Isaievych, and others at the socialist conference in Lucerne, Switzerland, in 1919. It is interesting to note that in the 1990s when he visited Toronto, Isaievych's son Iaroslav (an important scholar in his own right) approached me and excitedly told me that shortly before the Gorbachev reform movement had got to Ukraine, the KGB had interrogated him on whether he had passed on this document to me during my brief trip to the Ukrainian SSR in 1981. Of course, I had gotten no such document out of the country at that time and all the KGB inquiries were in vain. Isaievych himself pointed out to me that I had clearly acknowledged from where I had gotten the picture in the credits of my book. Still, he thought it important to let me know something of the effect that the publication of my book had had on the Soviet secret police.

Finally, I also visited the library of the Ukrainian National Home (*Ukrainskyi narodnyi dim*) in Toronto. Although this was the oldest Ukrainian library that I used in Toronto, dating back to the pioneer period before 1920, it was the most poorly organized and difficult to access. Nevertheless, I was able to peruse its shelves, which were loaded with dusty old pamphlets of all kinds, and examine the annual almanacs of several Ukrainian Canadian newspapers for the revolutionary years. From them, I was able to get a good feeling of how the Ukrainian colony in Canada greeted the events of 1917–18, the time of Hrushevsky's political apogee. Unfortunately, after the collapse of Communism, the Toronto Ukrainian National Home Library was dissolved or dispersed and its treasures are no longer available to the interested researcher.

Ukrainian Collections in Winnipeg

Because I had close personal connections with Winnipeg, I was able to make good use of some Ukrainian libraries in that city. Until the 1970s, Winnipeg was widely known as the Ukrainian capital of Canada, and, in the early 1980s, its library and archival facilities were extensive. Ukrainian scholars in Winnipeg were then able to use the University of Manitoba library, the library of Saint Andrew's College, the library of the Ukrainian Free Academy of Sciences in Canada (UVAN), the library of the Ukrainian Cultural and Educational Centre, the library of the Prosvita Reading Society, and the very old and rich library of the Winnipeg Ukrainian National Home. In Winnipeg, my work on Hrushevsky was carried out primarily at the Ukrainian Cultural and Educational Centre (Oseredok), which was organized during the Second World War and which, to the present, remains the best-organized and most easily accessible private Ukrainian library in Winnipeg. The "Centre," or "Oseredok," as it is called for short, possesses a rich collection of Ukrainian pamphlets and booklets from all periods during the twentieth century and I was able to discover a number of unique titles in its collection.

One of the most interesting of these was a first-hand account by Ostap Voinarenko of the voting in the Central Rada on the Fourth Universal, which proclaimed Ukrainian independence in early 1918. Voinarenko was writing as a conservative opponent of the Central Rada, but his account shines as a document produced by an actual participant in the events he describes.[28] It was also at the Centre that I discovered a copy of Ievhen Chykalenko's invaluable and (at that time) very rare diary, which described Ukrainian politics in Kyiv before the revolution of 1917. Chykalenko (1861–1929) was the publisher of Kyiv's daily newspaper *Rada* and his relations with Hrushevsky were close and fairly amicable. Entire letters from Hrushevsky to Chykalenko are reproduced in this diary.[29] The Centre also possessed a number of old journals and periodicals that proved to be of use. An example of these was the rare and valuable *Vistnyk* (Herald) of the Vienna-based Union for the Liberation of Ukraine. In 1916, a special issue was devoted to Hrushevsky, who was then living in exile in Moscow, where he was watched by the tsar's police. I reproduced two interesting photographs from this issue in my section of illustrations.[30] I made less use of the other Winnipeg libraries, though, without a doubt, they contained considerable material that would have been of value to me. (Unfortunately, at the beginning of the twenty-first century, both the UVAN library and the library of Prosvita Chytalnia [Prosvita Reading Society] were dissolved, the former, it is said, even being shipped off to Ukraine for the use of patrons there.) In the 1980s, however, I did visit the University of Manitoba library, where I used several pre-1914 copies of the *Zapysky Naukovoho Tovarystva im. Shevchenka* (Memoirs of the Shevchenko scientific society), an almost complete set of which was hard-bound and sitting on the library shelves. (Most North American libraries, if they had this periodical, had it only in microform, which, of course, is more difficult to peruse.) I also visited the Saint Andrew's College library, a Ukrainian Orthodox institution affiliated with the University of Manitoba. In the Saint Andrew's College library I found a unique copy of Hrushevsky's fictional stories called *Pid zoriamy* (Under the stars), published in Kyiv in 1928 but containing some of his earliest non-historical writings. Also, I eventually became acquainted with the Winnipeg scholar Mykhailo Marunchak (1914–2004), an important figure in the Ukrainian Free Academy of Sciences in Canada, who had earlier published some materials on Hrushevsky's relations with the Ukrainian colony in Canada.[31] On another level, at the bookstore of Trident Publishers (Tryzub) in Winnipeg, I was able to purchase several old items published in Winnipeg many years before, which turned out to be valuable to me in my study of Hrushevsky. The best example of this kind of book was the little volume of early memoirs of Dmytro Doroshenko, who resided in Winnipeg briefly after the Second World War and, at the suggestion of the Winnipeg activist Olha Woycenko, composed these memoirs there. Dmytro Doroshenko had helped to found the branch of the Ukrainian Free Academy of Sciences in Winnipeg, and, in spite of his short stay in the city, was quite productive during his time there. Doroshenko's early memoirs are valuable for their dispassionate tone and broad perspective on the Ukrainian national movement before the revolution.

A Research Trip to New York and Boston

In 1981, I made an important research trip to New York and Boston in search of Hrushevsky materials. In New York, I made some use of the public library, the Slavonic collection of which is quite extensive and boasts a published catalogue in many large volumes.[32] In this collection, I discovered the published but little-known diary of Hrushevsky's rival for the leadership of the Ukrainian Party of Socialist Revolutionaries, Mykyta Shapoval (1882–1932). Although less extensive than the parallel diary of Chykalenko, this diary contained several direct references to Shapoval's relations with Hrushevsky and illuminate a different phase of his life.[33] Similarly, I used the collection of published and archival materials in the library of Columbia University. I was able to acquire some rare pamphlets dealing with the revolution and learned about the diary of the Ukrainian Social Democratic leader Volodymyr Vynnychenko (1880–1951). This diary was stored at Columbia but I was able to use it in published form shortly afterwards. Vynnychenko's diary is remarkable for its bitter references to Hrushevsky, but, together with the diaries of Chykalenko and Shapoval, forms an interesting primary base for further considerations of Hrushevsky's career. As to diaries in general, which are always written as the events themselves transpire, rather than years later, they are generally a base that is more reliable than memoir material written long after the events in question.[34]

Finally, I also briefly visited the library of the Ukrainian Free Academy of Sciences in the US (UVAN), which is located in New York City. (One of the elderly female librarians there had actually known Hrushevsky in Kyiv in the 1920s and had served him at the library of the All-Ukrainian Academy of Sciences just as she was now serving me!) The group of distinguished scholars working at UVAN, which, like its counterpart in Winnipeg, was founded by émigrés from central Ukraine after the Second World War, was responsible for publishing some original material on Hrushevsky. Perhaps the most important such manuscript they published was the memoir of Ievhen Chykalenko, which retold and expanded on the story told earlier in his diary.[35] One of the most eminent UVAN scholars, Oleksander Ohloblyn (1899–1992), originally from Kyiv, had known Hrushevsky personally in the 1920s, and, on the pages of *Ukrainskyi istoryk,* summed up his evaluation of the historian's role in Ukrainian political and intellectual life. Unfortunately, I did not get a chance to meet Ohloblyn during my short research trip to the United States, but I later heard that he eventually read and liked my dissertation on Hrushevsky.[36]

However, while I was in New York, I did visit the Shevchenko Scientific Society (NTSh) building, where I had hoped to use the library. Unfortunately, the institution was then in the process of moving to new quarters and I was unable to utilize its collection. On the other hand, I did meet and interview Dr Vasyl Lev (1903–1991), a prominent NTSh scholar who had been active in the society in Galicia between the wars. Lev, a specialist on Ukrainian philology, told me of the society's traditions and Hrushevsky's role in them; we also discussed Hrushevsky's views on language, which were anything but dogmatic.

From New York, I passed on to Boston and the Harvard Ukrainian Research Institute (HURI), where I was welcomed by Omeljan Pritsak and discussed with him his famous article criticizing Hrushevsky. Although it was clear that Pritsak disagreed with Hrushevsky's historical methodology and political positions, it was also clear to me that he had an enormous respect for the man, which did not come out at all in his article. Pritsak suggested to me that I spend an hour or so every morning reading Hrushevsky's ten-volume *Istoriia Ukrainy-Rusy* (History of Ukraine-Rus') and in this way go through the whole set in preparation for my biography. As I already had my hands full going through the hundreds of his political, polemical, and literary articles, as well as the many articles about him, and knew that his historical style did not make for easy reading (especially in the original Ukrainian), I thought this suggestion impractical and quietly ignored it. But Pritsak did turn out to be quite helpful: he arranged for me to stay in Harvard for a full week (in the Ukrainian Research Institute guestroom) and ensured that my stay was comfortable and academically profitable.

At Harvard, I discovered photocopies of several important pamphlets published by Hrushevsky after 1905. The most important of these were his *Osvobozhdenie Rossii i Ukrainskii Vopros* (The liberation of Russia and the Ukrainian question), which came out in Saint Petersburg in 1907, and his *Ukrainskii vopros* (The Ukrainian question), which was published in the same city in the same year. At Harvard, I also was able to use a great variety of Soviet materials from the 1920s and 1930s that had not been available to me in Toronto. These included both primary documentation on the revolutionary era and political and historical debates in which Mikhail Pokrovsky, Matvii Iavorsky, Osyp Hermaize, M. A. Rubach, and others had participated. At Harvard, I also examined in hard copy the journal *Boritesia-poborete!* (Fight and you will win!), which Hrushevsky had edited as a Socialist Revolutionary leader in Vienna during the early 1920s. Also at Harvard, I consulted in hard cover the pre-revolutionary

Universitetskie izvestiia (University news) of Kyiv University, which is extremely rare in North America. In general, my trip to New York and Boston was very useful in filling out my portrait of Hrushevsky and provided me with an opportunity of examining materials that I would not have had otherwise.

Of course, there were several other library collections in the United States that contained rich Ukrainian collections, but I was unable to use them all. Mention should be made, however, of the collection of the Library of Congress in Washington, DC, of which I was able to make some use through the interlibrary loan system, and the University of Illinois at Urbana-Champaign, where Dmytro Shtohryn (b. 1923) had overseen a very extensive collection of Ucrainica. The latter institution, for many years, ran a summer workshop that made access to the collection especially easy for researchers and at present is of considerable use to visitors from Ukraine. As to interlibrary loans in general, I also obtained some important books through this system from the libraries that I briefly visited during my various research trips. One of the most important of these items was the anti-Ukrainian tract by the Kyiv censor and tsarist bureaucrat S. N. Shchegolev. This document was a kind of "police handbook" on the pre-revolution Ukrainian national movement in the Russian Empire but nevertheless was of great use in outlining the history of this movement and reflecting how the tsar's officials viewed it. Its characterization of Hrushevsky as "*heresyarch*" ("ruler of the heretics") was particularly pointed. I photocopied this book from a unique copy obtained from the Columbia University Library in New York City.[37]

An Exploratory Trip to Europe

Finally, I should mention that I did make a research trip to Europe, including Soviet Ukraine, where I visited several libraries in search of Hrushevsky materials. Unfortunately, however, when I visited Ukraine, as I had expected, it was made very clear to me that Hrushevsky was completely off-limits to researchers. I had expected better of western Europe. But even in the West, I was very disappointed to learn that all the great private Ukrainian libraries in western Europe were destroyed or disrupted during the war and much, if not all, of their collections also dispersed or destroyed. I already knew that this was true of the Ukrainian libraries in Berlin, Prague, and Warsaw, but I was surprised to find out this was also true of the Petliura Library in Paris, where I had hoped to find some old published materials and perhaps also some archival materials. This

was not to be, however, since the Nazis confiscated the original collection during their occupation of France in the 1940s and, so I was told at
the time, most of it was destroyed or disappeared. Thus, western Europe
was not much better for my purposes than Soviet Ukraine itself.[38]

In all of Europe, both west and east, the only library where I was able
to find and use rare and unknown Hrushevsky materials was the
Ossolineum Library in Wrocław, Poland. This was because when I made
my trip to eastern Europe and the Soviet Union in 1981, only in Poland
were political conditions suitable for primary research on a Ukrainian
subject as controversial as Hrushevsky. (This summer of 1981, I should
add, was the springtime of the Solidarity movement in Poland; martial
law was imposed only in the following winter.) At the Ossolineum, which
was a major Polish research library that had been transferred from Lviv
to Wrocław after 1945, I was able to obtain several rare pamphlets on
Hrushevsky and on Ukrainian life in old Galicia, where the library had
originally been located. These materials, which consisted primarily of
various Polish criticisms of Hrushevsky's history and politics, were then
unavailable in the West.[39]

Conclusions

During the course of three solid years of working on nothing but
Hrushevsky, I discovered that even during the height of the Cold War (it
should be recalled that while I was beginning work on Hrushevsky, the
Soviet Union invaded Afghanistan), it was entirely possible to carry out a
major research project on a controversial Ukrainian subject that was politically proscribed in the Soviet Union. I was able to do this almost entirely on the basis of library and archival materials in North America.
Moreover, most of this research was carried on entirely at my home university, the University of Toronto; or, alternatively, at private Ukrainian
libraries located elsewhere in Toronto and to some degree in Winnipeg.
Research trips to New York and Boston were valuable in expanding my
source base and filling out many of the details, but the general picture
was drawn on the basis of materials found in Toronto.

Of course, there were several limits to the kind of research I could
undertake in North America. First, despite the riches of the Robarts
Library and the Ukrainian libraries in Toronto and Winnipeg, many important political pamphlets, and journal and newspaper articles, including some by Hrushevsky himself, remained beyond my reach. This
was especially true of rare political pamphlets and newspapers produced

during the revolution of 1917–18. Second, archival materials on Hrushevsky were then, as now, almost completely non-existent in the West, and Soviet Ukrainian archives, which I suspected to be quite rich, remained closed to me. With regard to archival materials, I might add that I was, in fact, able to use only a few unpublished items dealing with "Hrushevsky and the Ukrainian Canadians," which were stored at the Public Archives of Canada in Ottawa. These materials did, however, throw considerable light on Hrushevsky's political positions during the short period that he spent in emigration.[40]

In general, however, it can be said that my biographical study of Hrushevsky, a political biography as I had planned it and as it in fact turned out, which I believed at the time to have been the first of its kind in any language, and, indeed, in some ways was unique, was produced almost entirely on the basis of published materials. My principal task had been the collection and ordering of these materials and the writing of a sensible and attractive narrative. I am content that I was able to codify and synthesize the materials then available into the book that I finally published on the eve of the collapse of Communism and the emergence of an independent and freer Ukraine, and this was done, I might reiterate, almost entirely on the basis of Ukrainian books and libraries in Canada and the United States.

14 Ukrainian Canada in the Encyclopedias, 1897–2010: An Historical Overview

Unum cum virtute multorum.

> (Motto of the City of Winnipeg,
> adopted in the 1970s. It had previously
> been: "Commerce, Prudence, Industry.")

Within fifty years, a moment in the sweep of history, our Canada has gone from aloofness, to tolerance, and beyond tolerance to respect for, indeed a deep desire for, the retention of differentiations of our heritage and culture.

> Edward Schreyer, newly appointed Governor General,
> reply at the installation, House of Commons, 22 January 1979.

The Ukrainian Canadians are one of Canada's major ethnic groups. According to the national census of 2006, Canadians of Ukrainian origin number some 1.2 million and rank tenth on the list of Canadian ethnicities, ninth if those who count themselves only "Canadian" are omitted; throughout most of the twentieth century, however, they were even more prominent, generally ranking fourth after the British groups, the French, and the Germans. Thus, from almost the onset of their settlement in Canada, which had identifiable roots by 1891 and began in earnest in 1896, they attracted the attention of various Canadian writers, journalists, and observers of the social scene. Some of this literature has been summarized and analyzed by the Edmonton historian Frances Swyripa in a pioneering work on the subject.[1]

However, there is one large lacuna in Swyripa's work and that is the encyclopedias, great compendia of knowledge organized in brief, dispassionate articles in alphabetical order. This is an important point, for not only are encyclopedias widely read because of their general synthetic approach, but they are also much trusted for their purportedly "objective" or non-partisan contents. As a matter of fact, encyclopedic knowledge of Ukrainian Canada is quite extensive and has steadily grown from very modest beginnings at the time of the first Ukrainian pioneers in this country. For the purposes of this study, materials on Ukraine and the Ukrainian Canadians have been examined in English- and French-language works, and materials on Canada have been examined in Ukrainian-language works. In this way, it is to be hoped, a fairly balanced portrayal of Ukrainian Canada may be obtained from at least two, and perhaps more, very different, though purportedly non-partisan, viewpoints.[2]

When the ancestors of most of today's Ukrainian Canadians first immigrated to this country in the 1890s and early twentieth century, Ukraine did not appear on the political map of Europe. At that time, the land that we now know as Ukraine was divided between two European empires: the Habsburg Monarchy, sometimes known as Austria-Hungary; and the Russian Empire ruled by the Romanov dynasty. Most of the pioneer or first great wave of Ukrainian immigrants came from the Crown Land of Galicia and the Duchy of Bukovina in the Austrian half of the Habsburg Monarchy, where they called themselves *Rus'ki* or *Rusyny* in their own language and were officially designated as *Ruthenen* by Austrian officialdom; in Canada, however, they quickly came to be called "Galicians" for the province of origin of the majority, though the English terms "Ruthenians" or "Ruthenes" were also somewhat known in educated English Canadian society.[3]

Turning to the subject of the encyclopedias, it may be observed that though the name and concept of "Ukraine" may have been generally unknown in Canada before 1914, the geopolitical term "Galicia" was not. In fact, Canadian scholars, if they cared to, could consult major European encyclopedias for basic information about this land. The three greatest, multivolume, western European encyclopedias of the time, the English-language *Encyclopaedia Britannica*, the French-language *La grande encyclopédie*, and the German language *Meyers Konversations-Lexikon*, all contained substantial articles on "Galicia."

The longest and most detailed was in *Meyers Konversations-Lexikon*, which was a cooperative publication venture shared by German and Austrian interests. This article was a full five pages in ten columns and discussed the population, geography, economy, administration, and history of the country. The article was accompanied by a table listing the various counties of Galicia and giving their area and population. This table would later be of use to Ukrainian Canadians wishing to find information about the area from which their forefathers came, but, as a whole, the article in *Meyers Konversations-Lexikon* was of little use with regard to the Ukrainian immigration to Canada, since it was published in 1897, only one year after the onset of the mass migration from Galicia to this country. Moreover, since German was less well known in Canada than either English or French, and the encyclopedia was printed in "*Fraktur*" or Old Gothic and not Roman type, it would have been less widely consulted than more easily read reference works in either French or English, which, of course, were printed in the more familiar Roman type.[4]

The second most extensive article on Galicia was published in *La grande encyclopédie*. It was three and a half pages long and was written by Louis Léger, in his day the foremost French expert on Slavonic Europe. Léger's article similarly treated geography, economics, history, and administration, but treated them less extensively. Instead, he devoted much more space to the ethnography, intellectual life, and the current political situation of the country. From Léger's article, the Canadian reader could get a clear picture of how Galicia was demographically divided into a Polish western half and a "Ruthenian" or Ukrainian eastern half. Léger also noted that the Ruthenians were then engaged in a political struggle to divide the province administratively along these ethnographic lines so that they could, in effect, get control over their own province. As well, he pointed out that while some Ruthenians were oriented towards "Little Russia" to the east, what we today call "Ukraine," Russia was using Ruthenian discontent in Galicia to promote an orientation on Great Russia and "Panslavism." (This would result in some Ruthenians' adopting a Russian national identity.) Thus, the Canadian reader could get a feel from Léger's article for the basic, as yet unresolved, question of developing national identity among Ruthenian Galicians at the time that they first started to emigrate to Canada. This question and its national labelling would not be fully decided until at least two decades after the first Ruthenian settlers set foot in this country.[5]

Léger's article would be extremely useful to contemporary Canadian observers of the new Galician immigration to Canada, but most of this immigration was directed towards Manitoba and the Northwest, which, by the 1890s, were already predominantly English-speaking. Thus, the *Encyclopaedia Britannica* was probably the reference work most widely used by Canadians in this region. But its article "Galicia" was only two pages long and, unlike the French-language article, was unsigned.

Nevertheless, it contained much basic information useful to the Canadian reader. Geography, climate, administration, and history are all briefly covered and the Polish–Ruthenian division clearly described. It was noted that Galicia was the largest province of the Austrian half of the empire and, after 1861, had more autonomy than any other part of this Austrian half. The *Encyclopaedia Britannica* recommended the Galicia volume of the monumental series *Die österreichisch-ungarische Monarchie in Wort und Bild* (The Austro-Hungarian monarchy in word and picture) and the works of the Galician German novelist Leopold von Sacher-Masoch (1841–1902) as further reading materials on Galician life.[6]

All three of these major European encyclopedias provided Canadian readers with some idea of who the new "Galician" settlers were and from where they came. But none of them mentioned the emigration to Canada in any of their articles. Also, they were very large and expensive editions that almost certainly were held only by major libraries in Canadian universities or by private scholars and individuals of considerable means. Thus, their influence in Canada was probably limited to certain segments of society.

To obtain information about the new Galician immigration to Canada, it would have been natural to turn to the major encyclopedias published at that time in Canada itself. There were, in fact, two such works in existence before the First World War. These were *Canada: An Encyclopedia of the Country* (six volumes, 1898–1900) and *Canada and its Provinces* (twenty-three volumes, 1913–1917). But both these works were topically and not alphabetically arranged, and, although the second contained two substantial volumes on the prairie provinces, where most of the Ruthenians were then settling, neither said a word about them.

This situation changed somewhat after the Great War, in the 1920s, when a new, alphabetically arranged encyclopedia of general knowledge, designed especially for use in Canadian schools, was published. This *Dominion Educator*, as it was called, was based on an American model but was geared to the use of Canadian schoolteachers and students; it was a "universal" encyclopedia of the Britannica type. It should be noted that, by the 1920s, when this encyclopedia first appeared, most of the settlers from Galicia had already largely abandoned the name "Ruthenian" and adopted the new name "Ukrainian." This they had done largely under the influence of the war and the revolutions in eastern Europe, where national governments actually bearing the Ukrainian name were briefly formed in Lviv (Lemberg), the capital of Galicia, and in Kyiv (Kiev), the short-lived capital of independent "Ukraine." Nevertheless, no article on

Ukrainian or even Galician immigration to either the United States or Canada appeared in this reference work. There was, however, a very respectable article on "Galicia" that gave a detailed political history of recent events in the province, including war events from 1914 to 1918 and ending with its annexation to the new Republic of Poland in 1918–19. (This annexation was not confirmed by the international powers until 1923.) However, the *Dominion Educator* somewhat garbled the ethnography of the province by referring to its inhabitants "who are Russians, Poles, Slovaks, Bohemians, and Ruthenians." In fact, the population of Galicia at the time was Polish, Ukrainian, and Jewish, in that order. Galicia's fourth-largest nationality to 1914 had been neither Russian nor Slovak but, rather, German. Further information on Galicia was given in this encyclopedia's article "Austria-Hungary or Austro-Hungarian Monarchy."[7]

Also, unlike the previous encyclopedias mentioned here, the *Dominion Educator* contained a brief but generally accurate article on "Ukraine." It noted that this region of the Russian Empire was inhabited by "Little Russians" or "Ruthenians," had declared its national independence in 1917, and had signed the Peace Treaty of Brest-Litovsk (1918) with the central powers. It concluded, however, by noting that Ukraine's claim to Galicia had been successfully disputed by Poland, and Ukraine ended by being annexed to the USSR in 1922.[8]

On a somewhat different level, the *Dominion Educator* contained the substantial article "Immigration and Emigration," which mainly dealt with American affairs. It noted the enormous immigration from Europe to the United States before 1914 and contained a whole section on "Immigration Problems," which reflected the nativist fears of the American public in the 1920s. The encyclopedia flatly stated:

> The great influx of aliens to the US occasioned many problems. While America has freely welcomed the people of other lands, it has realized the danger attending unrestricted immigration of the weak, the vicious, and the ignorant alien. Laws have been passed which forbid entrance into the country of certain classes of 'undesirables' including criminals, those afflicted with contagious disease, the feeble-minded, and moral degenerates.

Thus, while no explicit statement of the new laws restricting immigration from eastern Europe was made and the new "quota" system limiting immigration from eastern Europe was not mentioned, they were implied nonetheless, and the encyclopedia noted that immigration patterns to Canada were similar to those to the United States, except that in Canada, so it claimed, about half of the new immigrants were "British." No mention of Ruthenian/Ukrainian immigration to Canada was made.[9]

Accurate information about Ukrainian immigration to Canada in the *Dominion Educator* could have been very influential during the Depression years in Canada, as this work was reprinted in 1933 in an attractive binding and widely distributed throughout the country. The year 1933, it should be remembered, was not only a terrible depression year in Canada, but also the year that the United States diplomatically recognized the USSR and the year of the Great Ukrainian Famine in which several million people perished. Thus, "Ukraine" was then making international headlines and the Ukrainian community in Canada, at least, began making publicity on behalf of its co-nationals in Europe.[10]

The 1930s also saw the publication of the first truly comprehensive, independent, alphabetically arranged encyclopedia devoted principally to Canadian subjects. This multivolume *Encyclopedia of Canada* was the first reference work to contain an article on the immigration of Ukrainians to Canada; in fact, there were two such articles. However, the first of these two articles, despite the almost universal adoption by that time of the term "Ukrainian" by the community in Canada, did not use this name at all. Instead, the article was titled "Galician Immigration."

The article updated previous information on Galicia by noting that this region was now a Polish province and Bukovina now a part of Romania. It stated that the "Ruthenian" immigrants from these areas "are commonly known in Canada as Galicians," and that, by 1920, there were some quarter of a million settled primarily in Manitoba, Saskatchewan, and Alberta, with a few in British Columbia. The article went on to say:

> Practically all the Galician immigrants to Canada are peasants, and come from a people so poor that some have not been accustomed to eat meat more than once or twice a year. They share some of the less attractive characteristics of the Slav race, such as a laxity of attitude toward sexual morality and a scantness (sic) of courtesy for women. But they are patient and industrious workmen, ambitious, and in many cases, eager to be Canadianized.

The article then noted that, on their arrival in Canada, the Ruthenians were mostly members of the Uniate Church (later the Ukrainian Catholic Church), which recognized Rome but held to its own customs and Slavonic liturgy; however, in Canada, the article approvingly stated, many had since shown a spirit of religious independence, the result being a Greek Independent Church that "has a strong evangelical tendency."

The article noted the important role of the Ruthenians as labourers in western Canadian industry and railway building and concluded by remarking on the considerable influence of "English culture" on the younger generation, though this was resisted in some quarters. Surprisingly, the article even noted that "many Galicians regard the government as bound to support Galician customs and language."[11]

Though brief, this first article in the *Encyclopedia of Canada* gave a good picture of how the Ukrainian Canadians were viewed by the English majority in the 1930s. It acknowledged their presence in Canada but stereotyped them as poor peasants, sexually lax, but good workers easily falling under the influence of English culture, which it equated with "Canadianization." Though, remarkably, this article mentioned the cultural claims of the Ukrainians, there was, of course, as yet no mention of the new name "Ukrainian" and no hint that Canada itself could ever accommodate to the Ukrainians or be changed by them.[12]

The second article in this encyclopedia was titled "Ukrainians" and gave a much clearer picture of the national identity of this Slavonic Canadian group. It stated that between 1896 and 1914, no fewer than 170,000 "Ukrainians" came to the country and settled principally on the Prairies, where they presently constituted "the third largest racial group ... probably the fourth largest in the Dominion." The article then repeated much of the same information contained in the first article, but with the patronizing air of Anglo-Saxon superiority somewhat toned down. It ended by saying that the Ukrainians "have been slow in assimilating Canadian ideals and education has made among them only moderate progress" but that they were starting to "drift into the cities" and their education and standard of living were presently rapidly rising.[13]

This peculiar pair of articles in the *Encyclopedia of Canada* was a true hallmark of its times with regard to the Ukrainians and the general history of ethnic relations in Canada. The first article was condescending and biased in the extreme; the second, much more careful in its judgments. The first totally ignored the nationality of the immigrants, focusing only on their "racial" or Slavic identity; the second more plainly acknowledged their now-accepted national name and made no reference to any particularly Slavic sexual morality. Thus, in its two somewhat varied treatments of the Ukrainians, this pioneering encyclopedia clearly reflected both the growth of national consciousness among these people and also increasing Canadian respect for them. Most interesting of all, of course, was the fact that the formation of this new Ukrainian national identity had occurred on this continent and in this country after immigration rather than before, and was noticed by at least some in the Anglo Canadian academic elite. Consequently, though it was influenced by events in Europe, this change was still a truly Canadian phenomenon.[14]

The 1930s *Encyclopedia of Canada* was the first alphabetically arranged encyclopedia of Canada and its appearance was an important cultural event in the country. Coincidentally, on the other side of the Atlantic, the first alphabetically arranged Ukrainian-language encyclopedia was published simultaneously in Lwów, in eastern Poland. Lwów (Lviv in Ukrainian) was the new official name given to Lemberg, the former capital of Austrian Galicia, where so many Ukrainians continued to live. This encyclopedia was called the *Ukrainska zahalna entsyklopediia* (Ukrainian general encyclopedia) and its publication in Poland in three large volumes caused the Soviet Ukrainian government in the neighbouring Soviet Ukraine to prepare the publication of an even larger Soviet Ukrainian encyclopedia. Unfortunately, political events in the USSR, where Stalin was then consolidating his rule, prevented this project from being carried out, but the *Ukrainska zahalna entsyklopediia* did contain the brief article "Canada," which pointed out that there were then about 300,000 Ukrainians in the country and they ostensibly formed the third-largest group after the British and French. The article mentioned that, from 1912, there had been a Greek Catholic bishopric in Canada and that the first bishops had been Nykyta Budka (1912 to 1929) and Vasyl Ladyka (from 1929). The encyclopedia also contained brief articles on various Ukrainian-language newspapers in Canada, an article on the Canadian Pacific Railway, which sponsored immigration and settled these immigrants on its lands adjacent to the various railway lines, and the general article "Emigration," which stated that, to 1909, some 470,000 people had emigrated from eastern Galicia to the USA and, between 1924 and 1929, from this same region (now ruled by Poland), some 75,123 people emigrated abroad. The article noted that this emigration had started with Brazil as a target, then changed to the USA and Canada, and then again to Brazil; the large seasonal migration to western Europe for work purposes, both prior to the war of 1914 to 1918 and afterwards, was also noted. Though very brief, these encyclopedia articles were important insofar as the appearance of the *Ukrainska zahalna entsyklopediia* was a major event in the history of twentieth-century Ukrainian culture, and, in the absence of a major Soviet Ukrainian encyclopedia, was to hold the field in this area for another three decades, until the Khrushchev thaw of the later 1950s made possible further significant advances in Ukrainian publishing and culture.[15]

Meanwhile, in Canada, the events of the early 1940s, especially the outbreak of the Second World War, led to substantial changes in the situation of the Ukrainian Canadians and certain other ethnic groups. In 1939, the Dominion of Canada followed Britain into the war against Germany and was quickly transformed by its wartime experience. Labour shortages in industry and the military, and the struggle against Nazi racism, greatly changed the country. The federal government made strenuous efforts to unite all Canadians behind the war effort, including the non-French and non-English groups like the Ukrainians. It was during this period that most of the Ukrainian parts of old "Galicia" were annexed to the Ukrainian SSR and that English Canadian society as a whole finally dropped the name "Galician" and completely went over to the new name "Ukrainian." Discrimination against the non-English, including the Ukrainians, was actively opposed by the government and a new "Canadians All" ethic began to grip the country.[16] At war's end, a new wave of Ukrainian refugees, generally referred to at the time as Displaced Persons (DPs), entered the country. In general, these DPs were better educated and more professional than their predecessors had been and they had a definite impact on how Ukrainians were seen by their fellow Canadians.[17]

As far as encyclopedias are concerned, the new respect shown the Ukrainian Canadians did not first appear in an encyclopedia published in Canada but, rather, in one published in the United States. This was the large-format *Slavonic Encyclopaedia* edited by the Czech American political scientist and sociologist Joseph S. Roucek. It contained the detailed article "Ukrainians in Canada" by the well-known polyglot Watson Kirkconnell of Acadia University, formerly of Wesley College in Winnipeg. This article stated that according to the 1941 census at 305,929 souls, the Ukrainians formed the sixth-largest "racial group" in the Dominion, after the French, English, Scottish, Irish, and Germans. Kirkconnell noted that 65.17 per cent of these had been born in the country and were concentrated in the prairie provinces. He gave exact figures as to religious breakdown, employment, and the professions, and devoted a long and detailed section to the history and organizations of the Ukrainian Canadians.

For example, he stated that the Ukrainian Catholic Church, the largest ecclesiastical institution of the group, had 345 parishes and 85 missions, 8 monasteries, 13 convents, 3 theological schools, 2 hospitals, 3 printing houses, 4 newspapers, 118 parish halls, and "a number of charitable institutions." Affiliated with it were the Brotherhood of Ukrainian

Catholics with 345 branches and 32,632 members, and also youth and women's organizations, as well as 121 schools, 278 choirs, and 236 drama clubs. The Ukrainian Orthodox Church was considerably smaller with only 163 parishes and 63 missions, though it also ran important student residences near the University of Saskatchewan in Saskatoon and the University of Alberta in Edmonton (the Petro Mohyla and Mykhailo Hrushevsky institutes, respectively). Similarly detailed descriptions of other political and social organizations were given and a generally accurate picture of the Ukrainian political spectrum in Canada emerged.

Of the pro-Communist organization, the Ukrainian Labour Farmer Temple Association (ULFTA), Kirkconnell wrote that it was "Communist controlled," and he quoted its program for "the mobilization of the working masses of this country for the revolutionary struggle of liberation." He stated that it was "alleged to have 108 halls, 200 orchestras, 120 choirs with an overall membership of 20,000." He noted that it had been suppressed during the early part of the war but later re-emerged as the Association of Ukrainian Canadians. Kirkconnell also listed numerous prominent individuals among the Ukrainian Canadians, various press organs, and some prominent literary and musical figures. All in all, his article was by far the most important such encyclopedia article to appear on the subject to the 1950s.[18]

Returning to Canada, when the *Encyclopedia of Canada* was revised and expanded in the 1950s and republished under the new title *Encyclopedia Canadiana*, it, too, contained a long, detailed, and very favourable article about the Ukrainian Canadians. This article was written by one of the most prominent of the post-war refugees, the linguist J. B. Rudnyckyj, founder of the Department of Slavic Studies at the University of Manitoba. Rudnyckyj later wrote that he had been so offended by the entry on "Galician immigration" in the 1936 *Encyclopedia of Canada* that when he discovered that a new *Encyclopedia Canadiana* was being planned, he made certain it would contain a full and favourable coverage of the then very large Ukrainian community in Canada.[19] This coverage included the article on the Ukrainians by Rudnyckyj himself, articles by his colleague Paul Yuzyk at the University of Manitoba on the two largest religious denominations, an article on "Slavonic or Slavic Studies" in Canada by the British Columbia Polish specialist William Rose, and significant Ukrainian-related content in the general article "Immigration" by W. A. Carruthers and Robert England.

Even the very title of Rudnyckyj's article broke with the precedent of the 1936 encyclopedia. Under "Galicians," the *Encyclopedia Canadiana* simply directed the reader to "Ukrainian origin, People of." And, again, this title, too, was the best of several different options since it omitted the words "immigrants" and "immigration," thus considering second-, third-, and even fourth-generation Ukrainian Canadians and avoiding giving the impression that the Ukrainians were new arrivals in the country, which, of course, they were not, since by this time the vast majority were Canadian-born. (It should be remembered that before 1939, the non-British and non-French were generally referred to as "foreigners" by British-origin people in English-speaking Canada.)

Rudnyckyj's article began with demography and stated there were 395,043 Ukrainians in Canada according to the census of 1951. Of these, 164,795 were Ukrainian (Greek) Catholic, and 111,045 Greek Orthodox, the rest being divided among various Protestant sects. He then named the first-known "Ukrainian" arrivals of 1891, Vasyl Eleniak and Ivan Pylypiw, but did not explain where the "Ukrainian" name came from or how it had spread throughout Canada. He identified three main waves of Ukrainian immigration to Canada: 1) the first pre-1914 wave; 2) a second, interwar, wave, which he mistakenly identified as "for the most part political refugees"; and 3) the post-1945 wave of Displaced Persons or true European political refugees.

Rudnyckyj then turned to the "characteristics of the people" and penned a description that deserves quotation at length:

> Physically the Ukrainians are strong, and capable of great endurance. As a peasant people, they are noted for deliberateness, modesty and an uneven temperament. The most important characteristics are their optimism, humour, and irony, which help them to face the blows and irritations of everyday life. Hard times have developed in them a certain cautiousness and increased their individualism. An intimate connection with the soil for more than a thousand years has left traces in their thoughts and actions, in their conduct of life, their view of the world. Of all the Slavic peoples, the Ukrainians have the most developed folk music. A rich repertoire of folk songs, choral music, folk dances, religious and family customs, traditional beliefs, legends, tales and proverbs has gained a world-wide reputation.

Rudnyckyj then turned to the Ukrainian language, which, he noted, was, together with Russian and Belarusan, a member of the east Slavic branch of the Slavic group; he described it as being similar to Russian in structure, to Polish in some of its vocabulary, and to Serbian and Croatian in sound. He mentioned the rich Ukrainian contribution to the folk arts in Canada and devoted a long section to Ukrainian organizational life in the country, especially concentrating on the umbrella Ukrainian Canadian Committee and its member organizations. He claimed that the pro-Communists formed only "a small minority" among the Ukrainian Canadians.

He then considered publishing activities, Ukrainian-language teaching, and folk festivals. He concluded with the Ukrainian "contribution to Canada," where he emphasized agriculture but also treated politics, education, the fine arts, and the military. His concluding sentence read: "If at the end of the nineteenth century [the Ukrainians] were an unknown factor, today they are taking part in the economic, cultural, scientific, and political life of Canada."[20]

Paul Yuzyk's two articles in the *Encyclopedia Canadiana* on religious affairs greatly added to the information supplied by Rudnyckyj. The article "Ukrainian Catholic Church" was two and a half pages long and described in detail the history and significance of this church. After summarizing its European background and describing its customs and usages, including communion with Rome, a liturgy in Old Church Slavonic, Byzantine art and architecture, and a married clergy in Europe, Yuzyk turned to its history in Canada. He noted the scarcity of priests during the pioneer era and the role of French-speaking priests in filling this void. (The roles of the Redemptorist and Basilian religious orders became important from very early times, since Rome insisted on the celibacy of priests ordained in North America.) Yuzyk noted that, unlike in the United States, where the first bishop came under the jurisdiction of the local Roman Catholic hierarchy, in Canada, the first bishop, Nicitas (or Nykyta) Budka, was independent of the local hierarchy and directly responsible to Rome. Yuzyk mentioned the great defection to Eastern Orthodoxy of large numbers of Greek Catholic "nationalists" who were unhappy with Budka's loyalty to the name "Ruthenian" and with his tolerance of "Latin" influences. The church reached its apogee under Budka's successor, Bishop Basil Ladyka, when the Canadian census of 1951 reported some 190,831 Ukrainian Catholics in the country. This same census reported that another 56,650 Ukrainians were now Roman Catholics, a tremendous leap from the 4,827 of the 1941 census; this seemed to indicate a strong assimilationist trend among the youth. The third presiding bishop or Metropolitan was Maxim Hermaniuk, who was of post-war DP background. Yuzyk concluded by outlining the rich Catholic periodical press of the 1950s and listing various organizations affiliated with the Ukrainian Catholic Church.[21]

Yuzyk's article "Orthodox Churches" was only slightly shorter than his article on the Ukrainian Catholics. He stated that, according to the census of 1951, there were 172,271 Greek Orthodox Christians in Canada, of whom the great bulk, 111,045, were of Ukrainian origin. Of the others, 12,219 identified themselves as Russian, 7,741 as Polish, and 3,468 as "others," which included both Greek and what Yuzyk called "Asiatic."

Yuzyk dealt first with the group called the Russian Orthodox Greek Catholic Church of North America, which, years later, took the name Orthodox Church of America. He noted its original dependence on the tsar's Holy Synod in Russia and the Ukrainian origin of most of its priests and faithful. He then treated the Ukrainian Greek Orthodox Church of Canada, which, at that time, was by far the largest of the Orthodox churches in Canada. He described its 1918 origins as a breakaway faction of the Ruthenian Greek Catholic Church in Canada, the fact that it used Ukrainian and not Church Slavonic in its liturgy, its temporary submission to Metropolitan Germanos Shegedi of the Syrian Greek Orthodox Church, the importance of the Rev S. W. Sawchuk as administrator of the church, its relatively independent position under the distant jurisdiction of various American bishops, and, finally, the assumption of the leadership of the church by Metropolitan Ilarion Ohienko in Winnipeg. By 1953, the church claimed to have 265 parishes and 69 priests in the country. In the 1950s, it was still growing: from 55,386 souls in 1931 to 88,874 in 1941 to 111,045 in 1951. Yuzyk concluded his article with a very brief treatment of the Greek Orthodox Church, composed of Greek immigrants, which at that time had only six parishes in the country, and the Syrian Orthodox Church, which had only three.[22]

The 1958 edition of the *Encyclopedia Canadiana* also contained the detailed article "Immigration" that gave some information on the Ukrainian Canadians. This article was authored by W.A. Carruthers and revised by the expert on central European immigrants in Canada, Robert England. The article was quite detailed and devoted much space to early immigration to French Canada and to the period following the British Conquest, which was dominated by the United Empire Loyalists who emigrated from the newly independent United States. It mentioned the Selkirk Settlement in Red River but noted that it "had been largely a failure." It noted the Dominion Lands Act of 1872 that offered free homesteads to prospective immigrants but acknowledged that the real settlement of the West occurred after the completion of the transcontinental railway in the 1880s, when Sir Clifford Sifton widely sought prospective immigrants in continental Europe. "In the nineties," wrote Carruthers and England, "large numbers of central and southern Europeans had begun to migrate to the United States, and Canada began to cast longing eyes on these sturdy peasants. As a result of the Sifton policy the numbers of foreign immigrants for a time exceeded those of British origin." The period from 1903 to 1914 was, in fact, the high point of Canadian immigration and saw 2,677,399 immigrants admitted to the Dominion.

The article noted the end of immigration during the Great War and an increase during the 1920s, when two-thirds all immigrants still came from Britain and northern Europe (175,766 came from "central Europe"). World War Two temporarily stopped immigration once again but, by 1949, it had increased. Between 1946 and 1954, 1.1 million immigrants were admitted to the Dominion, of whom 165,697 were Displaced Persons from the continent. As to immigration policy, Carruthers and England maintained that no country had a longer history of "directed" settlement and after-care than Canada. Canadian immigration agents were in Europe long before there were any Canadian diplomats there. The article was accompanied by charts explaining the ethnic diversity of the Canadian population. These graphics showed that in 1951, 6.5 per cent of Canadians were of eastern European origin and 2.8 per cent were Ukrainian. A revised chart in a later edition of the encyclopedia (1972) showed that, by 1961, Ukrainians were the fourth-largest Canadian group at 2.6 per cent of the total population after the British, French, and Germans. They were followed closely by the Italians and the Dutch.[23]

One final point may be made about the *Encyclopedia Canadiana*: this great reference work even contained the article "Slavonic or Slavic studies" by the first Canadian-born Slavist, William J. Rose, who had lived in England for many years but had returned to Canada after 1945 to teach at the University of British Columbia. This article gave a detailed description of the growth of Slavic Studies in the Dominion, emphasizing their expansion after the war. Although, because of its current political status in the world, the importance of Russian and Russian studies was stressed in this article, Polish and Ukrainian studies were considered and it was noted that Polish literature was far older than Russian and that the Ukrainians were, after the British and French, so Rose claimed, "by far the largest ethnic group in the Dominion ... numbering nearly 400,000." He continued: "These hard-working and freedom-loving people have become part of the country's business and political life; the younger generation has found in Canadian colleges and universities something that their parents never knew, and the Ukrainian organizations have made annual contributions (especially in Manitoba) in support of Slavonic studies."

The author also made special mention of Constantine Andrusyshen's great Ukrainian-English dictionary (1955) and the work of J. B. Rudnyckyj of the University of Manitoba, especially the *Slavica Canadiana* series of pamphlets edited by him.[24]

About the same time that the *Encyclopedia Canadiana* was published in English in Canada, the first really large-scale, detailed, universal, alphabetically arranged encyclopedia in the Ukrainian language was published in the Ukrainian SSR. It was the successor of the planned but never published general Soviet Ukrainian encyclopedia of the 1930s. This impressive multivolume *Ukrainska radianska entsyklopediia* (Ukrainian Soviet encyclopedia, or URE) was a product of the Khrushchev thaw in the USSR, during which the tight censorship of Stalin's time was slightly loosened. The encyclopedia contained a detailed article on Canada in which extensive treatment was given to the subject of Ukrainian Canada.

The URE article on Canada treated the population, structure, climate, geography, economics, and politics of the country, but most striking was its subsection "Ukrainians in Canada," which was a full two pages long and was illustrated with two photographs. The section on population began by stating that Canada's 1951 population consisted primarily of the descendants of Europeans: 6.7 million "Anglo-Canadians," 4.3 million Franco-Canadians, one million Slavs, 620,000 Canadians of German ancestry, 566,000 of Scandinavian ancestry, and others. The section "Ukrainians in Canada" claimed that there were then 700,000 Ukrainians in the country and that they formed the third-largest nationality in terms of numbers and were settled primarily in the western provinces. (They were, in fact, still fourth after the British groups, the French, and the Germans, and still numbered considerably less than 700,000.) The article described the first Ukrainian migrants who came from western Ukraine and claimed that by 1914, they numbered 170,000. The article then mentioned Canadian immigration policy and the important role of Clifford Sifton. It discussed the difficult working conditions of the early immigrants who helped to build the basic infrastructure of the West, including roads and railways. This was followed by descriptions of the economic crises of 1908 to 1913 and 1929 to 1933 when "the immigrants knew unemployment, hunger, and homelessness." The URE continued:

The principle of discrimination was applied to the Ukrainians. They were the last to be hired and the first to be fired. Discrimination was also apparent in the fact that for a long time Ukrainian immigrants were not given citizenship rights. In spite of much loss, savage exploitation, and discrimination,

they made a significant contribution to the economic and cultural development of Canada, especially in the provinces of Alberta, Manitoba, and
Saskatchewan.

The URE then turned to social questions. It mentioned Galician Metropolitan Andrei Sheptytsky's sending of priests, especially Basilians, to
Canada and the role of Bishop Budka, but it devoted most space to the
leftist pro-Communist organizations and their press. It noted their participation in the Winnipeg General Strike of 1919, their support for the
revolution in Russia in 1917 and their subsequent support for the USSR,
their fight against fascism in the 1930s, including participation in the
International Brigades in the Spanish Civil War, and their struggle
against fascism in the Second World War that followed. The article mentioned by name the various pro-Communist Ukrainian organizations,
especially the Association of United Ukrainian Canadians (AUUC), and
contrasted them to the Ukrainian Canadian Committee, which it labelled as "bourgeois nationalist." (There was, moreover, no mention of
Ukrainian support for the non-Communist democratic socialists of the
Co-operative Commonwealth Federation, which was popular from the
1940s to the 1960s.) The article ended with a contrast between the pro-
Communist leftists who erected a statue to the Ukrainian national poet
Taras Shevchenko, in Palermo, Ontario, in 1951, and the nationalists
who did the same in Winnipeg in 1961, but for supposedly purely propa-
gandistic purposes. The final sentence of this article, reflecting the usual
Soviet concern about the international legitimacy of the USSR, stated
that "many delegates of the Ukrainian Canadians have visited Soviet
Ukraine during the post-war period."[25]

In spite of its detailed treatment of the Ukrainian community in Canada,
which was made possible by the Khrushchev thaw, the article on Canada
in the URE was still subject to very strict Soviet censorship and had a
clearly "pro-Communist," not to say "leftist," bias. It was balanced, however, by articles appearing in Ukrainian émigré encyclopedias, which
were then being simultaneously published abroad. The most openly "nationalist" and anti-Communist of these was Ievhen Onatsky's *Ukrainska
mala entsyklopediia* (Small Ukrainian encyclopedia).

Onatsky's encyclopedia contained a substantial article on Canada but
much of this article was simply a description of the Ukrainian community
given in a Radio Canada International broadcast by Paul Yuzyk, who, like
Onatsky, supported the rightist Organization of Ukrainian Nationalists
(Melnyk branch). Onatsky's article on Canada, like the previous articles

discussed above, stated that, as of 1951, there were 395,043 Ukrainians in Canada and they formed 2.8 per cent of the total population. Moreover, 90 per cent of them lived in the prairie provinces. Onatsky then mentioned Ivan Pylypiw and Vasyl Eleniak and noted that Eleniak lived to see the sixtieth anniversary of Ukrainian settlement in the country in 1951, when he turned ninety-two years old. He quoted Yuzyk at length on Ukrainian life in Canada: many communities had been founded by the Ukrainians and given Ukrainian names (Ukraina, Ternopil, Petlura, and so on); the Ukrainians excelled in agriculture but also were to be found in the professions as doctors, lawyers, engineers, and prominent businessmen; many were elected to town councils, provincial legislatures, and even the federal parliament, where four prominent Ukrainian politicians had already held seats – Mykhailo Luchkovych, Fred Zaplitny, Antin Hlynka, and Ivan Dykur (John Decore). The last of these had even been appointed Canadian representative to the United Nations. Yuzyk concluded by saying that the Ukrainian churches were flourishing in Canada and there were 400 Greek Catholic and 250 Orthodox Ukrainian churches in the country, that there were numerous cultural organizations, and that the Ukrainian language was taught in both schools run by the Ukrainian community (*ridny shkoly*) and in four different universities.[26]

Onatsky's *Ukrainska mala entsyklopediia* was plainly ideological and its article on the Ukrainians in Canada thoroughly optimistic and brief. It was the work of one very dedicated individual. In contrast to this, during this same period, a group of scholars in western Europe, with numerous contributors in Canada and the United States and led by the Paris-based geographer Volodymyr Kubiiovych, produced a much larger *Entsyklope-diia ukrainoznavstva* (Encyclopedia of knowledge about Ukraine, or EU); this venture was more non-partisan in tone, devoted much more space to Canada, and contained numerous separate articles on various Ukrainian Canadian institutions and people.[27] Its article on Canada was, in fact, seventeen pages long with sections devoted to demography, the history of Ukrainian settlement, religious life, social life, participation in Canadian public life, the press, literature, art, theatre, libraries and archives, economics, and assimilation. It was co-authored by several prominent Ukrainian Canadian scholars including Ivan Teslia (demography and geography), Bohdan Kazymyra (the Catholic Church), Vladimir Kysilewskyj (the orthodox Church), V. Borovsky (Protestant churches), Constantine Andrusyshen (literature), and Z. Yankovsky (economics).

The article was accompanied by five maps, six illustrations, and several tables and graphs. It contained much the same material as the *Encyclopedia*

Canadiana (describing the country in 1951 as did that encyclopedia) but went into greater detail on all subjects, giving more statistical data and identifying by name many prominent Ukrainian Canadian leaders in political, religious, and social life. It also made occasional comparisons with the history and position of the Ukrainians in the United States. For example, it maintained that the Ukrainian immigration to Canada post-dated that to the United States by about twenty years, and, while Galicians and Bukovinians made up the bulk of the Ukrainian immigrants to Canada, unlike the United States, they were not accompanied by immigrants from Transcarpathia (today in western Ukraine) or the Lemko region (today in the Polish Carpathians).

The EU article on Canada gave the same figures as the other encyclopedias as to the Ukrainian population of Canada, but also pointed out that while in 1951, they made up the fourth-largest nationality in Canada as a whole, on the Prairies, they came in third after the British and the Germans, thus surpassing the French in this part of Canada. It outlined the three great "waves" of Ukrainian immigration to Canada, giving the number of immigrants for each as 100,000, 70,000, and 35,000. The article stated that, in 1951, there were 395,000 Canadians of Ukrainian ancestry and gave the ethnic breakdown of the country per 1,000 people at that time, as shown in table 14.1.

Furthermore, the article broke down the Ukrainian population in 1951 as follows: 69.5 per cent born in Canada and 30.5 per cent immigrants, of whom 13.5 per cent arrived before 1914, 11.0 per cent arrived between the wars, and 6.0 per cent after 1945. Two-thirds still lived in the prairie provinces. The article contained a map showing the Ukrainian population density throughout the Prairies. This map clearly showed the areas of most dense settlement along the northern edge of the Prairies (the so-called poplar belt) where the grasslands gradually turned into bush country.

The sections on religion authored by Bohdan Kazymyra and Vladimir Kysilewskyj gave a detailed church history of the group. The former mentioned the Catholic prelates Sheptytsky, Budka, Ladyka, and Hermaniuk by name and outlined their contributions, while the latter mentioned Myroslav Stechishin, Vasyl Svystun, V. Kudryk, S. Sawchuk, and Julian Shechishin as founders of the Ukrainian Orthodox Church. The section on Protestant churches mentioned Ivan Bodrug as a founder of the Independent Greek Orthodox Church, most of whose leaders eventually went over to the Protestants.

Table 14.1 Ethnic Composition of Canada, 1951 (per thousand).

Rank	Origin	All Canada	Prairies
1	British	479	457
2	French	308	68
3	German	44	117
4	Ukrainian	28	104
5	Scandinavian	20	65
6	Dutch	19	40
7	Polish	17	37
8	Jewish	13	10
9	Others	72	102
	Total	1,000	1,000

The section on organizational life was particularly detailed. It gave an outline of the various political organizations from right to left and included the many new political organizations founded by the post-1945 political immigrants. The organizations affiliated with the churches were the most influential, and the umbrella organization, the Ukrainian Canadian Committee, was particularly noted. The Communist organizations, however, were not discussed or even mentioned. As to academic organizations, the émigré Ukrainian Free Academy of Sciences in Winnipeg and the Shevchenko Scientific Society in Toronto were described. Detailed descriptions of the participation of the Ukrainians in Canadian political, social, and cultural life followed with a very detailed description of the Ukrainian-language press (by Kazymyra) and of Ukrainian literature in Canada (by Andrusyshen). The article closed with Yankovsky's description of economics and assimilation, which was quite remarkable by even the second generation.[28]

In addition to this very large article on Canada, the EU also contained articles on individual Ukrainian Canadian organizations and press organs. The detail of these articles was remarkable and immediately made the EU the most useful general reference work on the Ukrainian Canadians ever published and certainly, in this regard, the most valuable encyclopedia. Thus, it was no coincidence that some two decades later, a project was undertaken to translate the entire work into English and update its contents for the use of the general public interested in almost anything to do with Ukraine. This project was carried out by the Canadian Institute of Ukrainian Studies (founded in 1976), Toronto Office, located at the University of Toronto.

Because it was published in Canada, the English-language edition of this translation, the *Encyclopedia of Ukraine,* made certain that Canadian topics were given accurate and full coverage in the work. It was also printed on much better paper than the original Ukrainian-language work and contained better quality illustrations, graphs, and maps, some in full colour.

The article "Canada" in this encyclopedia was about the same length as the original Ukrainian-language version, sixteen pages, but also contained three additional pages of coloured maps of the prairie region, describing the areas of most intense Ukrainian settlement from 1921 to 1971. These maps demonstrated a steady ethnic dispersion of the Ukrainian population to areas south of the poplar belt where the original immigrants had settled. The article updated basic information about the Ukrainians in Canada, stating that, by 1981, there were 775,000 Canadians of Ukrainian origin who made up Canada's fifth-largest ethnic group after the British, French, Germans, and now also Italians. In 1981, they constituted 3.1 per cent of the total population. The article also stressed the new "multicultural" character of the country (from its beginnings, the multicultural movement had been led by the Ukrainians) and described the continuing urbanization and modernization of the Ukrainian community. Interestingly, the section on organizations, unlike the Ukrainian original, also contained some information on the pro-Communist organizations, especially the Ukrainian Labour Farmer Temple Association (ULFTA; later the Association of United Ukrainian Canadians, or AUUC), which reached its heyday during the 1930s and 1940s. By the time of the Cold War, it was already in decline, suffering severe losses after de-Stalinization in the USSR and with the Soviet invasion of Czechoslovakia in 1968. In general, however, like its Ukrainian-language predecessor, the updated *Encyclopedia of Ukraine* immediately became an invaluable reference work on Ukrainian Canada.[29]

If, in the 1960s, the *Entsyklopediia ukrainoznavstva* was meant to supplement and correct the heavily censored URE published in the Ukrainian SSR, the *Encyclopedia of Ukraine* of the 1980s and early 1990s was meant to do the same for the new, somewhat shortened 1980s edition of the URE, which was similarly – in fact, in some ways more tightly – censored. This new URE contained the article "Canada," similar to that in its predecessor, complete with the subsection "Ukrainians in Canada." It was authored by V. B. Ievtukh, a specialist on Ukrainians abroad. This article stated that, according to the census of 1971, there were 580,700 Ukrainians in Canada, 80 per cent of whom had been born there. By this time, of course, these Ukrainians were settled in the cities as well as the countryside, including Vancouver and Montreal. (Curiously, the article did not mention Toronto.) It continued with a somewhat more cautious indictment of Canadian discrimination than that expressed by its Soviet predecessor:

> From the very beginning of Ukrainian settlement in Canada, the Ukrainian emigrants experienced exploitation and discrimination, especially in years of production decline and economic crisis. Many migrants from Ukraine returned to the fatherland.... To the present time, discrimination on the basis of ethnic characteristics is continuing. The somewhat lower than average educational level, wages, and standard of life of immigrants from Ukraine, testify to this.

The article's section "Ukrainians in Canada" concluded with a detailed history of the pro-Communist left among them, in particular the ULFTA and the AUUC. The final words were devoted to the recently established (1960) Tovarystvo 'Ukraina' (The Ukraine Society) to aid friendly Ukrainian organizations and individuals in Canada and the West in their relations with Soviet Ukraine.[30]

The next major encyclopedia that contained materials on Ukrainian Canada was the *Canadian Encyclopedia* published by the Canadian nationalist Mel Hurtig in Edmonton. This encyclopedia was not an updating or expansion of the earlier *Encyclopedia Canadiana* but, rather, a completely new work, considerably briefer, but still containing the substantial articles "Ukrainians" by Frances Swyripa and "Ukrainian Writing" by Yar Slavutych, both Edmonton scholars.

Swyripa's article stated that as of 1986, there were 420,210 Canadians of Ukrainian origin (possibly referring only to those of wholly Ukrainian background, since the total number of persons with some Ukrainian background was much higher). Of these, only 59.1 per cent now lived in the prairie provinces, while 25.3 per cent lived in Ontario. Swyripa outlined the three major waves of Ukrainian immigration to Canada and noted the shift in settlement to the east, particularly Ontario. Unlike Rudnyckyj in the *Encyclopedia Canadiana*, she stated that the interwar immigration had been *both* peasants and politicals; and the post-1945 immigrants, war refugees. She noted the shift from farm to city and from agriculture to industry, and believed that, while Ukrainians were still under-represented in the professions, they were now close to the Canadian average in other ways. She gave an outline of the organizational history of Ukrainian Canadians and stated that by 1986, only 10 to 15 per cent of them belonged to such organizations or took part in the organized Ukrainian community, but the rest, she explained to the reader, "identify with its cultural but not its national-political goals." She also stated that "many Ukrainian Canadians no longer find the ethnic press relevant."

In the area of religion, too, the Ukrainian institutions were suffering a decline. In 1981, only 30.0 per cent and 18.6 per cent belonged to the Ukrainian Catholic and Orthodox churches, respectively. Nevertheless, Swyripa noted, hybrid Ukrainian Canadian country music and church architecture, which mixed Byzantine and North American design, were flourishing. She concluded by saying that "overt discrimination has largely disappeared and many Canadians of Ukrainian origin retain few distinctive ethnic values." Her last sentence reads: "Since the 1960s, the Canadian born have countered assimilation by reviving interest in their heritage, aided by [government] multicultural policies."[31]

Yar Slavutych's somewhat shorter article "Ukrainian Writing" divided it into three distinct periods: 1) the pioneer period permeated with folklore and realism; 2) the interwar period marked by an expansion of themes and artistry; and 3) the post-1945 period, which discarded realism for modernism and other trends. Among writers mentioned were Mykyta Mandryka, who authored the long poem *"Kanada,"* and Ulas Samchuk, who treated Canadian Prairie themes as well as European ones. Slavutych concluded by saying there were only about fifteen Ukrainian Canadian authors "whose artistic accomplishments place their literature on a level equal to that in Ukraine or higher."[32]

Only two years after the publication of the *Canadian Encyclopedia,* the Gorbachev reforms were underway in Soviet Ukraine, the censorship loosened, and new contacts with Western countries like Canada were opened up. At this point, a new *Ukrainska literaturna entsyklopediia* (Ukrainian literary encyclopedia) started publication in Kyiv. The second volume, which appeared in 1990, contained the substantial article "Canadian Literature" by N. F. Ovcharenko and R. P. Zorivchak with the subsection "Literature in the Ukrainian Language." This article basically repeated the content of Slavutych's article in the *Canadian Encyclopedia,* including his threefold periodization of Ukrainian literature in Canada, with a considerable amount of new detail added. For example, N. Dmytriv's *Kanadiiska Rus': Podorozhni vspomyny* (Canadian Rus': A traveller's recollections) (1897) was mentioned as the first story about the Ukrainians in Canada and T. Fedyk's *Pisni pro Kanadu i Avstriiu* (Songs about Canada and Austria) (1908) was singled out as particularly important. The works of Ulas Samchuk and Yar Slavutych, as well as many others, were mentioned and the literary histories of Peter Krawchuk and Mykyta Mandryka cited. Translators such as Florence Livsay, Alexander Hunter, and especially the very prolific Watson Kirkconnell and Constantine Andrushyshen were discussed. Finally, George Luckyj's *Shevchenko and the Critics*, which was a work of literary criticism published in English, and Pavlo Zaitsev's biography of Shevchenko (edited by Luckyj), which also appeared in English, were mentioned. Much of this material, non-Communist in approach, was completely new to readers in Ukraine who had long been isolated by the severe censorship. The article ended with a detailed account of the new contacts between Canadian and Ukrainian authors.[33]

The late 1980s and the 1990s were not only a period of new contacts between Canada and Ukraine, which gained state independence in 1991, but also of impressive growth in the multicultural movement in Canada. During these years, ethnic Canadians exercised increased political, social, and cultural influence, as symbolized by the appointments of the first two Governors General of non-British and non-French background: Edward Schreyer from Manitoba, who was of Galician German ancestry, and Raymond Hnatyshyn from Saskatchewan, who was of Ukrainian ancestry. This period also saw the flourishing of new multicultural institutions such as the Multicultural History Society of Ontario founded by Robert Harney in Toronto; under Harney's successor Paul Magocsi, a specialist in Ukrainian history at the University of Toronto, the society undertook to compile and publish an ambitious *Encyclopedia of Canada's Peoples,* which aimed to demonstrate the ethnic diversity in Canada's life and history. Not only did this encyclopedia contain detailed articles on almost every identifiable Canadian ethnic group, but it also contained a number of thematic articles such as the "Definitions and Dimensions of Ethnicity" (by the sociologist Wsevolod Isajiw), "Immigration Policy" (by historians Roberto Perin and Harold Troper), "Multiculturalism" (again by Troper), and several on other subjects. The article "Ukrainians" by Frances Swyripa was especially impressive, being thirty-one pages long in sixty-two columns.

Swyripa's article closely followed the tight format of the volume by dividing the subject into the following sections: origins, migration, arrival and settlement, economic life, community life, family and kinship, culture, education, religion, politics, intergroup relations, group maintenance and ethnic commitment, and bibliography. After giving an excellent general survey of Ukrainian history, Swyripa outlined the three main waves of Ukrainian migration to Canada and suggested that a fourth post-Soviet wave was presently beginning. She noted that in 1991, there were slightly over a million Canadians of Ukrainian origin: 647,650 of partly and 406,645 of wholly Ukrainian background. She remarked on the continued ethnic dispersion of Ukrainians across the country and the rising importance of Ontario, and noted the continuing process of assimilation and integration of Ukrainians into Canadian society. She continued:

> In the early 1990s, Ukrainians were found throughout the Canadian economic spectrum. Prejudice and discrimination had all but disappeared, as had ignorance of English, lack of business experience, and education, and material poverty. Though the interplay of age, immigration, generation, and gender continued to disadvantage older Ukrainian Canadians, the foreign born, and women, ethnicity had virtually no effect on the occupational and career patterns of younger, Canadian born generations.

She noted that by the 1990s, only some 10 per cent of Canadians of Ukrainian origin participated in Ukrainian organizational life in Canada, and the traditional churches were losing members fast. This was especially remarkable among the children of mixed marriages who now formed the new majority.

Swyripa's outline of Ukrainian organizational life was especially detailed, and she clearly described the divisions between the nationalist right and the Communist left, as well as the fierce divisions among the post-1945 nationalists. She also intimated the prominent Ukrainian role in the struggle for multiculturalism in Canada and the creation of a Civil Liberties Commission to represent Ukrainian Canadians before the Commission of Inquiry on War Crimes headed by Judge Jules Deschenes. This was especially important for the post-1945 DPs who had lived under Nazi occupation. Her final paragraph read:

> By the early 1990s, only a minority of Ukrainian Canadians (albeit a vocal minority) spoke Ukrainian, participated in Ukrainian activities, and related closely with the [European] homeland. Nevertheless, a strong sense of ethnic identity persisted. Non-linguistic and non-political, it drew on the folk culture introduced by the peasant pioneers, selectively reinforced by two subsequent immigrations, often as art, and frequently transformed into something uniquely 'Ukrainian Canadian,' particularly on the Prairies. On

the eve of the twenty-first century, Ukrainian Canadians' future as a distinct collectivity rested on voluntary identification with their heritage by the group members, increasingly distant from their group's roots, and expressing their Ukrainian Canadian identity in different ways.[34]

Thus, Swyripa gave a clear picture of the assimilationist trends apparent in Ukrainian Canadian life on the eve of, and during, the initial stage of the new fourth wave of Ukrainian immigration to Canada. Her article in the *Encyclopedia of Canada's Peoples* stands to the present day as the most detailed such article to appear in any encyclopedia in either the English or Ukrainian language.

Over the next decade, however, three other encyclopedias were published in English that contained articles on the Ukrainian Canadians. These were all provincial encyclopedias: the *Encyclopedia of British Columbia* (2000), the *Encyclopedia of Saskatchewan* (2005), and the *Encyclopedia of Manitoba* (2007). All were large-format, single-volume works. The *Encyclopedia of Saskatchewan* was the largest of the three.

The *Encyclopedia of British Columbia* contained only a brief article on Ukrainians. This article gave a short outline of the history of Ukrainians in the province and mentioned the migration of Prairie Ukrainians to British Columbia, especially during the depression years of the 1930s, which struck the Prairies very hard. The article also mentioned the internment of some Ukrainians in Canada, and in British Columbia in particular, during the First World War. It also stated that by 1996, there were 168,765 Canadians of Ukrainian origin in the province.[35]

The somewhat larger *Encyclopedia of Saskatchewan* contained the general article "Ukrainian Settlements" (by political scientist Bohdan Kordan) and smaller articles on specific Ukrainian organizations in the province: the Ukrainian Catholic Brotherhood, the Ukrainian Catholic Women's League, Ukrainian Catholics, the ULFTA, and the Ukrainian Sisters of Saint Joseph of Saskatoon. Kordan's article indicated the areas and towns of original Ukrainian settlement in Saskatchewan, concentrated along the poplar belt from Yorkton, through Ituna, to Saskatoon and beyond. He gave a brief statistical description of Ukrainian Saskatchewan. In 1996, he wrote, the total number of people in the province of either wholly or partly Ukrainian origin was 125,395, or 12.7 per cent of the total population.[36]

In his article "Ukrainian Catholics," Paul Laverdure explained the large-scale losses of the Ukrainian Catholic Church to the Orthodox, the Roman Catholics, and the Protestants during the early years in Canada,

the stabilization of the church during the middle period, and then renewed losses with the onset of assimilation of the Ukrainians into general Canadian culture and the English language. He noted, however,
that by the early 2000s, the Ukrainian Catholic Church in Saskatchewan
was attracting many non-Ukrainians and slowly becoming not so much a
specifically Ukrainian church as a general Eastern Catholic Church with
a Byzantine rite; and he believed this to be "distinctive of Saskatchewan,"
due to the province's unusual demographic stability and lack of new
immigrants.[37]

The *Encyclopedia of Saskatchewan* also contained brief articles on influential individuals connected to Ukrainian culture. Thus, there were articles on the historian George W. Simpson and the literary scholar
Constantine Andrusyshen by Victor Buyniak, as well as an article on the
Ukrainian-origin premier Roy Romanow. There was, however, no article
on the important grammarian/historian/lawyer Julian Stechishin, one
of the most influential Ukrainian Canadians of the twentieth century.
Also, quite surprisingly, there was no article on the Ukrainian Orthodox Church of Canada, which had its origins in Saskatchewan. In the
brief article "Orthodox Churches," it was, however, noted that 108 of
135 Orthodox congregations in the province were Ukrainian.[38]

The *Encyclopedia of Manitoba* was somewhat briefer in its treatment of
Ukrainians than the *Encyclopedia of Saskatchewan*. Nevertheless, this encyclopedia contained a wide-ranging article on Ukrainians by Orysia Tracz.
This article gave a general history of Ukrainians in Manitoba and stated
that in 2001, there were 157,655 individuals of Ukrainian background
in the province, 102,635 in Winnipeg alone.[39] (The latter figure would
amount to about 15 per cent of the city's total population.) The *Encyclopedia of Manitoba* also contained the significant article "Ukrainian Cultural
and Educational Centre of Winnipeg" or Oseredok, one of the premier
Ukrainian cultural institutions in the country.[40] But there was no article
on either of the Ukrainian churches or on either the historian/senator
Paul Yuzyk or the linguist/royal commissioner J. B. Rudnyckyj, two of the
most important Ukrainians in Canadian history.

As these three provincial encyclopedias were going to press, a new
multivolume *Entsyklopediia istorii Ukrainy* (Encyclopedia of the history of
Ukraine) appeared in Kyiv, now capital of the independent Ukrainian
state. This encyclopedia was geared especially for the use of professional
historians and students of history. Volume 4 (2007) contained a long article on Canada with an especially long subsection, "Ukrainians in Canada."
This article, by O. O. Kovalchuk, noted that of its 2003 population of

32.2 million, 45.0 per cent were what it called "English-speaking," 29.0 per cent "French-speaking," and the rest "of various national minorities." In religion, over 45.0 per cent were Catholic. Kovalchuk's article traced the growth of the Ukrainian population from 1941 to 2004 as follows: 1941: 306,000 or 2.7 per cent of the total population; 1951: 395,000 or 2.8 per cent; 1961: 473,300 or 2.6 per cent; 1971: 580,300 or 2.7 per cent; 1981: 529,600 (seemingly an error by way of underestimation) or 2.2 per cent; 1991: 1,054,000 or 3.7 per cent; 2001: 1,071,060 or 3.6 per cent. By 2001, 90.0 per cent had been born in Canada.

This article also gave interesting data on the 2001 makeup of certain major cities: Edmonton had 125,720 Canadians of Ukrainian origin or 13.6 per cent of the total population; Toronto, 104,490 or 2.2 per cent; Winnipeg, 102,635 or an amazing 15.5 per cent; Vancouver, 76,525 or 3.9 per cent; Calgary, 65,040 or 6.9 per cent; Saskatoon, 34,385 or 15.4 per cent; Hamilton, 24,070 or 3.7 per cent; and Regina, 23,220 or 12.2 per cent. Kovalchuk's article then passed on to politics and education, mentioning prominent Ukrainian politicians, from Andrew Shandro, who was elected to the Alberta Provincial Legislature in 1915, to Ray Hnatyshyn, who was appointed twenty-fourth Governor General in the early 1990s, and outlining the bilingual educational system that existed in Manitoba at the beginning of the twentieth century. Higher education was not ignored and the article listed the work of George W. Simpson in Saskatchewan, who helped start Ukrainian studies at the university there; Constantine Andrushyshen, who founded the first department of Slavic Studies at this same university; Rudnyckyj and Yuzyk at the University of Manitoba; V. Kaye-Kysilewskyj and Constantine Bida at the University of Ottawa; George Luckyj at the University of Toronto; and O. Starchuk at the University of Alberta. Many of these scholars, particularly historians such as George Simpson, Ivan Lysiak-Rudnytsky, Orest Subtelny, and Paul Magocsi, were scheduled to have their own entries in later volumes of this encyclopedia, which, of course, was primarily aimed at historians. (An article by H. P. Harasymov on Kaye-Kysilewskyj had already appeared.) Kovalchuk's article, however, did contain some information about some of these figures and also gave a very detailed outline of the Ukrainian-language press in Canada and a relatively full bibliography.[41] It was followed by a separate article by D. S. Virsky on the Canadian Institute of Ukrainian Studies (CIUS, founded 1976), which outlined this institution's history and functions, especially its relations with scholars and institutions in Ukraine. The Petro Jacyk Centre for Ukrainian Historical Research (founded 1989), which was a part of the CIUS, was noted for its important project translating into English Mykhailo Hrushevsky's ten-volume *Istoriia Ukrainy-Rusy* (History of Ukraine-Rus').[42]

Finally, it should be noted that many of the encyclopedias discussed above are now available on-line as well as in print. These include the *Canadian Encyclopedia*, the *Encyclopedia of Ukraine*, the *Encyclopedia of Canada's Peoples*, and the *Entsyklopediia istorii Ukrainy*. Some of them, such as the *Canadian Encyclopedia*, are continually being updated. This includes the article on Canada in the *Encyclopedia of Ukraine* and the article on Ukrainians in the *Canadian Encyclopedia*.

In addition to this, other on-line encyclopedias such as the *Wikipedia*, which contains over three million articles in its English-language version and several hundreds of thousands of articles in other language versions, all on one Web site and easily transferred to with the click of a mouse, must be mentioned. There is considerable Ukrainian Canadian content in the English-language version, including a list of prominent Ukrainian Canadians, and there is the article *"Kanada"* in the Ukrainian version. But since there is very little editorial control in the *Wikipedia* and anyone can contribute, and many of the articles change from day to day, the material is difficult to summarize or analyze. Nevertheless, the *Wikipedia* is presently the most widely consulted encyclopedia in the world and exercises a powerful influence on public opinion internationally.

By way of general conclusion, several important points may be made. First, the breadth of treatment of Ukrainian Canada in these encyclopedias is truly large. From very modest beginnings in various European encyclopedias that published useful articles on "Galicia" at the time of the pioneer immigration, through early Canadian encyclopedias such as the *Dominion Educator* and the *Encyclopedia of Canada*, which displayed a noticeably anti-Slavic, not to say anti-Ukrainian, bias, through the great encyclopedic publications of the mid-twentieth century, most of whose contributors made a sincere effort to give Ukrainian Canada its due, to later treatments when the Ukrainians in Canada were already largely acculturated to English Canadian society, these volumes traced Ukrainian Canadian history from the 1890s through to the early years of the twenty-first century.

Second, the two major encyclopedias that appeared in the 1950s were important; both the *Encyclopedia Canadiana* and the Ukrainian-language EU were both surprisingly detailed and accurate in their treatments. Third, because of the reality of the Cold War, by the 1960s, two starkly different views were available about Ukrainian Canada: a) a pro-Communist view stressing the importance of what it considered to be "progressive" organizations, as revealed in the URE; and b) a pro-nationalist view stressing non-Communist organizations, available as revealed in the EU. Both views had to be considered to obtain a full picture of Ukrainian life in this country. Fourth, the most detailed and one of the most balanced descriptions of Ukrainian Canada was definitely the essay by Frances Swyripa published in the *Encyclopedia of Canada's Peoples* at a time when the Ukrainian community in Canada was still very important but already in decline because of assimilation. Fifth, the regional encyclopedias published in Saskatchewan and Manitoba were fairly weak in their treatment of Ukrainian Canada. This is especially remarkable insofar as the Ukrainians on the Prairies formed the third-largest ethnic group in that region throughout most of the twentieth century. This brief treatment is, perhaps, indicative of the decline of ethnic consciousness and the progress of assimilation in the region. And, finally, and on a somewhat different level, several of the encyclopedias considered here erroneously maintained that the very numerous Ukrainian Canadians actually formed the third-largest ethnic group, not just in the Prairie region, but in the whole country at the time that they were published. This error was understandable in view of the fact that the group actually standing in third place after the British groups and the French was the Germans, who generally had a lower profile than the Ukrainian group and could also be divided into various, very distinct, subgroups. Moreover, as mentioned above, the Ukrainians actually did form the third-largest group on the Prairies (after the British groups and the Germans) throughout most of the twentieth century.

In sum, it may be noted that examination of the encyclopedias, despite their very real limitations and repeated failure to attain the ideal of "objectivity," gives a good overview of the general history of Ukrainian Canada from the 1890s, when significant Ruthenian settlement first began, to the early twenty-first century, when Canadians of Ukrainian origin were already very numerous and the Ukrainian community in Canada was institutionally well developed. These encyclopedias also clearly reflect the changing attitudes of English Canadian society towards them, from disdain through tolerance to full acceptance. This change paralleled the continuing process of the acculturation, integration, and assimilation of the group into general Canadian society. The recent appearance of a new fourth wave of Ukrainian immigration to this country reveals that this process is still ongoing and will probably continue for many years to come.

Concluding Thoughts

15 Ukrainian Canadians and Ukrainian Americans: Some Reflections and Comparisons

Nor knowest thou what argument Thy life to Thy neighbor's creed has lent. All are needed by each one; Nothing is fair or good alone.

Ralph Waldo Emerson

Some years ago, I attended an unusual conference at the University of Toronto. It was unusual because it dealt in a comparative way with the Ukrainian experience in Canada and the United States. Although, in casual conversations, members of the two Ukrainian communities often make comparisons between the United States and Canada, this is seldom done in the context of a formal academic conference. "Cross-Stitching Cultural Borders," as this particular conference was titled, was held 29–31 October 1998 and drew numerous visitors from Edmonton, Winnipeg, Ottawa, and various places in the United States, mainly in New England and the Midwest. The most memorable paper that stuck closely to the scheme of the organizers was probably that of Toronto historian Orest Subtelny, who compared the PLAST scouting organizations in Canada and the United States; but my favourite paper was undoubtedly that of Ottawa archivist Myron Momryk, who unearthed a treasure of Canadian government materials – including a great deal of RCMP snooping – on the Ukrainian communities in both countries. (This paper was later published in a special issue of the Toronto-based *Journal of Ukrainian Studies*, which was devoted to "Ukrainians in Canada between the Great War and the Cold War.")[1] The conference was memorable because of its warm and engaging tone and was the occasion to see many old friends and colleagues from all over North America. Afterwards, I wrote a brief account of its course and, on 27 January to 9 February 1999, published it in

Ukrainski visti (The Ukrainian news), a bilingual Ukrainian-English news-paper in Edmonton. I should like to recall some of these observations here and expand on them a little.

Certainly, the most important conclusion I drew from this conference, and one I still hold to today, is that, while there are many parallels be-tween the Ukrainian experiences in Canada and the United States, there are also many differences. Both parallels and differences, in my opinion, can be traced back to the very origins of the Ukrainian emigration to North America and deserve serious consideration.

To begin with, mass emigration from what the first immigrants called the "Old Country" to the "New" one began at about the same time: the first wave of large-scale Ukrainian labour immigration began in the 1880s in the United States and only slightly later, in the 1890s, in Canada. Moreover, they involved pretty much the same social classes (villagers and country folk generally). This gave a consistency and a certain social psychology to the new communities the immigrants founded in Canada and the United States. But the regions of origin and the regions of settle-ment differed considerably and this had a profound effect on the devel-opment of the young Ukrainian communities in North America.

Immigrants to Canada came mostly, though not exclusively, from Galicia and Bukovina in the Austrian half of the Habsburg Monarchy, where the Ukrainian national movement and Ukrainian national con-sciousness were about to make rapid progress; immigrants to the United States, however, came from Transcarpathia as well as Galicia and Buko-vina, and in Transcarpathia, which was in the Hungarian half of the Habsburg Monarchy, there were many obstacles to the rapid develop-ment of Ukrainian national consciousness. As a result of these divergent geographical factors, within a generation, a "Ukrainian" community emerged in Canada from the original "Ruthenian" settlements, while the Ruthenian community in the United States split into a Carpatho-Ruthenian community, which was not concerned about Ukrainian in-dependence or the ties of the Transcarpathian people to Ukraine, and a Galician-oriented "Ukrainian" community, which firmly accepted the idea of an independent Ukrainian nationality and looked forward to eventual Ukrainian independence. In large part, this organic unity in the Ukrainian Canadian community (the convergence of the Bukovinians and the Galicians) and this basic split in the American community (the divergence between Carpatho-Ruthenians and Ukrainians) continue to the present day.

Differing destinations had almost as profound an effect as differing regions of origin. Most Ukrainians coming to Canada settled in the Prairie West and took up farming, while most Ukrainians going to the United States settled in industrial or mining towns in the East or the Midwest and became industrial workers. Ukrainians in western Canada were pioneers and original settlers who, for the most part, homesteaded the open prairie, while Ukrainians in the United States seemingly were just one more wave of immigration to an already heavily settled industrial area from an increasingly distant and unknown part of Europe. This contextual difference seems to have had a profound effect on the feelings of self-worth, ethnic pride, and civil status of Ukrainians in the two countries. While both were discriminated against in the early days, the Prairie Ukrainians gradually became a force to be reckoned with in Canadian culture and politics, while, in the United States, the mining and industrial experience left little room for a parallel development.

The bald fact that Ukrainians made up a far greater proportion of the population in Canada than they did in the United States was also of enormous cultural and political import. As a result of settlement in a well-defined and compact region (and of settlement in blocks within this region), Ukrainians in Canada were electing their representatives to school boards and municipal governments and then provincial and federal parliaments from relatively early days, and they won important premierships in two prairie provinces (Saskatchewan and Manitoba), and a third briefly in British Columbia as well, and an appointment as head of state (Governor General Ray Hnatyshyn) by the 1990s. (A fourth provincial premiership followed a decade later in Alberta.) Moreover, outstanding politicians such as former Saskatchewan premier Roy Romanow continued to play an important role in Canadian politics long after their term in office had ended. No parallel developments ever occurred in the United States, where Ukrainians were always a small minority, where no governors or senators of Ukrainian origin were ever elected, and where the mere appointment of a Ukrainian activist (Myron Kuropas) as an ethnic advisor to President Gerald Ford was seen as, and probably really was, a great victory.

Indeed, in certain very fundamental ways, a more apt comparison might be between the Ukrainian Canadians and Polish Americans rather than Ukrainian Americans. This is because the Ukrainian Canadians, from their arrival in this country, formed by far the largest and most influential Slavic or Slavonic group in the country. In the United States, this honour is held not by the Ukrainian Americans, who constitute a relatively small group in American terms, but by the Polish Americans, who number almost 9.5 million. In other words, Polish Americans, or, at least, Americans of wholly or partly Polish ancestry, constitute about 3 per cent of the total American population; this is about the same as the Ukrainian Canadians, who, at 1.2 million, form about 3 per cent of the total Canadian population. Similarly, Polish Americans outnumber all other Slavonic groups in the United States combined. For a long time, this was also true of the Ukrainian Canadians, who outnumbered all other Slavonic groups in Canada combined. Polish Americans have a "heartland" in the American Midwest with a capital in Chicago (where many Ukrainian Americans are also settled); until recently, Ukrainian Canadians had a heartland on the Canadian Prairies with a capital in Winnipeg. The great bulk of Polish Americans trace their origins to the Great Economic Immigration from Europe that occurred between 1880 and 1914, and they tended to vote Democrat; thereafter, the greatest change in Polish American organizational life came after 1945 with the arrival of a new immigration of Displaced Persons (DPs) of more conservative anti-Communist opinion. For at least two generations, these post-1945ers tended to vote Republican. The older immigration and their children, grandchildren, and great-grandchildren, still predominately democrats, are now very assimilated into the dominant American culture; the more recent arrivals, somewhat less so.

All these things are also true of the Ukrainian Canadians, the bulk of whom trace their origins to this same Great Economic Immigration and a significant part of whom held left-of-centre views (sometimes even being pro-Communist, especially before 1956) or supported various forms of Prairie populism, in Manitoba and Saskatchewan, of a plainly social democratic variety. For their organizational life, as well, the arrival of the DPs constituted an important break, since these DPs also tended to be very much more conservative and anti-Communist in their political views. Moreover, the descendants of this older immigration are also much assimilated to English Canadian culture; later arrivals, somewhat less so. But there, the similarities seem to end.

Ukrainian Canadians have been much more successful in Canadian political life than Polish Americans in American political life. As mentioned above, they have elected premiers of all three prairie provinces, federal cabinet ministers, and even a head of state, who was in office during the 1991 centennial of Ukrainian settlement in Canada and the 1991

Ukrainian Declaration of Independence in Europe. They have elected mayors of most major Prairie Canadian cities where they live, including Winnipeg, where Steven Juba governed for many long years. Very few Polish Americans have ever been elected governors of American states, none has ever been elected governor of either Illinois or Michigan, or even mayor of Chicago (where so many Polish Americans continue to live), and only a very small handful has been appointed to the federal cabinet in Washington. The first to be appointed to Washington was John A. Gronouski, who became President John Kennedy's postmaster general (responsible for the introduction of the famous "zip code"), and the most influential was probably either Zbigniew Brzezinski, who was President Jimmy Carter's national security advisor in the late 1970s, or former Maine governor and senator Edmund Muskie, who served as Carter's secretary of state. Of course, these last were very influential positions indeed and coincided with the election of the Polish Pope John Paul II and the appointment of Michel Poniatowski as foreign minister of France during this same period. Moreover, certain Polish American politicians, such as congressmen Dan Rostenkowski and Roman Pucinski, wielded considerable influence in their time. Nevertheless, there is little doubt that on certain levels at least, the Ukrainian Canadians constitute a much more important and influential political force in Canada than do Polish Americans in the United States.

Returning to the comparison between the Ukrainian Canadians and the Ukrainian Americans, it may be observed that the differing patterns of settlement in Canada and the United States also seem to have promoted differences in the assimilation of values from the host societies. Thus, the Ukrainians in western Canada assimilated a certain amount of Prairie regionalism from their surrounding society (feelings of distance from the East, of frontier independence, and of resentment against the central government), while Ukrainians in the United States seem to have been much more influenced by the American patriotism and American nationalism within which they had to carry on their daily lives. (This became especially strong and coincided with anti-Soviet sentiments most acutely expressed during the tense years of the Long Cold War.)

A concomitant effect of this Canadian regionalism versus American patriotism may well be the attention paid to ethnic affairs and ethnic history in Canada (witness the extensive attention given the Prairies in the Canadian-based *Encyclopedia of Ukraine*) and the general indifference to such questions in the United States. Of course, Ukrainian Americans partly made up for this lack by paying more attention to international affairs and the Soviet repression of human and national rights in Ukraine than did the Ukrainian Canadians. This, in part, I think, explains the success of more internationally oriented newspapers such as *Svoboda* (Liberty) and the *Ukrainian Weekly* during the period up to 1991. Canada never had anything quite like the New York/New Jersey-based *Ukrainian Weekly*, which could always rely on a solid phalanx of highly motivated, so to speak, "cold-warrior" contributors, though I hasten to add that at least a few of these contributors were based in Canada.

Of course, the collapse of the USSR and the emergence of an independent Ukraine changed this situation considerably. A new fourth wave of immigrants began coming to North America. But, whereas in the United States, these new immigrants soon found a voice on the pages of *Svoboda*, and reoriented the newspaper to a certain extent, in Canada, they founded new papers such as the Toronto-based *Meest* (The bridge) and *Slovo* (The word), which catered to their special needs and interests, and they left older newspapers such as Toronto's *Novyi shliakh* (New pathway), Winnipeg's *Ukrainskyi holos* (Ukrainian voice), and Edmonton's *Ukrainski visti* (Ukrainian news) to become even more Canadian-oriented. As a result, these latter three newspapers turned ever more frequently to articles in the English language to be read by third, fourth, and even fifth generations of Ukrainian Canadians whose knowledge of the Ukrainian language was minimal or even non-existent. Of course, these general differences between Americans and Canadians were never quite absolute and the American papers never completely neglected local affairs, while the Canadian papers never completely ignored international politics and human rights issues.

Ukrainian academic life in Canada and the United States also invites comparisons. During the DP period and after, Canada had the Ukrainian Free Academy of Sciences (UVAN in Canada) in Winnipeg, while the United States had the Ukrainian Academy of Arts and Sciences (UVAN in the US) in New York. Both these organizations could be described as émigré institutions founded by post-World War Two refugees, and their publication programs, especially during the 1950s and 1960s, reflected this fact. But, with the passage of time, UVAN in Canada turned its attention more and more to the culture of the older pioneer immigration, its history, language, literature, and folklore, while UVAN in the United States, which largely had been founded by émigrés from eastern Ukraine, remained concentrated on Ukrainian culture in eastern Europe, not the United States.

A similar situation might have occurred (but did not) with regard to the Shevchenko Scientific Society, also founded by post-Second World War refugees, with branches in New York City, Ottawa, Montreal, and Toronto. The New York branch undertook a very extensive publication program, concentrating on the publication of almanacs and materials dealing with western Ukraine under the Poles, which was the background of most of its members; meanwhile, the Ottawa and Toronto branches never had quite the same publishing program as the American branch, although they did not engage in the celebration of pioneer Ukrainian culture in the same way as did the Winnipeg UVAN. Perhaps this was due to the fact that Toronto, and eastern Canada generally, was the main centre of Ukrainian DP culture in Canada, whereas Winnipeg was the metropolitan centre of the pioneer immigration right through to the 1970s. Moreover, both the New York and the Toronto Shevchenko Scientific Society branches cooperated with each other in major ventures such as the multivolume encyclopedia of Ukraine, titled in Ukrainian *Entsyklopediia ukrainoznavstva*. The Paris headquarters of the society was the focal point of this major project from the 1940s through to the 1980s.

However, the difference between American and Canadian academic institutions was revealed once again in the 1970s and 1980s with the emergence of new scholarly centres of Ukrainian studies attached to major universities: in Canada, the Canadian Institute of Ukrainian Studies at the University of Alberta, and, in the United States, the Harvard Ukrainian Research Institute in the Boston area. From their very foundations in the 1970s, these institutions differed in their atmospheres and directions. For many years, the former concentrated on modern Ukrainian history and literature while the latter primarily addressed the medieval and Cossack periods. To some outside critics, the former seemed more practical and courageous; the latter, more esoteric and cautious. Moreover, once again, the Canadian institution produced a whole string of publications dealing with Ukrainian Canadian topics and issues, including the idea of multiculturalism that was pioneered in Canada, while the latter virtually ignored the Ukrainian American experience. During the 1990s, however, personnel changes in both institutes changed their profiles somewhat and the situation became more balanced. During the early years of the twenty-first century, new contacts with Ukraine and the influx of scholars from that country affected both institutions, and the older distinctions became even more blurred. Nevertheless, both Alberta and Harvard have found their respective niches in the North American academic community and each retains a spirit of its own.

On a more general level, of course, there lies the important question of how Ukrainians have fit into, or contributed to, the realities of diversity and assimilation in Canadian and American life. Traditionally, the United States has been known for its "melting-pot" approach to the assimilation of immigrants from various places all over the world. Various American and foreign observers remarked on this phenomenon as early as the 1790s and throughout the nineteenth century. Thus, in 1845, when the major non-English and non-Protestant wave of new immigrants to the United States still consisted of the Irish and the Germans, the American philosopher and essayist Ralph Waldo Emerson, who was a strong advocate of an independent American literature and culture, penned the following words on a mixing of peoples, which not only foretold new immigration from elsewhere, including eastern Europe, but also predicted a new racial harmony that as yet did not exist in the antebellum republic. Although not mentioning Ukrainians by name (this was impossible at that time, since they had not yet adopted their modern name), the words contain an allusion to what might be interpreted as the Cossacks of the Ukrainian and Kuban steppe regions. Such an allusion would later warm the heart of many a Ukrainian American:

> As in the old burning of the Temple at Corinth, by the melting and intermixture of silver and gold and other metals, a new compound more precious than any, called Corinthian brass, was formed; so in this continent – asylum of all nations – the energy of Irish, Swedes, Poles, and Cossacks, and all the European tribes – of the Africans, and of the Polynesians, will construct a new race, a new religion, a new state, a new literature, which will be as vigorous as the new Europe which came out of the smelting-pot of the Dark Ages, or that which earlier emerged from Pelasgic and Etruscan barbarism.[2]

This prediction, mathematically encapsulated by the algebraic formula $A+B+C = D$, was to be repeated by others later in American history.

Meanwhile, in Canada, there was as yet no talk of any "melting pot" or mixture of this sort, but only the supremacy of British institutions and the British way of life. This was also the time that the amalgamation of Upper and Lower Canada into one Crown colony took place. This was done to promote the assimilation of the French, who were firmly resisting the English language, the Protestant religion, and British influences in general. The colony that resulted was the most populous and important part of what was then unequivocally known as "British North America."

By slightly more than a half-century later, however, the situation had changed somewhat. By then, the Austrian Crown Land of Galicia was providing settlers for the newly opened Canadian prairies, which had been acquired only recently by the once-again-reorganized British colonies, a new federation within British North America, the young Dominion of Canada, which, according to the terms of its confederation, had divided the formerly united Upper and Lower Canada into two separate provinces, English-speaking Ontario and French-speaking Quebec. Meanwhile, in the United States, immigrants from all over eastern and southern Europe, including Ukrainians from Austrian Galicia and elsewhere, who were generally known in the sources as "Ruthenians," were flooding into the United States. It was at this crucial time that in New York, Israel Zangwell's play *The Melting Pot* was first staged. The play glorified the new American mixing of nationalities and gave American ideas about diversity and assimilation a new descriptive catchphrase, albeit one that had already been anticipated a half-century previously by Ralph Waldo Emerson. It was also at this time that in Canada, the interior minister Clifford Sifton welcomed what he believed to be the "sturdy" peasants from eastern Europe, and from Galicia in particular, who would conquer the severe climate and master the difficult conditions of Canadian Prairie life.

However, some very clear differences between the two countries remained. While the United States continued to build its newly independent culture, Canada remained part of the British Empire and still was generally known as British North America. So, while in the United States, immigration from continental Europe was predominant, in Canada, immigrants from the British Isles still formed the majority.

In other ways, though, there were parallel developments in the two countries. For example, in both countries, the outbreak of war in 1914 put an abrupt end to this migration from Europe. And, when the war ended, a deep reaction against the new immigrants set in. In the United States, new laws restricting immigration from southern and eastern Europe were enacted, and almost the same thing happened in Canada. However, the distinction between the United States and Canada, though now somewhat attenuated, remained, and, in 1929, was put in the following way by George Exton Lloyd, the Anglican bishop of Saskatchewan, a strong promoter of British immigration to Canada, who simultaneously objected to the immigration of what he called "continentals."

Among the many fallacies one meets in discussions on nation building by immigration none is more misleading than the 'melting pot.' The exponents of this theory would open the doors of Canada as wide as possible. They say, 'let all these continentals come: Canada will soon make good

Canadians of them.' I notice that persons holding this view always seem to have in the back of their minds a distinction between Canadian and British. A distinction can, of course, properly be made between a Canadian and a Scotchman, an Irishman, a Welshman, or an Englishman. But there can be no distinction between 'Canadian' and 'British' unless and until the Prime Minister of the dominion repudiates his adherence to the constitution of Empire agreed to at the last Imperial Conference. That he is not prepared to do. Therefore, there cannot be a good Canadian who is not at the same time a loyal son of the Empire and, therefore, a 'Britisher.'[3]

Thus, for the Prairie prelate George Exton Lloyd, the algebraic formula to which he acceded (though with only the greatest reluctance and some disbelief) was: A+B+C = A, a formula that has since been labelled not a "melting pot," of course, but, rather, "Anglo-conformity."

However, Lloyd, it should be noted, was bishop of a province with one of the highest percentages of eastern Europeans, predominantly Ukrainians, in the country; the population included also Poles, Doukhobors, and many others. In Saskatchewan, ethnics such as Ukrainians and Germans, even though most of them had been born and raised in this country, were then usually still called "foreigners" by many of Lloyd's "Britishers," who were sometimes loath to admit that these "continentals" pretty much equalled them in numbers. One of the few "Britishers" who did, however, openly admit this fact was the young polyglot Watson Kirkconnell, a proud Scottish Canadian who nonetheless welcomed the mingling of peoples in western Canada and criticized what he called the bishop's "un-Christian fulminations."[4]

Thus, by this time, diversity as well as assimilation was a fact of life in both the United States and Canada. By the 1930s, however, while the melting pot continued to dominate American life, a new mosaic concept began to arise in Canada. Promoted by publicists such as J. M. Gibbon, it took account not only of the French–English dualism of the country, but also of diversity within the British group and the diversity of settlement on the Prairies. Gibbon faced much opposition, of course, but the war of 1939 to 1945, with its "Canadians All" campaign, reduced anti-foreign sentiment considerably, at least towards those groups that could not be counted among so-called enemy nations. Of course, the Americans, too, had their "Americans All" campaign, which also seems to have generally reduced anti-ethnic prejudices. The trends established during the war continued for many years – in fact, for some twenty-five years – at the end of which the new ideology of multiculturalism emerged in Canada.

As it arose, the ideology encompassed at least three separate elements: 1) a recognition of the reality of ethnic or cultural pluralism; 2) the placement of a positive value on this pluralism, especially in terms of mutual respect and equality; and 3) the adoption of a set of government policies that were supposed to support this pluralism. Thus, the establishment of a clear algebraic formula for a multicultural country is somewhat more complex than for a primarily "melting-pot" country, or an "Anglo-conformist" country. Perhaps there is room for all three of these principles in a truly multicultural land. Nevertheless, defenders of multiculturalism are often also defenders of the concept of "hyphenated Canadians" or even "hyphenated Americans." With this in mind, the following algebraic formula may be proposed: $A+B+C = AD+BD+CD$, where D stands for citizenship in the Canadian state, ever-changing with the steady arrival of different newcomers, and changing these newcomers in turn. In other words, as Canadian Prime Minister Joe Clark put it in his 1980 address to the Empire Club of Canada in Toronto: "Canada is where diversity comes together."[5]

The general question of how Ukrainians fit into the spirit of multiculturalism, which originated in Canada but quickly spread to the United States, is important. From the very beginning, Ukrainians played a prominent role in the elaboration of multiculturalism in Canada; Canadian Senator Paul Yuzyk, who had earlier done a PhD in ethnic history at the University of Minnesota, introduced the word "multiculturalism" itself to the Canadian Parliament; the president of the Winnipeg UVAN, J. B. Rudnyckyj, saw that some of its most important aspects were introduced into public discourse to accompany official French/English "bilingualism"; and the first director of the Canadian Institute of Ukrainian Studies, Manoly Lupul, in particular, was influential in its implementation on the Prairies. The preservation of the ancestral cultures and languages was of growing importance in Canada, which, on an official level, at least, beginning with French Canada, now rejected the idea of the melting pot, and this complemented ideas of mutual respect, cultural and ethnic tolerance, and the proper "integration," not to say "assimilation," of minorities, which were at the base of the new multicultural policies. The Ukrainians, in particular, who led the movement, and also the Poles and the usually low-profile Germans, were very much concerned about the preservation of their ancestral languages and cultures, which, in some ways, at least, were already on the wane because of the passing away of the pioneers. The latter was less true of the French.

In the United States, however, "white ethnics" such as the Ukrainians were always neighbours to larger and more numerous ethnocultural or racial groups such as the African Americans and Hispanics, who also strove for greater integration, if not always outright assimilation, into American society and public life; thus, American multiculturalism had a somewhat different political profile from that of the Canadian phenomenon. Right from the beginning, the fight against racism and associated feelings, as well as cultural preservation, was very important in the United States. Moreover, in the United States, the term also came to denote a particular constellation of special-interest groups including women, the physically and mentally challenged, homosexuals, and the economically disadvantaged, as well as ethnic and racial groups. This never quite happened the same way in Canada, where multiculturalism continued to be most closely focused on ethnicity.[6]

Also right from the beginning, however, multiculturalism had its enemies in both countries. In Canada, for instance, voices have always been raised that condemned it as a threat to English or French interests and a mere "pandering" to the "ethnic vote." Later on, by the 1990s and early 2000s, official multiculturalism came under pressure from the extreme right in Canada, and voices as varied as those of writer Neil Bissoondath, journalist Richard Gwyn, and rightist politician Preston Manning, the leader of the Alberta-based Reform Party, were raised against it. Parallel multicultural ideas were severely criticized in the United States, where historian Arthur M. Schlesinger Jr. wrote an influential book criticizing them. But, through several years of great difficulty, the multicultural idea weathered the storm. Sophisticated political thinkers such as Will Kymlicka defended Canada's multicultural record and pointed out that the concept had neither inhibited the integration of newcomers nor reduced use of the English language by them. Kymlycka argued that the so-called walls that writers like Gwyn accused it of erecting between various cultural and ethnic groups simply did not exist.[7]

On a different level, the new non-discriminatory immigration rules that had been first promulgated in the 1960s were now having a transformational effect on society in both the United States and Canada. The large influx of immigrants from Third World countries to North America, which began in the 1970s and reached truly great proportions by the year 2000, had a considerable effect on the ethnic and cultural makeup of both Canada and the United States and considerably changed the tincture of multiculturalism. For one thing, new groups took up the cause. For another, other groups such as the Ukrainian Canadians no longer held the prominent place in the Canadian ethnic mosaic that they once held and they became more like Ukrainian Americans, just another ethnic minority group, and an "older," largely assimilated, white one at that.

Then, something entirely unexpected happened: the terrorist attacks on New York and Washington. After 11 September 2001, American suspicion of foreigners, especially foreigners from the Middle East, grew immensely, and even in Canada, in the wake of alleged terrorist conspiracies by members of certain immigrant groups, multiculturalism came under question once again. Just how Ukrainian Canadians fit into this new constellation of factors and events remains to be seen, but their positive role in the pioneering of Canadian multiculturalism is already a subject for the historians. Similarly, just how Ukrainian Americans fit into the new security situation in the United States is as yet unclear, but there is no doubt that the days of the Long Cold War, when they had a special niche of their own, are long gone.

Many further themes deserve to be investigated: the weakening though continuing British monarchist connection in Canada, which has traditionally, at least in part, sheltered the idea of group identities and rights, versus the continuing republican ethic in the United States, which has always espoused liberalism, individualism, and the skirting of the concept of group rights; the influence of French-speaking Quebec on the Canadian ethnic climate versus the role of visible minorities such as the African Americans and Hispanics in the United States; the existence during the Cold War of a viable Communist Party and Ukrainian pro-Communists in Canada and their relative weakness in the United States; during the 1980s and 1990s, the varying course of the war-criminals issue in Canada and in the United States; comparisons of Ukrainian life in cultural metropolises such as Toronto and New York, and of the cultural climate in the Canadian West and the American Midwest; ethnic dispersion to Ontario and British Columbia in Canada, and to the south and California and the Southwest in the United States; and the implications of "snow birding" or the wintering of numerous elderly Prairie Canadians of Ukrainian background in Arizona, Nevada, and southern California; and, through it all, parallel political allegiances in largely left-leaning Ukrainian Winnipeg in the Canadian West and places such as Scranton and the mining country in Pennsylvania (both centres of the older labour immigration), and, as well, similarly parallel political allegiances in largely right-leaning Ukrainian Toronto and Ukrainian New York City (both very important to the post-1945 DP immigration); and finally, the relative positions of the post-Soviet fourth wave of immigrants to Canada and the United States. A comparative study of the experience of the

Ukrainian Canadians and Ukrainian Americans over the course of the last century or so has yet to be done, but, as indicated by these brief ruminations, may lead in many unexpected directions and may prove to be a fruitful topic attracting the attention of future scholars.

The Ukraina
358 Redwood Ave.
Winnipeg, Man.
Canada

Logo of the Ukrainian Bookstore, Winnipeg, 1918.

Appendix

Publishing Histories

1) "The Great Migration: East Central Europe to the Americas in the Literatures of the Slavs: Some Examples," *Ethnic Forum* 12, no. 2 (1992): 31–47.
2) "Recent Soviet Scholarship on the Economic Emigration from Imperial Russia to Western Europe and North America, 1880–1914," *Ethnic Forum* 11, no. 1 (1991): 47–58.
3) "Ivan Franko and Mass Ukrainian Emigration to Canada," *Canadian Slavonic Papers* 26, no. 4 (1984): 307–17. Summary of revised and expanded version in the newspaper *Novyi shliakh/New Pathway* (Toronto), 77, 22, 1 June 2006, 6.
4) "Recent Scholarship on Polyethnic Emigration from the Republic of Poland to Canada between the Wars," *Canadian Ethnic Studies* 23, no. 1 (1991): 58–70.
5) "Dmytro Doroshenko and Canada," *Journal of Ukrainian Studies* 30, no. 2 (2005): 1–25.
6) "General Histories of Ukraine Published in English during the Second World War," *Ab Imperio* 2 (2003): 455–76. Ukrainian version (with translator Nadia Zavorotna): "Zahalni istorii Ukrainy drukovani anhliiskoiu movoiu pid chas Druhoi Svitovoi Viiny," *Ukrainskyi istoryk* 44-5, nos. 3–4, 1–2 (2007–2008): 168–88.
7) "George Simpson, the Ukrainian Canadians, and the 'Pre-history' of Slavic Studies in Canada," *Saskatchewan History* 41, no. 2 (1988): 53–66.
8) "The Post-Secondary Teaching of the 'History of Ukraine' in Canada: An Historical Profile," *Ukrainskyi istoryk* 28, no. 1–2 (1991): 71–81. Ukrainian version: "Vykladannia istorii Ukrainy v universytetakh Kanady: Istorychna retrospektyva," *Novi dni* 44, no. 523 (1993): 12–14; no. 524: 8–9. Also abridged as "Vykladannia istorii Ukrainy v universytetakh Kanady," *Kyivska starovyna* 1 (1995): 90–97.

9) "Ukrainian Scholarship in the West During the 'Long Cold War,'" in *Rossiis-kaia istoricheskaia mozaika. Sbornik nauchnykh statei/Russian Historical Mosaic/ Collection of Scientific Articles*, ed. A. L. Litvin (Kazan: Izdatelstvo kazanskogo matematicheskogo obshchestva, 2003), 272–85.

10) "Lubomyr Wynar and the Ukrainian Historical Association in the United States and Canada," *Journal of Ukrainian Studies* 31, nos. 1–2 (2006): 205–16.

11) (Chapter 12) "J. B. Rudnyckyj on Ukrainian Culture, Books, and Libraries in the West During the 'Long Cold War,'" *Canadian Slavonic Papers* 51, no. 1 (2009): 53–76.

12) (Chapter 14) "Ukrainian Canada in the Encyclopedias: An Historical Over-view," photocopied in a limited private edition in *Winnipeg Papers on Ukrai-nian Arts Culture in Canada*, comp. Robert B. Klymasz (Winnipeg: Centre for Ukrainian Canadian Studies, University of Manitoba, 2010), 112–34.

13) (Chapter 15) "Ukrainian Canadians and Ukrainian Americans: Some Re-flections and Comparisons." This chapter is partly based on a brief news-paper article of the same name published in *Ukrainski visti/Ukrainian News* (Edmonton), 72, no. 17, September 8–21, 1999, p. 14.

Notes

Introduction

1 I refer here to the work of certain European historians cited by Paul Robert Magocsi in his attempt to apply such stages to the Ukrainian case. See his article "The Ukrainian National Revival: A New Analytical Framework," *Canadian Review of Studies in Nationalism* 16, nos. 1–2 (1989): 45–62. Also see Ivan L. Rudnytsky, "The Intellectual Origins of Modern Ukraine," in his *Essays in Modern Ukrainian History* (Edmonton: Canadian Institute of Ukrainian Studies, 1987), 123–41.

2 "Galician Immigration," in *Encyclopedia of Canada* (Toronto: University Associates of Canada, 1936), 3:3–4, and "Ukrainians," ibid. (Toronto, 1937), 4:185. On the church, see Paul Yuzyk, *The Ukrainians in Manitoba: A Social History* (Toronto: University of Toronto Press, 1953), 36.

3 On the question of the "Third Generation Immigrant," which I prefer to rephrase as the "Third Generation Ethnic," see, in particular, Peter Kivisto and Dag Blanck, eds., *American Immigrants and their Generations: Studies and Commentaries on the Hansen Thesis After Fifty Years* (Urbana and Chicago: University of Illinois Press, 1990). On the importance of selectivity in identity maintenance, see the two sociological studies by Wsevolod W. Isajiw, "The Process of Maintenance of Ethnic Identity: The Canadian Context," in *Sounds Canadian: Languages and Cultures in Multi-ethnic Society*, ed. Paul M. Migus (Toronto: Peter Martin, 1975), 129–38, and *idem, Understanding Diversity: Ethnicity and Race in the Canadian Context* (Toronto: Thompson Educational, 1999), 32–3, 196–7. For an establishment historian's vociferous attack on some abuses of Canadian ethnic history, which throws the baby out with the bathwater, see in particular, J. L. Granatstein, *Who Killed Canadian History?* (Toronto: Harper, 1998), esp. ch. 4: "Multicultural

Mania," 79–108. The very idea that ethnic Canadians can even have a
history is criticized in Roberto Perin, "Writing About Ethnicity," in *Writing
About Canada: A Handbook for Modern Canadian History*, ed. John Schultz
(Scarborough, ON: Prentice-Hall, 1990), 207–31. Perin, turning sociologist
Raymond Breton on his head, argues that since ethnic groups in North
America form "incomplete cultures" and are ever-changing and "evanes-
cent," the term "ethnic history" should be dropped altogether and only the
term "immigrant history" should be used. Granatstein and Norman Hillmer
seem to have done just this in their otherwise interesting *Land Newly Found:
Eyewitness Accounts of the Canadian Immigrant Experience* (Toronto: Thomas
Allen, 2006). Indeed, even Gerald Friesen in his influential book *The
Canadian Prairies: A History* (Toronto: University of Toronto Press, 1987),
242–73, largely dismissed the general ethnic histories of the region,
restricted his attention to "immigrants" on the Prairies from 1870 to 1940,
and pretty much followed the same approach as Perin. He gives some good
brief vignettes of various groups in their relation to assimilation, but
thereafter ignores them. Indeed, his account of the very numerous
Germans is brief to the point of embarrassment. However, Margaret Conrad
and Alvin Finkel have made an attempt to integrate some ethnic content,
including some mentions of Ukrainians, into their survey bearing the
admirable title *History of the Canadian Peoples*, vol. 2, *1867 to the Present*, 5th
ed. (Toronto: Pearson Longman, 2009). This distinction between immigrant and ethnic, over which mainstream Canadian historians such as
Granatstein, Perin, and Friesen run roughshod, is, moreover, very clear
– indeed, in my opinion, indisputable – when it comes to folklore. See, for
example, Robert B. Klymasz, "From Immigrant to Ethnic Folklore: A
Canadian View of Process and Transition," *Journal of the Folklore Institute* 10
(1973): 131–9; repr. in *Canadian Music: Issues of Hegemony and Identity*, ed.
Beverly Diamont and Robert Witmer (Toronto: Canadian Scholars' Press,
1994), 351–8.

4 See the discussion of Leacock's remark in Franz A. J. Szabo, "The Austrian
Immigrant and the Canadian Multicultural Spectrum," in *Austrian
Immigration to Canada: Select Essays*, ed. Franz A. J. Szabo (Ottawa: Carleton
University Press, 1996), 8. As to Cossacks, it should be noted that they were
always a more characteristic motif of eastern Ukraine under the Russians
than western Ukraine under the Austrians, and it was western Ukraine that
provided most of the early Ukrainian settlers to the Prairies. Thus, while
there are no monumental statues of Ukrainian Cossacks gracing the skylines
of prairie towns (such statues are a prominent example of prairie kitsch),
there is a giant painted Ukrainian Easter egg (called a *pysanka* in

Ukrainian) outside Vegreville, Alberta, which attracts the bemused curiosity of many passing tourists. Of course, it must also be noted that there were, until recently, large bronze statues of the Ukrainian national poet Taras Shevchenko in both Winnipeg, Manitoba (erected by the nationalists in 1961), and Palermo, Ontario (erected by the Communists in 1951), and Shevchenko was an exemplary bard of Cossack glory.

5 Only some of the earlier points mentioned in this paragraph have been fully treated in the scholarly literature. See, for example, Jaroslav Petryshyn, *Peasants in the Promised Land: Canada and the Ukrainians 1891–1914* (Toronto: James Lorimer, 1985); Frances Swyripa, *Ukrainian Canadians: A Survey of Their Portrayal in English-language Works* (Edmonton: University of Alberta Press, 1978); Frances Swyripa and John Herd Thompson, eds., *Loyalties in Conflict: Ukrainians in Canada During the Great War* (Edmonton: Canadian Institute of Ukrainian Studies Press, 1983), and, especially, Orest Martynowych, *Ukrainians in Canada: The Formative Years 1891–1924* (Edmonton, Toronto: Canadian Institute of Ukrainian Studies Press, 1991). For one particularly interesting interwar development, see Myron Momryk, "Ukrainian Volunteers from Canada in the International Brigades, Spain, 1936–39," *Journal of Ukrainian Studies* 1–2 (1991): 181–95. For other interwar developments and the Conscription Plebiscite of 1942, see my *Maple Leaf and Trident: The Ukrainian Canadians during the Second World War* (Toronto: Multicultural History Society of Ontario, 1988). On multiculturalism, see especially Julia Laland, "The Roots of Multiculturalism: Ukrainian Canadian Involvement in the Multiculturalism Discussion of the 1960s as an Example of the Position of the 'Third Force'," *Canadian Ethnic Studies* 38, no. 1 (2006): 47–64. On the latest period, only the controversy over alleged Nazi war criminals has been treated in any depth, though even this treatment, even when scholarly, usually contains a certain amount of bias. See, for example, Harold Troper and Morton Weinfeld, *Old Wounds: Jews, Ukrainians, and the Hunt for Nazi War Criminals in Canada* (Markham, ON: Penguin, 1988), which does make some attempt to be even-handed, and John-Paul Himka, "A Central European Diaspora under the Shadow of World War II: The Galician Ukrainians in North America," *Austrian History Yearbook* 37 (2006), also available on-line to subscribers at the Gale Cengage Learning Web site, which is well attuned to, but critical of, the views of the organized Ukrainian community in both Canada and the United States.

6 Perhaps, at this point, it is fitting to note that in the early 1970s, Canadians of Slavonic background were instrumental in the establishment of the Canadian Ethnic Studies Association and its journal *Canadian Ethnic Studies*. The association originated as the Inter-University Committee on Canadian

Slavs, which, in the 1960s, had published three stout volumes of scholarly papers under the title *Slavs in Canada.*

7 V. J. Kaye-Kysilevskyj [Kysilewskyj], *Slavic Groups in Canada,* in the series *Slavistica,* no. 12 (Winnipeg: Ukrainian Free Academy of Sciences, 1951), esp. 19.

8 For a survey of historical writing on the problem, see Jason McDonald, *American Ethnic History: Themes and Perspectives* (New Brunswick, NJ: Rutgers University Press, 2007), 3–24, who outlines the influential work of Werner Sollors, Rudolph J. Vecoli, and others. For a manifesto-like declaration of this "inventionist" position, see, in particular, K. Conzen, D. Gerber, E. Morawska, G. Pozzetta, and R. Vecoli, "The Invention of Ethnicity: A Perspective from the USA," *Journal of American Ethnic History* 12 (Fall 1992): 3–41. Also see Werner Sollors, ed., *Theories of Ethnicity: A Classical Reader* (New York: New York University Press, 1996), esp. the section giving the etymology and history of the word "ethnic" in the English language, 2–12. Another relevant selection of readings is Montserrat Guibernau and John Rex, eds., *The Ethnicity Reader: Nationalism, Multiculturalism and Migration* (Cambridge: Polity Press, 1997).

9 Ivan Franko, *Zibrannia tvoriv u 50-ty tomakh* (Kyiv: Naukova dumka, 1986), 50:44–45.

10 John J. Bukowczyk, *And My Children Did Not Know Me: A History of the Polish Americans* (Bloomington and Indianapolis: Indiana University Press, 1986).

11 See, in particular, Charles Verlinden, "L'origin de *sclavus*=esclave," *Archivum Latinitatis medii aevi* 17 (1942): 97–128. Further on this subject, see the concluding sections of the brief study by J. B. Rudnyckyj, *The Origin of the Name "Slav"* in the series *Onomastica,* no. 21 (Winnipeg: Ukrainian Free Academy of Sciences, 1961). On anti-Slavic sentiment in general in the United States, which undoubtedly had an effect on the emotional content of the word "Slavic" as used on this continent, see, for example, the extensive bibliography in Josephine Wtulich, *American Xenophobia and the Slav Immigrant: A Living Legacy of Mind and Spirit* (Boulder, CO: East European Monographs, 1994), and Caroline Golab, "Stellaaaaaa.....!!!!!!: The Slavic Stereotype in American Film," in *The Kaleidoscopic Lens: How Hollywood Views Ethnic Groups,* ed. Randall M. Miller (Englewood, NJ: Ozer, 1980), 135–55.

12 See, for example, the impressively comprehensive study of James S. Olson, *The Ethnic Dimension in American History* (New York: Saint Martin's Press, 1994). For some account of the Canadian situation, with an excellent bibliography, see Ninette Kelley and Michael Trebilcock, *The Making of the Mosaic: A History of Canadian Immigration Policy* (Toronto: University of Toronto Press, 1998).

13 For the Polish debate from which the above quotations are taken, see James S. Pula, *Polish Americans: An Ethnic Community* (New York: Twayne, 1995), 138–9. On the first three waves of Ukrainian immigrants to Canada, see Vladimir J. Kaye (Kysilewsky) and Frances Swyripa, "Settlement and Coloniza- tion," in *A Heritage in Transition: Essays in the History of Ukrainians in Canada,* ed. Manoly R. Lupul (Toronto: McClelland and Stewart, 1982), 32–58. Certain authors deny the economic, less-political spirit of the second wave and liken it more to the third wave. See, in particular, Yuzyk, *The Ukrainians in Manitoba,* 37-8. Although a child of the first wave, Yuzyk also identified closely with the more politically nationalist wing of the second wave.

14 I recall that the Nixon/Brezhnev détente of the 1970s, in particular, seemed to dull the edge of the Cold War in the eyes of many observers. This general process is well illustrated by a perusal of the articles on the Cold War in various editions of the *Encyclopedia Britannica* of those years. In the 1970 edition, Walter Millis (d. 1968) declared that the Cold War had lost its meaning after the Sino–Soviet split, while, shortly afterwards in the 1972 edition, William H. McNeill observed the proliferation of nuclear weapons in his time and stated that, with this, the bipolar world and the "end of the Cold War era of international relations seemed to have arrived." In fact, by the 1974 edition, when the encyclopedia was divided into a Macropedia and a Micropedia, no longer did a separate article appear under the term "Cold War" in the Macropedia section and only the briefest of articles was printed in the Micropedia.

15 Alla Atamanenko, *Ukrainske istorychne tovarystvo: Idei, postati, diialnist* (Ostroh: UIT, 2010). This work appeared too late for its data to be incorpo- rated into the text of the present volume.

1 The Great Migration

1 See, for example, Stephen Castles and Mark J. Miller, *The Age of Migration: International Population Movements in the Modern World,* 2nd ed. (New York, London: Guilford Press, 1998), esp. ch. 3: "International Migration before 1945," 48–66, which puts the Great Transatlantic Migration from Europe to the Americas into an even wider geographical and chronological perspec- tive. Also see Franklin Daniel Scott, ed., *World Migration in Modern Times* (Englewood Cliffs, NJ: Prentice Hall, 1986); C. Erickson, ed., *Emigration from Europe 1815–1914: Selected Documents* (London: Adam & Charles Black, 1976); and the classic study by Frank Thistlewaite, "Migration from Europe Overseas in the Nineteenth and Twentieth Centuries," in *Population Movements in Modern European History,* ed. Herbert Moller (New York: Macmillan, 1964), 73–92. For a synthetic treatment from the European

perspective, see Philip Taylor, *The Distant Magnet: European Emigration to the USA* (New York: Eyre & Spottiswoode, 1971); and, for some general observations from an American perspective, see Roger Daniels, *Coming to America: A History of Immigration and Ethnicity in American Life* (New York: HarperCollins, 1990); L. Edward Purcell, *Immigration* (Phoenix: Greenwood Publishing Group, 1995); Leonard Dinnerstein, Roger Nichols, and David Reimers, *Natives and Strangers: A Multicultural History of Americans* (New York, Oxford: Oxford University Press, 1996); and Paul Spickard, *Almost All Aliens: Immigration, Race, and Colonialism in American History and Identity* (London, New York: Routledge, 2007), who give further references.

2 The volume of essays edited by Julianna Puskás, *Overseas Migration from East-Central and Southeastern Europe 1880–1940* (Budapest: Akadedmai Kiado, 1990), contains essays on Polish, Czech, Slovak, and Croatian migration to the Americas. The first chapter of Michael Just, *Ost und Südosteuropäische Amerikawanderung 1881–1914* (Stuttgart: F. Steiner Verlag, 1988), is quite comprehensive, and so is the statistical study by V. M. Kabuzan, *Emigratsiia i reemigratsiia v Rossii v XVIII-nachale XX veka* (Moscow: Nauka, 1998), the last chapter of which directly treats our theme and contains much information on Russian, Ukrainian, and Belarusan migration overseas. Also see V. M. Kobuzan and N. V. Chorna, "Zaokeanska mihratsiia Slov'ian y XIX-na pochatku XX st.," *Narodna tvorchist ta etnohrafiia* 6 (1989): 3–14; Andrej Pilch, "Migrations of the Galician Populace at the Turn of the Nineteenth and Twentieth Centuries," in *Employment-Seeking Migration of the Poles World Wide* (Cracow: PWN, 1975); Anna Reczyńska, "Emigration from Polish Territories to Canada up until World War Two," *Polyphony* 6, no. 2 (1984): 11–19; and Hans Chmelar, *Höhepunkte der Österreichischen Auswanderung ... 1905–1914* (Vienna: ÖAW, 1974).

3 On Kościuszko and Pułaski, see the article on Poles in the *Harvard Encyclopedia of American Ethnic Groups*, ed. Stephan Thernstrom (Cambridge, MA: Belknap Press of Harvard University Press, 1980), 787–803, which gives further references. On Poles in Latin America and the remark of Pedro I, see Marcin Kula, "The Curing of Complexes: Poles on Brazilians, Brazilians on Poles, up to 1939," *Acta Poloniae Historica* 50 (1984): 141–56.

4 All these personalities are mentioned in the various entries of their respective nationalities in the *Harvard Encyclopedia of American Ethnic Groups*, which gives further references.

5 For general studies of Sienkiewicz published in English, see Mieczyslaw Giergielewicz, *Henryk Sienkiewicz* (New York: Twayne, 1968) and Wacław Lednicki, *Henryk Sienkiewicz: A Retrospective Synthesis* (The Hague: Mouton, 1960). For a highly respected synthesis in Polish, see Julian Krzyżanowski,

Henryk Sienkiewicz (Warsaw: PWN, 1972). Also see Cheryl A. Pula, "Sienkiewicz, Henryk," in *The Polish American Encyclopedia*, ed. James S. Pula (Jefferson, NC, and London: McFarland and Co., 2011), 482–3.

6 Lednicki, *Henryk Sienkiewicz*, 29–34; Giergielewicz, *Henryk Sienkiewicz*, 25–7; Krzyżanowiski, *Henryk Sienkiewicz*, 47. Sienkiewicz's California experiences are also described in Arthur Prudden and Marion Moore Coleman, *Wanderers Twain: Modjeska and Sienkiewicz: A View from California* (Cheshire, CT: Cherry Hill Books, 1964).

7 Giergielewicz, *Henryk Sienkiewicz*, 48, briefly describes these works.

8 The most convenient Polish edition of *Listy z podróży do Ameryki* was edited with a lengthy introduction by Zdzisław Najder (Warsaw: PWN, 1956); see esp. 594–606 for the section on the peasant immigrants. I have used the English translation by Charles Morley published under the title *Portrait of America: Letters of Henry Sienkiewicz* (New York: Columbia University Press, 1959).

9 Julian Krzyżanowski, *Henry Sienkiewicz: Kalendarz życia i tworczości* (Warsaw: PWN, 1956), 84–5. "For Bread" was translated into English in the 1890s by Jeremiah Curtin and was reprinted more than a dozen times. See, for example, Henryk Sienkiewicz, *Sielanka: A Forest Picture and Other Stories*, trans. Jeremiah Curtin (Boston: Little Brown, 1899), 25–110. There also exists a specialized study by J. Maciejewski, *"Za chlebem" H. Sienkiewicza* (Poznań: PWN, 1956), which I did not consult for this writing.

10 For biographical details on Kukučin, see Cyril H. Potoček, "Martin Kukučin: Pioneer of Slovak Realism," *Slavonic and East European Review* 22, no. 2 (1944): 47–60; *idem, Martin Kukučin: A Link Between Two Worlds* (Passaic, NJ: Slovak Catholic Sokol 1943); and Stanislav Mečiar *Kukučin živý* (n.d., n.p.), which deals primarily with his experiences in Latin America. (My study of Kukučin was limited to materials available in English.)

11 See Monika Glettler, *Pittsburgh–Wien–Budapest: Programm und Praxis der Nationalitätenpolitik bei der Auswanderung der ungarischen Slowaken nach Amerika um 1900* (Vienna: ÖAW, 1980), and the detailed English-language review article on this book by Julianna Puskás in *Acta Historica Academiae Hungaricae* 29, nos. 2–4 (1983): 311–15. Also see M. M. Stolárik, "Slovak Migration from Europe to North America, 1870-1918," *Slovak Studies* 20 (1980): 1–137.

12 Both are available in English with an introduction by Norma Leigh Rudinsky, "Two Stories by Martin Kukučin," *Slovak Studies* XVIII (1978): 65–151.

13 For background, see Laurie Nock, "The Croatians in Punta Arenas, Chile," in *Symposium: Emigrants from Croatia and Their Achievements*, ed. V. Markotic (Calgary: Western Publishers, 1987), 57–77.

14 Unlike *Dom v stráni*, which was translated into Croatian during the 1920s, *Mat' volá* has never been translated into a second language. I have relied on the summary in Potoček, "Martin Kukučin." For a complete bibliography of English-language titles dealing with Kukučin, see W. L. Rudinsky, "Annotated Bibliography of English Language Sources on Martin Kukučin," *Slovak Studies* 18 (1978): 169–79.

15 For biographical details on Konopnicka, see Maria Szypowska, *Konopnicka jakiej nie znamy* (Wrocław: PIW, 1962), which pays considerable attention to *Pan Balcer w Brazylii*. See especially 392–414. More briefly, see the article on Konopnicka by Jan Baculewski in the *Polski Słownik Biograficzny* (Wrocław, 1967–8), 13:576–81. In English, there is only the highly slanted Soviet treatment by Mark Zhivov, "Maria Konopnicka: Poetess and Patriot," *International Literature* 10 (1944): 53–5.

16 See Tadeusz Czapyński, *"Pan Balcer w Brazylii" jako poemat emigracyjny* (Łódz: Ossolinium, 1957), which was the principal source for my study of Konopnicka.

17 See ibid., 15–28, in which a great deal of background material on the emigration to Brazil and on the genesis of Konopnicka's poem is given. About one-third of the migrants eventually returned to their European homeland. For a brief overview of the mass migration of the Polish peasantry, see Edward Strzelecki and M. Latuch, "Emigracja zarobkowa z Polski," in *Wielka Encyklopedia Powszechna PWN* (Warsaw: PWN 1964), 3:419–20, who, by way of comparison, report that between 1899 and 1914, some 595,000 Poles migrated to the United States. For a more detailed treatment of the American situation, see Florian Stasik, *Polska emigracja zarobkowa w Stanach Zjednoczonych Ameryki 1865–1914* (Warsaw: PWN, 1985). Marcin Kula, "Polska diaspora w Brazylii," in *Polska diaspora*, ed. Barbara Górska (Cracow: Wydaw. literackie, 2001), 118–28, esp. 118, puts the number of Polish immigrants to Brazil during this period much lower. He writes that some 40,000 to 80,000 arrived to the 1890s, another 25,000, mostly from Galicia, in the next two decades, and another 10,000 from Podlasia and the Lublin area in 1910–11.

18 For the text of the poem, see Maria Konopnicka, *Pan Balcer w Brazylii* (Warsaw, Cracow: Gebethner i Wolff, 1925), which I was able to peruse. I am unaware of the existence of any English translation of this work.

19 See especially the discussion in Czapyński, *"Pan Balcer w Brazylii,"* 42.

20 Ibid., 6–9.

21 Julian Krzyżanowski, *Dzieje literatury polskiej* (Warsaw: PWN, 1972), 456–7.

22 See, for example, A. G. Piotrovskaia, "Mariia Konopnitskaia," in *Istoriia polskoi literatury* (Moscow: Nauka, 1968), I:596–615; V. B. Obolevich, *Istoriia*

polskoi literatury (Leningrad: Leningradskii gosudarstvennyi universitet, 1960), 252–60; and M. T. Rylsky, "Mariia Konopnitska," in his *Statti pro literaturu* (Kyiv: Dnipro, 1980), 450–60.

23 Ivan Franko, "Maria Konopnicka," *Die Zeit* (Vienna), no. 421, October 25, 1902; used by me as reprinted in Ukrainian translation in Franko's *Zibrannia tvoriv u p'iatdestiaty tomakh* (Kyiv: Naukova dumka, 1982), 33:375–83. See especially 375 for the quoted passage. More generally, see I. Hlynsky, "Velykyi Kameniar i Mariia Konopnitska," *Vsesvit* 5 (1966): 82–6, and M. Kupłowski, "Iwan Franko o twórczości Marii Konopnickiej," *Slavia Orientalis* 4 (1976): 473–81.

24 Most of Franko's journalistic writings on the emigration theme are collected in his *Zibrannia tvoriv u p'iatdesiaty tomakh,* vol. 44, Book 2 (Kyiv: Naukova dumka, 1985). More generally, see Thomas M. Prymak, "Ivan Franko and Mass Ukrainian Emigration to Canada," *Canadian Slavonic Papers* 26, no. 4 (1984): 307–17. A fuller version of this paper appears as Chapter 3 in this volume.

25 *Istoriia Ukrainskoi RSR* (Kyiv: Naukova dumka, 1978), 4:305. Also see Chemlar, *Höhepunkte der Österreichischen Auswanderung,* 96–107. A more recent study of this phenomenon also takes account of seasonal migration to western Europe. See Stepan Kacharaba and Mykola Rozhyk, *Ukrainska emihratsiia: Emihratsiinyi rukh zi skhidnoi Halychyny ta pivnichnoi Bukovyny u 1890–1914 rr.* (Lviv, 1995).

26 See Prymak, "Ivan Franko." Prince Rudoph is also sometimes mentioned in modern Brazilian accounts of early Ukrainian immigration to Brazil. See, for example, Mariano Chaikovsky, "Pochatok immihratsii do Brazylii ta svidchennia pershykh immihrantiv," in *Ukraintsi Brazylii,* ed. Andriy Nahachewsky and Maryna Hrymych (Kyiv: Duliby, 2011), 45n38.

27 Ivan Franko, *Zibrannia tvoriv u p'iatdesiaty tomakh* (Kyiv: Naukova dumka, 1975), 2:491.

28 See ibid., 263–71, for the text of the poem.

29 E. S. Lysenko, "Tema emihratsii u tvorchosti I. Franka ta inshykh prohresyvnykh ukrainskykh pysmennykiv," *Ukrainske literaturoznavstvo* 7 (1970): 42–7; A. L. Biletska, "Tema emihratsii halytskoho selianstva v tvorchosti I. la Franka," *Ukrainske literaturoznavstvo* 42 (1984): 74–80. Of the works mentioned above, only Stefanyk's *The Stone Cross,* trans. Joseph Wiznuk and C. H. Andrushyshen (Toronto: McClelland and Stewart, 1971), has been put into English. This story describes the enormous grief and pain felt by an elderly peasant landholder when forced by circumstances to leave with his family for Canada. Many years later, Stefanyk's son did, in fact, emigrate to Canada.

30 The fullest biography of Korolenko is Maurice Comtet, *Vladimir Gataktionovic Korolenko (1853–1921): L'homme et l'oeuvre*, 2 vols. (Lille, Paris: Université Lille, 1975). For a Soviet treatment, see G. A. Bialyi, *V. G. Korolenko* (Leningrad: Khudozhnaia literatura, 1983). Also see R. F. Christian, "V. G. Korolenko (1853–1921): A Centennial Appreciation," *Slavonic and East European Review* 32, no. 79 (1954): 451–63.

31 The fullest description of Korolenko's American tour is in Comtet, *Vladimir Gataktionovic Korolenko*, I:308–16.

32 N. L. Tudorianu, *Ocherki rossiiskoi trudovoi emigratsii perioda imperializma* (Kishinev: Shtintsa, 1986), 166–85. If we can believe Tudorianu, 173, eastern Slavs – that is, Russians, Belarusans, and Ukrainians – or *Russkie*, to use his vocabulary, grew to make up some 12 per cent of American immigrants from imperial Russia in the years before the First World War. From 1899 to 1913, this supposedly amounted to some 165,000 people.

33 The 1902 text of *Bez iazyka* is printed in Vladimir Galaktionovich Korolenko, *Sobranie sochinenii* (Moscow: Gos. izd. Khudozhnoi literatury, 1953), 4:7–145, and has been translated into English by Gregory Zilboorg under the title *In a Strange Land* (Westport, CN, 1925; repr.: Greenwood Press, 1975). I have perused the former and made full use of the latter.

34 See, in particular, I. S. Mukhyn, *Za viru batkiv: Uniiaty v khudozhnykh tvorakh V. G. Korolenka* (Chicago: Ukrainskyi katolytskyi universytet im. Papy Klymentii v Rymi, Filiia Chicago, 1976), especially 69–81.

2 A Little-Known Book

1 For some synthetic treatments, see the titles listed in note 1 to Chapter 1 of the present volume.

2 See, for example, Celina Bobinska and Andrzej Pilch, eds., *Employment Seeking Emigration of Poles World Wide, XIX and XX Centuries* (Cracow: PWN, 1975); K. Groniowski, "Emigracja z ziem zaboru rosyjskiego (1864–1918)," in *Emigracja z ziem polskich w czasach nowozytnych i najnowszych*, ed. A. Pilch (Warsaw: PWN, 1984), 196–251; Keijo Virtanen, *Settlement or Return: Finnish Emigrants 1860–1930, in the International Overseas Return Migration Movement* (Helsinki: Finnish Historical Society, 1979).

3 For the Habsburg Monarchy, see the two studies by Johann Chmelar, "The Austrian Emigration, 1900–1914," *Perspectives in American History* 7 (1973): 275–378, and *Höhepunkte der Österreichischen Auswanderung . . . 1905–1914* (Vienna: Verlag der Österreichischen Akademie der Wissenschaften, 1974). On the Russian Empire, see V. M. Kabuzan, *Emigratsiia i reemigratsiia v Rossii v XVIII-nachale XX veka* (Moscow: Nauka, 1998). Also see V. M. Kabuzan and

N. V. Chorna, "Zaokeansksa mihratsiia Slov'ian u XIX-na pochatku XX st.," *Narodna tvorchist ta etnohrafiia* 6 (1989): 3–14. The most recent work of this type deals specifically with Belarusan and Ukrainian labour migration from the western parts of the Russian Empire to Canada. See Vadim Kukushkin, *From Peasants to Labourers: Ukrainian and Belarusan Immigration from the Russian Empire to Canada* (Montreal, Kingston: McGill-Queen's University Press, 2008), which gives further references.

4 *Istoriia litovskoi SSR* (Vilnius: Mokslas, 1978), 230; *Istoriia ukainskoi RSR* (Kyiv: Naukova dumka, 1978), IV:305.

5 Arnold N. Shlepakov, *Ukrainska trudova emihratsiiai SShA i Kanady* (Kyiv: Akademia nauk ukrainskoi RSR, 1960); Andrei A. Strelko, *Slavianskoe naselenie v stranakh latinskoi Ameriki* (Kyiv: Naukova dumka, 1980).

6 E. S. Lysenko, "Tema emihratsii u tvorchosti I. Franka ta inshykh prohresyvnykh ukrainskykh pysmennykiv," *Ukrainske literaturoznavstvo* 7 (1970): 42–7; A. L. Biletska, "Tema emihratsii halytskoho selianstva v tvorchosti I. Ia. Franka," *Ukrainske literaturoznavstvo* 42 (1984): 74–80.

7 Arnold N. Shlepakov, *Immigratsiia i amerikanskii robochii klass v epokhu imperialzma* (Moscow, 1966); Sh. A. Bogina, *Immigrantskoe naselenie SShA* (Leningrad: Nauka, 1976).

8 N. L. Tudorianu, *Ocherki rossiiskoi trudovoi emigratsii perioda imperializma (v Germaniiu, Skandavskie strany, i SShA)* (Kishinev: Shtiintsa, 1986). Tudorianu conventionally uses the word *rossiiskii* (Russian) in a non-ethnic way in the general sense of belonging to the Russian Empire. He uses the word *russkii* (Russian) to refer to ethnic Russians.

9 Tudorianu, *Ocherki rossiiskoi trudovoi emigratsii*, 28–9, added that after 1907, the government of Peter Stolypin consciously encouraged peasant migration. In central Russia and the eastern Ukrainian lands, this movement was directed toward Siberia. (Between 1905 and 1913, about three million people crossed the Urals for Siberia.) In the western borderlands of the empire, where, Tudorianu argues, there was more rural poverty, peasant migration was directed toward western Europe and the Americas. Although, after 1910, internal migration to Siberia sharply decreased, emigration abroad continued to increase. It usually increased by a factor of two or three times per year, although, in some years, it even reached a factor of four.

10 Paul Magocsi, in his article "Russians" in the *Harvard Encyclopedia of American Ethnic Groups* (Cambridge, MA: Belknap Press of Harvard University, 1980), 885, which, of course, was published shortly before Tudorianu did his study, was somewhat more conservative in his totals and made the following generalization: "At the present time less than 50 percent of the population of the Soviet Union is Russian, and in the past an even smaller percentage

of immigrants arriving from Russia have been ethnic Russians. U.S. Census Bureau figures for 1910, 1920, and 1930 indicate that only 17 percent of the 1.5 million immigrants entering the United States from Russia were actually Russian, and this category has often included Belorussians and Ukrainians as well. The vast majority were Jews (58 percent), Poles (11 percent), and Germans (8 percent)."

11 Vladimir Ilich Lenin, "Capitalism and Workers' Immigration," in *Lenin on the United States of America*, ed. C. Leiteizen (Moscow: Progress Publishers, 1967), 82–5. This article had originally been published in *Za pravdu*, no. 22, Oct. 29, 1913, at the very climax of the immigration movement.

12 Information is provided in Chapter 1 in the present volume.

13 See, for example, the summaries and references in John Bodnar, *The Transplanted: A History of Immigrants in Urban America* (Bloomington: Indiana University Press, 1987) and Jean R. Burnet, *Coming Canadians: An Introduction to a History of Canada's Peoples* (Toronto: McClelland and Stewart, 1988).

3 Ivan Franko and Emigration

1 One of the last pre-independence Soviet biographies of Franko was O. I. Dei, *Ivan Franko zhyttia i dialnist* (Kyiv: Dnipro, 1981), who paid some attention to the emigration question. Although a critical and sophisticated treatment, it portrays Franko as a pro-Russian "revolutionary democrat," according to the Leninist formula. By contrast, the émigré Luka Lutsiv, in *Ivan Franko: Borets za natsionalnu i sotsiialnu spravedlyvist* (New York: Svoboda 1967), stressed his role as a national leader. This interesting product of the Cold War also contained some information on the theme of "Franko and America." On Franko and Canada, in particular, see Petro Kravchuk, *Vony obraly Kanadu: Pershyi period emihruvannia ukraintsiv do Kanady, 1891–1914* (Toronto: Kobzar, 1991), 63–6, which was published after the first version of the present essay appeared in *Canadian Slavonic Papers* 26, no. 4 (1984): 307–17, and repeats some of the information contained in it. On Franko and the emigration question more generally, see Volodymyr Levynsky, *Franko iak economist* (Scranton, PA: Ukrainskyi robotnychyi soiuz, 1957), 94–103, and S. M. Zlupko, *Ivan Franko: Ekonomist* (Lviv: Male pidpryiemstvo slovo, 1992), 87–99. There is no decent biography of Franko in English, but the old biographical introduction to Percival Cundy's translation, *Ivan Franko, The Poet of Western Ukraine; Selected Poems* (New York: Philosophical Library, 1948), is still somewhat serviceable.

The last Soviet edition of Franko's collected works was planned over many years and was advertised as a complete critical edition. *Zibrannia tvoriv u p'iatdesiaty tomakh* (Kyiv: Naukova dumka, 1976–86) maintained a fairly high level of scholarship, especially in the last volumes, which were published on the eve of the Gobachev reforms and their consequent "openness." The first twenty-five volumes contained Franko's literary works, while the remaining twenty-five were devoted to his scholarship, political polemics, and letters. Censorship remained an issue in Soviet Franko scholarship right to the demise of the USSR. During the Cold War, with a view to succouring his unfortunate Soviet colleagues and challenging their censors, the Ukrainian émigré scholar Bohdan Kravtsiv published an interesting edition of Franko's more controversial political tracts under the title *Ivan Franko pro sotsiializm i marksyzm: retsenzii i statti 1897–1906* (New York: Proloh, 1966). For a fuller Franko collection of both literature and scholarship censored out of the last great Soviet edition of his works, see *Ivan Franko: Mozaika*, ed. Z. I. Franko and M. H. Vasylenko (Lviv: Kameniar, 2001). Unfortunately, this last work contained nothing on the emigration question, though the Soviet *Zibrannia tvoriv* omitted at least two seemingly important articles on this theme. See, for example, notes 23 and 28 below.

2   "Vidpovid I. Franka na pryvitannia na vechori prysviachenomu 25 richchiu ioho literaturnoi diialnosti," *Literaturno-naukovyi vistnyk* 4, no. 11 (1898): 128–30, and reprinted in *Ivan Franko, Dokumenty i materiialy 1856–1965* ed. I. Butych (Kyiv: Naukova dumka, 1966), 223–35.

3   For some remarks by Franko himself, see his study, first published in 1887, "Zemelna vlasnist u Halychyni," *Tvory v dvadtsiaty tomakh* 19 (Derzhavne vydavnytstvo 'Khudozhnoi literatury', 1955–6): 278–304. More generally, see *Istoriia Ukrainskoi RSR*, 10 vols. in 8 (Kyiv: Naukova dumka, 1977–1979), 4:292–8.

4   For a general statistical table of Austrian emigration abroad (1896 to 1910), broken down by destination, see Hans Chmelar, *Höhepunkte der Österreichischen Auswanderung . . . 1905–1914* (Vienna: ÖAW, 1974), 24. According to Andzej Pilch, "Migrations of the Galician Populace at the Turn of the Nineteenth and Twentieth Centuries," in *Employment-Seeking Emigrations of the Poles World Wide*, ed. Celina Bobińska (Cracow: PWN, 1975), 97, within the empire, Silisia and Lower Austria were the largest recipients of Galician immigrants. Bukovina was also a large recipient and there was an exclusively Ukrainian migration to Russia and Romania. Also see the survey by V. Kubiiovych and V. Markus', "Emigratsiia," in *Entsyklopediia ukrainoznavstva* (Paris, New York: NTSh, 1955–7), 2:629–37; available in English by the same authors as "Emigration," in *Encyclopedia of Ukraine*, ed. V. Kubijovyč (Toronto: University of Toronto Press, 1984), I:818–24. For more detailed general surveys in Ukrainian, see B. D. Lanovyk

et al., *Istoriia ukrainskoi emihratsii* (Kyiv: Vyshcha shkola, 1997), and Stepan Kacharaba and Mykola Rozhyk, *Ukrainska emihratsiia: Emihratsiinyi rukh zi skhidnoi Halychyny ta pivnichnoi Bukovyny u 1890–1914 rr.* (Lviv, 1995). Most recently, see O. V. Ias, "Emihratsiia ukrainskoho naselennia," in *Entsyklopediia istorii Ukrainy* (Kyiv: Naukova dumka, 2005), 3:33–7, with a bibliography. For some Canadian perspectives, see Jaroslav Petryshyn, *Peasants in the Promised Land: Canada and the Ukrainians 1891–1914* (Toronto: Lorimer, 1985); Stella Hryniuk, "Sifton's Pets: Who Were They?" in *Canada's Ukrainians: Negotiating an Identity,* ed. Lubomyr Luciuk and Stella Hryniuk (Toronto: University of Toronto Press, 1991), 3–116; and the first chapters of Orest Martynowych, *Ukrainians in Canada: The Formative Years 1891–1924* (Edmonton: Canadian Institute of Ukrainian Studies, 1991).

5 *Lystuvannia I. Franka i M. Drahomanova,* ed. Mykhailo Vozniak (Kyiv: UVAN, 1928), 271. *Ameryka* (1886–1890) was the first Ukrainian periodical to be published in the United States. At first, it appeared irregularly about every two weeks; later, it became a weekly and was published by the Ukrainian Greek Catholic parish of Shenandoah, Pennsylvania.

6 Ibid. Though he had been a co-founder of the Polish socialist movement, Franko had long been dissatisfied by Polish reluctance to accept the existence of the Ukrainian nationality in Galicia. He was to break firmly with the Poles in 1897. See H. D. Verves, *Ivan Franko i pyttania ukrainsko-polskykh literaturno-hromadskykh vzaiemyn 70-90-kh rokiv XIXst.* (Kyiv: Akademiia nauk URSR, 1957). The Franko and America (USA) theme remains largely unexplored.

7 Vozniak, *Lystuvannia Franka i Drahomanova,* 272. Both Drahomanov and Franko saw the more narrow-minded of the village clergy and the conservative hierarchy as obstacles to the work of popular enlightenment. In Soviet literature, Franko, in particular, is portrayed as a militant atheist, though "anti-cleric" would be a better term. For a typical Soviet treatment, see the introduction to Ivan Franko, *Monoloh ateista,* ed. A. Khalimonchuk (Lviv: Kameniar, 1973), which is a carefully selected compilation of Franko's criticism of organized religion. (The title is the editor's and not Franko's.) This should be compared with V. Doroshenko, *Velykyi Kameniar; Zhyttia i zasluhy Ivan a Franka* (Winnipeg: Nakladom Komitetu Ukraintsiv Kanady, 1956), 35–46, who demonstrates that Franko was not entirely without religious sensitivities. Also see the brief observations of Konstantyn Bida, *Relihiini motyvy v tvorakh I. Franka* (Munich: n.p., 1956).

8 Vozniak, *Lystuvannia Franka i Drahomanova,* 275–6. According to John-Paul Himka, "Ivan Volianskyi: The Formative Years of the Ukrainian Community in America," *Ukrainskyi istoryk* 3–4 (1975): 61–72, Voliansky was very much "a

radical priest" who sympathized with worker grievances and should have gotten along well with Franko.

9 *Istoriia Ukrainskoi RSR*, 4:305. Compare Chmelar, *Höhepunkte der Österreichischen Auswanderung*, 96–107, who analyzes the statistics for Galicia and Bukovina. A more recent study by the Ukrainian demographer living in Russia, V. M. Kabuzan, *Ukraintsi v mire* (Moscow: Nauka, 2006), 248–9, counts 272,300 eastern Galician emigrants, 65 per cent of whom were Ukrainians, "at the beginning of the twentieth century."

10 On Pylypiw, see William A. Czumer, *Recollections About the Life of the First Ukrainian Settlers in Canada*, trans. L. Laychuk (Edmonton: Canadian Institute of Ukrainian Studies, 1981), 16. On the conservative gentry and the Galician *Sejm*, or provincial legislature, which they controlled, see Benjamin P. Murdzek, *Emigration in Polish Social-Political Thought 1870–1914* (New York: East European Monographs, 1977), 79ff., 111–12, and, on Caro, 135–6.

11 I. Franko, "Die Auswanderung der galizischen Bauern," reprinted in *Beiträge zur Geschichte und Kultur der Ukraine*, ed. Eduard Winter (Berlin: Akademie Verlag, 1963), 277–81, and also as "Emihratsiia halytskykh selian," *Tvory v dvadtsiaty tomakh* 19: 311–24. Franko, like many other socially concerned observers, was greatly impressed by the work of the Polish economist Stanisław Szczepanowski, whose *Nędza Galicyi w cyfrach i program energicznego rozwoju gospodarstwa krajowego* [Galician misery in statistics and a program for the energetic development of the economy of the country] (Lwów, 1888) is sometimes considered the most influential book of its kind published in Polish in the nineteenth century. (This volume was not available to me, but see Murdzek, *Emigration in Polish Social-Political Thought*, 140.) Szczepanowski claimed that, in Galicia, 50,000 people perished annually as a result of poverty and hunger. It was he who coined the popular aphorism: "Each Galician produces what is necessary for one fourth person and consumes the equivalent for one half person." He saw massive industrialization as the only practical solution.

12 Franko, "Emihratsiia," 313. Compare Murdzek, *Emigration in Polish Social-Political Thought*, 133ff.

13 Franko, "Emihratsiia," 314. Also see John-Paul Himka, "Hope in the Tsar: Displaced Naive Monarchism among the Ukrainian Peasants of the Habsburg Empire," *Russian History* 7, pts. 1–2 (1980): 125–38.

14 Sister Severyna, "Emigratsiia v ukrainskim pysmenstvi," in *Propamiatna knyha vydana z nahody soroklitnoho iuvyleiu Ukrainskoho Narodnoho Souizu*, ed. L. Myshuha (Jersey City: UNS, 1936), 408–11. Also see Murdzek, *Emigration in Polish Social-Political Thought*, 103–9, who points out that the Polish Commercial-Geographical Association, which had been established in Lviv

in 1894, exposed Gargoletti, but considered that mass emigration to Brazil could be beneficial provided that it was restricted to the southern and temperate Brazilian province of Parana. Prospective emigrants were warned against availing themselves of free transportation to the Brazilian states of Sao Paulo and Espirito Santo, which had been needing workers on their coffee and sugar plantations since 1888 when slavery was finally abolished in Brazil.

15 Konopnicka's *Pan Balcer w Brazylii* (Mr Balcer in Brazil) was intended to be the historical epic of the Polish peasant in the same way that Mickiewicz's *Pan Tadeusz* had been one for the *szlachta* or Polish gentry. It was begun in 1893, as Franko points out, "at the time of the most powerful emigration fever," and was continued in 1897, and then again later. Franko turned to versification on the Brazilian theme in 1898 and may well have been influenced by Konopnicka, whom he thought to be "certainly the greatest Polish poetess, and together with Eliza Orzeszkowa, the most talented woman not only in Polish, but in all Slavic literature." See Franko's "Mariia Konopnitska," in *Tvory v dvatsiaty tomakh*, 18:171–8, which is also available in Polish in Ivan Franko, *O literaturze Polskiej*, ed. Mikolaj Kupłowski (Cracow: Wydawnictwo literackie, 1979), 202–13. The latter edition contains some valuable annotations. Also see I. Hlynsky, "Velykyi Kameniar i Mariia Konopnitska," *Vsesvit*.5 (1966): 82–6.

16 Franko, "Mii izmarahd," in *Tvory v dvadtsiaty tomakh*, 11:133–44. In this poem, Franko paints a stirring picture of the simple villager's view of the good life in a peaceful kingdom. It was to be an abundant kingdom without oppressive Polish landlords or Jewish tavern-keepers. The pseudo-Rudolph assures his loyal country folk that there would be land aplenty and that even the monkeys from the forests would be available to help with any hard work.

17 See E. S. Lysenko, "Tema emihratsii u tvorchosti I. Franka ta inshykh prohresyvnykh ukrainskykh pysmenykiv," *Ukrainske literaturoznavstvo* 7 (1969): 42–7.

18 This translation, together with all others in this paper, is mine. See "Na temat duru emigratsiinoho," *Dilo*, no. 255, November 14, 1895, which gives a typical description of both the "emigration fever" among the peasantry and of the near hysteria of local officials who could not control it.

19 As early as 1887, Franko had dedicated his short story "Misiia" to him. See Franko, *Zibrannia tvoriv*, 16:495. Sixteen years later, on the occasion of his premature death, Franko penned his obituary for *Literaturno-naukovyi vistnyk* 24 (1903): 147–8.

20 O. Oleskiv, *Pro vilni zemli* (Lviv: Prosvita, 1895; repr. Winnipeg: UVAN, 1975). The original edition is cited in Vladimir J. Kaye [Kysilewskyj], *Early*

Ukrainian Settlements in Canada 1895–1900: Dr. Josef Oleskow's Role in the Settlement of the Canadian Northwest (Toronto: University of Toronto Press, 1964), 12–18. Mykhailo Ivanchuk, "Ti shcho promostyly shliakh Ukrainskii imigratsii v Novyi Svit," *Kalendar-almanakh Ukrainskoho Holosu na 1966 rik* (Winnipeg), 55–8, has suggested that Oleskiv's discovery of the Canadian idea is linked to articles in the Galician press sent by California-based Ahapii Honcharenko, who was a friend of the famous Russian political émigré Alexander Herzen, and was the first-known Ukrainian political immigrant in North America.

21 Franko, *Zibrannia tvoriv*, 50:44–5; also see Kravchuk, *Vony obraly Kanadu*, 66.

22 Oleskiv's trip to Canada is described in detail by Kaye, *Early Ukrainian Settlements*, 19–44.

23 M. O. Moroz, *Ivan Franko: Bibliohrafiia tvoriv 1874–1964* (Kyiv: Naukova dumka, 1966), 276, 280, lists: "Starosta tarnopolski w sprawie emigracji," *Kurier Lwowski*, no. 100, April 10, 1895, and "Znowu odysseja emigrantów galicyjskich," *Kurier Lwowski*, no. 142, May 23, 1895. The last of these, together with several more of Franko's emigration pieces, is reprinted in Ukrainian translation in *Zibrannia tvoriv*, 44:pt. 2.

24 The Lviv newspapers did not report this event until Oleskiv sent them a descriptive letter. See "Vid D-ra Iosyfa Oleskova," *Dilo*, no. 249, November 6, 1895, and "V dele emigratsii selian," *Galichanin*, no. 250, November 7, 1895; M. Marunchak, *The Ukrainian Canadians: A History* (Winnipeg, Ottawa: UVAN, 1970), 32–3, notes that "the more progressive younger generation took an active part in the discussions at the conference which the older generation failed to attend."

25 A few days later, the conservative Russophile newspaper *Galichanin*, no. 252, November 10, 1895, reported Oleskiv's ideas and contrasted his positive attitude toward emigration to Canada with the negative attitude of certain Polish landlords who had petitioned the Vienna government to put a stop to the Brazilian fever. Also see Kaye, *Early Ukrainian Settlements*, 44.

26 "Mizerja emigracyjne," *Kurier Lwowski*, no. 316, November 14, 1895, listed in Moroz, *Bibliohrafiia tvoriv*, 276. Also available in Ukrainian translation as "Mizeriia emihratsiina," *Zibrannia tvoriv*, 44, pt. 2:449–50.

27 M. Mochulsky, "Z ostannikh desiatylit zhyttia Franka 1896–1916," in *Za sto lit* (1928): 3:227–28. This memoir is reprinted in *Spohady pro Ivana Franka*, ed. Mykhailo Hnatiuk (Lviv: Kameniar, 1997), 364–92.

28 Moroz, *Bibliohrafiia tvoriv*, 275–7, lists: "Bezholowie emigracyjne," *Kurier Lwowski*, no. 329, 27 November 1895; "Czy emigracja z Galicji jest konieczna?" *Kurier Lwowski*, nos. 353–7, 21-5 December 1895; "O piekle brazylijskiem I–II," *Kurier Lwowski*, nos. 340, 344, 8 and 12 December 1895. These

articles are also noted by Dei, *Ivan Franko*, 197, and the first two are reprinted in Ukrainian translation in Franko's *Zibrannia tvoriv*, 44, pt. 2:551–5, and 559–67.

29 For a general introduction to Ukrainian politics in Galicia, see I. L. Rudnytsky, "The Ukrainians in Galicia under Austrian Rule," in *Nationbuilding and the Politics of Nationalism: Essays on Austrian Galicia*, ed. A. Markovits and F. Sysyn (Cambridge, MA: Harvard Ukrainian Research Institute, 1982), 23–67. On the Radical Party, see John-Paul Himka, "Ukrainskyi sotsializm u Halychyni," *Journal of Ukrainian Graduate Studies* 7 (1979): 33–51. Also see Iaroslav Hrytsak, "Ivan Franko pro politychnu samostiinist Ukrainy," *Zeszyty naukowe Uniwersytetu Jagielonskiego, Prace histoyczne* 103 (1993): 45–53, and other works by this author.

30 Franko set his view of the Galician elections before Austrian public opinion in his "Die jungste galizische Wahl," *Die Zeit*, no. 50, November 9, 1895; reprinted in *Beiträge zur Geschichte und Kultur der Ukraine*, 299–309. Also see Matvii Stakhiv's introduction to Ivan Makukh, *Na narodnii sluzhbi* (1958), 43–7. On an earlier occasion, when the emperor visited Galicia, Badeni had ensured order through equally brutal methods, which directly affected the emigration question. Special precautions – including a "state of siege" – were taken to halt peasant emigration during the emperor's tour. Franko writes: "The police received an order to hold and confine the emigrants, '*and shoot like a dog whoever does not want to abide by the order, obey commands, or begins to flee,*'" (Franko's emphasis). See his "Emihratsiia halytsykh selian," 316.

31 The *vichovyi rukh*, which can be translated literally, but rather awkwardly, as "the mass meeting movement," had begun during the last quarter of the nineteenth century and continued to gather momentum up to 1914. There were some fifty-nine such assemblies before 1900. Soviet accounts tried hard to link the movement's further growth to the influence of the Russian revolution of 1905 to 1907. See, for example, P. V. Svezhynsky's article "Vichovyi rukh," in *Radianska entsyklopediia istorii Ukrainy*, 4 vols. (Kyiv, 1969–1972), I:323.

32 M. Vozniak, "Ivan Franko v dobi radykalizmu," *Ukraina* 6 (1926): 133.

33 "Povidomlennia pro vystup I. Franka na narodnomu vichi v Velkykh Mostakh," *Hromadskyi holos*, nos. 10–11, 15 December 1895; reprinted in *Dokumenty i materiialy*, 195–7. Compare Franko's words with the report in the Russophile newspaper *Galichanin*, no. 265, 26 November–8 December 1895, whose editor, in fact, sat on Oleskiv's committee. *Galichanin* objected to Franko's position that emigration was a necessity, and seemed to view the prospective movement to Canada as the lesser of two evils. *Galichanin* also

claimed that the Radicals were split, some standing with the Austrian Saint Rafael Society, which favoured emigration to Brazil, and others, like Franko, trying to redirect the movement northward. Perhaps religion played some role in this split, even among the generally anti-clerical Radicals. Brazil was supposedly Catholic, like Austria, while North America was predominantly Protestant.

34 In Kaye, *Early Ukrainian Settlements*, 91.

35 The proposal is given in full in Kaye, *Early Ukrainian Settlements*, 92, from a translation made at the time by the Canadian High Commission in London.

36 Ivan Franko, "Die Auswanderungsagenten in Galizien," in *Beiträge zur Geschichte und Kultur der Ukraine*, 326–31; and "Emihratsiini ahenty v Halychyni," *Tvory v dvatsiaty tomakh* 19:318–24.

37 Kaye, *Early Ukrainian Settlements*, 92–4. Badeni, as described by Kaye, *passim*, does not appear to have been a strong opponent of emigration, as long as it did not assume massive proportions. Murdzek, *Emigration in Polish Social-Political Thought*, 118ff, does not even mention Badeni in his chapter on imperial government policy, but establishes that, as emigrant savings began to flow back to the homeland, the price of land rose and the landowning gentry began to take a more favourable view of the movement.

38 Kaye, *Early Ukrainian Settlements*, 381. For a description of these first arrivals and the kinds of tools they brought, see Czumer, *Recollections*, 35–7, and the richly illustrated oral history by Zonia Keywan and Martin Coles, *Greater Than Kings* (Montreal: Harvest House, 1977), 13ff. Individual travellers were often not so well financed. It was necessary to show $25 in cash upon arrival in Halifax, and, at least on one occasion, three prospective immigrants had to combine their meagre resources, show the money to the immigration officer, and then hand it on secretly to each other as each one passed. See V. Trishchuk's memoir "Koby bida, a hroshi naidutsia," in J. B. Rudnyckyj, *Materiialy do Ukrainsko-kanadiiskoi folklorystyky i diialektolohii* (Winnipeg: UVAN, 1958), 3:393–4.

39 See Kaye, *Early Ukrainian Settlements*, 78–9, who also gives a short biography of Genyk on pp. 381–2. The most thorough study of Genyk is by the veteran Ukrainian Canadian Communist Petro Krawchuk, *Kanadskyi druh Ivana Franka* (Toronto: Kobzar, 1971). An example of Genyk as legend is his mention in immigrant folksongs. For a recorded sample sung by a surviving pioneer, see the collection of Robert B. Klymasz, *Introduction to the Ukrainian-Canadian Immigrant Folksong Cycle* (Ottawa: National Museum of Canada, 1970), and the accompanying audio recording, which is included in the bookend pocket.

40 In Kaye, *Early Ukrainian Settlements*, 362.
41 Johann Chmelar, "The Austrian Emigration, 1900–1914," *Perspectives in American History* 7 (1973): 275–8, esp. 318.
42 In Krawchuk, *Kanadskyi druh Ivana Franka*, 84. The letter is dated 18 September 1903. Presumably, Krawchuk discovered this document in the Franko archives in Kyiv.
43 Krawchuk, *Kanadskyi druh Ivana Franka*, 88.
44 Genyk's letter with Franko's commentary appeared in *Literaturno-naukovyi vistnyk* (Lviv, 1901): 8:18, and is reprinted by Krawchuk, *Kanadskyi druh Ivana Franka*, 102–3.
45 For a thorough but strictly Communist account of the Franko cult in Canada, see Petro Krawchuk, *Ivan Franko sered kanadskykh ukraintsiv* (Lviv: Kameniar, 1966), which should be compared with the mélange of non-Communist materials collected in *I. Franko i Frankiiana na zakhodi: statti i materiialy*, ed. J. B. Rudnyckyj (Winnipeg: UVAN, 1957). More recently, a major collection of Franko's prose fiction was published in Canada. See Ivan Franko, *Turbulent Times: A Trilogy*, trans. Roma Franko, 3 vols. (Toronto: Language Lanterns, 2006); and *idem, Behind Decorum's Veil*, trans. Roma Franko (Toronto: Language Lanterns, 2006).

4 A Polish Scholar

1 For references to some synthetic treatments, see note 1 to Chapter 1 in the present volume..
2 See Robert England, *The Central European Immigrant in Canada* (Toronto: Macmillan, 1928), and Charles H. Young, *The Ukrainian Canadians: A Study in Assimilation* (Toronto: Thomas Nelson, 1931).
3 Józef Okolowicz, *Wychodźstwo i osadnictwo polskie przed wojną swiatową* (Cracow: Nakladem urzędu emigracyjnego, 1920); Roman Mazurkiewicz, *Polskie wychodźstwo i osadnictwo w Kanadzie* (Warsaw: Nakladom naukowego instytutu emigracyjnego, 1929). (I was able to peruse these two volumes only in microform, and the second was missing the last chapters; that is, pp. 79ff.) The relative importance of Canada in the thinking of Okołowicz is revealed in the space accorded to it in his book: there are eight sections on the US, five on Brazil, three on Canada, and only one or two on most other countries.
4 Victor Turek, *Poles in Manitoba* (Toronto: Polish Research Institute, 1967); Paul Yuzyk, *The Ukrainians in Manitoba: A Social History* (Toronto: University of Toronto Press, 1953); Vladimir J. Kaye [Kysilewskyj], *Early Ukrainian*

Settlements in Canada 1895–1900: Dr. Josef Oleskow's Role in the Settlement of the Canadian Northwest (Toronto: University of Toronto Pre ss, 1964).

5 Henry Radecki and Benedykt Heydenkron, *Member of a Distinguished Family: The Polish Group in Canada* (Toronto: McClelland and Stewart, 1976); Manoly R. Lupul, ed., *A Heritage in Transition: Essays in the History of Ukrainians in Canada* (Toronto: McClelland and Stewart, 1982).

6 Aloysius Balawyder, *The Maple Leaf and the White Eagle: Polish-Canadian Relations, 1918–1978* (Boulder, CO: East European Monographs, 1980); Donald Avery, *"Dangerous Foreigners": European Immigrant Workers and Labour Radicalism in Canada, 1896–1932* (Toronto: McClelland and Stewart, 1979); Irving Abella and Harold Troper, *None Is Too Many: Canada and the Jews of Europe, 1933–1948* (Toronto: Lester and Orpen Dennys, 1982).

7 J. Matejko, "Kanadyjska polityka imigracyjna w stosunku do Polaków w latach 1896–1939," *Studia Polonijne* 3 (1979): 23–60.

8 Anna Reczyńska, *Emigracja z Polski do Kanady w okresie międzywojennym* (Wrocław: Ossolineum, 1986). An abridged translation of this work also exists: Anna Reczynska, *For Bread and a Better Future* (Toronto: Multicultural History Society of Ontario, 1996). All references in the present essay are to the fuller Polish edition. There is an unpublished study in English on a related subject: Myron Gulka-Tiechko, "Interwar Ukrainian Immigration to Canada, 1919–1939," MA thesis, University of Manitoba, 1983. A brief summary of this thesis has also been published as Myron Gulka-Tiechko, "Ukrainian Immigration to Canada under the Railways Agreement, 1925–30," *Journal of Ukrainian Studies* 16, nos. 1–2 (1991): 29–60, but all references in the present work are to the longer unpublished thesis. Finally, there is a major study in Ukrainian by S. P. Kacharaba, *Emihratsiia z zakhidnoi Ukrainy 1919–1939* (Lviv: Lvivskyi natsionalnyi universytet im. Ivana Franka, 2003). For the section on Canada, see 176–93.

9 Reczyńska, *Emigracja z Polski do Kanady*, 10, citing Mazurkiewicz, *Polskie wychodźstwo i osadnictwo w Kanadzie*, 3. Actually, the reference is to the preface of Mazurkiewicz's book, written by G. Załęcki. The author of these lines calls these Ukrainians "Rusini z Polski" (Ruthenians from Poland).

10 Mazurkiewicz, *Polskie wychodźstwo i osadnictwo w Kanadzie*, 70, readily admitted that, before 1914, illiteracy had been a very real problem among the immigrants. Even in 1921, he maintained, 20 per cent of people "from Poland" were illiterate. Among "Ruthenians," the problem supposedly was worse, at that time reaching, he estimated, 30 to 40 per cent.

11 Gulka-Tiechko, "Interwar Ukrainian Immigration to Canada," 304, puts it somewhat differently. He writes that this migration was made up primarily

of "agricultural labourers" and domestics, who were not necessarily homesteaders or independent farmers, although some entire families (more
likely to become homesteaders) immigrated and also some dependents of
men who had come earlier, during the pre-1914 era.

12 See, in particular, Stella Hryniuk, *Peasants with Promise: Ukrainians in
Southeastern Galicia 1880–1900* (Edmonton: Canadian Institute of Ukrainian
Studies, 1991). The endpapers to this book contain a detailed map of this
area showing almost all the individual villages that existed there c. 1900.
Hryniuk also published this map separately in full colour (Winnipeg, 1991),
but I did not consult it for this writing. For a very interesting "Guidebook"
to this same area, which was first published during the interwar period and
contains much historical information on the individual villages from which
these immigrants to Canada came, see *Przewodnik po Województwie
Tarnopolskiem z mapą* (Ternopil: Nakladem Wojewódzkiego Towarzystwa
Turystyczno-krajoznawczego, 1928; reprinted in the 1990s). But the map
accompanying this Polish publication is inferior in detail and clarity to the
Hryniuk map.

13 See, in particular, Avery, "Dangerous Foreigners," 90–115, and Vadim
Kukushkin, *From Peasants to Labourers: Ukrainian and Belarusan Immigration
from the Russian Empire to Canada* (Montreal and Kingston: McGill-Queen's
University Press, 2007), 93–117.

14 Caro's most important book in this regard (not seen by me in the original)
was *Emigracja i polityka emigracyjna ze szczególnym uzględieniem stosunków polskich*
(Poznan: Ksieg. Sw. Wojciecha, 1914). According to Reczyńska, *Emigracja z
Polski do Kanady,* 100, Oleskiv's Canadian project, which, it seems, ran counter
to a Polish scheme to build a "New Poland" in Latin America, specifically
Brazil, was criticized at the time not only by Polish publicists in Europe, but
also by Polish newspapers in the United States. As one example of anti-
Oleskiv criticism, she cites J. Siemiradzki, "Pare słów pod adresem dra
Oleskowa i jego kanadyjskich projektów," *Przewodnik Handlowo-Geograficzny,*
no. 10, 1895, 73. On Ukrainian immigration to South America more gener-
ally, see *Ukraintsi Brazylii,* ed. Andriy Nahachewsky and Maryna Hrymych
(Kyiv: Duliby, 2011), and Serge Cipko, *Ukrainians in Argentina 1897–1950:
The Making of a Community* (Edmonton, Toronto: Canadian Institute of
Ukrainian Studies Press and the Shevchenko Scientific Society, 2011).

15 See also Radecki and Heydenkorn, *Member of a Distinguished Family,* 113, and
Benedykt Heydenkorn, *The Organizational Structure of the Polish Canadian
Community* (Toronto: Polish Research Institute, 1979), 33.

16 Compare Avery, *"Dangerous Foreigners,"* 90, 101–2; Balawyder, *Maple Leaf and
White Eagle,* 4–9; and Kacharaba, *Emihratsiia z zakhidnoi Ukrainy,* 193.

Kacharaba, who, of course, is concerned only with those Polish provinces that later entered the Ukrainian SSR, lists a total of 79,480 such "Polish" emigrants of all nationalities to Canada for the period from 1926 to 1938. According to Gulka-Tiechko, "Ukrainian Interwar Immigration to Canada," 8, some 55,000 Ukrainians from Poland entered Canada under the railway agreement. Gulka-Tiechko was the first Ukrainian Canadian scholar to stress the importance of the railway agreement.

17 Personal communication from the late Professor Bohdan Budurowycz of the University of Toronto, formerly of Ternopil, eastern Galicia, who recalled these verses and their origin over half a century later, and translated them for use in this paper. The manuscript of the communication in the hand of Professor Budurowycz is in the author's archive, Toronto. I have not tried to verify the text in *Komar*, which was published in Lviv from 1933 to 1939.

18 Victor Turek, author of the pioneering study *Poles in Manitoba*, was a post-1945 immigrant to Canada who was profoundly impressed by the then-existing good relations between Poles and Ukrainians on the Prairies, and commented extensively on what he called "the amazing linguistic assimilation of the Polish group to the Ukrainian" (65), and the "Ukrainization or de-nationalization of the Polish ethnic group by the Ukrainian majority" (66). For Edward Kołodziej's remark, see his *Dzieje Polonii w zarysie 1918–1939* (Warsaw: Książka i Wiedza, 1991), 237. For an example of Polish diplomatic intervention against Ukrainian nationalists in Canada, see the introductory chapter of my *Maple Leaf and Trident: The Ukrainian Canadians during the Second World War* (Toronto: Multicultural History Society of Ontario, 1988), 21–2. Also see Andrzej A. Zięba, *Ukraińcy w Kanadzie wobec Polaków i Polski 1914–1939* (Cracow: Instytut polonijny, 1998), which, however, says more about how Ukrainian Canadians viewed Poland than about how the Polish government viewed Ukrainian Canadians.

5 Dmytro Doroshenko and Canada

1 For general introductions to Doroshenko and his work, see Thomas M. Prymak, "Dmytro Doroshenko: A Ukrainian Émigré Historian of the Interwar Period," *Harvard Ukrainian Studies* 25, nos. 1–2 (2001): 31–56, and Lubomyr Wynar [Liubomyr Vynar], "Dmytro Ivanovych Doroshenko: Zhyttia i diialnist (u 50-littia smerty)," *Ukrainskyi istoryk* 38, nos. 1–4 (2001): 9–67, which give further references. The original version of this article was dedicated to my mentor and friend of many years, the late Bohdan Budurowycz, Professor Emeritus of Slavic Languages and Literatures,

University of Toronto, on the occasion of the sixtieth anniversary of his emigration from Ternopil, western Ukraine, to western Europe and then Manitoba, 1944–2004.

2 For some general treatments of the early history of the Ukrainian Canadians, see Orest Martynowych, *Ukrainians in Canada: The Formative Years 1891–1924* (Edmonton: Canadian Institute of Ukrainian Studies, 1991); Jaroslav Petryshyn, *Peasants in the Promised Land: Canada and the Ukrainians 1891–1914* (Toronto: Lorimer, 1985); and the relevant chapters of *A Heritage in Transition: Essays on the History of Ukrainians in Canada*, ed. Manoly R. Lupul (Toronto: McClelland and Stewart, 1982). For a general encyclopedic-style work on all periods of Ukrainian Canadian history, see M. H. Marunchak, *The Ukrainian Canadians: A History* (Winnipeg and Ottawa: Ukrainian Academy of Arts and Sciences in Canada, 1970).

3 M. Zabarevsky, "V. Lypynsky i ioho 'Lysty do brativ-khliborobiv'," *Ukrainskyi holos* (Winnipeg), nos. 35–41, 27 Aug.–8 Oct. 1924. For a list of Doroshenko's publications from this period, see *Bibliohrafiia prats Prof. D. Doroshenka za 1899–1942 roky* (Prague: Vydavnytstvo T. Tyshchenka, 1942), esp. 31. For a bibliography of his later publications, see Hryhorii Kuras, "Do prodovzhennia bibliohrafii Dmytra Doroshenka (1942–2006)," in *Visti UVAN* (New York, 2007), 4:255–79.

4 The Doroshenko–Stechishin correspondence is in the Julian Stechishin Papers, vol. 8, file 41, MG30 D307, National Archives of Canada, Ottawa. On Stechishin more generally, see Hryhory Udod, *Julian W. Stechishin: His Life and Work* (Saskatoon: Mohyla Institute, 1978).

5 Prof. D. Doroshenko, "From Short Course of the History of Ukraine. Ukrainiana," *Kanadiiskyi farmer*, no. 101, 13 September 1929, 14–15; *idem*, "Moi spomyny pro nedavne-mynule (1914–1918) ... Drukuietsia z tekstu, avtorom nanovo perehlianutoho i vypravlenoho," ibid., nos. 26–52 (1934) and nos. 1–43 (1935), listed in *Bibliohrafiia Prats Prof. D. Doroshenka za 1899–1942 roky*, 34, 39, and 40. This corrected text of Doroshenko's revolutionary memoirs has, to my knowledge, never been reprinted. The Munich reprint of 1969 is based on the original uncorrected Lviv edition (1923).

6 Olha Woycenko, letter of 1 February 1986 to the author (hereafter, Woycenko, letter). On Lazarowich more generally, see the article on him in Mykhailo H. Marunchak, *Biohrafichnyi dovidnyk do istorii ukraintsiv Kanady* (Winnipeg: Ukrainska vilna akademiia nauk, 1986), 376.

7 For a general introduction to the USRL, which stresses its liberal position in Canadian politics, see Oleh Gerus, "Consolidating the Community: The Ukrainian Self-Reliance League," in *Canada's Ukrainians: Negotiating an*

Identity, ed. Lubomyr Y. Luciuk and Stella M. Hryniuk (Toronto: University of Toronto Press, 1991), 157–86.

8 Woycenko, letter. Also see the brief remarks of Lazarowich himself in his pamphlet, *Soiuz ukraintsiv samostiinykiv i ukrainska vyzvolna sprava* (Winnipeg: SUS, 1951).

9 Dmytro Burim, "Varshavskyi period zhyttia i diialnosty D. I. Doroshenka (1936–1939)," in *Naukovi zapysky: Zbirnyk prats molodykh vchenykh ta aspirantiv* (Kyiv: Institut ukrainskoi arkheohrafii ta dzhereloznavstva im. M. S. Hrushevskoho, 1999), 4:283–96.

10 "Po vidizdi Profesora Doroshenka," *Ukrainskyi holos* (Winnipeg), no. 38, 29 Sept. 1937. Olha Woycenko [Olha Voitsenko], *Litopys ukrainskoho zhyttia v Kanadi,* 8 vols. (Winnipeg: Tryzub, 1961–92), 4:360, identifies the author of this piece as the Rev Ye. Hrycena (Ieronym Hrytsyna). The press did, however, make a few observations on the visit with which Hrycena took some offence. For example, I. Esaiw, the editor of Edmonton's Catholic *Ukrainski visti* (The Ukrainian news), noted that the idea of bringing Doroshenko to Canada was hardly new since as early as 1930 he had discussed the matter with the prominent Ukrainian Canadian intellectual and supporter of the monarchist idea, Orest Zerebko; Hrycena replied that it was only the USRL that had dared to finance the venture and actually brought it to fruition. *Ukrainski visti* also observed that Doroshenko had been surprised to discover on arriving in Canada that the Mohyla Institute was not a scholarly research institution but merely an ordinary student residence (*zvychaina bursa*); Hrycena retorted that this was so but that Doroshenko had taken no offence by this fact and that his trip had gone very smoothly.

11 Burim, "Varshavskyi period," 289–90, gives a brief outline of this first tour. As well, see Woycenko, *Litopys,* 4:340, 354–56, 358, 360, which summarizes the reports in *Ukrainskyi holos.* For the original report on the unexpected success of the Edmonton history course, see "Nespodivanyi uspikh kursiv Prof. D. Doroshenka v Edmontoni," *Ukrainskyi holos* (Winnipeg), 28 July 1937.

12 Dmytro Doroshenko, letter of 24 Nov. 1937 to Doris Yanda, in Doris Yanda Papers, vol. 2, file 11, MG30 D393, National Archives of Canada, Ottawa. I am indebted to Professor Bohdan Budurowycz of Toronto for helping me to decipher Doroshenko's handwriting in this letter.

13 *Idem,* letter of 23 Dec. 1937, in ibid. The full Ukrainian-language texts of the Doroshenko–Yanda correspondence are also available as: Tomas Pryimak [Thomas M. Prymak] and Nadiia Zavorotna, "Lystuvannia Dmytra Doroshenka z Doris Iandoiu," *Ukrainskyi istoryk* 43, nos. 1–3 (2006): 211–27.

14 "Ukrainske zhyttia v Kanadi pulsuie zhyvym rytmom: Interviu z Prof. Dmytrom Doroshenkom," *Dilo* (Lviv), 3 Oct. 1937, and Voitsenko [Woycenko], *Litopys*, 4:364.

15 Dmytro Doroshenko, letter of 30 Dec. 1937 to Liudmyla Kraskovska, in Mykola Mushynka, "Edmonton 1937 roku ochyma Dmytra Doroshenka," in *Zakhidnokanadskyi zbirnyk*, ed. Mykola Soroka (Edmonton, Ostroh, 2008), 5:496–501. I am indebted to Roman Senkus of the Canadian Institute of Ukrainian Studies Press, Toronto, for this reference.

16 Burim, "Varshavskyi period," 289–90; Voitsenko, *Litopys*, 4:390–4.

17 Woycenko, letter.

18 Ibid. Also see chapter 7 in the present volume.

19 See Thomas M. Prymak, *Maple Leaf and Trident: The Ukrainian Canadians During the Second World War* (Toronto: Multicultural History Society of Ontario, 1988), Appendix E: "Ukrainian History and the War," 144–9, and chapter 6 in the present volume.

20 Dmytro Doroschenko, "Die ukrainische ostliche-orthodox Kirche in Kanada und in den Vereinigten Staaten von Amerika," *Kyrios* 1–2 (1940): 153–7.

21 Dmytro Doroschenko, "Die Ukrainer in Kanada," *Volksforschung* 5, nos. 2–3 (1942): 179–87.

22 By "English" [*Engländern*], Doroshenko evidently meant the various groups originating in the British Isles: English, Scots, Irish, and Welsh. If these groups were counted separately, then the Ukrainians of the time would have fallen below fourth place in the census of 1936; that is, to sixth place behind the Scots and the Irish, but before the Welsh and all others. Borys Myhal, "Ethnicity and Ethnic Origins," in *A Statistical Compendium on the Ukrainians in Canada 1891–1976*, ed. William Darcovich and Paul Yuzyk (Ottawa: University of Ottawa Press, 1980), 21, writes: "Response from the field in the 1921, 1926, and 1931 censuses continued to provide the Galician, Bukovinian, Ruthenian, and Ukrainian designations, though by 1931 the numbers of the first three had fallen to insignificance.... Starting in 1936 only the Ukrainian was reported." The census of 1931 listed 225,113 Ukrainians in Canada (ibid., 26).

23 In fact, mass Ukrainian immigration to Canada began only in the mid-1890s; that is, at least a decade later than to the United States.

24 Doroschenko, "Die Ukrainer in Kanada," 183.

25 For a more detailed description of these organizations on the eve of the war, and their political orientations, see Prymak, *Maple Leaf and Trident*, 16–33. In terms of actual size, the pro-Communist ULFTA (*tovarystvo Ukrainskyi robitnycho-farmerskyi dim*) was by far the largest and most important Ukrainian secular organization in the country, followed by the liberal

democratic USRL, then the revolutionary nationalist/rightist UNF (*Ukrainske natsionalne ob'iednannia*), and only lastly by the pro-German but traditionally conservative UHO. After the pro-Communists, the USRL was stronger in western Canada and the UNF stronger in the East (personal communication from Orest Martynowych of Winnipeg).

26 Much of the correspondence concerning Doroshenko's possible admission to Canada in 1945, including his handwritten letter in English to Simpson, is in the George Simpson Papers, Ukrainian files, 1945–49, University of Saskatchewan Archives, Saskatoon. A portion of this material is summarized in Chapter 7 of the present volume.

27 At a conference on Ukrainian DPs sponsored by the Multicultural History Society of Ontario (held in Toronto in the mid-1980s), one of these DPs, a member of the audience, publicly thanked one of these servicemen, Bohdan Panchuk, on behalf of Doroshenko. More generally, see Bohdan Panchuk, *Heroes of their Day: The Reminiscences of Bohdan Panchuk*, ed. Lubomyr Y. Luciuk (Toronto: Multicultural History Society of Ontario, 1983). During this confused initial period of occupation, Panchuk and his colleagues roamed western Germany, distributing homemade identification cards in English to Ukrainian DPs; these cards stated that the bearers were under the protection of Panchuk's organization, the London-based Ukrainian Canadian Servicemen's Association. On numerous occasions, it seems, this simple tactic saved otherwise documentless refugees from forcible deportation east. For Krupnytsky's remarks, see his "Dmytro Doroshenko: Spohady uchnia," in *Naukovyi zbirnyk* (New York: Ukrainian Academy of Arts and Sciences in the United States, 1952), 1:20–1.

28 Nataliia Doroshenko, "Uryvky spomyniv," in *Ukrainskyi litopys* (Augsburg, 1953), 1:139–51, esp. 147. The author of this memoir was Doroshenko's wife.

29 Quoted in Wynar, "Dmytro Doroshenko," 51. As early as March 1947, Doroshenko had informed the UVAN administration of his plan to go to Canada and had begun making arrangements to transfer the institution to the North American Dominion.

30 See Woycenko's covering note in the Olha Woycenko Collection, vol. 23, file 12, Doroshenko, 1937–49, MG30 D212, National Archives of Canada, Ottawa (hereafter, Woycenko, covering note). Also see Voitsenko, *Litopys*, 5:304.

31 Information from the Saint Andrew's College academic calendar for 1948–9, and from Oleh Krawchenko, Winnipeg, who at that time was a student of Doroshenko's. I am indebted to Raisa Moroz, formerly librarian at the college, for conveying this information to me. Also see Voitsenko, *Litopys*, 5:307.

32 Ivan Krypiakevych and Mykloa Holubets, *Velyka istoriia Ukrainy*, 2nd ed., with
additional material by Dmytro Doroshenko (Winnipeg: Ivan Tyktor, 1948).
In this volume, Doroshenko, for the first time, had an opportunity to
describe both Polish oppression of the western Ukrainians between the
wars, a phenomenon he had been compelled to gloss over in his previous
work published while he was a professor at the University of Warsaw, and
Nazi ravages in Ukraine from 1941 to 1944, which he obviously could not
discuss in his previous *Istoriia Ukrainy z maliunkamy dlia shkoly i rodyny*
(Cracow, 1940; repr. New York: Bulava, 1957). As well, in this *Velyka istoriia
Ukrainy*, he described the ukrainianization program in Soviet Ukraine in the
1920s and the recurrent purges of the 1930s. Amazingly, however, unlike in
his previous English-language *History of the Ukraine*, in this volume he made
no mention of the Great Famine of 1932–3 in which, it is generally agreed,
millions perished.

33 According to the Finding Aid to the Paul Yuzyk Collection, the card file of
this bibliography is preserved in the National Archives of Canada, Yuzyk
Papers, MG32 C67, vol. 6, file 7.

34 *Propamiatna knyha Ukrainskoho Narodnoho Domu u Vinipegu*, ed. Dmytro
Doroshenko (Winnipeg: Ukrainskyi narodnyi dim, 1949). This volume also
contains a brief memoir about Doroshenko's first visits to Canada: "Z moikh
spohadiv pro podorozh do Kanady v 1937–1938 rokakh," 551–60.

35 Dmytro Doroshenko, *Moi spomyny pro davnie-mynule (1901–1914 roky)*
(Winnipeg: Tryzub, 1949). On the title page of a copy of this volume
(a photocopy of which is preserved in the Olha Woycenko papers),
Doroshenko inscribed the following dedication in Ukrainian: "To the
very honoured [*vysokopovazhnii*] and dear Mrs. Olha Woycenko, on whose
initiative and with whose help this book was published. I am very thankful.
The author. Winnipeg, 24, V, 1949." Woycenko added some marginalia
noting that the book was written in a "few weeks time," solely from memory
only a few months after the historian's arrival in Canada, and was first
published serially in *Ukrainskyi holos*. See the Olha Woycenko Collection,
MG30 D212, vol. 23, file 12, Doroshenko, 1937–49.

36 Dmytro Doroshenko, *Korotkyi narys istorii khrystianskoi tserkvy* (Winnipeg:
Eklesia, 1949); *idem, Pravoslavna tserkva v mynulomu i suchasnomu* (Berlin,
1940; repr. Winnipeg ?, n.d.). It is unclear to me whether the second of
these works was reprinted before or after Doroshenko's death.

37 Nataliia Doroshenko, "Uryvky spomyniv," 148.

38 Information from Bohdan Budurowycz, Toronto. Shortly afterward,
Malaniuk was successful in immigrating to the United States and settled
in New York.

39 Woycenko, letter. Also see Vynar, "Dmytro Ivanovych Doroshenko," 52.
40 See "Ukrainian Academy of Arts and Sciences," in *Encyclopedia of Ukraine* (Toronto: University of Toronto Press, 1993), 5:347–8; Ya. Rudnytsky [J.B. Rudnyckyj], "Ukrainska vilna akademiia nauk u Kanadi: Pochatkovyi period, roky 1949–1955," in *Zhyttievyi dosvid ukraintsiv u Kanadi: Reflksii/The Ukrainian Experience in Canada: Reflections*, ed. Oleh W. Gerus et al. (Winnipeg: Ukrainian Academy of Arts and Sciences in Canada, 1994), 163–72.
41 Quoted in Vynar, "Dmytro Ivanovych Doroshenko," 52.
42 Woycenko, covering note.
43 Nataliia Doroshenko, "Uryvky spomyniv," 147–8. Oleh Gerus, letter of 13 February 2000 to the author (hereafter, Gerus, letter), also notes the bouts of depression. Gerus seems to have got this information from Sawchuk, whom he interviewed in the early 1970s, in connection with a new edition of Doroshenko's *History of the Ukraine*. Gerus re-edited and updated this book under the more accurate title *A Survey of Ukrainian History* (Winnipeg: Humeniuk Publication Foundation, 1975; repr. 1980).
44 See Nataliia Doroshenko, "Uryvky spomyniv"; also see Woycenko, covering note. Woycenko even held Sawchuk, of whom she had a very low opinion, responsible for Doroshenko's premature death. On Ohienko's dispute with Sawchuk and his group, see Paul Yuzyk, *The Ukrainian Greek Orthodox Church of Canada* (Ottawa: University of Ottawa Press, 1981), 191. This dispute was later resolved and Ohienko was eventually elected Metropolitan of the Church, taking the name Metropolitan Ilarion. Gerus, letter, does not believe that Sawchuk was vindictive toward Doroshenko. He writes: "It seems that Doroshenko was a victim of circumstance and indifference rather than of ill will." On Sawchuk more generally, see Oleh Gerus, "The Reverend Semen Sawchuk and the Ukrainian Greek Orthodox Church of Canada," *Journal of Ukrainian Studies* 16, nos. 1–2 (1991): 61–88.
45 Olha Woycenko, marginalia and letter of 23 October 1949 to P. Lazarowich, Olha Woycenko Collection, vol. 23, file 13, Jubilee Committee, 1949, MG 30 D212, National Archives of Canada, Ottawa. Also see "Vshanuvaly Prof. Doroshenka," *Ukrainskyi holos* (Winnipeg), no. 42, 19 Oct. 1949, which reports that at the Saint Andrew's gathering, Sawchuk wished Doroshenko a quick recovery from his health problems, and it was noted that the throat ailment did not allow the professor to continue his lectures.
46 Woycenko, covering note. See also Leonid Biletsky, *Dmytro Doroshenko* (Winnipeg: UVAN, 1949). This pamphlet was the first in the UVAN series *Ukrainski vcheni*.
47 Nataliia Doroshenko-Savchenko, "Dmytro Ivanovych Doroshenko: Z nahody 5-richchia smerty," *Svoboda* (New York), 2 May 1956. The author of this

memoir was not Doroshenko's wife but, rather, another relative with the same first name.

48 See "Liudy i spletni," *Ukrainskyi holos* (Winnipeg), no. 40, 4 Oct. 1950, citing *Ukrainski visti* (Edmonton) 15 August 1950, and quoting from *Novyi shliakh* (Winnipeg), no. 59, 1950.

49 S. Nahai, "Khronolohichnyi pokazhchyk vazhlyvishykh podiiakh z zhyttia D. I. Doroshenka," in *Ukrainskyi litopys* (Augsburg, 1953), 1:18; Nataliia Doroshenko, "Uryvky spomyniv"; *Ukrainskyi holos* (Winnipeg), no. 13, 28 March 1951, announced the death of Doroshenko on its front page, and in no.14, April 4, ran an obituary by Leonid Biletsky, which stated that "this news passed through Winnipeg like a bolt of electricity and shook all Ukrainian society."

50 Nataliia Doroshenko, "Uryvky spomyniv," 151.

6 General Histories of Ukraine

1 This essay is a slightly revised version of a paper that was first published in the English language in the bilingual (Russian/English) journal *Ab Imperio* 2 (2003): 455–76. A Ukrainian translation under the title "Zahalni istorii Ukrainy drukovani anhliiskoiu movoiu pid chas Druhoi Svitovoi Viiny" appeared in *Ukrainskyi istoryk*, 44–45 (2007–2008): 168–86. I also made some introductory remarks on this subject in my book *Maple Leaf and Trident: The Ukrainian Canadians during the Second World War* (Toronto: Multicultural History Society of Ontario, 1988). See especially Appendix E: "Ukrainian History and the War," 144–9.

2 Some of the most important scholars were R. Nisbet Bain (1854–1909), who worked in both Russian and Polish history; W. R. Morfill (1834–1909), who also worked primarily in Russian and Polish history; and Sir Bernard Pares (1867–1949), who was primarily a "Russianist." Pares had begun his career prior to 1939, but reached full maturity as a scholar between the wars.

3 Perhaps the most significant pre-1939 pamphlet to treat Ukrainian history was published during the First World War; it was authored by the distinguished Ukrainian historian and national leader, the author of a multivolume history of his country, Mykhailo Hrushevsky (1866–1934). See his *The Historical Evolution of the Ukrainian Problem* (London: Published in English for the SVU, 1915; repr. Cleveland: John T. Zubal, 1981). This work surveyed Ukrainian history from its origins in Kyivan Rus' through Cossackdom to modern times and provided a general framework for a national interpretation of the history of the country. It was translated into English by George Raffalovich (Bedwin Sands), a Ukrainian propagandist of Jewish background

active in England during this first war. The title page indicates that the SVU (*Soiuz vyzvolennia Ukrainy*) (League for the Liberation of Ukraine) sponsored the publication. For a general bibliography of pre-1936 English-language imprints about Ukraine, see V. J. Kaye-Kysilewsky [Kysilewskyj], *Ukraine, Russia, and Other Slavic Countries in English Literature … 1912–1936*, in the series *Slavistica*, no. 40 (Winnipeg: UVAN, 1961).

4 Pierre Bregy and Prince Serge Obolensky, *The Ukraine: A Russian Land*, trans. George Knupfer (London: Selwyn and Blount, 1940). I consulted this book over twenty-five years ago and summarized it in my *Maple Leaf and Trident*, 146. The information given here is based on that summary.

5 Hugh P. Vowles, *Ukraine and Its People: The Essential Background of One of Europe's Vital Problems* (London: W. and R. Chambers, 1939).

6 C. Milnes Gaskell, "A Submerged Nation: The Ukrainian Case," typescript, author's archive, Toronto. There are six pages missing from this copy of the ms. On the reasons why this book was never published, see my *Maple Leaf and Trident*, 146–47.

7 W. E. D. Allen, *The Ukraine: A History* (Cambridge: Cambridge University Press, 1940; repr. New York: Russell and Russell, 1963).

8 One of Allen's unnamed "collaborators" was George Vernadsky (1887–1973) of Yale University, who was one of the most prominent historians of Russia working in the United States prior to 1939. Vernadsky was of Ukrainian origin but generally accepted the traditional scheme of Russian history, with modifications along "Eurasian" lines. It is unclear to me whether Allen considered Vernadsky to be "Russian" or "Ukrainian" or perhaps both at the same time. Over thirty years ago, I had the opportunity to examine the correspondence between them in the George Vernadsky Papers, Bakhmeteff Archive, Columbia University Library, New York. As to Allen himself, he had some very conservative views and sympathized with at least one radical rightist organization in pre-war Britain. See Alastair Hamilton, *The Appeal of Fascism: A Study of British Intellectuals and Fascism* (London: Blond, 1971), 297.

9 B. H. Sumner in *English Historical Review* 57, no. 226 (1942): 264–67.

10 Harold R. Weinstein in *American Historical Review* 47, no. 3 (1942): 255–56.

11 A few years later, Frederiksen also wrote the chapter "The Ukraine" for *A Handbook of Slavic Studies*, ed. Leonid I. Strakhovsky (Cambridge, MA: Harvard University Press, 1949), 346–66, and contributed articles on Ukrainian subjects to the *Slavonic Encyclopaedia*, ed. J. Roucek (New York: Philosophical Library, 1949).

12 First published in Ukrainian in 1911, this work was reprinted many times in Ukrainian before and during the revolution. At that time, it was also

translated into, and published, in Russian. Long proscribed in the USSR, it once again appeared in print in both Ukrainian and Russian editions during and after the Gorbachev reforms. For a bibliography of Hrushevsky's works, which lists the earlier editions, see Lubomyr R. Wynar, *Mykhailo Hrushevs'kyi 1866–1934: Bibliographic Sources* (New York, Munich, Toronto: Ukrainian Historical Association, 1985). On Hrushevsky more generally, see my *Mykhailo Hrushevsky: The Politics of National Culture* (Toronto: University of Toronto Press, 1987), and Serhii Plokhy, *Unmaking Imperial Russia: Mykhailo Hrushevsky and the Writing of Ukrainian History* (Toronto: University of Toronto Press, 2005).

13 On Vernadsky and the Ukrainians, see Charles J. Halperin, "Russia and the Steppe: George Vernadsky and Eurasianism," *Forschungen zur osteuropäischen Geschichte* 36 (1985): 159–63, and Ernest Gyidel, "Ob 'Ukrainofilstve' Georgiia Vernadskogo, ili variatsiia na temu natsional'nykh i gosudarstvennykh loial'nostei," *Ab imperio* 4 (2006): 329–69, esp. the Appendix, which includes his 1940 letter to Luke Myshuha, editor of New York's Ukrainian newspaper *Svoboda,* where he explains to him "*Povazhaiu sebe za ukraintsia ta rus'koho odnochasno* (I consider myself to be Ukrainian and Russian at the same time)." Also see Igor Torbakov, *Rethinking the Nation: Imperial Collapse, Eurasianism, and George Vernadsky's Historical scholarship,* Occasional Paper, no. 302 (Washington: Woodrow Wilson Center, 2008), which devotes considerable attention to Vernadsky's Ukrainian family background.

14 Michael Hrushevsky, *A History of Ukraine,* ed. O. J. Frederiksen (New Haven: Yale University Press, 1941).

15 Dmytro Doroshenko, *History of the Ukraine,* trans. Hanna Chikalenko-Keller, ed. G. W. Simpson (Edmonton: The Institute Press, 1939; repr. 1940). On Simpson, see my "George Simpson, the Ukrainian Canadians, and the 'Pre-history' of Slavic Studies in Canada," *Saskatchewan History* XLI, no. 2 (1988): 52–66; revised edition printed in this volume. Many years later, Oleh Gerus of the University of Manitoba revised and updated Simpson's edition of Doroshenko and published it under the more exact title *A Survey of Ukrainian History* (Winnipeg: Trident Press, 1975; repr. 1980).

16 On Doroshenko, see Lubomyr Wynar [Liubomyr Vynar], "Dmytro Ivanovych Doroshenko: Zhyttia i diialnist (u 50-littia smerty)," *Ukrainskyi istoryk* 37, nos. 1–4 (2001): 9–67, which gives further references. Also see my synthetic essay "Dmytro Doroshenko: A Ukrainian Emigre Historian of the Inter-war Period," *Harvard Ukrainian Studies* 25, nos. 1–2 (2001): 31–56.

17 Simpson returned to these themes in separate publications. See his *Ukraine: A Series of Maps and Explanations Indicating the Historic and Contemporary Geographical Position of the Ukrainian People* (London: Oxford University

Press, 1941), and his "The Names 'Rus' and 'Ukraine' and Their Historical Background," *Slavistica*, no. 10 (Winnipeg: UVAN, 1951).

18 Alfred A. Skerpan in *Journal of Modern History* 14, no. 1 (1942): 92–95.

19 John Shelton Curtiss in *American Historical Review* 48, no. 2 (1943): 316–17.

20 Michael T. Florinsky in *Russian Review* 1, no. 1 (1941): 109–10.

21 George W. Simpson in *Journal of Central European Affairs* 2, no. 1 (1942–43): 94–97.

22 Stuart R. Tompkins in *Journal of Central European Affairs* 1, no. 1 (1941): 104–5. More general reviews appeared in Ukrainian magazines and at least one major Canadian newspaper. See, for example, Roman Lapica, "Doroshenko's History of Ukraine," *The Trident* 4, no. 4 (1940): 39–41, and Watson Kirkconnell, "The Ukrainian Nation," *The Tribune* (Winnipeg), 3 Feb. 1940.

23 The term "Ruthenian" is used by Frank E. Sysyn, *Between Poland and the Ukraine: The Dilemma of Adam Kysil* (Cambridge, MA: Harvard Ukrainian Research Institute, 1985); the term "Rus'ian" by Nicholas L. Chirovsky, *Introduction to Ukrainian History*, 3 vols. (New York: Philosophical Library, 1981–6); and the term "Ukrainian" by Orest Subtelny, *Ukraine: A History* (Toronto: University of Toronto Press, 1988).

24 Paul Robert Magocsi, *A History of Ukraine* (Toronto: University of Toronto Press, 1996), esp. 67–8.

25 *A Handbook of Slavic Studies*, ed. Leonid I. Strakhovsky (Cambridge, MA: Harvard University Press, 1949), xviii–xix. "Allen is remote and aloof, an Englishman looking from the calm heights of an ancient empire upon the petty struggles of a little Eastern European people, and finding the picture sordid at best. He is anti-Russian, anti-Polish, and anti-Ukrainian, and to him the struggle for independence is a curious anachronism in the modern world, fascinating to observe, but to be pitied rather than praised."

26 William Henry Chamberlin, *The Ukraine: A Submerged Nation* (New York: Macmillan, 1944). This work was positively reviewed by Simpson in the *Journal of Central European Affairs* 5, no. 2 (1945); by C. H. Andrusyshen in the *American Slavic and East European Review* 4, nos. 1–2 (1945): 210–13; by O. J. Frederiksen in the *Russian Review* 4, no. 2 (1945): 97–9; and by Longin Cehelsky in the *Ukrainian Quarterly* 1, no. 2 (1944): 181–3. All the reviewers cited here were skeptical about Chamberlin's hopeful musings.

27 The book in question was the general history of Ukraine published in Ufa in 1942 by the Ukrainian Academy of Sciences. It was quickly reprinted by a group of Ukrainian pro-Communists in Canada. See *Narys istorii Ukrainy*, ed. K. Huslysty and others (n.p.: Nakladom Ukrainskoho Zhyttia, 1944). The original was reviewed favourably by George Vernadsky in the *American Historical Review* 49, no. 3 (1944): 470–1; to the 1980s, the only example of

which I am aware of a major history in the Ukrainian language being reviewed in this journal. It was less favourably reviewed by O. J. Frederiksen in the *American Slavic and East European Review* 4, nos. 3–4 (1945): 220–2, and by N. D. Czubaty in the *Ukrainian Quarterly* 1, no. 3 (1944–5): 291–3, who pointed out that wartime pressures forced the Soviet regime to make these concessions to Ukrainian national sentiment.

7 George W. Simpson

1 "In memoriam: Professor George Wilfred Simpson, 1893–1969," *Canadian Slavonic Papers* 11 (1969): 1. The original version of this paper was dedicated to Professor Peter Brock (1920–2006) of the University of Toronto, who was my doctoral thesis supervisor (1980 to 1984). Since it first appeared, a study incorporating some new archival materials unavailable to me was published by Viktor O. Buiniak [Buyniak], "Profesor Dzhordzh Sympson: Pryiatel Ukraintsiv," in *Zakhidnokanadskyi zbirnyk*, ed. Iar Slavutych (Edmonton: Naukove tovarystvo im. Shevchenka, 2000), 4:230–44. Buyniak also authored a brief article on Simpson for the *Encyclopedia of Saskatchewan* (Regina: Canadian Plains Research Center, 2005), 862.

2 "In memoriam," *Canadian Slavonic Papers.*

3 See "The Problem of the Ethnic Name," in Vladimir J. Kaye [Kysilewskyj], *Early Ukrainian Settlements in Canada 1895–1900: Dr Josef Oleskow's Role in the Settlement of the Canadian Northwest* (Toronto: University of Toronto Press, 1964), xxiii–xxvi, and Nestor Makuch, "The Influence of the Ukrainian Revolution on Ukrainians in Canada, 1917–1922," *Journal of Ukrainian Graduate Studies* 6 (1979): 42–61.

4 George Simpson, "Memorandum on Ukrainian Files," University of Saskatchewan Archives, George Simpson Papers, Ukrainian files, vol. 1.

5 Ibid. Oleh Gerus of the University of Manitoba informs me that, in the 1960s, he heard Simpson deliver a Ukrainian-language speech before the Ukrainian Students Club on the Manitoba campus but that, on that occasion at least, Simpson's Ukrainian was far from fluent. However, the very fact that he made the effort to speak the Ukrainian language, which was at that time still not the official language of any sovereign state, is remarkable.

6 Interview with Savella Stechishin, Saskatoon, April 1985. On Stechishin, see Hryhory Udod, *Julian W. Stechishin: His Life and Work* (Saskatoon: Mohyla Institute, 1978). His special historical interests included the Ukrainian political leader and historian Mykhailo Hrushevsky (1866–1934), and the history of Ukrainian pioneer settlements on the Prairies. At his death, he left extensive, in fact, book-length, unpublished manuscripts on both subjects.

7 Vladimir Kysilewsky [Kysilewskyj], "Things We Remember," *Canadian Slavonic Papers* 11 (1969): 144.
8 For the text of the Budka proposal, see Bohdan S. Kordan and Lubomyr Y. Luciuk, *A Delicate and Difficult Question: Documents in the History of Ukrainians in Canada* (Kingston: Limestone Press, 1986), 25–7. On Arsenych, see V. Buyniak, "The Beginnings of Ukrainian Scholarship in Canada," in *Ethnic Canadians: Education and Culture*, ed. M. L. Kovacs (Regina: Canadian Plains Research Center, 1978), 112.
9 See G. E. Lloyd, "Immigration and Nation Building," *Empire Review* (February 1929): 105–6; reprinted in Howard Palmer, ed., *Immigration and the Rise of Multiculturalism* (Toronto: Copp Clark, 1978), 55–6.
10 For Kirkconnell's criticism of Lloyd's program, see his "Western Immigration," in Palmer, *Immigration and the Rise of Multiculturalism*, 56–8. On Luchkovich, see his memoirs, *A Ukrainian Canadian in Parliament* (Toronto: Ukrainian Canadian Research Foundation, 1965), 61ff.
11 George Simpson, "Memorandum on Establishment of the Department of Slavic Studies," University of Saskatchewan Archives, George Simpson Papers, vol. 2. On the Hospodyn proposal, see Volodymyr Zhyla, *Z istorii ukrainoznovstva i slavystyky v kanadi* (Winnipeg: Ukrainska vilna akademiia nauk, 1961), 16–19. About the turn of the nineteenth century, the Toronto political economist James Mavor had interested himself in the history of Russia. He published a bulky two-volume *Economic History of Russia* (1914) and helped bring the Doukhobors to Canada, but founded no school and left no successors. W. J. Rose, probably the first Canadian-born professional Slavist, studied in Europe and the United States in the 1930s and eventually became director of London's School of Slavonic Studies, but he did not return to Canada until after the war. V. J. Kaye [Kysilewskyj], "The Ten Years Leading to the Formation of the CAS," *Canadian Slavonic Papers* 7 (1965): 3–4, writes: "In my enquiries in the early twenties, I was unable to locate in Canada another graduate of the East European Institute of the University of Vienna. Even later, during post-graduate studies at the School of Slavonic and East European Studies in London, England, I did not encounter a single Canadian student following similar courses."
12 See Simpson's correspondence and explanatory memo in the University of Saskatchewan Archives, George Simpson Papers, vol. 1.
13 Olha Woycenko, letter of 1 February 1986 to the author. Compare Udod, *Julian Stechishin*, 32.
14 For a detailed description of Canadian reactions to the Carpatho-Ukraine affair, see my *Maple Leaf and Trident: The Ukrainian Canadians during the Second World War* (Toronto: Multicultural History Society of Ontario, 1988),

ch. 1. More generally, see J. Motyl, "Ukrainian Nationalist Political Violence in Inter-war Poland," *East European Quarterly* 19, no. 1 (1985): 45–55.

15 For Simpson's detailed response to England, which maintained that Ukrainian Canadians were "seriously concerned that the creation of a Ukrainian national state should not be merely a German creation," see his letter of 9 December 1939 to Robert England, University of Saskatchewan Archives, George Simpson Papers, vol. 1.

16 Simpson's speech, together with a similar radio talk by the UNF figure Wasyl Swystun, was immediately published as *The Ukrainian Cause on Radio Waves* (Saskatoon: Ukrainian National Federation, 1939).

17 Saskatchewan Archives Board, Saskatoon, George Simpson Papers, Ukrainian files, file 14.

18 "Radio-promova Prof. Simpsona," *Novyi shliakh* (Saskatoon), no. 2, 5 January 1949. On 16 January, *Novyi shliakh* printed the full text of Simpson's speech.

19 P. J. Lazarowich to George Simpson, 16 March 1939, in the University of Saskatchewan Archives, George Simpson Papers, vol. 1. For Simpson's evaluation of these "March events,"' see his review of Winch's "Republic for a Day," *Novyi shliakh* (Saskatoon), 23 December 1940.

20 Loc. cit.

21 For the texts of Simpson's radio broadcasts, see his *The Ukrainian Question and the Present Crisis* (Saskatoon: Ukrainian National Federation, 1939) and his *Ukraine under Hungarian, Polish, and Russian Occupations* (Saskatoon, n.d.).

22 For Simpson's correspondence with Bachynska, see the University of Saskatchewan Archives, George Simpson Papers, Ukrainian files 1940–1944.

23 V. J. Kysilewsky [Kysilewskyj] to George Simpson, 19 February 1940, in ibid. A second edition of Doroshenko's *History* never was published in London, but the book was reprinted in Edmonton, and, later in the war, the London-based Ukrainian-Canadian Servicemen's Association (UCSA) distributed many copies in England. On the UCSA, see L. Y. Luciuk, ed., *Heroes of their Day: The Reminiscences of Bohdan Panchuk* (Toronto: Multicultural History Society of Ontario, 1983).

24 Oleh W. Gerus, "The Ukrainian Canadian Committee," in *A Heritage in Transition*, ed. M. R. Lupal (Toronto: McClelland and Stewart, 1982), 198–9; Bohdan Kordan, "Disunity and Unity: Ukrainian Canadians and the Second World War," MA thesis, Carleton University, 1981, 33–4, 43–7, stresses the involvement of Tracy Philipps, but Simpson, "Memorandum on the Ukrainian files," University of Saskatchewan Archives, vol. 1, considered the creation of the UCC to be his own personal achievement as well.

25 James Gardiner to George Simpson, 23 November 1940, in ibid.

26 For a discussion of these projects, see Simpson to Wasyl Swystun, 9 November 1940, in ibid., and Udod, *Julian Stechishin*, 33. Also see George Simpson, *Ukraine: A Series of Maps and Explanations Indicating the Historic and Contemporary Geographical Position of the Ukrainian People* (London: Oxford University Press, 1941), which contained nineteen hand-drawn maps printed on fine paper with accompanying commentaries.

27 For Buchko's original statement, see *The Trident* 4, no. 6 (1940): 7–21. Also see Simpson to Buchko, 17 October 1940, and Buchko to Simpson, 14 November 1940, in the University of Saskatchewan Archives, George Simpson Papers, vol. 1.

28 George Simpson to Wasyl Swystun, 29 November 1940, in ibid. He continued: "I think that with you, more than with any other single person in Western Canada, lies the opportunity for energetic and wise action." (Swystun had been a founding member of the moderate USRL and had only recently gone over to the rightist UNF.)

29 George Simpson, "Memorandum Regarding File on Citizenship Division," in ibid., vol. 2.

30 See the report: "Advisory Committee on Co-operation in Canadian Citizenship (Nationalities Branch)," in ibid., esp. 10–11. Watson Kirkconnell, who was a member of the committee, took charge of the translation proposal.

31 Ibid., 11–12. Many of these directly concerned Prairie ethnic groups, as, for example, *Iceland on the Prairies* (1941), *Ukrainian Christmas* (1941), *Poland on the Prairies* (1943), *New Home in the West* (1943), etc. The release of *New Home in the West*, in the words of the report, "used the celebration at Mundare, Alberta, of the fiftieth anniversary of the coming of the Ukrainians to Canada as part of the picture."

32 George Simpson, "Memorandum Regarding File on Citizenship Division," in George Simpson Papers, vol. 2. The "Nationalities Branch" under the committee remained intact, however, even after 1945, and was eventually transferred to the Secretary of State, where it was renamed the "Citizenship Branch." It eventually became the kernel of the Multiculturalism Directorate of the 1970s.

33 Watson Kirkconnell, *The Place of Slavic Studies in Canada*, in the series *Slavistica*, no. 31 (Winnipeg: Ukrainian Free Academy of Sciences, 1958), 9. It is unknown whether Simpson played any role in the establishment of this course. He does not mention it in any of his memos on Slavic Studies, which is quite peculiar.

34 George Simpson, "Memorandum on Establishment of the Department of Slavic Studies," and letter to J. B. Rudnyckyj, 14 July 1950, in the University of Saskatchewan Archives, George Simpson Papers, vol. 1.

35 Victor O. Buyniak, "Slavic Studies in Canada: An Historical Survey," *Canadian Slavonic Papers* 9, no. 1 (1967): 6.

36 Simpson to Rudnyckyj, loc. cit.

37 George Simpson, "Memorandum to Dr. J. S. Thompson, President, Regarding the Establishment of a Department of Slavic Languages in the University of Saskatchewan," University of Saskatchewan Archives, George Simpson Papers, vol. 1, undated.

38 On Andrusyshen, see V. Buyniak, "Pam'iati Prof. D-ra Kostia Andrusyshyna," *Novyi shliakh* (Toronto), June 25, 1983. Also see June Dutka, *The Grace of Passing Constantine H. Andrusyshen: The Odyssey of a Slavist* (Edmonton: Canadian Institute of Ukrainian Studies, 2000).

39 Since 1912, the *Kanadiiskyi farmer* was not owned by a Ukrainian but, rather, by the Czech Frank Dojacek, who ran the paper as a business venture rather than as a political tribune. During the 1920s and 1930s, the paper inclined towards the Liberals, but, by the 1930s, T. Datzkiw, a strong supporter of the conservative Hetman Skoropadsky, was editor. By early 1941, pressure to toe the national line with regard to Canada's war effort was mounting and "ethnic" editors came under increasing pressure. It was at this time that Dojacek suddenly fired Datzkiw, denounced him to the local RCMP, and hired Andrusyshen to replace him. See the Manitoba Provincial Archives, Frank Dojacek Papers, 533, file Datzkiw, and my *Maple Leaf and Trident*, ch. 2.

40 Loc. cit.

41 S. H. Cross to C. H. Andrusyshen, n.d., in the University of Saskatchewan Archives, George Simpson Papers, vol. 1.

42 See Andrusyshen's correspondence with Simpson in ibid. Also see Buyniak, "Slavic Studies in Canada," 7.

43 See the secret RCMP report on the Eighth National UNF Convention, in Kordan and Luciuk, *Documents*, 80–90, esp. 87–8.

44 For the printed proceedings of the congress containing Simpson's address, see *The All-Canadian Congress of Ukrainians in Canada* (Winnipeg: Ukrainian Canadian Committee, 1943), which should be consulted in conjunction with the secret RCMP report on the affair in the National Archives of Canada, RG 25. Gl, vol. 1896, file 165, part 4.

45 R. A. Davies [Rudolf Shohan], *This Is Our Land: Ukrainian Canadians Against Hitler* (Toronto: Progress Books, 1943), esp. 68.

46 Saskatchewan Archives Board, Saskatoon, George Simpson Papers, file 25, "The Ukrainian Canadian Committee, 1942–1962." Unlike Watson Kirkconnell, Simpson was no avid anti-Communist crusader. Of the ULFTA, for example, he explained to one correspondent that it "did fall under Communist influence. Many of its members, however, were not members of

the Communist Party. They felt themselves under special social and economic pressure and their group was an extreme protest group." See Simpson to Sgt. Walter Katarenchuk, 3 March 1944, in the University of Saskatchewan Archives, George Simpson Papers, vol. 2, file "Citizenship Division."

47 See George Simpson, "Suggestions Regarding the Objectives of the KUK [UCC] Delegation to San Francisco," in the University of Saskatchewan Archives, George Simpson Papers. Ukrainian files, 1945–1949, and the UCC "Memorandum to the Canadian Delegation ...," *Novyi shliakh* (Winnipeg), 26 May 1945.

48 The correspondence concerning Doroshenko's possible admission to Canada in 1945 is in the University of Saskatchewan Archives, George Simpson Papers, Ukrainian files, 1945–1949. It was only in 1947 that Doroshenko finally came to Canada, where he briefly taught at Winnipeg's Saint Andrew's College and presided over the organization of the Ukrainian Free Academy of Sciences in Canada. But he fell ill in Winnipeg and returned to Europe in 1950. See Leonid Biletsky, *Dmytro Doroshenko* (Winnipeg: Ukrainska vilna akademiia nauk, 1949).

49 Lev. Dobriansky to Simpson, 28 February 1946, and Simpson to Dobriansky, 11 March 1946, in George Simpson Papers, Ukrainian files, 1945–1949. "In these days," Simpson wrote, "when the ordinary decencies of civilization are collapsing over wide areas it is necessary for all people of good will to join in rescue work."

50 George Luckyj, interview of 16 March 1988, Toronto. Luckyj later did a PhD in Slavic Studies at Columbia and became an early chairman of the Department of Slavic Languages and Literatures at the University of Toronto. Even forty years later, he remembered Simpson and his Saskatoon colleagues with some warmth.

51 George W. Simpson, *The Names 'Rus' 'Russia' and 'Ukraine' and Their Historical Background*, in the series *Slavistica*, no. 10 (Winnipeg: Ukrainian Free Academy of Sciences, 1951), and "Hrushevsky: A Historian of Ukraine," *Ukrainian Quarterly* 1 (1944): 132–9.

52 Paul Yuzyk, interview of 7 April 1984. Ottawa.

53 J. B. Rudnyckyj [Ia. Rudnytsky], *Z podorozhei po Kanadi 1949–1959* (Winnipeg: Ivan Tyktor, n.d.), 83–5. On post-war Slavistics in Canada generally, see Buyniak, "Slavic Studies in Canada," and Zbigniew Folejewski, "Slavistics in Canada," in Josip Hamm and Günther Wytrzens, eds., *Beiträge zur Geschichte der Slawistik in Nichtslawischen Ländern* (Vienna: ÖAW, 1985), 529–38.

54 For statements by Simpson, Yuzyk, and others, and the text of the Canadian Association of Slavists brief, see *Canadian Slavonic Papers* 7 (1965): 23–62. Twenty years before, Simpson appeared to be a precursor of multiculturalism

when he addressed a gathering of Canadian historians in Montreal. See G. W. Simpson, "The Blending of Traditions in Western Canadian Settlement," *The Canadian Historical Association Report* (1944): 46–52.

55 *Canadian Slavonic Papers* 11 (1969): 1. Also see J. B. Rudnyckyj [Ia. Rudnytsky], "Pam'iati Dz. V. Simpsona," *Ukrainskyi holos* (Winnipeg), no. 15, 1969.

8 Post-Secondary Teaching of Ukrainian History

1 The history of Canadian nativist sentiment during this period is well documented. See, for example, Frances Swyripa, *Ukrainian Canadians: A Survey of Their Portrayal in English Language Works* (Edmonton: CIUS, 1978), 1–25; Howard Palmer, *Patterns of Prejudice: A History of Nativism in Alberta* (Toronto: McClelland and Stewart, 1982).

2 Victor Buyniak, "The Beginnings of Ukrainian Scholarship in Canada," in *Ethnic Canadians: Culture and Education*, ed. L. Kovacs (Regina: Canadian Plains Research Center, 1978), 109–16, esp. 111.

3 Mykhailo Hrushevsky, undated letter, "To the distinguished Organization of Ukrainian Teachers in Canada," in Mykhailo Marunchak, "M. Hrushevsky i ukraintsi Kanady," *Vilne slovo* (Toronto), 19 November 1966. There is a good-quality photograph of this letter in the original Cyrillic handwriting of the author in Mykhailo Marunchak, *The Ukrainian Canadians: A History* (Winnipeg, Ottawa: Ukrainian Free Academy of Sciences, 1970), 251.

4 Nicetas Budka, "Memorandum On the Status and Improvement of the Ruthenians of Canada," in *A Delicate and Difficult Question: Documents in the History of Ukrainians in Canada 1899–1962*, ed. Bohdan S. Kordan and Lubomyr Y. Luciuk (Kingston: Limestone Press, 1986), 25–7.

5 V. Mihaichuk, "Uchytelskyi zhurnal i vyshcha osvita," *Ukrainskyi holos* (Winnipeg), no. 30, July 29, 1914; cited in Volodymyr Zhyla, *Z istorii ukrainoznavstva i slavistyky v Kanadi* (Winnipeg: UVAN, 1961), 13–14.

6 Buyniak, "Beginnings of Ukrainian Scholarship," 112.

7 See, in particular, Iu. Stechyshyn [J. Stechishin], *Iuvileina knyha 25-littia Instytutu im. Petra Mohyly v Saskatuni* (Winnipeg: *Ukrainskyi holos*, 1945).

8 There were, however, a few exceptions. For example, as early as the turn of the century, the Toronto political economist James Mavor had interested himself in the history of Russia. He published a two-volume *Economic History of Russia* (1914) and helped bring the Doukhobors to Canada, but founded no school and left no successors. W. J. Rose, probably the first Canadian-born professional Slavist, studied in Europe and in the United States in the 1930s, and eventually became director of London's School of Slavonic Studies, but he did not return to Canada until after the Second World War.

9 P. I. Lazarovych [P. I. Lazarowich], *Soiuz Ukraintsiv Samostiinykiv i ukrainska vyzvolna sprava* (Winnipeg: The Trident Press, 1951).

10 On the Hospodyn proposal, see Zhyla, *Z istorii ukrainoznavstva*, 16. On George Simpson, see my "George Simpson, the Ukrainian Canadians, and the 'Prehistory' of Slavic Studies in Canada," *Saskatchewan History* 41, no. 2 (1988): 53–66, or Chapter 7 in the present volume.

11 Lazarovych, *Soiuz ukraintsiv samostiinykiv.*

12 Dmytro Doroshenko, *History of the Ukraine*, trans. H. Chikalenko-Keller, ed. George Simpson (Edmonton: The Institute Press, 1939).

13 See my "George Simpson," for a fuller quote and more information on this subject.

14 See Clarence A. Manning, *History of Slavic Studies in the United States* (Milwaukee: Marquette University Press, 1957), 62, who wrote that "on the surface, the reactions in 1939 differed little from those in 1914. This is well illustrated by the fact that at the opening exercises of Columbia University in 1939, President Nicholas Murray Butler repeated large extracts from his talk of 1914 on a similar occasion." Of course, American academics could excuse themselves by the fact that the United States was not yet at war. English Canadian academics had no such excuse.

15 For a detailed discussion of the origin of these and other works, see my "Ukrainian History and the War," in *Maple Leaf and Trident: The Ukrainian Canadians during the Second World War* (Toronto: Multicultural History Society of Ontario, 1988), 144–9.

16 Watson Kirkconnell, *The Place of Slavic Studies in Canada*, in the series *Slavistica*, no. 31 (Winnipeg: UVAN, 1958), 9.

17 Victor O. Buyniak, "Slavic Studies in Canada: An Historical Survey," *Canadian Slavonic Papers* 9, no. 1 (1967): 6.

18 On Andrusyshen, see V. Buyniak, "Pam'iati Prof. D-ra Kostia Andrusyshyna," *Novyi shliakh* (Toronto), 25 June 1983; June Dutka, *The Grace of Passing: Constantine H. Andrusyshen The Odyssey of a Slavist* (Edmonton: CIUS, 2000).

19 On Rudnyckyj, see *Scripta Manent: A. Bio-bibliography of J. B. Rudnyckyj* (Winnipeg, Ottawa, 1975), which contains a biographical sketch by Olha Woycenko. On Luckyj, see the *Journal of Ukrainian Studies* 26 (1989), which is a festschrift in his honour, and Roman Senkus and Bohdan Klid, "In Memoriam: Prof. George S. N. Luckyj (1919–2001)," *Ukrainian News/ Ukrainski visti* (Edmonton), December 12–25, 2001, p. 13.

20 "Ukrainska vilna akademia nauk," in *Entsyklopedia ukrainoznavstva* (Paris: NTSh, 1980), 9:3342–3. Also see Jaroslav Rozumnyj, "UVAN in Canada: Fifty Years of Service," in his *Yesterday Today Tomorrow: The Ukrainian Community in Canada* (Winnipeg: UVAN, 2004), 117–54.

21 Lubomyr R. Wynar, "Ukrainian Scholarship in Exile: The DP Period, 1945–1952," *Ethnic Forum* 8, no. 1 (1988): 40–72.
22 On the logic behind the establishment of Ukrainian studies at Harvard, see Omelian Pritsak, *Chomu Katedry ukrainoznavstva v Harvardi?* (Cambridge, MA: Fond ukrainoznavstva, 1973), and *idem*, "The Present State of Ukrainian Studies," *Canadian Slavonic Papers* 14, no. 2 (1972): 139–52.
23 See, in particular, Omelian Pritsak, "Ivan Lysiak-Rudnytsky, Scholar and Communicator," in Ivan L. Rudnytsky, *Essays in Modern Ukrainian History* (Edmonton: CIUS, 1987), xv–xxii.
24 See Dmytro Doroshenko and Oleh Gerus, *A Survey of Ukrainian History* (Winnipeg: Trident Press, 1984). The first Gerus edition appeared in 1975.
25 Information from Robert Klymasz, who at that time was one of Yuzyk's students. Both Yuzyk and Baran after him used Oscar Halecki, *Borderlands of Western Civilization* (New York: Ronald Press, 1952), as their textbook. From the 1940s, Yuzyk was also doing primary research on Canadian ethnic, particularly Ukrainian Canadian, history, but I have not been able to determine whether he taught any courses in this area at the University of Manitoba. Certainly, at that time, the published literature to serve as readings for such a course would have been minimal.
26 Manoly Lupul, "The Canadian Institute of Ukrainian Studies," in *The Jubilee of the Ukrainian Free Academy of Sciences*, ed. O. Gerus et al. (Winnipeg: UVAN, 1976), 522–40.
27 Bohdan Krawchenko, "Ukrainian Studies in Canada," *Nationalities Papers* 6, no. 1 (1978): 30.
28 See "The Chair of Ukrainian Studies at the University of Toronto," *UNESCO Information* (Moscow: International Association for the Study and Dissemination of the Slavonic Cultures, 1989), 20:34–44; Joanna Bielecki et al., *The Chair at Thirty* (Toronto: John Yaremko Chair in Ukrainian Studies, 2011). On Magocsi, see *Paul Robert Magocsi: A Bibliography 1964–1985*, ed. Luba Pendzey (Toronto: Chair of Ukrainian Studies, 1985); *Paul Robert Magocsi: A Bibliography 1964–2011*, ed. Ksenya Kiebuzinski (Toronto: Chair of Ukrainian Studies, 2011); and "An Interview with Paul Robert Magocsi [1993]," in Paul Robert Magocsi, *Of the Making of Nationalities There Is No End*, 2 vols. (New York: East European Monographs, 1999), 2:228–48. Also on Magocsi, see the special section of the journal *Nationalities Papers* 39, 1 (2011), titled: "The Scholar, Historian and Public Advocate. The Academic Contributions of Paul Robert Magocsi."
29 See Orest Subtelny, *Ukraine: A History* (Toronto: University of Toronto Press, 1988). In view of the enormous changes that transpired in eastern Europe after 1988, Subtelny added some new materials to this work and brought out several new editions. The fourth "revised" edition was published in 2010.

30 See my "The History of Ukraine at the University of Saskatchewan and its
    Antecedents," *Promin* 4 (1985): 15–18. Several years later, however, a Prairie
    Centre for Ukrainian Culture was established at Saint Thomas More College
    at the University of Saskatchewan and began to promote courses, lectures,
    and publications in Ukrainian studies. The political scientist Bohdan
    Kordan was active in this effort.
31 On the first years of the Jacyk Centre, see "Peter Jacyk Centre for Ukrainian
    Historical Research Inaugurated," *Canadian Institute of Ukrainian Studies
    Newsletter* (Fall/Winter 1989) and (Spring/Summer 1990).
32 For example, a second Canadian Chair of Ukrainian Studies was eventually
    established (1993) at the University of Ottawa, where the focus was not on
    history but on political studies of contemporary Ukraine. The political
    scientist Dominique Arel, a French speaker and specialist in language
    politics in contemporary Ukraine, was appointed to this chair. There is some
    information on such developments, especially those in folklore, in *Champions
    of Philanthropy: Peter and Doris Kule and their Endowments*, ed. Serge Cipko and
    Natalie Kononenko (Edmonton: Kule Endowment Group, 2009).
33 Paul Robert Magocsi, *A History of Ukraine* (Toronto: University of Toronto
    Press, 1996). This volume, a detailed work of some 784 pages, was thorough-
    ly revised in a second edition with a newly added subtitle: *A History of Ukraine:
    The Land and Its Peoples* (Toronto: University of Toronto Press, 2010).

11 In the Shadow of a Political Assassination

1 The standard biography is François Ricard, *Gabrielle Roy: A Life*, trans. Patricia
   Claxton (Toronto: McClelland and Stewart, 1999). Also see Linda Clemente
   and Bill Clemente, *Gabrielle Roy: Creation and Memory* (Toronto: ECW, 1997),
   and Andre Vanasse, *Gabrielle Roy: A Passion for Writing* (Montreal, Toronto:
   XYZ, 2007). For a brief introduction, see the article on Gabrielle Roy in the
   Dictionary of Canadian Biography Online: www.biographi.ca. Accessed
   17 March 2014. In this chapter, translations from French are from the
   editions given in the notes; translations from Ukrainian are by the author.
2 Michel Biron, Francois Dumont, and Elisabeth Nardout-Lafarge, *Histoire de
   la littérature québécoise* (Montreal: Boréal, 2007), 302; Carol J. Harvey, *Le cycle
   manitobain de Gabrielle Roy* (Saint Boniface: Les Éditions des Plaines, 1993).
   Also see Ismène Toussaint, *Gabrielle Roy et le nationalisme québécois* (Paris:
   Lanctot, 2006), 70, who enigmatically concludes that, in the end, Gabrielle
   Roy remained a *"petite fille déchirée entre un Canada et un Québec trop vastes pour
   elle, et dont le seul véritable pays fut en fait l'écriture."*
3 See, in particular, the discussion of this important point in M. G. Hesse,
   "'There Are No More Strangers': Gabrielle Roy's Immigrants," *Canadian*

Children's Literature/Littérature canadienne pour la Jeunesse 35/36 (1984): 27–37, esp. 28.

4 Gabrielle Roy, *Rue Deschambault*, 3rd ed. (Quebec City: Stanké, 1980), 141–2; reprinted as *Street of Riches*, trans. Henry Binsse (Toronto: McClelland and Stewart, 1967), 73. There is a brief discussion of this excerpt in Rosemary Chapman, *Between Languages and Culture: Colonial and Postcolonial Readings of Gabrielle Roy* (Montreal, Kingston: McGill-Queen's University Press, 2009), 218–23.

5 Gabrielle Roy, *Where Nests the Water Hen*, trans. Harry L. Binsse (Toronto: McClelland and Stewart, 1951), 151–52. Also see the discussion in Clemente and Clemente, *Gabrielle Roy*, 57, who believe that the model for Nick Sluzick was Gabrielle's father Léon.

6 For a general introduction to this question, and a particularly interesting example of a French Canadian priest who became sincerely devoted to the Ukrainian national cause, see Zonia Keywan, *A Turbulent Life: A Biography of Josephat Jean OSBM (1885–1972)* (Verdun, QC: Éditions Clio, 1990).

7 Gabrielle Roy, *Ces enfants de ma vie* (Montreal: Éditions du Boréal, 2012), 50–1; reprinted as *Children of My Heart*, trans. Alan Brown (Toronto: McClelland and Stewart, 1979), 37–53. In this same work, Roy also recalls the Demetrioff family, who were ethnic Russians, though she notes that there were more Poles and Ukrainians than Russians in the area called "Little Russia" ("*la petite Russie*") where they lived.

8 See V. J. Kaye-Kysilevskyj [Kysilewskyj], *Slavic Groups in Canada* (Winnipeg: Ukrainian Free Academy of Sciences, 1951), and *A Statistical Compendium on the Ukrainians in Canada 1891–1976*, ed. William Darcovich and Paul Yuzyk (Ottawa: University of Ottawa Press, 1980), 21. The possibility also exists that Léon Roy used the term "Little Ruthenians" as a hybrid under the influence of the term "Little Russians" (*Malorussy* in Russian), which was the official name for Ukrainians in imperial Russia before 1917, and the term "Ruthenians" (*Ruthenen* in German), which was the official name for Ukrainians in Austrian Galicia before 1918. As indicated above, Gabrielle always wondered about the origin of this term.

9 For a succinct overview of the Ukrainian Canadian political spectrum of the 1930s, see the first chapter of my *Maple Leaf and Trident: The Ukrainian Canadians during the Second World War* (Toronto: Multicultural History Society of Ontario, 1988), 11–34. For a general introduction to these times written from the viewpoint of a conservative participant who was at one time a member of the UNF, see Paul Yuzyk, *The Ukrainians in Manitoba: A Social History* (Toronto: University of Toronto Press, 1953).

10 On Kysilewskyj, who was later "encouraged" to change his name to Kaye, see "Kaye-Kysilewskyj, Vladimir," in the *Encyclopedia of Ukraine*, 5 vols. (Toronto:

University of Toronto Press, 1984–93), 2:432; and H. N. Harasymova, "Kaiie-Kysilevsky, Volodymyr Iulianovych," in *Entsyklopediia istoriia Ukrainy* [Encyclopedia of the history of Ukraine], many vols. (Kyiv: Naukova dumka, 2003–in progress), 4:24. On Seton-Watson's attitude toward Ukrainian studies, see Roman Syrota, "Ukrainian Studies in Interwar Great Britain: Good Intentions, Major Obstacles," *Harvard Ukrainian Studies* 27, nos. 1–4 (2004–05), 149–80. For Seton-Watson's confidential, but generally positive, assessment of Kysilewskyj's academic abilities, see 167.

11 Information from Stephen Pawluk in various conversations and an interview carried out on 12 July 1984, in Toronto. Also, "Biography of Stephen Pawluk," author's archive, Toronto.

12 There is an article on "Hubytskyi, Taras," in Mykhailo Marunchak, *Biohrafichnyi dovidnyk do istorii ukrainskiv Kanady* (Biographical guide for the history of the Ukrainians of Canada) (Winnipeg: UVAN, 1986), 163, but no articles on his brother Bohdan or sister Honoré. However, there are pictures of both Taras and Bohdan and some information about them in *Kalendar Kanadiiskoho Farmera za 1929 rik* (Calendar of the 'Ukrainian farmer' for the year 1929) (Winnipeg), 122–3. There is a picture of Honoré with some information about her planned trip to Europe in the *Ukrainian Review* (February–March 1938): 7. (I am endebted to Orest Martynowych of Winnipeg for these last two references.) Information about Gabrielle's residence and outings with Olga Pawluk is from Andrew Gregorovich, Toronto, who is Stephen Pawluk's nephew.

13 Ievhen Stotsko, "Za voliu ridnoi zemli: Spohad pro Stepana Davydovycha" (For the freedom of the native land: A recollection of Stephen Davidovich), *Novyi shliakh/The New Pathway* (Toronto), 4 July 1987, and 11–18 July 1987. There are two early photographs of Stephen Davidovich printed along with this article. A photo of him from about 1942 is also available online: www.ukrainiansintheuk.info/eng/01/davidovich-e.htm. Accessed 17 October 2013.

14 For general introductions to the OUN, see M. Yurkevich, "Organization of Ukrainian Nationalists," in *Encyclopedia of Ukraine*, 3:708–10, and Orest Subtelny, *Ukraine: A History*, 4th ed. (Toronto: University of Toronto Press, 2009), 441–6. For an apologetic history of the organization, see Petro Mirchuk, *Narys istorii OUN* (An outline history of the OUN), vol. 1 (1920–1939) (Munich, London, New York: Ukrainske vydavnytstvo, 1968). (Mirchuk was a spokesman for the more radical "Bandera" wing of the OUN, which arose during the war.) For some remarks on the OUN's relations with the Canadian UNF, see my *Maple Leaf and Trident*, 19–22. Orest T. Martynowych maintains that veterans of the Ukrainian War of Independence from 1917 to 1921 were instrumental in the founding of the

328   Notes to pages 176–80

UNF and in keeping it on an extremely rightist course. See his "Sympathy for the Devil: The Attitude of Ukrainian War Veterans in Canada to Nazi Germany and the Jews," in *Re-Imagining Ukrainian Canadians: History Politics and Identity*, ed. Rhonda L. Hinther and Jim Mochoruk (Toronto: University of Toronto Press, 2011), 173–222.

15 Stotsko, "Za voliu."

16 Interview with Stephen Davidovich, Toronto, July 1984. There is a tape recording of this interview in the author's archive, Toronto.

17 Gabrielle Roy, *La détresse et l'enchantement* (Paris: Éditions Boréal Express, 1984), 342–4; reprinted as *Enchantment and Sorrow: The Autobiography of Gabrielle Roy*, trans. Patricia Claxton (Toronto: Lester and Orpen Dennys, 1987), 277. This work has also been translated into Ukrainian. See Gabrielle Roy, *Tuha i zacharovannia*, tr. Karina Maistrenko (Kyiv: Kyivske naukove tovarystvo im. Petra Mohyly, 1996).

18 The most detailed study of this autobiography, though with an emphasis on literary theory rather than history, is Cécilia [Wiktorowicz] Francis, *Gabrielle Roy: Autobiographie subjectivité passions et discourse* (Quebec City: Les presses de l'université Laval, 2006).

19 The Davidovich–Konovalets correspondence is in the Konovalets Collection, Box II, file 307/18, Ukrainian Cultural and Educational Centre (Oseredok), Winnipeg. I am indebted to Orest T. Martynowych of Winnipeg for sending me copies of this material and to Nadia Zavorotna of Toronto for helping me to decipher Davidovich's Cyrillic handwriting.

20 Ibid. Within less than a year, Davidovich was successful at publishing at least one volume of essays in Ukrainian: *Almanakh: Ideia v nastupi* (Almanac: An idea on the offensive) (London: Ukrainian National Information Service, 1938). In 1985, I had the opportunity of seeing a copy of this very rare publication in the private library of the historian Marko Antonovych of Montreal, formerly of Prague, Czechoslovakia, who was active in the OUN during the war.

21 Roy, *La détresse et l'enchantement*, 353–5; *Enchantment and Sorrow*, 286–8.

22 For a brief survey in English of Konovalets's life and contribution to Ukrainian politics, see V. Yaniv, "Konovalets, Yevhen," in *Encyclopedia of Ukraine*, 2:599–600. Amazingly, Konovalets's assassin, who escaped to the USSR, survived the Stalin purges of the Soviet security apparatus, the war, and the Khrushchev purge, and, after the collapse of the USSR, published his memoirs about his various unsavoury exploits as a secret agent. He was also instrumental in the 1940 assassination of Leon Trotsky. See Pavel Sudoplatov and Anatolii Sudoplatov, *Special Tasks: The Memoirs of an Unwanted Witness – A Soviet Spymaster* (Boston: Little Brown, 1994), 12–29.

This memoir contains an account of Sudoplatov's meeting with Stalin at which the Soviet dictator ordered him to kill Konovalets.

23 Michael Sharik [Sharyk], *Z viddali 50 lit* (From fifty years ago) (Toronto: Proboiem, 1969), 2:145. Also see Prymak, *Maple Leaf and Trident*, 26.

24 "Vozhd OUN zamordovanyi" (The OUN leader has been murdered), *Novyi shliakh/The New Pathway* (Saskatoon), no. 22, 31 May 1938. The reaction of Winnipeg's staunchly liberal democratic *Ukrainskyi holos/ Ukrainian voice*, no. 22, was considerably more restrained. On 1 June, it printed a small but prominent notice of Konovalets's death on its front page and stated: "Although we were not in agreement with the organization whose leader Colonel Konovalets was, we never doubted his patriotism and dedication to the cause of the liberation of the Ukrainian people from the Polish and Muscovite yokes. We bow our heads before the grave of one of the most outstanding sons [*naivydnishykh syniv]* of the Ukrainian people of our times." For a survey of Ukrainian émigré press reaction to the assassination, see *Ievhen Konovalets* (Paris: Première imprimerie ukrainienne en France, 1938? in Ukrainian). The Soviet press passed over the assassination in silence. See, for example, "Chomu Moskva movchyt pro vbyvstvo Konovaltsia?" (Why is Moscow quiet about the murder of Konovalets?) *Ukrainskyi holos/Ukrainian voice* (Winnipeg), no. 26, June 29, 1.

25 Orest Martynowych, "The Ukrainian Bureau in London: Diplomacy, Propaganda, and Political Consolidation" (2005), unpublished paper; on the basis of Kysilewskyj's unpublished London diary, in the National Archives of Canada, Vladimir J. Kaye Collection, MG 31 D69. Shortly afterwards, Davidovich penned a brief biographical article about Konovalets, which was published later that same year by Lancelot Lawton. See Stepan Davidovich, "Colonel Eugene Konowalets," *Contemporary Russia* 2, no. 3 (August–October 1938): 344–7. This article clearly identified the NKVD/OGPU as the culprit in the Konovalets murder and stressed the colonel's "constant contact with the nationalists in Ukraine, preparing for the day when they will make another bid for freedom."

26 Roy, *La détresse et l'enchantement*, 356–8; *Enchantment and Sorrow*, 289–93.

27 Ibid.

28 Conversations between Stephen Pawluk and the author carried out in the 1980s. In one of these conversations, Pawluk claimed that he had played a role in introducing Gabrielle to Stephen. Many years later, in conversation with Pawluk's nephew Andrew Gregorovich, Olga claimed that Stephen had asked her if he should marry Gabrielle and she had replied "No." Information from Andrew Gregorovich..

29 London diary, October 2, 1938, cited in Martynowych, "The Ukrainian Bureau in London."

30 For brief introductions, see V. Kubijovič and others, "Transcarpathia," in *Encyclopedia of Ukraine*, 5:262–63; Paul Robert Magocsi, *A History of Ukraine* (Toronto: University of Toronto Press, 1996), 613–16; and Subtelny, *Ukraine: A History*, 448–51.

31 Roy, *La détresse et l'enchantement*, 412–21; *Enchantment and Sorrow*, 333–42. Gabrielle's political convictions at this point are a source of some confusion. On the one hand, some authors point to the supposed existence of a card that purported to show that she was a member of "the Communist Party of London" (*Parti communiste de Londres*) (*sic!*), a card that is said to have "disappeared" in 1969; on the other hand, in 1938 and 1939, she published some of her first successful journalistic articles for the rightist Paris magazine *Je suis partout*. It may have been these articles that Stephen himself, who knew some French, read together with her before publication, as her autobiography indicates that he did read and praise some of her work at that time. At any rate, after her return to North America, she never had anything to do with the Communist Party of Canada and most certainly was never a member of that organization. For a brief discussion her 1938 politics, see Toussaint, *Gabrielle Roy et le nationalisme québécois*, 21, 75.

32 Stepan Davidovich, "Carpatho-Ukraine," *Contemporary Russia* 2, no. 4 (Winter 1938), 421–6.

33 Martynowych, "Ukrainian Bureau in London," on the basis on Kysilewskyj's London diary. Stephen Davidovich's ideas about the Ukrainian national movement and Germany were shared by at least one of the best-informed Canadian observers of the Carpatho-Ukraine crisis of early 1939. This observer was George W. Simpson, a professor of history at the University of Saskatchewan in Saskatoon, who often advised the UNF leadership in Canada and in January 1939 spoke out on CBC Radio on the subject. Simpson thought that the Ukrainian national liberation movement in Europe moved in harmony with German expansionist aims, but that this was only a coincidence. He compared underground nationalist Ukraine's relationship with Nazi Germany to the old alliance between revolutionary America and absolutist France. Just as America would have achieved its independence anyway and eventually have turned against absolutist France, with which it differed in principle, so, too, said Simpson, would Ukraine gain its independence and throw off German influence at the earliest opportunity. *Novyi shliakh/The New Pathway* commented approvingly: "With these words, the honourable professor rebutted those opponents of the Ukrainian cause who try to turn Ukrainian nationalism and the whole

Ukrainian problem into a 'German intrigue.'" See "Radio-promova Prof. Simpsona" (The radio speech of Professor Simpson), *Novyi shkiakh/The New Pathway* (Saskatoon) 5 January 1939. Also see Prymak, *Maple Leaf and Trident*, 28, 154n55.

34 See my *Maple Leaf and Trident*, Appendix D: "The UNF Mission to Europe and the 'Legend of the Gold Watch'," 138–43. Rumour had it that on this trip to Europe, the leader of the rightist UNF, Kossar, had presented a gold watch to Hitler on behalf of the Ukrainian Canadians. This rumour was, of course, completely false and, indeed, illogical in view of Hitler's recent abandonment of Carpatho-Ukraine in favour of the Hungarians. This move by Hitler was, in fact, the first step towards the Molotov–Ribbentrop Non-Aggression Pact concluded five months later between Nazi Germany and Stalin's USSR, according to which eastern Europe, starting with Poland, was to be divided between them. The pact amounted to a tacit alliance between the two powers until Hitler turned on Stalin in June 1941.

35 Mirchuk, *Narys istorii OUN*, 574–75.

36 For some remarks about this series, as well as about Roy's journalistic career in general, see Paul Socken, "Gabrielle Roy as a Journalist," *Canadian Modern Language Review/Revue canadienne des langues vivantes* 30, no. 2 (1974): 96–100.

37 Gabrielle Roy, *Fragiles lumières de la terre: Écrits divers 1942–1970* (Montreal, Paris: Stanké, 1978), 77–86; reprinted as *The Fragile Lights of Earth: Articles and Memories 1942–1970*, trans. Alan Brown (Toronto: McClelland and Stewart, 1982), 75–85.

38 Stephen Davidovich, "The Ukrainian Problem," *The Nineteenth Century and After* 126 (December 1939): 717–22.

39 Interview with Stephen Davidovich. In the 1980s, Stephen Pawluk, who greatly admired Milnes Gaskell, also suggested to the author that he might have been a British secret agent. Milnes Gaskell's history was titled "A Submerged Nation: The Ukrainian Case." An incomplete copy survives in the author's archive, Toronto. Milnes Gaskell was one of those scholars for whom Olga Pawluk translated Ukrainian and Russian materials.

40 Interview with Stephen Davidovich.

41 Ibid. Information about the Chair of Ukrainian Studies from Ihor Bardyn of Toronto. The author also gleaned some information from the late George Luckyj, from the early 1950s a professor of Slavic Languages and Literatures at the University of Toronto, who arrived in England from the Continent in the summer of 1939 to study English literature and seems to have become acquainted with Stephen at that time. The two men remained on good terms later on, and, several years after Stephen's death in 1987, Luckyj encouraged the author of these lines to take up the subject of Gabrielle and Stephen.

42 See the articles cited in note 10 above.

43 "Obituary: Margaret Hubicki," *The Guardian* (London), January 19, 2006; also available on-line; "Margaret Hubicki," *The Telegraph* (London), February 3, 2006; also available on-line.

44 "Biography of Stephen Pawluk"; conversations with Stephen Pawluk.

12 Inveterate Voyager

1 J. B. Rudnyckyj, *An Etymological Dictionary of the Ukrainian Language*, 2 vols. (Winnipeg: Ukrainian Free Academy of Sciences, 1962–1982); J. B. Rudnyckyj and Zenon Kuzela, *Ukrainisch-Deutsches Wörterbuch* (Leipzig: Otto Harrassowitz, 1943; repr. 1983 and 1987); Iaroslav Rudnytsky [J. B.Rudnyckyj], *Slovo i nazva "Ukraina"* (Winnipeg: Ukrains'ka vil'na akademiia nauk, 1951).

2 For bibliographies of Rudnyckyj's writings, see *Scripta Manent: A Biobibliography of J. B. Rudnyckyj* (Winnipeg, Ottawa: Published by Students and Friends, 1975). This work was updated twice, the last being *J. B. Rudnyckyj: Repertorium Bibliographicum: Addenda 1984–1994* (Ottawa: Ukrainian Language Association, 1995). The total number of listed titles reaches a very impressive 2,967, although most of these are shorter pamphlets and newspaper articles. *Scripta Manent* (1975) also contains a useful biographical sketch of Rudnyckyj by his collaborator and close friend Olha Woycenko. Two related titles are: [Olha Woycenko and W. J. Couch], *Scripta Manent II: J. B. Rudnyckyj's Papers at the Public Archives of Canada: An Inventory* (Winnipeg, Ottawa: Friends and Students, 1977); and Olha Woycenko et al., *Scripta Manent III: An Annotated Bibliography of Theses Directed or Evaluated by J. B. Rudnyckyj* (Ottawa: Alumni and Friends, 1980). At this point, it should also be noted that towards the end of his life, Rudnyckyj's friends at the Ukrainian Language Association (Ottawa) sponsored an entire journal dedicated to his life and work. See *Rudnyckiana* 1 (1985). Eleven issues of this unusual journal were published before Rudnyckyj's death in 1995. No further issues appeared thereafter. Some additional material for this paper was also gleaned from conversations or correspondence with Rudnyckyj's surviving colleagues, protégés, and students. These include long-time University of Manitoba Slavic librarian Ivan Muchin, Winnipeg-based Ukrainian Free Academy of Sciences librarian Olenka Negrych, Ottawa archivist Myron Momryk, and Rudnyckyj's sometime student, the historian Oleh Gerus, now Professor of History Emeritus at the University of Manitoba.

3 In addition to the biographical sketch by Olha Woycenko cited in note 2 above, also see Tania Nosko-Oboroniv, *Iaroslav Bohdan Rudnytskyi/J. B.*

Rudnyckyj (n.p.: Ukrainian Mohylo-Mazepian Academy of Sciences, 1992). This Ukrainian-language sketch repeats much of the information available in English in Woycenko. Rudnyckyj also wrote but did not finish his autobiography. The manuscript is preserved in his voluminous papers stored in the National Archives of Canada, Ottawa, MG31 D58. On his Winnipeg period, which was the most lengthy, and his manifold contributions to the UVAN, see the general remarks of Jaroslav Rozumnyj, "UVAN in Canada: Fifty Years of Service," in his *Yesterday Today Tomorrow: The Ukrainian Community in Canada* (Winnipeg: Ukrainian Academy of Arts and Sciences in Canada, 2004), 117–54.

4 For some remarkably impartial general remarks on Slavonic Studies in the West made during the height of the Cold War, see Clarence A. Manning, *History of Slavic Studies in the United States* (Milwaukee: Marquette University Press, 1957). For a more specific and recent appraisal, see Thomas M. Prymak, "Ukrainian Scholarship in the West during the 'Long Cold War'," in *Rossiiskaia istoricheskaia mozaika/Russian Historical Mosaic,* ed. A. L. Litvin (Kazan: Izdatelstvo kazanskogo matematicheskogo obshchestva, 2003), 272–85 (or Chapter 9 in the present volume), which gives further references. The *Russian Historical Mosaic* is a festschrift for John Keep, professor emeritus of Russian history at the University of Toronto.

5 Iaroslav Rudnytsky [J. B. Rudnyckyj], *Z podorozhi navkolo pivsvitu 1955* (Winnipeg, Toronto: Ivan Tyktor, 1955).

6 Ibid., 11–29.

7 Ibid., 30–33. The archives of *La revue ukrainienne,* together with materials on Drahomanov and a great deal of material on the Ukrainians in Switzerland and France, were transferred to Canada in the late 1970s and are stored in the Batchinsky Collection, Special Collections, Carleton University Library, Ottawa. This archive is described in John S. Jaworsky and Olga S. A. Szkabarnicki, *The Batchinsky Collection, Carleton University Library: Finding Aid,* ed. Jeremy Palin (Edmonton: Canadian Institute of Ukrainian Studies Press, 1995).

8 Rudnyckyj, *Z podorozhi navkolo pivsvitu,* 34–55.

9 See Arkady Joukovsky, "The Symon Petliura Library in Paris," *Harvard Ukrainian Studies* 14, nos. 1–2 (1990): 218–35; and Jaroslava Josypszyn, "Le rôle culturel de la Bibliothèque ukrainienne de Paris dans le monde occidental," in *Histoire de la slavistique: Le rôle des institutions,* ed. Antonia Bernard (Paris: Institut d'études slaves, 2003), 169–77. Also see Patricia Kennedy Grimstead, "The Odyssey of the Petliura Library and the Records of the Ukrainian National Republic during World War Two," in *Cultures and Nations of Central and Eastern Europe: Essays in Honor of Roman Szporluk,* ed. Zvi

Gitelman et al. (Cambrdge, MA: Harvard Ukrainian Research Institute, 2000), 181–208. More generally, see Jacques Chevtchenko, *Ukraine: Bibliographie des ouvrages en français XVIIe–XXe siècles* (Paris: Publications de l'Est Européen, 2000).

10 Rudnyckyj, *Z podorozhi navkolo pivsvitu*, 60–106. For some general remarks on the development of Slavic Studies in western Europe (though with an emphasis on the pre-1945 period), see the essays by Helmut Schaller (Germany), Jacques Veyrenc (France), Claude Backvis (Belgium), A. H. van Den Baar (Holland), and Gerald Stone (Great Britain), in *Beiträge zur Geschichte der Slawistik in Nichtslawischen Ländern*, ed. Josip Hamm and Günther Wytrzens (Vienna: Verlag der Österreichischen Akademie der Wissenschaften, 1985). Schaller mentions Rudnyckyj's contribution to pre-1945 Slavic Studies in Germany on p. 166.

11 The electrifying effect of Sputnik was mentioned by Omeljan Pritsak in speeches and addresses delivered in the 1970s and 1980s in Toronto, Hamilton, and elsewhere.

12 Iaroslav Rudnytsky [J. B. Rudnyckyj], *Z podorozhei po Kanadi 1949–1959* (Winnipeg, Montreal, Vancouver: Ivan Tyktor, n.d.).

13 Ibid., 1–2. For a more recent account of Ukrainian Winnipeg and Manitoba in general, see Orysia Tracz, "Ukrainians," in *The Encyclopedia of Manitoba* (Winnipeg: Great Plains Publications, 2007), 696–98. Tracz was a Slavic librarian at the University of Manitoba during Rudnyckyj's last years there.

14 Rudnytsky, *Z podorozhei po Kanadi*, 30–3. In this connection, also see J. B. Rudnyckyj, *Ukrainian Books for Public Libraries* (Winnipeg: UVAN and the Ukrainian Cultural and Education Centre, 1956), which is a well-annotated bibliography of recommended titles with a list of Ukrainian bookstores in North America on the final page.

15 In spite of his considerable influence on the development of Ukrainian studies in Canada, there is very little appreciative literature on Constantine Bida. For a festschrift with a select bibliography of his publications, see *Living Record: Essays in Memory of Constantine Bida*, ed. Irena R. Makaryk (Ottawa: Ottawa University Press, 1991).

16 Rudnytsky, *Z podorozhei po Kanadi*, 56–72. Luckyj, in particular, went on to become one of the most prolific literary scholars in the Ukrainian emigration. On him, see Roman Senkus and Bohdan Klid, "In Memoriam: Prof. George S. N. Luckyj (1919–2001)," *Ukrainian News/Ukrainski visti* (Edmonton), 12–25 December 2001, 13. Many years later, Christine Worobec compiled a bibliography of Toronto materials on Ukrainians in Canada and Paul Magocsi compiled one on University of Toronto Ucrainica in general. See Halyna Myroniuk and Christine Worobec, *Ukrainians in North America:*

A Select Bibliography (St. Paul, Toronto: Multicultural History Society of Ontario and Immigration History Research Center, 1981), and Paul R. Magocsi, *Ucrainica at the University of Toronto Library*, 2 vols. (Toronto: University of Toronto Press, 1985). Unlike Winnipeg, which at that time was the metropolitan centre of the pioneer immigration, the DP immigration dominated Ukrainian cultural life in Toronto and lobbied successfully for the inclusion of a Ukrainian collection in the Toronto Public Library. The results were impressive. See *Ukrainski knyzhky/Ukrainian Books: On Deposit in the Public Libraries of Toronto*, 2nd ed. (Toronto: Metropolitan Toronto Library Board, 1983).

17 On Saskatoon more generally, see Thomas M. Prymak, "George Simpson, the Ukrainian Canadians, and the 'Pre-history' of Slavic Studies in Canada," *Saskatchewan History* 41, no. 2 (1988): 53–66. (A slightly revised edition of this essay appears as chapter 7 of the present book.) On Andrusyshen in particular, see June Dudka, *The Grace of Passing: Constantine H. Andrusyshen, The Odyssey of a Slavist* (Edmonton, Toronto: Canadian Institute of Ukrainian Studies, 2000). On Stechishin, see Hryhory Udod, *Julian W. Stechishin: His Life and Work* (Saskatoon: Mohyla Institute, 1978).

18 Rudnytsky, *Z podorozhei po Kanadi*, 88–111. Forvyn Bohdan later published a detailed *Dictionary of Ukrainian Surnames in Canada* (Winnipeg, Vancouver: Ukrainian Free Academy of Sciences, 1974), which was a revision of a MA thesis done under Rudnyckyj's supervision.

19 In fact, when it was finally published, this new reference work even contained an article on the development of Slavic studies in the Dominion. See W. J. Rose, "Slavonic or Slavic Studies," in *Encyclopedia Canadiana*, 2nd ed. (Toronto: Grolier, 1975), 9:328–30. Unfortunately, this article underestimated the importance of Rudnyckyj's scholarly home, the University of Manitoba. For a useful corrective, see Volodymyr Zhyla, *Z istorii ukrainoznavstva i slavistyky v Kanadi* (Winnipeg: UVAN, 1961). More generally, see the essay by Rudnyckyj's younger colleague Victor O. Buyniak, "Slavic Studies in Canada: An Historical Survey," *Canadian Slavonic Papers* 9, no. 1 (1967): 3–23, and accompanying discussion papers, 24–49. Also see Zbigniew Folejewski, "Slavistics in Canada," in *Beiträge zur Geschichte der Slawistik in Nichtslawischen Ländern*, 529–38. For a more detailed treatment of Rudnyckyj's remark, see my "Two Encyclopedias: The Difference a War Made," *Ukrainski visti/Ukrainian News* (Edmonton), 16–29 April 2009, 7.

20 Two generations later, Catherine Owen, "Allophone Publishing," in *History of the Book in Canada*, ed. Patricia Fleming, vol. 3, 1918–1980 (Toronto: University of Toronto Press, 2007), 3:297–304, briefly noted that, unlike some groups such as the Prairie Icelanders and the Finns, whose publishing

activity lasted only a generation or two, Ukrainian-language publishing in
Canada enjoyed a certain longevity.

21 Iaroslav Rudnytsky [J. B. Rudnyckyj], *Z podorozhi po Amerytsi 1956* (Winnipeg,
Washington: Ivan Tyktor, 1956).

22 Ibid., 1–19. Many years later, the Slavic librarian at the Immigration History
Research Center, Halyna Myroniuk, surveyed the centre's holdings on
Ukrainian Americans, and Ukrainian émigré literature in general, in the
bibliography she co-compiled with Christine Worobec, *Ukrainians in North
America*. On Granovsky and his efforts to have Ukrainians in the West
represented at the United Nations, see my *Maple Leaf and Trident: The
Ukrainian Canadians During the Second World War* (Toronto: Multicultural
History Society of Ontario, 1988), 123–25.

23 For a bibliography concerning the society's most prestigious periodical,
the *Zapysky NTSh*, see Maksym Boiko, *Index to the Memoirs of the Shevchenko
Scientific Society 1892–1982: A Guide to the Holdings at the Indiana University
Library* (Bloomington, IN: Volhynian Bibliographic Center, 1984).

24 Rudnytsky, *Z podorozhi po Amerytsi*, 35–56. The results of Rudnyckyj's work
as special consultant were never published in whole, but many photocopies
of his report exist. For a small published excerpt of his findings, see his
"History of the Ukrainian Holdings in the Library of Congress," *Annals of the
Ukrainian Academy of Arts and Sciences in the US* 6 (1958): 1406–10. For the
full mimeographed report, see his "Ukrainica in the Library of Congress:
A Preliminary Survey" (Washington: Library of Congress, 1956), and
"Operational Document for Administrative Use Only." For some general
remarks on the history of the library, see the beautifully illustrated book by
James Conaway, *America's Library: The Story of the Library of Congress 1800–2000*
(New Haven and London: Yale University Press, 2000); for a Ukrainian-
language account that contains something on the Slavonic collections and
compares the Library of Congress to the earlier Alexandrine and imperial
Byzantine libraries, see Eugene Slon [Ievhen Slovinsky], *Istorychne znachennia tro'kh vydatnykh bibliotek/[The] Historical Significance of Three Distinguished
Libraries* (Ithaca, New York: Author, 1977).

25 Rudnytsky, *Z podorozhi po Amerytsi*, 56–85. On the New York UVAN, see
Marko Antonovych, "50-richchia Ukrains'koi vil'noi akademii nauk,"
Ukrains'kyi istoryk 32, nos. 1–4 (1995): 73–81, and, in the same volume,
Iurii Lutsky [George S.N. Luckyj], "Annaly UVAN": 82–6. In Luckyj's article,
there is some mention of Ukrainian studies at Columbia and, in particular,
of Philip Mosely, who helped to set up the UVAN's scholarly journal, the
Annals. On the UVAN manuscript collection, see Yury Boshyk, *A Guide to the
Archival and Manuscript Collection of the Ukrainian Academy of Arts and Sciences*

in the US, New York City: A Detailed Inventory (Edmonton: Canadian Institute of Ukrainian Studies, 1988). On the New York Public Library, see Robert H. Davis Jr., *Slavic and Baltic Library Resources at the New York Public Library: A First History and Practical Guide* (New York: New York Public Library and Charles Shlacks Jr, 1994).

26 There is a significant literature in Ukrainian or Russian on both Vernadsky and Chyzhevsky but less on Shevchenko. In English, see the respective articles on them in the *Encyclopedia of Ukraine*, 5 vols. (Toronto: University of Toronto Press, 1984–1993). Chyzhevsky was uncomfortable at Harvard and soon returned to Germany, and Shevchenko's scholarship only touched on Ukraine peripherally, but Vernadsky actually wrote or edited entire volumes on Ukrainian history while teaching at Yale. On Vernadsky, in particular, who attempted to found a Ukrainian research institute in the US during the Second World War, see Charles J. Halperin, "Russia and the Steppe: George Vernadsky and Eurasianism," *Forschungen zur osteuropäischen Geschichte* 36 (1985): 55–194, esp. 159–63; my *Maple Leaf and Trident*, Appendix E: "Ukrainian History and the War," 144–49; and Ernest Gyidel, "Ob 'Ukrainofilstve' Georgiia Vernadskogo, ili variatsiia na temu natsional'nykh i gosudarstvennykh loialnostei," *Ab imperio* 4 (2006): 329–69, esp. the Appendix, which includes his 1940 letter to Luke Myshuha, editor of New York's Ukrainian newspaper *Svoboda*, where he explains to him "*Povazhaiu sebe za ukraintsia ta rus'koho odnochasno*" (I consider myself to be Ukrainian and Russian at the same time).

27 Rudnytsky, *Z podorozhi po Amerytsi*, 120–1. For a more recent general survey, see Allan Urbanic and Beth Feinberg, *A Guide to Slavic Collections in the United States and Canada* (Binghamton, NY: Haworth Press, 1994). Also see William B. Edgerton, "The History of Slavistic Scholarship in the United States," in *Beiträge zur Geschichte der Slawistik in Nichtslawischen Ländern*, 491–528 (emphasis on literature), and Robert F. Byrnes, *A History of Russian and East European Studies in the United States: Selected Essays* (Lanham, New York; London: University Press of America, 1994) (emphasis on history). For a bibliography of Canadian and American Ukrainian studies compiled about the time of Rudnyckyj's retirement, see Roman Weres, *Ukraine: Selected References in the English Language*, 2nd ed. (Chicago: Ukrainian Research and Information Institute, 1974). Weres lists twelve titles in English by Rudnyckyj himself.

28 Iaroslav Rudnytsky [J. B. Rudnyckyj], *Z podorozhi po Italii* (Winnipeg: Novyi shliakh, 1965). *Idem, Z podorozhi po Skandynavii* 1957 (Winnpeg: Ivan Tyktor, n.d.).

29 See, for example, Iaroslav Rudnytsky [J. B. Rudnyckyj], *Z podorozhi na Maltu 1962 r.* (Valleta, Munich, Winnipeg: Ukrains'ke tovarystvo zakordonnykh

studii, n.d.); *idem, Navigare Necesse ... Z podorozhi 1981* (n.p.: Author, n.d.); *idem, Academia Mohylo-Mazepiana CCCL ... Z podorozhi 1982* (n.p.: Author, n.d.).

30 Iaroslav Rudnytsky [J. B. Rudnyckyj], *Biblioteka 'Oseredku ukrainskoi kultury i osvity'* (Winnipeg: Kultura i osvita, 1955); *idem, Biblioteka 'Chytalni Prosvity' u Vinnipegu*, 2nd ed. (Winnipeg: UVAN, 1956); *idem, Biblioteka tovarystva 'Prosvita' v Fort Villiumi*, 2nd ed. (Winnipeg: UVAN, 1957).

31 Iaroslav Rudnytsky [J. B. Rudnyckyj], *Ukrainski biblioteky v Kanadi*, 2nd expanded ed. (Winnipeg: UVAN, 1954); *idem*, "Ukrainica Congressiana: A Survey of Ukrainian Holdings at the Library of Congress" (Washington DC: Library of Congress, 1979); *idem*, "The Pre-1950 Ukrainica in the National Library of Canada: A Survey of Holdings as of 1980" (Ottawa: [National Library of Canada], 1981).

32 On the colourful life of one of the founders of the Mundare Museum, see Zonia Keywan, *A Turbulent Life: A Biography of Josephat Jean OSBM (1885–1972)* (Verdun, QC: Éditions Clio, 1990).

33 Rudnytsky, *Ukrainski biblioteky*, 1–14. On the library of Saint Andrew's College, which, many years later, after its acquisition of the private library of Ivan Ohienko (Winnipeg-based "Metropolitan Ilarion" of the Ukrainian Orthodox Church of Canada), became one of the largest Slavic ecclesiastical libraries in Canada, see Raisa Moroz, *Pokazhchyk ridkisnoi literatury v bibliotetsi Kolegii Sv. Andreia* (Winnipeg: Saint Andrew's College, 2002).

34 On this and other works in Cyrillic, see the amply illustrated catalogue of Iraida I. Gerus-Tarnawecka, *East Slavic Cyrillica in Canadian Repositories: Cyrillic Manuscripts and Early Printed Books* (Winnipeg: Society of Volyn, 1981). On the University of Manitoba library in particular, see J. S. Muchin, *[The] Slavic Collection of the University of Manitoba Libraries* (Winnipeg: University of Manitoba Press and UVAN, 1970). Almost two decades later, a survey conducted by Paul Magocsi revealed that the University of Manitoba library had the highest percentage of Ucrainica relative to its Slavic holdings of any major library in North America (60 per cent). Surprisingly, the New York Public Library had one of the lowest (5.2 per cent). See his "*Ucrainica* Collections and Bibliography in North America: Their Current Status," *Journal of Ukrainian Studies* 23 (1987): 77–91.

35 Rudnytsky, *Ukrainski biblioteky*, 14–26.

36 Ibid., 26–41.

37 Bohdan Budurowycz, *Slavic and East European Resources in Canadian Academic and Research Libraries* (Ottawa: National Library of Canada, 1976), xi. Also see Andrew Gregorovich, "Canadian Library Resources for Slavic Studies," in *Slavs in Canada*, ed. C. Bida (Ottawa: Inter-University Committee on

Canadian Slavs, 1968), II:191–203, who, as well, seems to have been very respectful of Rudnyckyj's achievement. However, Gregorovich adds some important new information on the history of the Slavic collection of the University of Toronto Library, which, by 1968, had clearly become the largest in the country and was rich in Ukrainian materials, especially concerning literature.

38 On Babine, see Edward Kasinec, "A. V. Babine (1866–1930): A Biographical Note," in his *Slavic Books and Bookmen: Papers and Essays* (New York: Russica, 1984), 73–7.

39 Rudnyckyj, *Ukrainica Congressiana*, 1–81.

40 Ibid. In fact, Harvard University had also acquired a copy in 1951.

41 Ibid., 82–140.

42 Ibid., 142.

43 Ibid., 158–72.

44 Ibid., 173–317.

45 In particular, Rudnyckyj defended Ukrainian scholars such as Mykhailo Hrushevsky (1866–1934) from the epithet "nationalist" while applying the same label to early LC librarians, such as Nicholas Rodionoff, whom he believed to be unsympathetic to Ukrainian viewpoints. Rudnyckyj did, however, praise Rodionoff's successors, such as Sergius Yakobson and Paul Horecky, whom he believed thought that, as he put it, Russia was Russia, and Ukraine was Ukraine. See J. B. Rudnyckyj, *LC Ukrainica* (Washington, DC: The Author, 1984).

46 Rudnyckyj, "Pre-1950 Ukrainica in the National Library of Canada." On p. 90, Rudnyckyj noted that it might be difficult to acquire certain titles because of two instances of the destruction of Ukrainian books in Canada, "in most cases [by] burning": in 1916, because of anti-immigrant war hysteria, and in the early 1940s (when Germany and the USSR seemed to be acting in concert) during the suppression of the pro-Communist Ukrainian labour-farmer temples.

47 Jaroslav B. Rudnyckyj, *Slavica Canadiana: A Selected Bibliography of Slavic Books and Pamphlets Published in or Relating to Canada* (Winnipeg: Ukrainian Free Academy of Sciences, 1952ff.) This serial, each number of which contained about twenty pages, was a subseries of the general series titled *Slavistica*.

48 J. B. Rudnyckyj and D. Sokulsky, *Ukrainica Canadiana* (Winnipeg: Ukrainian Free Academy of Sciences, 1954ff.) Again, the average length of a volume in this series was about twenty pages.

49 The bridge between Rudnyckyj's bibliographies and those appearing in *Canadian Slavonic Papers* was a nicely produced booklet by Daniel Dorotich, *A Bibliography of Canadian Slavists 1951–1971* (Saskatoon: Canadian

Association of Slavists, 1972). This bibliography contained academic journal articles as well as separate imprints.

50 Iu. Shevelov [Iurii Sherekh], *Ia-mene-meni..(i dovkruhy): Spohady*, 2 vols. (Kharkiv-New York: Berezil'-Kots', 2001), 2:279: "... *nevtomnyi, nerozbirlyvyi, i trokhy proidysvitskyi i velmy khlestakovskyi.*"

13 Scholarship on Mykhailo Hrushevsky

1 This chapter concerns the background and circumstances of the conduct of research on my doctoral thesis titled "Mykhailo Hrushevsky and the Politics of National Culture," defended at the University of Toronto, November 1983. It was published shortly later as Thomas M. Prymak, *Mykhailo Hrushevsky: The Politics of National Culture* (Toronto: University of Toronto Press, 1987). Just as Communism was collapsing in the USSR, it was also made available in a paraphrasing Ukrainian translation as "Mykhailo Hrushevsky: Polityka natsionalnoi kultury," *Vsesvit* 3 (1991): 183–9; 4: 179–90; 5: 207–25. Simultaneously, I was able to publish in Soviet Ukraine an excerpt from some of my other work on Hrushevsky: Tomas M. Pryimak, "Konstytutsiinyi proiekt M. Hrushevskoho z 1905 roku," *Ukrainskyi istorychnyi zhurnal* 1 (1991): 127–36. Both these publications were innovative for that time and place: the complete collapse of censorship, which had begun to loosen shortly before, and the Ukrainian declaration of independence, occurring only in the summer of 1991, confirmed by plebiscite the following winter.

2 Omelian [Omeljan] Pritsak, "U stolittia narodyn M. Hrushevskoho," in *Idei i liudy vyzvolnykh zmahan* (New York: Bulava, 1968), 187–230.

3 Mykhailo Hrushevsky, *Vybrani pratsi: Vydano z nahody 25-richchia z dnia ioho smerty (1934–1959)*, ed. M. Halii (New York: Association of Ukrainians of Revolutionary-Democratic Persuasions in the USA, 1960).

4 Unfortunately, Halii's edition of this work, although very full, was not complete. For some reason, Halii omitted the discursive essay titled "Istoriia i ii sotsialno-vykhovuiuche znachennia" (History and its social-educational significance) and a few other smaller pieces. These works, which, in particular, reveal Hrushevsky's non-racial idea of nationalism, became generally available in the West, and available to me personally, only much later. See the full reprints of *Na porozi novoi Ukrainy* in Mykhailo Hrushevsky, *Na pororzi novoi Ukrainy: Statti i dzerelni materiialy* (New York: Ukrainske Istorychne Tovarystvo, 1992), and *idem, Khto taki ukraintsi i choho vony khochut* (Kyiv: Znannia, 1991).

5 Volodymyr Doroshenko, "Pershyi prezydent vidnovlenoi ukrainskoi der-zhavy," *Ovyd* 1 (1957); 25–6; 2–3 (1957): 27–32; "Zasluhy M. Hrushevskoho

dlia ukrainskoi kultury," ibid., 5 (1957): 18–22; "M. Hrushevsky: Hromadskyi diiach, polityk, i publitsyst," ibid., 6 (1957): 15–19; 10: 23–26; and 11: 18–19. The name *Ovyd* refers to the Roman poet who was said to have been exiled to the Crimean peninsula or perhaps elsewhere on the western or northern Black Sea coast, in classical antiquity.

6 "V stolittia z dnia narodyn Akademika Mykhaila S. Hrushevskoho (1866–1934–1966)," *Ukrainskyi istoryk* 3, nos. 1–2 (1966). Also see "'Ukrainskyi istoryk' i rozvytok hrushevskoznavstva (U 135-littia narodzhennia M. Hrushevskoho)," *Ukrainskyi istoryk* 39, nos. 1–4 (2002): 11–16; and "Bibliohrafiia hrushevskiany v zhurnali 'Ukrainskyi istoryk'," *Ukraisnkyi istoryk* 43-4, no. 4 (1–2) (2006–07): 406–23.

7 In addition to his activities as a librarian, Gregorovich was well known as the editor of the popular magazine *Forum: A Ukrainian Review*, in which he published an enormous number of antique illustrations for Ukrainian history, eventually including pictures of Hrushevsky and his times. In my book on Hrushevsky, I reproduced from *Forum* an excellent photograph of the Central Rada building in Kyiv. (Because he had contacts with Soviet Ukraine at that time, which he did not wish to endanger, Gregorovich asked that I not credit the picture to *Forum* but rather to a "Private Collection, Toronto," which I did.) Antique maps of Ukraine were already at that time Gregorovich's specialty, but his major contribution to Ukrainian scholarship is his later work titled *Cossack Bibliography* (Toronto: Forum, 2008).

8 "Mykhailo Hrushevsky: Statti spohady dokumenty i komenari," *Zapysky Naukoho Tovarystva im. Shevchenka* 117 (1978). Stakhiv eventually became an historian in his own right, publishing books and articles on nineteenth- and twentieth-century Galicia and on the revolutionary period of Ukrainian history.

9 Thomas M. Prymak, "Mykhailo Hrushevsky: Populist or Statist?" *Journal of Ukrainian Studies* 10 (1981): 65–78. Some twenty years later, I returned to this theme in an article that analyzed how historians in independent Ukraine were then adopting positions first staked out by Ukrainian historians in emigration during the interwar period and during the Cold War. See Thomas M. Prymak, "The Hrushevsky Controversy at the End of the 1990s," *Journal of Ukrainian Studies* 26 (2001): 323–43.

10 Paul R. Magocsi, *Ucrainica at the University of Toronto Library: A Catalogue of Holdings*, 2 vols. (Toronto: University of Toronto Press, 1985).

11 Mykhailo Hrushevsky, "Volodymyr Antonovych: Osnovi idei ioho tvorchosty i diialnosty," *Zapysky Ukrainskoho Naukovoho Tovarystva* 3 (1909): 5–13. This article was later reprinted in *Ukrainskyi istoryk* 22, nos. 1–4 (1984): 193–9.

12 Paul R. Magocsi, *The Peter Jacyk Collection of Ukrainian Serials: A Guide to Newspapers and Periodicals [In the University of Toronto Library]* (Toronto: Chair of Ukrainian Studies, 1983). Also see Sofija Škorič and Wasyl Sydorenko, *Newspapers from Central and Eastern Europe in the University of Toronto Library* (Toronto: Petro Jacyk Central and East European Resource Centre, 2000).

13 Volodymyr Doroshenko, "Ivan Franko i Mykhailo Hrushevsky," *Suchasnist* 1 (1962): 16–36; Liubomyr Vynar [Lubomyr Wynar], "Potribna bibliohrafiia tvoriv Mykahila Hrushevskoho," ibid., 7 (1966): 228–35.

14 Liubomyr Vynar [Lubomyr Wynar], "Naivydatnishyi istoryk Ukrainy Mykhailo Hrushevsky (U 50-littia smerty, 1934–1984)," *Suchasnist*, scattered across various issues beginning no. 11 (1984). This work was shortly later reprinted in booklet form under the same title (no place). The cover of this publication states that it was published in 1986, but the title page states 1985. The small, pocket-sized format of this work was obviously used to facilitate its relatively easy import into the USSR, where such works were strictly forbidden. (At that time baggage was thoroughly checked by the Soviet border police but individuals of non-Soviet or Western origin were not usually frisked.)

15 Ievhenia Krychevska, "Pozhezha budynku Mykhaila Hrushevskoho," *Novi dni* 105 (1958): 13–20.

16 N. Polonska-Vasylenko, "Z moikh spohadiv pro M. Hrushevskoho," *Ukraina* 9 (1953): 744–47; *idem*, "Ahatanhel Krymsky," ibid., 2 (1949): 121–28.

17 Bohdan Budurovych [Bohdan Budurowycz], "Mykhailo Hrushevsky v otsintsi zakhidno-europeiskoi i amerykanskoi istoriohrafii," *Vyzvolnyi shliakh* 20 (1967): 171–81. Ivan Lysiak-Rudnytsky also came to Toronto to sit on my examination committee and, during the thesis defence, engaged Budurowycz in a spirited debate on Kyivan Rus', which was only tangentially connected to Hrushevsky's politics, or so I believed at the time.

18 Oleksander Lototsky, *Storinky mynuloho*, 4 vols. (Warsaw: Naukovo-Bohoslovskyi Instytut, 1932–1939; repr. in the USA: Vydannia Ukrainskoi Pravoslavnoi Tserkvy v SShA, 1966).

19 Ivan Makukh, *Na narodnii sluzhbi* (Detroit: Vydavnytstvo ukrainskoi vilnoi hromady Ameryky, 1958; repr. Kyiv: Osnovni tsinnosti, 2001). (I have not yet examined the reprint *de visu*.) Makukh was later active in the government of the Western Ukrainian People's Republic and then in Radical politics during the interwar period in Poland, where he was twice elected to the Polish Senate. He emigrated to Austria in 1944, where he wrote his detailed memoirs covering all these periods.

20 Dmytro Doroshenko, *Moi spomyny pro davnie-mynule 1901–1914* (Winnipeg: Tryzub, 1949; repr. Kyiv: Tempora, 2007).

21 Dmytro Doroshenko, *Moi spomyny pro nedavne-mynule 1914–1921* (Munich: Ukrainske vydavnytstvo, 1969; repr. Kyiv: Tempora, 2007). Also see his

general history of the revolution: *Istorii Ukrainy 1917–1923*, 2 vols. (Uzhhorod: Svoboda, 1930–1932; repr. New York: Bulava, 1954).

22 Mykola Kovalevsky, *Pry dzherelakh borotby* (Innsbruck: Nakladom Marii Kovalevskoi, 1960); N. Hryhoriiv, *Spohady 'Ruinnyka' Iak my ruinuvaly tiurmu narodiv a iak my buduvaly svoiu khatu* (Lviv: n.p., 1938). Hryhoriiv, in particular, immigrated to the United States in the late 1930s, remained a firm defender of "Ukrainian democracy" during the Second World War when many Ukrainians in Europe were forced to choose between Communism and Naziism as a lesser evil, and then worked for the Ukrainian-language service of Voice of America during the early years of the Cold War.

23 N. Polonska-Vasylenko, *Ukrainska Akademiia Nauk: Narys istorii*, 2 vols. (Munich: Institute for the Study of the USSR, 1955–1958). This work was later reprinted in independent Ukraine (Kyiv: Naukova Dumka, 1993; 2 vols.), though I have not yet examined the reprint *de visu.*

24 See, in particular, M. Halii, "M. Hrushevsky i 'Ukrainska radianska entsyklopediia'," *Vilna Ukraina* 42 (1964): 29–38; Dmytro Solovei, "U spravi zhyttiepysu M.S. Hrushevskoho," ibid., 17 (1958): 9–21; and Panas Fedenko, "Mykhailo Hrushevsky v nautsi i politytsi," ibid., 52 (1966): 1–17.

25 Anna Franko-Kliuchko, *Ivan Franko i ioho rodyna: Spomyny* (Toronto: Liga vyzvolennia Ukrainy, 1956). Also see note 13 above.

26 Mykyta Shapoval, "Narodnytstvo v ukrainskomu vyzvolnomu rukhovi," *Vilna Spilka* 3 (1927–1929): 95–128.

27 Symon Narizhny, *Ukrainska emigratsiia: Kulturna pratsia ukrainskoi emigratsii mizh dvoma svitovymy viinamy* (Prague: Vydavnytstvo im. Oleny Telyhy, 1942; repr. Ostroh: Ukrainske Istorychne Tovarystvo, 2008). I later discovered that this important book was widely used by the Soviet secret police to locate and persecute Ukrainians in Czechoslovakia after the Soviet occupation of that country in 1945.

28 Ostap Voinarenko, *Pro samostiinist UNR: De koly i iak vono proholoshuvalas ta iakyi buv ii zmist* (Winnipeg, 1966).

29 Ievhen Chykalenko, *Shchodennyk 1907–1917* (Lviv, 1931; repr. 2 vols. Kyiv: Tempora, 2004).

30 *Vistnyk soiuza vyzvolennia Ukrainy* 128 (1916).

31 See, for example, Mykhailo Marunchak, "M. Hrushevsky i ukraintsi Kanady," *Vilne slovo* (Toronto), no. 47, November 19, 1966.

32 New York Public Library, *Dictionary Catalogue of the Slavonic Collection*, 2nd ed., 44 vols. (New York: G.K. Hall, 1974). This catalogue contains some references to journal articles as well as to books and pamphlets published under separate cover. Needless to say, before the advent of the Internet, it was a basic reference tool for almost all Slavists in the Western world, and I made some use of it in my work.

33 Mykyka Shapoval, *Shchodennyk*, 2 vols. (New York; n.p., 1958).
34 Volodymyr Vynnychenko, *Shchodennyk*, vol. I (Edmonton: Canadian Institute of Ukrainian Studies, 1980).
35 Ievhen Chykalenko, *Spohady 1861–1907* (New York: UVAN, 1955). More generally, see Yury Boshyk, *A Guide to the Archival and Manuscript Collection of the Ukrainian Academy of Arts and Sciences in the US* (Edmonton: Canadian Institute of Ukrainian Studies, n.d.).
36 Oleksander Ohloblyn, "Mykhailo Hrushevsky i ukrainske natsionalne vidrodzhennia," *Ukrainskyi istoryk* 2–3 (1964): 1–6; *idem,* "Mykhailo Serhiievych Hrushevsky 1866–1934," ibid., 1–2 (1966): 6–14.
37 S. N. Shchegolev, *Ukrainskoe dvizhenie kak sovremennyi etap iuzhnorusskago separatizma* (Kyiv, 1912). The work has since been reprinted under a new title by an extreme Russian nationalist organization in Moscow. See Sergei Shchegolev, *Istoriia 'ukrainskogo' separatizma* (Moscow: Imperskaia traditsiia, 2004), with an introduction, notes, and an afterword on more recent developments by Mikhail Smolin.
38 Many years later, it was revealed that the Petliura Library had been captured by the Soviets during the war and much of its contents preserved. See Patricia Kennedy Grimstead, "The Odyssey of the Petliura Library and the Records of the Ukrainian National Republic during World War Two," in *Cultures and Nations of Central and Eastern Europe: Essays in Honor of Roman Szporluk,* ed. Zvi Gitelman et al. (Cambridge, MA: Harvard Ukrainian Research Institute, 2000), 181–208.
39 On the Ossolineum, see Karol Heintsch, *Guide à travers la bibliothèque de l'institut national Ossolinski de l'Academie polonaise des sciences à Wrocław* (Wrocław: Ossolineum, 1967), and Krystyna Korzon, *Biblioteka Ossolineum we Wrocławiu: Przewodnik* (Wroclaw: Ossolineum, 1975).
40 The most important file in this regard is the Olha Woycenko Collection, MG 30 D 212, vol. 12, which contained a large manuscript collection of Hrushevsky's circular letters to the Ukrainians of North America. These letters were long preserved in the office files of the newspaper *Ukrainskyi holos* (The Ukrainian voice) in Winnipeg. More generally, see Myron Momryk, *A Guide to Sources for the Study of Ukrainian Canadians* (Ottawa: Public Archives of Canada, 1984).

14 Ukrainian Canada in the Encyclopedias

1 Frances Swyripa, *Ukrainian Canadians: A Survey of their Portrayal in English Language Works* (Edmonton: University of Alberta Press, 1978).
2 For a brief article on the history of Canadian encyclopedias, see "Encyclopedias," in *The Canadian Encyclopedia* (Edmonton: Hurtig, 1988),

2:694. For a general article evaluating Ukrainian-language encyclopedias and giving something of their history, see Wasyl Veryha, "Encyclopedias, Ukrainian," in *The Modern Encyclopedia of Russian and Soviet Literatures (including non-Russian and Émigré Literatures)* (Gulf Breeze, FL: Academic International Press, 1982), 6:193–204.

3 The changing nomenclature of the Ukrainian people is an important and recurring problem for both European and North American historians, but, at least as far as Canada is concerned, there is very little scholarly literature devoted to it. See, for example, Vladimir J. Kaye [Kysilewskyj], *Early Ukrainian Settlements in Canada 1895–1900: Dr Josef Oleskow's Role in the Settlement of the Canadian Northwest* (Toronto: University of Toronto Press, 1964), esp. the section "The Problem of the Ethnic Name," xxii–xvi; and Robert B. Klymasz, "Introduction" and "Generalities and the Name Question," in his *Searching for 'Kanadiiska Rus'* (Winnipeg: Privately printed for the Centre for Ukrainian Canadian Studies, University of Manitoba, 2011), 4–10. Both Paul Yuzyk, *The Ukrainians in Manitoba: A Social History* (Toronto: University of Toronto Press, 1953), 36, and Orest Martynowych, *Ukrainians in Canada: The Formative Period 1891–1924* (Edmonton: Canadian Institute of Ukrainian Studies Press, 1991), xxvii–xviii, make only passing reference to this problem and anachronistically project the term "Ukrainian" backwards to the pre-1914 period. This is also standard and accepted practice for many historians writing on European developments. See, for example, Orest Subtelny, *Ukraine: A History* (Toronto: University of Toronto Press, 1988).

4 "Galizien," in *Meyers Konversations-Lexikon* (Leipzig, Vienna: Verlag der Bibliographischen Instituts, 1897), 7:16–20.

5 L. Léger, "Galicie," in *La grande encyclopédie* (Paris: H. Lamirault, undated, but certainly before 1914), 18:379–82.

6 "Galicia," in *Encyclopaedia Britannica*, 11th ed. (Cambridge: Cambridge University Press, 1910), 11:401–2. Sacher-Masoch's unusual stories of sexual deviance in Galician village life gave rise to the modern term "masoschism." Also see *Die österreichisch-ungarische Monarchie* in Wort und Bild, vol. 11, *Galizien* (Vienna: K.K. Hof-und Staatdruckerei, 1898). This series was published under the patronage of the Archduke Rudolph, son of the Emperor Francis Joseph and heir to the Austrian throne, who died mysteriously at Meyerling in the 1890s. Rudolph soon became a legend among the Galician Ukrainian peasantry, who for a long time refused to believe he was dead, but, rather, believed he had escaped the evil nobles and went to Brazil where he called his faithful Ruthenian peasants to join him. The legend of the Archduke Rudolph had a certain impact on the early wave of Ukrainian immigration to Canada. See the discussion in Thomas M. Prymak, "Ivan

Franko and Mass Ukrainian Immigration to Canada," *Canadian Slavonic Papers* XXVI, no. 4 (1984): 307–18, or the expanded version of this essay that forms chapter 3 of the present volume.

7 I have used the 1933 reprint. See *The Dominion Educator*, 8 vols. (Toronto: General Research Foundation, 1933): articles "Galicia," 3:1431–2, and "Austria-Hungary or Austro-Hungarian Monarchy," 1:296–301. The latter article stated that there were five million Poles and "almost four million Ruthenians" in Galicia.

8 Ibid., 10:3665.

9 Ibid., 4:1773–74. Strangely, in its article "Dukhobors" (sic), a Russian pacifist dissident sect (3:1151), unlike in its article "Galicia," the encyclopedia did note that "numbers" of what it called this "industrious harmless people" had immigrated to Canada in 1902. In view of the fact that by the 1920s, when this reference work was first published, the Ruthenian/Ukrainian immigration to Canada was many times greater than the Doukhobor immigration, such an omission of all reference to the Ruthenians/Galicians/Ukrainians is curious, to say the least.

10 See, in particular, Mykhailo Marunchak, *Natsiia v borotby za svoie isnuvannia 1932 i 1933 v Ukraini i diiaspori* (Winnipeg: Ukrainska vilna Akademiia nauk, 1985), 44–9, and George P. Kulchytsky, "Western Relief Efforts during the 'Stalin' Famine," *Ukrainian Quarterly* 44, no. 2 (1993): 152–64.

11 "Galician Immigration," in *Encyclopedia of Canada* (Toronto: University Associates of Canada, 1936), 3:3–4.

12 The cultural and linguistic claims of the "Galicians" mentioned here probably refer to the bilingual school system that existed in Manitoba and, to a lesser extent, Saskatchewan and Alberta, to 1916, when it was closed down in a wave of nativist war hysteria among English Canadians, led in particular by J. W. Dafoe and the *Winnipeg Free Press*. See Martynowych, *Ukrainians in Canada*, 357–72. Also see Cornelius Jaenen, "Ruthenian Schools in Western Canada, 1897–1919," *Paedagogica Historica* 10, no. 3 (1970): 517–41. Robert Craig Brown and Ramsay Cook, *Canada 1896–1921: A Nation Transformed* (Toronto: McClelland and Stewart, 1974), 258–9, see the language question in Manitoba mainly in terms of the English–French conflict.

13 "Ukrainians," *Encyclopedia of Canada* (Toronto: University Associates of Canada, 1937), 6:185.

14 A further angle glossed over in the *Encyclopedia of Canada* was the fact that not all Galician immigrants to the country were of Ukrainian/Ruthenian nationality and eastern Christian heritage. There was also a significant number of Roman Catholics who came to identify themselves as "Poles," and there were Germans and Jews, as well. In fact, the first Governor

General of Canadian "ethnic" background, Edward Schreyer from Manitoba, was of Galician German ancestry, though even he identified to some extent with his Ukrainian neighbours, speaking briefly in both German and Ukrainian as well as in French, Polish, and Italian at his installation ceremony in 1979.

15 "Kanada," in *Ukrainska zahalna entsyklopediia*, 3 vols. (Lviv: Ridna shkola, 1930–34), 2:cols. 184–5; "Emigratsiia," ibid., 1:cols. 1220–1. On the claim that the Ukrainians formed the third-largest "group" in Canada, see note 24 below.

16 Thomas M. Prymak, *Maple Leaf and Trident: The Ukrainian Canadians during the Second World War* (Toronto: Multicultural History Society of Ontario, 1988). This book may be consulted on-line at the Multicultural Canada Web site, hosted by Simon Fraser University.

17 See Ihor Stebelsky, "The Resettlement of Ukrainian Refugees in Canada after the Second World War," in *Canada's Ukrainians: Negotiating an Identity*, ed. Lubomyr Luciuk and Stella Hryniuk (Toronto: University of Toronto Press, 1991), 123–54. Also see *The Refugee Experience: Ukrainian Displaced Persons after World War II*, ed. Wsevolod W. Isajiw, Yury Boshyk, and Roman Senkus (Edmonton, Toronto: Canadian Institute of Ukrainian Studies Press, 1992), which contains several pieces on Canada.

18 W[atson] K[irkconnell], "Ukrainians in Canada," in *Slavonic Encyclopaedia*, 4 vols., ed. Joseph S. Roucek (New York: Philosophical library, 1949; repr. 1969), 4:1327–30. (The 1949 edition had appeared in one large volume.) This reference work also contained the substantial article "Ukrainians in the US," 1330–3.

19 See Thomas M. Prymak, "Two Encyclopedias: The Difference a War Made," *Ukrainski visti/Ukrainian News* (Edmonton), 16–29 April 2009, 7. Also see *idem*, "Inveterate Voyager: J. B. Rudnyckyj on Ukrainian Culture, Books, and Libraries in the West During the 'Long Cold War'," *Canadian Slavonic Papers* 51, no. 1 (2009): 53–76, or chapter 12 in the present volume.

20 J. B. Rudnyckyj, "Ukrainian Origin, People of," in *Encyclopedia Canadiana*, 10 vols. (Ottawa: Grolier, 1958), 10:168–71.

21 Paul Yuzyk, "Ukrainian Catholic Church," ibid., 166–8.

22 *Idem*, "Orthodox Churches," ibid., 8:65–6.

23 W. A. Carruthers and Robert England, "Immigration," ibid., 5:230–9. See, in particular, the graph in the 1972 edition on 237.

24 W. J. Rose, "Slavonic or Slavic Studies," ibid., 9:328–30. The claim that the Ukrainians formed the largest "ethnic group" in the 1950s Dominion can be sustained only if the various German-speaking groups are broken down into their religious and other components. Indeed, there is some basis for

arguing that groups such as the Hutterites and Mennonites formed independent ethno-religious entities and that "Austrians" and perhaps also "Swiss" should be counted separately from "Germans."

25 "Kanada," in *Ukrainska radianska entsyklopediia,* 17 vols. (Kyiv: URE, 1959–65), 6:134–42, esp. 136–8. The detailed (but unsigned) treatment of the Ukrainian Canadians in this encyclopedia should be contrasted to the brief treatment of Polish Canadians in the contemporary Polish encyclopedia: "Kanada," in *Wielka encyklopedia PWN,* 13 vols. (Warsaw: PWN, 1962–70), 5:413–18. This latter article devoted only a few lines to "the Polish emigration in Canada." It stated that, by 1961, there were some 324,000 Poles in the country. Similarly, the otherwise substantial article "Kanada" in the Russian-language *Bolshaia sovetskaia entsiklopediia,* 3rd ed. 30 vols. (Moscow: BSE, 1973), virtually ignored ethnic Canada, though it did briefly note in the subsection "Population" (p. 873) that about 20 per cent of the country was made up of "immigrants and their offspring," and that there were 1,050,000 Germans, 473,000 Ukrainians, 450,000 Italians, 430,000 Dutch, 324,000 Poles, 125,000 Russians, and 240,000 native Canadian Indians in the country.

26 "Kanada," in *Ukrainska mala entsyklopediia,* ed. Ievhen Onatsky, 4 vols. (Buenos Aires: UAPTS, 1957–63), 2:587–8.

27 In a pamphlet promoting the EU, Volodymyr Kubiiovych and Vasyl Markus, *Dvi ukrainski entsyklopedii* (New York: Proloh, 1961), argued that while their venture strove to balance the heavily censored URE, it was necessary to maintain as much objectivity as possible.

28 "Kanada," in *Entsyklopediia ukrainoznavstva,* 10 vols. (Paris, New York: Shevchenko Scientific Society, 1955–84), 3:932–48.

29 "Canada," in *Encyclopedia of Ukraine,* 5 vols. (Toronto: University of Toronto Press, 1983–93), 1:344–58.

30 "Kanada," in *Ukrainska radianska entsyklopediia,* 2nd ed., 12 vols. (Kyiv: URE, 1977–85), 4:546–50. The subarticle by Ievtukh, "Ukraintsi v Kanadi," was on page 547.

31 Frances A. Swyripa, "Ukrainians," in *The Canadian Encyclopedia,* 4 vols. (Edmonton: Hurtig, 1985), 4:2206–8.

32 Yar Slavutych, "Ukrainian Writing," ibid., 2206.

33 N. F. Ovcharenko and R. P. Zorivchak, "Kanadska literatura," in *Ukrainska literaturna entsyklopediia,* 3 vols., unfinished (Kyiv: URE, 1988ff.), 2:393–99. This work was originally projected to be comprised of five volumes but only three were published.

34 Frances Swyripa, "Ukrainians," in *Encyclopedia of Canada's Peoples,* ed. Paul R. Magocsi (Toronto: University of Toronto Press, 1999), 1280–1311.

35 "Ukrainians," in *Encyclopedia of British Columbia*, ed. Daniel Francis (Madeira Park, BC: Harbour Publishing, 2000), 725–26.
36 Bohdan Kordan, "Ukrainian Settlements," in *Encyclopedia of Saskatchewan* (Regina: Canadian Plains Research Center, 2005), 904–5.
37 Paul Laverdure, "Ukrainian Catholics," ibid., 962–63.
38 Yaroslav Lozowchuk and Gerald Luciuk, "Orthodox Churches," ibid., 674.
39 Orysia Tracz, "Ukrainians," in *The Encyclopedia of Manitoba* (Winnipeg: Great Plains Publications, 2007), 696–8.
40 "Ukrainian Cultural and Educational Centre in Winnipeg," ibid., 695.
41 0. 0. Kovalchuk, "Kanada," in *Entsyklopediia istorii Ukrainy* (Kyiv: Naukova dumka, 2007), 4:71–7. It is expected that, when completed, this encyclopedia should constitute about ten volumes.
42 D. S. Virsky, "Kanadskyi instytut ukrainskykh studii," ibid., 77–8. It is interesting to note that the predecessor of this encyclopedia, the Soviet-era *Radianska entsyklopediia istorii Ukrainy*, 4 vols. (Kyiv: URE, 1969–72), which was published during a period of relative thaw in the censorship, still contained no article on Canada.

15 Ukrainian Canadians and Ukrainian Americans

1 Myron Momryk, "The Royal Canadian Mounted Police and the Surveillance of the Ukrainian Community in Canada," *Journal of Ukrainian Studies* 28, no. 2 (2003): 89–112.
2 In Vincent N. Parrillo, *Diversity in America*, 3rd ed. (Los Angeles: Pine Forge Press, 2009), 10–11.
3 In Howard Palmer, *Immigration and the Rise of Multiculturalism* (Vancouver: Copp Clark, 1975), 55–6. This little volume is an interesting compilation of primary materials of various sorts.
4 See ibid., 56–8.
5 In John Robert Colombo, *Dictionary of Canadian Quotations* (Toronto: Stoddart, 1991), 355.
6 This point is clearly made by Harold Troper in his synthetic article "Multiculturalism" in the *Encyclopedia of Canada's Peoples*, ed. Paul Robert Magocsi (Toronto: University of Toronto Press, 1999), 997–1006, esp. 998. The explanation of this difference, perhaps, lies in the fact that the "foreign-born" remained a much higher percentage of the population in Canada than in the USA throughout the period in question.
7 Will Kymlicka, *Finding Our Way: Rethinking Ethnocultural Relations in Canada* (Toronto: Oxford University Press, 1998). A decade later, Kymlicka defended multiculturalism from accusations by Toronto political scientist Janice

Stein that it sheltered unequal religious practices (such as discrimination against women in the Jewish and Roman Catholic traditions) that contradicted the Canadian Charter of Rights and Freedoms. Kymlicka argued that these practices were protected by very old ideas about freedom of religion and had nothing to do with modern multiculturalism. In fact, Kymlicka pointed out, orthodox and fundamentalist religious groups often opposed multiculturalism because they feared it would present alternate lifestyles in a positive manner to which they objected and did not wish their young exposed. See the essays by these two authors in the book by Janice Stein et al., *Uneasy Partners: Multiculturalism and Rights in Canada* (Waterloo: Wilfred Laurier University Press, 2007), the very title of which assumes rather a lot.

Index

Makohin, Jacob, Ukrainian American millionaire 120; finances Ukrainian Bureau in London 173; ambitions 179
Makovei, Osyp, 33
Makuch, Andrij, xiii
Makukh, Ivan, 222; Radical Party activist and memoirist 342n19
Malaniuk, Yevhen or Ievhen, 95
Malofij, A., 86
Malone, Cecil, 177-8
Mandryka, Mykyta, 254
Manitoba, xi, 54-5, 57-8, 257-60; large Ukrainian population of 172, 173-4; Roy leaves 173
Manning, Clarence, 145, 203
Manning, Preston, 276
Martynovsky, Professor at St Andrew's College, 96
Marx, Karl, 46
Matseiko, H., 175
Mat' volá (The motherland is calling) (Kukučin), 27-8
Mazepa, Ivan, 202
Mazepa, Ivan, Hetman, 161
Mazurkiewicz, Roman, 62
Meest (The Bridge), 270
The Melting Pot (Zangwell), 273
Mennonites, 42-3, 186
Métis, 5
Meyers Konversations-Lexikon, 234; on Galicia 235
Miakotyn, Russian historian, 106
Miedzybrocki, Edward, 11
Miiakovsky, Volodymyr, archivist, 145
Milnes Gaskell, Charles, 102-3, 117, 188
Miłosz, Czesław, 15
Mochulsky, Mykhailo, 55
Momryk, Myron, 265

Montcalm, 5
Montreal, 89, 170, 187
Mosley, Philip, S., 147, 336n25
multiculturalism discussion, 275-77; and human rights 349-50n7
Murgas, Joseph, 24
Mykhailo Hrushevskyi: Bibliographic Sources 1866-1934 (Wynar), 168

Narodna volia (The peoples will), 219
Narys istorii Ukrainy (Survey of Ukrainian history) (Doroshenko), 87
National Library of Canada, 209-10
Nazi war crimes, 7
Newberry Library in Chicago, 202
New York, Ukrainian libraries of 228-30
New York Public Library, 203
New York Times Book Review, 15
Nineteenth Century and After, 187
Nixon/Brezhnev détente, 287n14
Nolde, Baron, 106
Novi dni (New days), 221
Novyi shliakh (The New Pathway), 97, 270; on Konovalets assassination 180; on Simpson 330-1n33

Obolensky, Serge, Prince, 101-2, 103
Ohienko, Ivan (later Metropolitan Ilarion), 96, 245
Ohloblyn, Oleksander, 93, 153, 168; active in New York UVAN 147; Wynar's mentor 158, 161; writes program for the Ukrainian Historical Association 163; writes on Hrushevsky 228
Okołowicz, Józef, 62, 69; on politics of Ruthenian/Ukrainian emigration to Canada 71

United Hetman Organization, 86, 173
University of Alberta, 124, 137, 140,
141, 142-3, 147-8, 206, 214, 271;
Gonsett Ukrainian Collection of
200
University of Manitoba, 138, 140-1,
194-5; Dafoe library of 205, 214;
libraries of 227
University of Ottawa, 195, 206; library
of 200
University of Saskatchewan, x,
119-42; early plans to introduce
Slavic Studies 127-9, 141, 145; first
Canadian university to introduce
Ukrainian language course 200
University of Toronto, 128, 138, 206;
Chair of Ukrainian Studies at
141, 143; Luckyj and 200; Robarts
Library of 219-23
University of Wisconsin Library, 202

Vasylenko, Mykola, 223
Velyka istoriia Ukrainy (Great History
of Ukraine), 94
Vernadsky, George, 108, 164, 203
Vernadsky, Vladimir, 108
Veryha, Wasyl, 219
Vetukhiv, Mykhailo, 147
Virsky, D. S., 259
Voinarenko, Ostap, 226
Voliansky, Ivan, 50
Voloshyn, Avhustyn, 122
Vowles, Hugh P., 102-3
Vyzvolnyi shliakh (The Liberation
Path), 221-2

Weinstein, Harold R., 107
Wikipedia, 260
Winnipeg, 4, 59-60, 72, 86, 97-8,
131, 139; Doroshenko's visit to

80; Orthodox Consistory at 88;
Gabrielle Roy and 170; Rudnyckyj
and 154-5; etymology of the name
of 199; Ukrainian libraries of
226-7; motto of 233; left-leaning
277
Winnipeg Public Library, 199-200
Woycenko, Olha, 86-7, 93, 94, 98,
310n35; on Sawchuk 311n44
Wynar, Lubomyr, 17, 19, 157-68,
212; distinguishes between
national and nationalistic history
160; as rankean 160; works on
Hrushevsky 217-18

Yanda, Doris, 83-4, 98
Young, Charles, 62
Yuzyk, Paul, 62, 94, 140, 199, 242-6,
324n25; contributes to *Ukrainskyi
istoryk* 162; contributes to *Encyclopedia Canadiana* 201; studies in
Minnesota 202; quoted by Onatsky
248; introduces word and concept
of "Multiculturalism" to Canadian
Parliament 275

Z podorozhi navkolo pivsvitu (Travels
across Half the World) (Rudnyck-
yj), 196-8
Z podorozhi po Amerytsi (Travels across
America) (Rudnyckyj), 201-3
Z podorozhi po Italii (Travels across
Italy) (Rudnyckyj), 204
Z po dorozhi po Kanadi (Travels across
Canada) (Rudnyckyj), 198-201
"Za Chlebem" (Sienkiewicz), 25-7,
36-7
Za Derzhavnist (For Statehood), 224
Zaitsev, Pavlo, 215
Zangwell, Israel, 273